Red Hat Enterprise Linux Troubleshooting Guide

Identify, capture, and resolve common issues faced by Red Hat Enterprise Linux administrators using best practices and advanced troubleshooting techniques

Benjamin Cane

[PACKT] open source✳

PUBLISHING   community experience distilled

BIRMINGHAM - MUMBAI

Red Hat Enterprise Linux Troubleshooting Guide

First published: October 2015

Production reference: 1131015

Published by Packt Publishing Ltd.
Livery Place
35 Livery Street
Birmingham B3 2PB, UK.

ISBN 978-1-78528-355-0

www.packtpub.com

Credits

Author
Benjamin Cane

Reviewers
Brian C Galura
Deepak G Kulkarni
Warren Myers
Siddhesh Poyarekar

Commissioning Editor
Nadeem Baghban

Acquisition Editor
Reshma Raman

Content Development Editor
Mamata Walkar

Technical Editor
Ryan Kochery

Copy Editors
Tani Kothari
Merilyn Pereira

Project Coordinator
Shipra Chawhan

Proofreader
Safis Editing

Indexer
Tejal Daruwale Soni

Production Coordinator
Aparna Bhagat

Cover Work
Aparna Bhagat

About the Author

Benjamin Cane has nearly 10 years of experience in Linux systems administration. His first systems administration role was in 2006. At that time, he worked for a web hosting company supporting thousands of FreeBSD and Linux systems.

Afterwards, he joined a managed services company that specialized in managing mission-critical systems. There, he worked his way to the position of a lead systems engineer, providing 24x7 support for highly critical enterprise systems that ran Red Hat Enterprise Linux.

Now, Benjamin is a systems architect. He focuses on building High and Continuous Availability environments within the financial services industry. He is also currently a Red Hat Certified Engineer and Certified Ethical Hacker.

With his experience in mission-critical environments, he has learned to identify and troubleshoot very complex issues quickly, because often these environments have a low tolerance for downtime. Being able to identify the root causes of very complex systems issues quickly is a skill that requires extensive knowledge of Linux and troubleshooting best practices.

In addition to this book, Benjamin writes about Linux systems administration and DevOps topics on his blog at http://bencane.com. He is also the project founder for Runbook (https://github.com/Runbook/runbook), an open source application designed to monitor and automatically resolve infrastructure and application issues.

About the Reviewers

Brian C Galura spent his childhood tinkering with subjects such as Java programming and Linux; his professional experience started with VoIP testing at 3Com in suburban Chicago. He then spent two years studying computer engineering at Purdue University before leaving to pursue freelance consulting in Los Angeles.

Following several years of freelancing, he developed his expertise in enterprise infrastructure and cloud computing by working for a variety of start-ups and large corporations. Later, he completed a bachelor's in IT while working at Citrix. Brian is currently working on Citrix's cloud engineering and systems architecture team in Santa Barbara, California.

Deepak G Kulkarni has around 10 years of experience in software engineering including nine years of strong experience in product development using C/C++/Java.

He has over four years of experience in JUnit, Core JAVA, Web Services, XML, Spring, Spring MVC, and Hibernate. He also has extensive software development experience using C/C++ on UNIX (HP-UX) and Sun-Solaris, shell scripting, and STL (Standard Template Library) and cross-platform development. Deepak also has over two years of experience in the Mac OS using Objective C/C++, Cocoa framework, Xcode, and MetroWorks IDE.

Deepak has a working knowledge of Perl/SNMP/TCP/IP, OS Internals, web services, XML, XSD, database (Oracle)/IPC (inter process communication)/system calls/Pro*C. He has been exposed to UML /use case diagrams /class diagrams / sequence diagrams / activity diagrams / state diagrams, IBM Rational Rose, and Design Patterns (GoF Patterns) / Design Principles. He has hands-on experience with Ant, Maven, JUnit, JProfiler, JProbe, JSON, Servlets, Python, and Ruby on Rails, as well as experience in remote service calls and client server programming.

Warren Myers has been a professional data center and cloud automation architect for over eight years, with exposure to dozens of platforms, scores of customers, and hundreds of interesting problems.

He was a reviewer on *Raspberry Pi Server Essentials* and wrote the freely-available e-book, *Debugging and Supporting Software Systems* (http://cnx.org/contents/ aa87c3d5-e350-458e-a948-8cd1a9bf8e36@2.4:1/Debugging_and_Supporting_ Softw).

Siddhesh Poyarekar has been a free and open source software programmer for over seven years and has worked on a variety of projects beginning with writing his own dialer program for an ISP that did not have a UI-based dialer for Linux. He spent a number of years troubleshooting problems in various domains from the Linux desktop, shell, and the kernel to the core system runtime on Linux systems, that is, the GNU C Library for which he is now a maintainer.

www.PacktPub.com

Support files, eBooks, discount offers, and more

For support files and downloads related to your book, please visit www.PacktPub.com.

Did you know that Packt offers eBook versions of every book published, with PDF and ePub files available? You can upgrade to the eBook version at www.PacktPub.com and as a print book customer, you are entitled to a discount on the eBook copy. Get in touch with us at service@packtpub.com for more details.

At www.PacktPub.com, you can also read a collection of free technical articles, sign up for a range of free newsletters and receive exclusive discounts and offers on Packt books and eBooks.

https://www2.packtpub.com/books/subscription/packtlib

Do you need instant solutions to your IT questions? PacktLib is Packt's online digital book library. Here, you can search, access, and read Packt's entire library of books.

Why subscribe?

- Fully searchable across every book published by Packt
- Copy and paste, print, and bookmark content
- On demand and accessible via a web browser

Free access for Packt account holders

If you have an account with Packt at www.PacktPub.com, you can use this to access PacktLib today and view 9 entirely free books. Simply use your login credentials for immediate access.

This book is dedicated to my wife Ruby and our two sons Ethan and Jacob. Ruby, without your love and support I would have never been able to write this book. Thank you for putting up with the long hours and sleepless nights while trying to complete this.

Table of Contents

Preface

Red Hat Enterprise Linux is a widely popular Linux distribution that is used in everything from Cloud to enterprise mainframe computers. If you include downstream distributions such as CentOS, the adoption of the Red Hat Enterprise Linux distribution is even greater.

As with most things, there is always someone responsible for resolving issues with all of these various systems running Red Hat Enterprise Linux. *Red Hat Enterprise Linux Troubleshooting Guide* is written to provide basic to advanced troubleshooting practices and commands for Linux systems, with these troubleshooting techniques specifically focused on systems running Red Hat Enterprise Linux.

This book is designed to provide you with steps and the knowledge required to remedy a wide variety of scenarios. The examples in this book use real-world issues with real-world resolutions.

While the examples in this book are situational, this book can also be used as a reference for Linux-related topics and commands. They provide the reader with the ability to reference both troubleshooting steps and specific commands to resolve complex issues.

What this book covers

Chapter 1, *Troubleshooting Best Practices*, covers the troubleshooting process at a high level. By equating the troubleshooting process with the scientific method, this book will explain how to break down a problem to identify the root cause, no matter how complicated the problem.

Chapter 2, Troubleshooting Commands and Sources of Useful Information, provides the reader with a simple introduction to common locations of useful information. It will also provide a reference for fundamental Linux commands that can be used for troubleshooting many types of issues.

Chapter 3, Troubleshooting a Web Application, takes the process learned in Chapter 1 and the commands learned in Chapter 2 to work through a complicated problem. The problem outlined in this chapter is "By example" meaning that the flow of this chapter is designed to walk you through the entire troubleshooting process, from end to end.

Chapter 4, Troubleshooting Performance Issues, deals with performance issues and some of the most complicated problems to troubleshoot. Often, the complications are compounded by the perception of users versus expected levels of performance. In this chapter, the tools and information discussed in Chapter 2 will, once again, be used to resolve a real-world performance problem.

Chapter 5, Network Troubleshooting, talks about networking being a critical component of any modern day system. This chapter will cover the core commands necessary for the configuration and diagnostics of Linux networking.

Chapter 6, Diagnosing and Correcting Firewall Issues, covers the complex nature of Linux firewalls, in a continuation of Chapter 5. This chapter will introduce and highlight commands and techniques necessary to troubleshoot Linux software firewalls.

Chapter 7, Filesystem Errors and Recovery, teaches you that being able to recover a filesystem could mean the difference between losing and retaining data. This chapter will introduce some core Linux filesystem concepts and will demonstrate how to recover a read-only filesystem.

Chapter 8, Hardware Troubleshooting, starts to touch on the process of troubleshooting hardware issues. This chapter will walk you through the restoration of a failed hard drive.

Chapter 9, Using System Tools to Troubleshoot Applications, explores how often a system administrator's role is not only to troubleshoot OS issues but also application issues. This chapter will show you how to utilize common system tools to identify the root cause of an application issue.

Chapter 10, Understanding Linux User and Kernel Limits, demonstrates that Red Hat Enterprise Linux has many components in place to prevent users from overloading the system. This chapter will explore these components and explain how to modify them to allow legitimate resource utilization.

Chapter 11, Recovering from Common Failures, walks you through troubleshooting out-of-memory conditions. This scenario is very common in heavily utilized environments and can be difficult to troubleshoot. This chapter will cover not only how to troubleshoot this issue, but also why the issue occurred.

Chapter 12, Root Cause Analysis of an Unexpected Reboot, puts the troubleshooting process and commands learned in the previous chapters to the test. This chapter walks you through performing a Root Cause Analysis on a server that has unexpectedly rebooted.

What you need for this book

Although this book can be standalone, readers will benefit greatly from having a system with Red Hat Enterprise Linux release 7, with the operating system available. You will more effectively learn the commands and resources discussed in this book when you have the ability to execute them on a test system.

While it is possible to use many of the commands, processes, and resources covered in this book with other Linux distributions, it is highly recommended to utilize a Red Hat downstream distribution such as CentOS 7 if Red Hat Enterprise Linux 7 is not available to the reader.

Who this book is for

If you are a competent RHEL administrator or consultant with a desire to increase your troubleshooting skills and your knowledge of Red Hat Enterprise Linux, then this book is perfect for you. A good knowledge level and understanding of basic Linux commands are expected.

Conventions

In this book, you will find a number of text styles that distinguish between different kinds of information. Here are some examples of these styles and an explanation of their meaning.

Code words in text, database table names, folder names, filenames, file extensions, pathnames, dummy URLs, user input, and Twitter handles are shown as follows: "Within reason, it is not required to include every `cd` or `ls` command executed."

When we wish to draw your attention to a particular part of a code block, the relevant lines or items are set in bold:

```
192.168.33.12 > 192.168.33.11: ICMP host 192.168.33.12
unreachable - admin prohibited, length 68
```

Any command-line input or output is written as follows:

```
# yum install man-pages
```

New terms and **important words** are shown in bold. Words that you see on the screen, for example, in menus or dialog boxes, appear in the text like this: "we will see a message on our screen that says **still here?**."

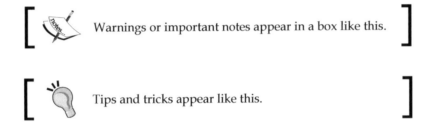

Warnings or important notes appear in a box like this.

Tips and tricks appear like this.

Reader feedback

Feedback from our readers is always welcome. Let us know what you think about this book—what you liked or disliked. Reader feedback is important for us as it helps us develop titles that you will really get the most out of.

To send us general feedback, simply e-mail feedback@packtpub.com, and mention the book's title in the subject of your message.

If there is a topic that you have expertise in and you are interested in either writing or contributing to a book, see our author guide at www.packtpub.com/authors.

Customer support

Now that you are the proud owner of a Packt book, we have a number of things to help you to get the most from your purchase.

Downloading the example code

You can download the example code files from your account at `http://www.packtpub.com` for all the Packt Publishing books you have purchased. If you purchased this book elsewhere, you can visit `http://www.packtpub.com/support` and register to have the files e-mailed directly to you.

Errata

Although we have taken every care to ensure the accuracy of our content, mistakes do happen. If you find a mistake in one of our books—maybe a mistake in the text or the code—we would be grateful if you could report this to us. By doing so, you can save other readers from frustration and help us improve subsequent versions of this book. If you find any errata, please report them by visiting `http://www.packtpub.com/submit-errata`, selecting your book, clicking on the **Errata Submission Form** link, and entering the details of your errata. Once your errata are verified, your submission will be accepted and the errata will be uploaded to our website or added to any list of existing errata under the Errata section of that title.

To view the previously submitted errata, go to `https://www.packtpub.com/books/content/support` and enter the name of the book in the search field. The required information will appear under the **Errata** section.

Piracy

Piracy of copyrighted material on the Internet is an ongoing problem across all media. At Packt, we take the protection of our copyright and licenses very seriously. If you come across any illegal copies of our works in any form on the Internet, please provide us with the location address or website name immediately so that we can pursue a remedy.

Please contact us at `copyright@packtpub.com` with a link to the suspected pirated material.

We appreciate your help in protecting our authors and our ability to bring you valuable content.

Questions

If you have a problem with any aspect of this book, you can contact us at `questions@packtpub.com`, and we will do our best to address the problem.

N

netstat -nap | grep 80
ps -elf | grep php.

1
Troubleshooting Best Practices

This chapter, which happens to be the first chapter, is probably the most important and least technical. Most chapters in this book cover specific issues and the commands necessary to troubleshoot those issues. This chapter, however, will cover some troubleshooting best practices that can be applied to any issue.

You can think of this chapter as the principles behind the practices being applied.

Styles of troubleshooting

Before covering the best practices of troubleshooting, it is important to understand the different styles of troubleshooting. In my experience, I have found that people tend to use one of three styles of troubleshooting, which are as follows:

- The Data Collector
- The Educated Guesser
- The Adaptor

Each of these styles have their own strengths and weaknesses. Let's have a look at the characteristics of these styles.

The Data Collector

I like to call the first style of troubleshooting, the **Data Collector**. The Data Collector is someone who generally utilizes a systematic approach to solve issues. The systematic troubleshooting approach is generally characterized as follows:

- Asking specific questions to parties reporting issues, expecting detailed answers
- Running commands to identify system performance for most issues
- Running through a predefined set of troubleshooting steps before stepping into action

The strength of this style is that it is effective, no matter what level of engineer or administrator is using it. By going through issues systematically, collecting each data point, and understanding the results before executing any resolution, the Data Collector is able to resolve issues that they might not necessarily be familiar with.

The weakness of this style is that the data collection is not usually the fastest method to resolve issues. Depending on the issue, collecting data can take a long time and some of that data might not be necessary to find the resolution.

The Educated Guesser

I like to call the second style of troubleshooting, the **Educated Guesser**. The Educated Guesser is someone who generally utilizes an intuitive approach to solve issues. The intuitive approach is generally characterized by the following:

- Identifying the cause of issues with minimal information
- Running a few commands before resolving the issue
- Utilizing previous experience to identify root cause

The strength of this style of troubleshooting is that it allows you to come up with resolutions sooner. When confronted with an issue, this type of troubleshooter tends to pull from experience and requires minimal information to find a resolution.

The weakness of this style is that it relies heavily on experience, and thus requires time before being effective. When focusing on resolution, this troubleshooter might also attempt multiple actions to resolve the issue, which can make it seem like the Educated Guesser does not fully understand the issue at hand.

The Adaptor

There is a third and often-overlooked style of troubleshooting; this style utilizes both the systematic and intuitive styles. I like to call this style the **Adaptor**. The Adaptor has a personality which enables it to switch between systematic and intuitive troubleshooting styles. This combined style is often faster than the Data Collector style and is more detail oriented than the Educated Guesser style. This is because they are able to apply the troubleshooting style appropriate for the task at hand.

Choosing the appropriate style

While it is easy to say that one method is better than the other, the fact of the matter is that picking the appropriate troubleshooting style depends greatly on the person. It is important to understand which troubleshooting style best fits your own personality. By understanding which style fits you better, you can learn and use techniques that fit that style. You can also learn and adopt techniques from other styles to apply troubleshooting steps that you would normally overlook.

This book will show both the Data Collector and Educated Guesser styles of troubleshooting, and periodically highlighting which personality style the steps best fit.

Troubleshooting steps

Troubleshooting is a process that is both rigid and flexible. The rigidity of the troubleshooting process is based on the fact that there are basic steps to be followed. In this way, I like to equate the troubleshooting process to the scientific method, where the scientific method has a specific list of steps that must be followed.

The flexibility of the troubleshooting process is that these steps can be followed in any order that makes sense. Unlike the scientific method, the troubleshooting process often has the goal of resolving the issue quickly. Sometimes, in order to resolve an issue quickly, you might need to skip a step or execute them out of order. For example, with the troubleshooting process, you might need to resolve the immediate issue, and then identify the root cause of that issue.

The following list has five steps that make up the troubleshooting process. Each of these steps could also include several sub-tasks, which may or may not be relevant to the issue. It is important to follow these steps with a grain of salt, as not every issue can be placed into the same bucket. The following steps are meant to be used as a best practice but, as with all things, it should be adapted to the issue at hand:

1. Understanding the problem statement.
2. Establishing a hypothesis.
3. Trial and error.
4. Getting help.
5. Documentation.

Understanding the problem statement

With the scientific method, the first step is to establish a problem statement, which is another way of saying: to identify and understand the goal of the experiment. With the troubleshooting process, the first step is to understand the problem being reported. The better we understand an issue, the easier it is to resolve the issue.

There are a number of tasks we can perform that will help us understand issues better. This first step is where a Data Collector's personality stands out. Data Collectors, by nature, will gather as much data as they can before moving on to the next step, whereas, the Educated Guessers generally tend to run through this step quickly and then move on to the next step, which can sometimes cause critical pieces of information to be missed.

Adaptors tend to understand which data collecting steps are necessary and which ones are not. This allows them to collect data as a Data Collector would, but without spending time gathering data that does not add value to the issue at hand.

The sub-task in this troubleshooting step is *asking the right questions*.

Asking questions

Whether via human or automated processes such as a ticket system, the reporter of the issue is often a great source of information.

Tickets

When they receive a ticket, the Educated Guesser personality will often read the heading of the ticket, make an assumption of the issue and move to the next stage of understanding the issue. The Data Collector personality will generally open the ticket and read the full details of the ticket.

While it depends on the ticketing and monitoring system, in general, there can be useful information within a ticket. Unless the issue is a common issue and you are able to understand all that you know from the header, it is generally a good idea to read the ticket description. Even small amounts of information might help with particularly tricky issues.

Humans

Gathering additional information from humans, however, can be inconsistent. This varies greatly depending on the environment being supported. In some environments, the person reporting an issue can provide all of the details required to resolve the issue. In other environments, they might not understand the issue and simply explain the symptoms.

No matter what troubleshooting style fits your personality best, being able to get important information from the person reporting the issue is an important skill. Intuitive problem solvers such as the Educated Guesser or Adaptor tend to find this process easier as compared to Data Collector personalities, not because these personalities are necessarily better at obtaining details from people but rather because they are able to identify patterns with less information. Data Collectors, however, can get the information they need from those reporting the issue if they are prepared to ask troubleshooting questions.

Don't be afraid to ask obvious questions

My first technical job was in a webhosting technical support call center. There I often received calls from users who did not want to perform the basic troubleshooting steps and simply wanted the issue escalated. These users simply felt that they had performed all of the troubleshooting steps themselves and had found an issue beyond first level support.

While sometimes this was true, more often, the issue was something basic that they had overlooked. In that role, I quickly learned that even if the user is reluctant to answer basic or obvious questions, at the end of the day, they simply want their issue resolved. If that meant going through repetitive steps, that was ok, as long as the issue is resolved.

Even today, as I am now the escalation point for senior engineers, I find that many times engineers (even with years of troubleshooting experience under their belt) overlook simple basic steps.

Asking simple questions that might seem basic are sometimes a great time saver; so don't be afraid to ask them.

Attempting to duplicate the issue

One of the best ways to gather information and understand an issue is to experience it. When an issue is reported, it is best to duplicate the issue.

While users can be a source of a lot of information, they are not always the most reliable; oftentimes a user might experience an error and overlook it or simply forget to relay the error when reporting the issue.

Often, one of the first questions I will ask a user is how to recreate the issue. If the user is able to provide this information, I will be able to see any errors and often identify the resolution of the issue faster.

Sometimes duplicating the issue is not possible

While it is always best to duplicate the issue, it is not always possible. Every day, I work with many teams; sometimes, those teams are within the company but many times they are external vendors. Every so often during a critical issue, I will see someone make a blanket statement such as "If we can't duplicate it, we cannot troubleshoot it."

While it is true that duplicating an issue is sometimes the only way to find the root cause, I often hear this statement abused. Duplicating an issue should be viewed like a tool; it is simply one of many tools in your troubleshooting tool belt. If it is not available, then you simply have to make do with another tool.

There is a significant difference between not being able to find a resolution and not attempting to find a resolution due to the inability to duplicate an issue. The latter is not only unhelpful, but also unprofessional.

Running investigatory commands

Most likely, you are reading this book to learn techniques and commands to troubleshoot Red Hat Enterprise Linux systems. The third sub-task in understanding the problem statement is just that—running investigative commands to identify the cause of the issue. Before executing investigatory commands, however, it is important to know that the previous steps are in a logical order.

It is a best practice to first ask the user reporting an issue some basic details of the issue, then after obtaining enough information, duplicate the issue. Once the issue has been duplicated, the next logical step is to run the necessary commands to troubleshoot and investigate the cause of the issue.

It is very common to find yourself returning to previous steps during the troubleshooting process. After you have identified some key errors, you might find that you must ask the original reporter for additional information. When troubleshooting, do not be afraid to take a few steps backwards in order to gain clarity of the issue at hand.

Establishing a hypothesis

With the scientific method, once a problem statement has been formulated it is then time to establish a hypothesis. With the troubleshooting process, after you have identified the issue, gathered the information about the issue such as errors, system current state, and so on, it is also time to establish what you believe caused or is causing the issue.

Some issues, however, might not require much of a hypothesis. It is common that errors in log files or the systems current state might answer why the issue occurred. In such scenarios, you can simply resolve the issue and move on to the *Documentation* step.

For issues that are not cut and dry, you will need to put together a hypothesis of the root cause. This is necessary as the next step after forming a hypothesis is attempting to resolve the issue. It is difficult to resolve an issue if you do not have at least, a theory of the root cause.

Here are a few techniques that can be used to help form a hypothesis.

Putting together patterns

While performing data collection during the previous steps, you might start to see patterns. Patterns can be something as simple as similar log entries across multiple services, the type of failure that occurred (such as, multiple services going offline), or even a reoccurring spike in system resource utilization.

These patterns can be used to formulate a theory of the issue. To drive the point home, let's go through a real-world scenario.

You are managing a server that both runs a web application and receives e-mails. You have a monitoring system that detected an error with the web service and created a ticket. While investigating the ticket, you also receive a call from an e-mail user stating they are getting e-mail bounce backs.

When you ask the user to read the error to you they mention `No space left on device`.

Let's break down this scenario:

- A ticket from our monitoring solution has told us Apache is down
- We have also received reports from e-mail users with errors indicative of a file system being full

Could all of this mean that Apache is down because the file system is full? Possibly. Should we investigate it? Absolutely!

Is this something that I've encountered before?

The above breakdown leads into the next technique for forming a hypothesis. It might sound simple but is often forgotten. "Have I seen something like this before?"

With the previous scenario, the error reported from the e-mail bounce back was one that generally indicated that a file system was full. How do we know this? Well, simple, we have seen it before. Maybe we have seen that same error with e-mail bounce backs or maybe we have seen the error from other services. The point is, the error is familiar and the error generally means one thing.

Remembering common errors can be extremely useful for the intuitive types such as the Educated Guesser and Adaptor; this is something they tend to naturally perform. For the Data Collector, a handy trick would be to keep a reference table of common errors handy.

 From my experience, most Data Collectors tend to keep a set of notes that contain things such as common commands or steps for procedures. Adding common errors and the meaning behind those errors are a great way for systematic thinkers such as Data Collectors to establish a hypothesis faster.

Overall, establishing a hypothesis is important for all types of troubleshooters. This is the area where the intuitive thinkers such as Educated Guessers and Adaptors excel. Generally, those types of troubleshooters will form a hypothesis sooner, even if sometimes those hypotheses are not always correct.

Trial and error

In the scientific method, once a hypothesis is formed, the next stage is experimentation. With troubleshooting, this equates to attempting to resolve the issue.

Some issues are simple and can be resolved using a standard procedure or steps from experience. Other issues, however, are not as simple. Sometimes, the hypothesis turns out to be wrong or the issue ends up being more complicated than initially thought.

In such cases, it might take multiple attempts to resolve the issue. I personally like to think of this as similar to trial and error. In general, you might have an idea of what is wrong (the hypothesis) and an idea on how to resolve it. You attempt to resolve it (trial), and if that doesn't work (error), you move on to the next possible solution.

Start by creating a backup

To those taking up a new role as a Linux Systems Administrator, if there were only one piece of advice I could give, it would be one that most have learned the hard way: *back everything up before making changes*.

Many times as systems administrators we find ourselves needing to change a configuration file or delete a few unneeded files in order to solve an issue. Unfortunately, we might think we know what needs to be removed or changed but are not always correct.

If a backup was taken, then the change can simply be restored to its previous state, however, without a backup. Thus reverting changes is not as easy.

A backup can consist of many things, it can be a full system backup using something like `rdiff-backup`, a VM snapshot, or something as simple as creating a copy of a file.

 For those interested in seeing the extent of this tip in practice, simply run the following command on any server that has more than four systems administrators and has been around for several years:

```
$ find /etc -name "*.bak"
```

Getting help

In many cases at this point the issue is resolved, but much like each step in the troubleshooting process, it depends on the issue at hand. While getting help is not exactly a troubleshooting step, it is often the next logical step if you cannot solve the issue on your own.

When looking for help, there are generally six resources available:

- Books
- Team Wikis or Runbooks
- Google
- Man pages
- Red Hat kernel docs
- People

Books

Books (such as this one) are good for referencing commands or troubleshooting steps for particular types of issues. Other books such as the ones that specialize on a specific technology are good for referencing how that technology works. In previous years, it was not uncommon to see a senior admin with a bookshelf full of technical books at his or her disposal.

In today's world, as books are more frequently seen in a digital format, they are even easier to use as references. The digital format makes them searchable and allows readers to find specific sections faster than a traditional printed version.

Team Wikis or Runbooks

Before **Team Wikis** became common, many operations groups had physical books called **Runbooks**. These books are a list of processes and procedures used daily by the operations team to keep the production environments operating normally. Sometimes, these Runbooks would contain information for provisioning new servers and sometimes they would be dedicated to troubleshooting.

In today's world, these Runbooks have mostly been replaced by Team Wikis, these Wikis will often have the same content but are online. They also tend to be searchable and easier to keep up to date, which means they are frequently more relevant than a traditional printed Runbook.

The benefit of Team Wikis and Runbooks are that not only can they often address issues that are specific to your environment, but they can also resolve those issues. There are many ways to configure services such as Apache, and there are even more ways that external systems create dependencies on these services.

In some environments, you might be able to simply restart Apache whenever there is an issue, but in others, you might actually have to go through several prerequisite steps. If there is a specific process that needs to be followed before restarting a service, it is a best practice to document the process in either a Team Wiki or Runbook.

Google

Google is such a common tool for systems administrators that at one point there were specific search portals available at `google.com/linux`, `google.com/microsoft`, `google.com/mac`, and `google.com/bsd`.

Google has depreciated these search portals but that doesn't mean that the number of times systems administrators use Google or any other search engine for troubleshooting has decreased.

In fact, in today's world, it is not uncommon to hear the words "I would Google it" in technical interviews.

A few tips for those new to using Google for systems administration tasks are:

- If you copy and paste a full error message (removing the server specific text) you will likely find more relevant results:

  For example, searching for *kdumpctl: No memory reserved for crash kernel* returns 600 results, whereas searching for *memory reserved for crash kernel* returns 449,000 results.

- You can find an online version of any man page by searching for `man` then a command such as `man netstat`.

- You can wrap an error in double quotes to refine search results to those that contain the same error.

- Asking what you're looking for in the form of a question usually results in tutorials. For example, *How do you restart Apache on RHEL 7?*

While Google can be a great resource, the results should always be taken with a grain of salt. Often while searching for an error on Google, you might find a suggested command that offers little explanation but simply says "run this and it will fix it". Be very cautious when running these commands, it is important that any command you execute on a system should be a command you are familiar with. You should always know what a command does before executing it.

Man pages

When Google is not available or even sometimes when it is, the best source of information on commands or Linux, in general, are the **man pages**. The man pages are core Linux manual documents that are accessible via the man command.

To look up documentation for the netstat command, for example, simply run the following:

```
$ man netstat
NETSTAT(8)
Linux System Administrator's Manual
NETSTAT(8)


NAME
        netstat - Print network connections, routing tables, interface
statistics, masquerade connections, and multicast memberships
```

As you can see, this command outputs not only the information on what the netstat command is, but also contains a quick synopsis of usage information such as the following:

```
SYNOPSIS
        netstat  [address_family_options]   [--tcp|-t]   [--udp|-u]
[--udplite|-U]  [--raw|-w]  [--listening|-l]  [--all|-a]
[--numeric|-n]  [--numeric-hosts]
        [--numeric-ports]  [--numeric-users]  [--symbolic|-N]
[--extend|-e[--extend|-e]]   [--timers|-o]   [--program|-p]
 [--verbose|-v]   [--continuous|-c]
        [--wide|-W]  [delay]
```

Also, it gives detailed descriptions of each flag and what it does:

```
        --route , -r
        Display the kernel routing tables. See the description in
route(8) for details.  netstat -r and route -e produce the same
output.


        --groups , -g
        Display multicast group membership information for IPv4 and
IPv6.


        --interfaces=iface , -I=iface , -i
        Display a table of all network interfaces, or the specified
iface.
```

In general, the base manual pages for the core system and libraries are distributed with the man-pages package. The man pages for specific commands such as top, netstat, or ps are distributed as part of that command's installation package. The reason for this is because the documentation of individual commands and components is left to the package maintainers.

This can mean that some commands are not documented to the level of others. In general, however, the man pages are extremely useful sources of information and can answer most day-to-day questions.

Reading a man page

In the previous example, we can see that the man page for netstat includes a few sections of information. In general, man pages have a consistent layout with some common sections that can be found within most man pages. The following is a simple list of some of these common sections:

- Name
- Synopsis
- Description
- Examples

Name

The **Name** section generally contains the name of the command and a very brief description of the command. The following is the name section from the ps command's man page:

```
NAME
        ps - report a snapshot of the current processes.
```

Synopsis

The **Synopsis** section of a command's man page will generally list the command followed by the possible command flags or options. A very good example of this section can be seen in the netstat command's synopsis:

```
SYNOPSIS
        netstat   [address_family_options]   [--tcp|-t]   [--udp|-u]
   [--raw|-w]   [--listening|-l]   [--all|-a]  [--numeric|-n]
   [--numeric-hosts]  [--numeric-ports]
        [--numeric-users]  [--symbolic|-N]  [--extend|-e[--extend|-
   e]]  [--timers|-o]  [--program|-p]  [--verbose|-v]  [--continuous|-c]
```

This section can be very useful as a quick reference for command syntax.

Description

The **Description** section will often contain a longer description of the command as well as a list and explanation of the various command options. The following snippet is from the `cat` command's man page:

```
DESCRIPTION
        Concatenate FILE(s), or standard input, to standard output.

        -A, --show-all
              equivalent to -vET

        -b, --number-nonblank
              number nonempty output lines, overrides -n
```

The description section is very useful, since it goes beyond simply looking up options. This section is often where you will find documentation about the nuances of commands.

Examples

Often man pages will also include examples of using the command:

```
EXAMPLES
        cat f - g
              Output f's contents, then standard input, then g's
infocontents.
```

The preceding is a snippet from the `cat` command's man page. We can see, in this example, how to use `cat` to read from files and standard input in one command.

This section is often where I find new ways of using commands that I've used many times before.

Additional sections

In addition to the previous section, you might also see sections such as **See Also**, **Files**, **Author**, and **History**. These sections can also contain useful information; however, not every man page will have them.

Info documentation

Along with man pages, Linux systems generally also contain **info documentation**, which are designed to contain additional documentation, which go beyond that, within man pages. Much like man pages, the info documentation is included with a command package, and the quality/quantity of the documentation can vary by package.

The method to invoke the info documentation is similar to man pages, simply execute the `info` command followed by the subject you wish to view:

```
$ info gzip
GNU Gzip: General file (de)compression
***************************************


This manual is for GNU Gzip (version 1.5, 10 June 2014), and
documents commands for compressing and decompressing data.

   Copyright (C) 1998-1999, 2001-2002, 2006-2007, 2009-2012 Free

Software Foundation, Inc.
```

Referencing more than commands

In addition to using man pages and info documentation to look up commands; these tools can also be used to view documentation around other items such as system calls or configuration files.

As an example, if you were to use man to search for the term `signal`, you would see the following:

```
$ man signal
SIGNAL(2)
Linux Programmer's Manual
SIGNAL(2)


NAME
       signal - ANSI C signal handling

SYNOPSIS
       #include <signal.h>

       typedef void (*sighandler_t)(int);

       sighandler_t signal(int signum, sighandler_t handler);

DESCRIPTION
       The  behavior of signal() varies across UNIX versions, and
has also varied historically across different versions of Linux.
Avoid its use: use sigaction(2) instead.  See Portability below.


signal() sets the disposition of the signal signum to handler,
which is either SIG_IGN, SIG_DFL, or the address of a
programmer-defined  function  (a "signal handler").
```

`Signal` is a very important system call and a core concept of Linux. Knowing that it is possible to use the `man` and `info` commands to look up core Linux concepts and behaviors can be very useful during troubleshooting.

Installing man pages

Red Hat Enterprise Linux based distributions generally include the `man-pages` package; if your system does not have the `man-pages` package installed, you can install it with the `yum` command:

```
# yum install man-pages
```

Red Hat kernel docs

In addition to man pages, the Red Hat distribution also has a package called **kernel-doc**. This package contains quite a bit of information on how the internals of the system works.

The kernel documentation is a set of text files that are placed into `/usr/share/doc/kernel-doc-<kernel-version>/` and are categorized by the topic they cover. This resource is quite useful for deeper troubleshooting such as adjusting kernel tunables or understanding how `ext4` filesystems utilize the journal.

By default, the `kernel-doc` package is not installed, however, it can be easily installed using the `yum` command:

```
# yum install kernel-doc
```

People

Whether it is a friend or a team leader, there is certain etiquette when asking others for help. The following is a list of things that people tend to expect when asked to help solve an issue. When I am asked for help, I would expect you to:

- **Try to resolve it yourself**: When escalating an issue, it is always best to at least try to follow the *Understanding the problem* statement and *Forming a hypothesis* steps of the troubleshooting process.

- **Document what you've tried**: Documentation is key to escalating issues or getting help. The better you document the steps tried and errors found, the faster it will be for others to identify and resolve the issue.

- **Explain what you think the issue is and what was reported**: When you escalate the issue, one of the first things to point out is your hypothesis. Often this can help expedite resolution by leading the next person to a possible solution without having to perform data collection activities.

- **Mention whether there is anything else that happened to this system recently**: Often issues come in pairs, it is important to highlight all factors of what is happening on the system or systems affected.

The preceding list, while not extensive, is important as each of these key pieces of information can help the next person troubleshoot the issue effectively.

Following up

When escalating issues, it is always best to follow up with that other person to find out what they did and how they did it. This is important as it will show the person you asked that you are willing to learn more, which many times will lead to them taking time to explain how they resolved and identified the issue.

Interactions like these will give you more knowledge and help build your system's administration skills and experience.

Documentation

Documentation is a critical step in the troubleshooting process. At every step during the process, it is key to take note and document the actions being performed. Why is it important to document? Three reasons mainly:

- When escalating the issue, the more information you have written down the more you can pass on to another

- If the issue is a reoccurring issue, the documentation can be used to update a Team Wiki or Runbook

- If, in your environment, you perform **Root Cause Analysis (RCA)**, all of this information will be required for a RCA

Depending on environments, the documentation can be anything from simple notes saved in a text file on a local system to required notes for a ticket system. Each work environment is different but a general rule is *there is no such thing as too much documentation*.

For Data Collectors, this step is fairly natural. As most Data Collector personalities will generally keep quite a few notes for their own personal use. For Educated Guessers, this step might seem unnecessary. However, for any issue that is reoccurring or needs to be escalated, documentation is critical.

What kind of information should be documented? The following list is a good starting point but as with most things in troubleshooting, it depends on the environment and the issue:

- The problem statement, as you understand it
- The hypothesis of what is causing the issue
- Data collected during the information gathering steps:
  - Specific errors found
  - Relevant system metrics (for example, CPU, Memory, and Disk utilization)
- Commands executed during the information gathering steps (within reason, it is not required to include every cd or ls command executed)
- Steps taken during attempts to resolve the issue, including specific commands executed

With the preceding items well documented, if the issue reoccurs, it is relatively simple to take the documentation and move it to a Team Wiki. The benefit to this is that a Wiki article can be used by other team members who need to resolve the same issue during reoccurrences.

One of the three reasons listed previously for documentation is to use the documentation during Root Cause Analysis, which leads to our next topic—Establishing a Root Cause Analysis.

Root cause analysis

Root cause analysis is a process that is performed after incidents occur. The goal of the RCA process is to identify the root cause of an incident and identify any possible corrective actions to prevent the same incident from occurring again. These corrective actions might be as simple as establishing user training to reconfiguring Apache across all web servers.

The RCA process is not unique to technology and is a widely practiced process in fields such as aviation and occupational safety. In these fields, an incident is often more than simply a few computers being offline. They are incidents where a person's life might have been at risk.

The anatomy of a good RCA

Different work environments might implement RCA processes differently but at the end of the day there are a few key elements in every good RCA:

- The problem as it was reported
- The actual root cause of the problem
- A timeline of events and actions taken
- Any key data points
- A plan of action to prevent the incident from reoccurring

The problem as it was reported

One of the first steps in the troubleshooting process is to identify the problem; this information is a key piece of information for RCAs. The importance can vary in reason depending on the issue. Sometimes, this information will show whether or not the issue was correctly identified. Most times, it can serve as an estimate of the impact of the issue.

Understanding the impact of an issue can be very important, for some companies and issues it could mean lost revenue; for other companies, it could mean damage to their brand or depending on the issue, it could mean nothing at all.

The actual root cause of the problem

This element of a Root Cause Analysis is pretty self-explanatory on its importance. However, sometimes it might not be possible to identify a root cause. In this chapter and in *Chapter 12, Root Cause Analysis of an Unexpected Reboot*, I will discuss how to handle issues where a full root cause is unavailable.

A timeline of events and actions taken

If we use an aviation incident as an example, it is easy to see where a timeline of events such as, when did the plane take off, when were passengers boarded, and when did the maintenance crew finish their evaluation, can be useful. A timeline for technology incidents can also be very useful, as it can be used to identify the length of impact and when key actions are taken.

A good timeline should consist of times and major events of the incident. The following is an example timeline of a technology incident:

- At 08:00, Joe B. phones the NOC helpline reporting an outage with e-mail servers in Tempe
- At 08:15, John C. logged into the e-mail servers in Tempe and noticed they were running out of available memory
- At 08:17, as per the Runbook, John C. began rebooting the e-mail servers one by one

Any key data points to validate the root cause

In addition to a timeline of events, the RCA should also include key data points. To use the aviation example again, a key data point would be the weather conditions during the incident, the work hours of those involved, or the condition of the aircraft.

Our timeline example included a few key data points, which include:

- Time of incident: 08:00
- Condition of e-mail servers: Running out of available memory
- Affected service: E-mail

Whether the data points are on their own or within a timeline, it is important to ensure those data points are well documented in the RCA.

A plan of action to prevent the incident from reoccurring

The entire point of performing a root cause analysis is to establish why an incident occurred and the plan of action to prevent it from happening again.

Unfortunately, this is an area that I see many RCA's neglect. An RCA process can be useful when implemented well; however, when implemented poorly they can turn into a waste of time and resources.

Often with poor implementations, you will find that RCAs are required for every incident big or small. The problem with this is that it leads to a reduction of quality in the RCAs. An RCA should only be performed when the incident causes significant impact. For example, hardware failures are not preventable, you can proactively identify hardware failure using tools such as `smartd` for hard drives but apart from replacing them you cannot always prevent them from failing. Requiring an RCA for every hardware failure and replacement is an example of a poorly implemented RCA process.

When an engineer is required to establish a root cause for something as common as hardware failing, they neglect the root cause process. When engineers neglect the RCA process for one type of incident, it can spread to other types of incidents causing quality of RCAs to suffer.

An RCA should only be reserved for incidents with significant impact. Minor incidents or routine incidents should never have an RCA requirement; they should however, be tracked. By tracking the number of hard drives that have been replaced along with the make and model of those hard drives, it is possible to identify hardware quality issues. The same is true with routine incidents such as resetting user passwords. By tracking these types of incidents, it is possible to identify possible areas of improvement.

Establishing a root cause

To give a better understanding of the RCA process, let's use a hypothetical problem seen in production environments.

 A web application crashed when writing to a file

After logging into the system, you were able to find that the application crashed because the file system where the application attempted to write to was full.

The root cause is not always the obvious cause

Was the root cause of the issue the fact that the file system was full? No. While the file system being full might have caused the application to crash, this is what is called a contributing factor. A contributing factor, such as the filesystem being full can be corrected but this will not prevent the issue from reoccurring.

At this point, it is important to identify why the filesystem was full. On further investigation, you find that it was due to a co-worker disabling a **cron job** that removes old application files. After the cron job was disabled, the available space on the filesystem slowly kept decreasing. Eventually, the filesystem was 100 percent utilized.

In this case, the root cause of the issue was the disabled cron job.

Sometimes you must sacrifice a root cause analysis

Let's look at another hypothetical situation, where an issue causes an outage. Since the issue caused significant impact, it will absolutely require an RCA. The problem is, in order to resolve the issue, you will need to perform an activity that eliminates the possibility of performing an accurate RCA.

These situations sometimes require a judgment call, whether to live with the outage a little longer or resolve the outage and sacrifice any chance of an RCA. Unfortunately, there is no single answer for these situations, the correct answer depends on both the issue and the environment affected.

While working on financial systems, I find myself having to make this decision often. With mission critical systems, the answer was almost always to restore service above performing the root cause analysis. However, whenever possible, it is always preferred to first capture data even if that data cannot be reviewed immediately.

Understanding your environment

The final section in this chapter is one of the most important best practices I can suggest. The final section covers the importance of understanding your environment.

Some believe that a systems administrator's job stops at the applications installed on the system and that the systems administrator should only be concerned with the operating system and the operating system's components, such as networking or file systems.

I do not follow this philosophy. In reality, it is often that a systems administrator will start to understand how an application works in production better than the development team who created it.

From my experience, in order to truly support a server, you must understand the service and applications running within that server. For example, in many enterprise environments the systems administrator is expected to handle the configuration and management of the web server (for example, Apache and Nginx). However, the same system admin is not expected to manage the application (for example, Java and C) behind Apache.

What makes Apache different from a Java application? The answer is nothing really; at the end of the day they are both applications running on the server. I have seen many administrators simply wash their hands off an issue once the issue is related to an application. Yet if the issue is related to Apache, they spring into action.

In the end, if those administration groups were to partner with the development group the issues could be solved faster. It is the administrator's responsibility to understand and help troubleshoot issues with any software loaded on their systems. Whether that software was distributed with the OS or installed later by an application team.

Summary

In this chapter, you learned that there are two main styles of troubleshooting, intuitive (Educated Guessers) and systematic (Data Collectors). We covered which troubleshooting steps work best for those two styles and that it is possible for some (Adaptors) to utilize both styles of troubleshooting.

In the following chapters of this book, as we troubleshoot real-life scenarios, I will utilize both the intuitive and systematic troubleshooting steps highlighted in the processes discussed in this chapter.

This chapter did not get into technical specifics; the next chapter will be full of technical details, as we cover and explore common Linux commands used for troubleshooting.

2

Troubleshooting Commands and Sources of Useful Information

In the first chapter, we covered troubleshooting best practices and the high level process involved. Where the first chapter was a 20,000 ft view on troubleshooting, this chapter starts to dive into the specifics.

This chapter will review common troubleshooting commands as well as common places to find helpful information. Within this book, we will utilize release 7 of Red Hat Enterprise Linux (also referred to as RHEL). All commands referenced in this chapter will be commands that are included with a default installation of RHEL 7.

We will reference commands that are installed by default, as I have found myself in situations where I could have used a specific command to identify an issue immediately but that command was not available to me. By limiting this chapter to default commands, you can be assured that the troubleshooting steps covered in this chapter are not only relevant to most RHEL 7 installations, but are also relevant to previous releases and other Linux distributions.

Finding useful information

Before starting to explore troubleshooting commands, I first want to cover locations of useful information. Useful information is a bit of a vague term, pretty much every file, directory, or command can provide *useful information*. What I really plan to cover are places where it is possible to find information for almost any issue.

Log files

Log files are often the first place to start looking for troubleshooting information. Whenever a service or server is experiencing an issue, checking the log files for errors can often answer many questions quickly.

The default location

By default, RHEL and most Linux distributions keep their log files in `/var/log/`, which is actually part of the **Filesystem Hierarchy Standard (FHS)** maintained by the Linux Foundation. However, while `/var/log/` might be the default location not all log files are located there (`http://en.wikipedia.org/wiki/Filesystem_Hierarchy_Standard`).

While `/var/log/httpd/` is the default location for Apache logs, this location can be changed with Apache's configuration files. This is especially common when Apache was installed outside of the standard RHEL package.

Like Apache, most services allow for custom log locations. It is not uncommon to find custom directories or file systems outside of `/var/log` created specifically for log files.

Common log files

The following table is a short list of common log files and a description of what you can find within them.

 Do keep in mind that this list is specific to Red Hat Enterprise Linux 7, and while other Linux distributions might follow similar conventions, they are not guaranteed.

Log file	Description
`/var/log/messages`	By default, this log file contains all syslog messages (except e-mail) of `INFO` or higher priority.
`/var/log/secure`	This log file contains authentication related message items such as: • SSH logins • User creations • Sudo violations and privilege escalation

Log file	Description
/var/log/cron	This log file contains a history of crond executions as well as start and end times of cron.daily, cron.weekly, and other executions.
/var/log/maillog	This log file is the default log location of mail events. If using postfix, this is the default location for all postfix-related messages.
/var/log/httpd/	This log directory is the default location for Apache logs. While this is the default location, it is not a guaranteed location for all Apache logs.
/var/log/mysql.log	This log file is the default log file for mysqld. Much like the httpd logs, this is default and can be changed easily.
/var/log/sa/	This directory contains the results of the sa commands that run every 10 minutes by default. We will utilize this data more in later sections in this chapter and throughout this book.

For many issues, one of the first log files to review is the /var/log/messages log. On RHEL systems, this log file receives all system logs of INFO priority or higher. In general, this means that any significant event sent to syslog would be captured in this log file.

The following is a sample of some of the log messages that can be found in /var/log/messages:

```
Dec 24 18:03:51 localhost systemd: Starting Network Manager Script
Dispatcher Service...
Dec 24 18:03:51 localhost dbus-daemon: dbus[620]: [system]
Successfully activated service 'org.freedesktop.nm_dispatcher'
Dec 24 18:03:51 localhost dbus[620]: [system] Successfully activated
service 'org.freedesktop.nm_dispatcher'
Dec 24 18:03:51 localhost systemd: Started Network Manager Script
Dispatcher Service.
Dec 24 18:06:06 localhost kernel: e1000: enp0s3 NIC Link is Down
Dec 24 18:06:06 localhost kernel: e1000: enp0s8 NIC Link is Down
Dec 24 18:06:06 localhost NetworkManager[750]: <info> (enp0s3): link
disconnected (deferring action for 4 seconds)
Dec 24 18:06:06 localhost NetworkManager[750]: <info> (enp0s8): link
disconnected (deferring action for 4 seconds)
Dec 24 18:06:10 localhost NetworkManager[750]: <info> (enp0s3): link
disconnected (calling deferred action)
Dec 24 18:06:10 localhost NetworkManager[750]: <info> (enp0s8): link
disconnected (calling deferred action)
```

```
Dec 24 18:06:12 localhost kernel: e1000: enp0s3 NIC Link is Up 1000
Mbps Full Duplex, Flow Control: RX
Dec 24 18:06:12 localhost kernel: e1000: enp0s8 NIC Link is Up 1000
Mbps Full Duplex, Flow Control: RX
Dec 24 18:06:12 localhost NetworkManager[750]: <info> (enp0s3): link
connected
Dec 24 18:06:12 localhost NetworkManager[750]: <info> (enp0s8): link
connected
Dec 24 18:06:39 localhost kernel: atkbd serio0: Spurious NAK on
isa0060/serio0. Some program might be trying to access hardware
directly.
Dec 24 18:07:10 localhost systemd: Starting Session 53 of user root.
Dec 24 18:07:10 localhost systemd: Started Session 53 of user root.
Dec 24 18:07:10 localhost systemd-logind: New session 53 of user root.
```

As we can see, there are more than a few log messages within this sample that could be useful while troubleshooting issues.

Finding logs that are not in the default location

Many times log files are not in /var/log/, which can be either because someone modified the log location to some place apart from the default, or simply because the service in question defaults to another location.

In general, there are three ways to find log files not in /var/log/.

Checking syslog configuration

If you know a service is using syslog for its logging, the best place to check to find which log file its messages are being written to is the **rsyslog** configuration files. The rsyslog service has two locations for configuration. The first is the /etc/rsyslog.d directory.

The /etc/rsyslog.d directory is an include directory for custom rsyslog configurations. The second is the /etc/rsyslog.conf configuration file. This is the main configuration file for rsyslog and contains many of the default syslog configurations.

The following is a sample of the default contents of /etc/rsyslog.conf:

```
#### RULES ####

# Log all kernel messages to the console.
# Logging much else clutters up the screen.
#kern.*                              /dev/console
```

```
# Log anything (except mail) of level info or higher.
# Don't log private authentication messages!
*.info;mail.none;authpriv.none;cron.none   /var/log/messages

# The authpriv file has restricted access.
authpriv.*                          /var/log/secure

# Log all the mail messages in one place.
mail.*                              -/var/log/maillog


# Log cron stuff
cron.*                              /var/log/cron
```

By reviewing the contents of this file, it is fairly easy to identify which log files contain the information required, if not, at least, the possible location of syslog managed log files.

Checking the application's configuration

Not every application utilizes syslog; for those that don't, one of the easiest ways to find the application's log file is to read the application's configuration files.

A quick and useful method for finding log file locations from configuration files is to use the grep command to search the file for the word log:

```
$ grep log /etc/samba/smb.conf
# files are rotated when they reach the size specified with "max
log size".
  # log files split per-machine:
  log file = /var/log/samba/log.%m
  # maximum size of 50KB per log file, then rotate:
  max log size = 50
```

The grep command is a very useful command that can be used to search files or directories for specific strings or patterns. This command will be used throughout this book in various methods. The simplest command can be seen in the preceding snippet where the grep command is used to search the /etc/samba/smb.conf file for any instance of the pattern "log".

After reviewing the output of the preceding grep command, we can see that the configured log location for samba is /var/log/samba/log.%m. It is important to note that %m, in this example, is actually replaced with a "machine name" when creating the file. This is actually a variable within the samba configuration file. These variables are unique to each application but this method for making dynamic configuration values is a common practice.

Other examples

The following are examples of using the grep command to search for the word "log" in the Apache and MySQL configuration files:

```
$ grep log /etc/httpd/conf/httpd.conf
# ErrorLog: The location of the error log file.
# logged here.  If you *do* define an error logfile for a
<VirtualHost>
# container, that host's errors will be logged there and not here.
ErrorLog "logs/error_log"

$ grep log /etc/my.cnf
# log_bin
log-error=/var/log/mysqld.log
```

In both instances, this method was able to identify the configuration parameter for the service's log file. With the previous three examples, it is easy to see how effective searching through configuration files can be.

Using the find command

The find command, which we will cover in depth later in this chapter, is another useful method for finding log files. The find command is used to search a directory structure for specified files. A quick way of finding log files is to simply use the find command to search for any files that end in ".log":

```
# find /opt/appxyz/ -type f -name "*.log"
/opt/appxyz/logs/daily/7-1-15/alert.log
/opt/appxyz/logs/daily/7-2-15/alert.log
/opt/appxyz/logs/daily/7-3-15/alert.log
/opt/appxyz/logs/daily/7-4-15/alert.log
/opt/appxyz/logs/daily/7-5-15/alert.log
```

The preceding is generally considered a last resort solution, and is mostly used when the previous methods do not produce results.

> When executing the find command, it is considered a best practice to be very specific about which directory to search. When being executed against very large directories, the performance of the server can be degraded.

Configuration files

As discussed previously, configuration files for an application or service can be excellent sources of information. While configuration files won't provide you with specific errors such as log files, they can provide you with critical information (for example, enabled/disabled features, output directories, and log file locations).

Default system configuration directory

In general, system, and service configuration files are located within the `/etc/` directory on most Linux distributions. However, this does not mean that every configuration file is located within the `/etc/` directory. In fact, it is not uncommon for applications to include a configuration directory within the application's home directory.

So how do you know when to look in the `/etc/` versus an application directory for configuration files? A general rule of thumb is, if the package is part of the RHEL distribution, it is safe to assume that the configuration is within the `/etc/` directory. Anything else may or may not be present in the `/etc/` directory. For these situations, you simply have to look for them.

Finding configuration files

In most scenarios, it is possible to find system configuration files within the `/etc/` directory with a simple directory listing using the `ls` command:

```
$ ls -la /etc/ | grep my
-rw-r--r--.  1 root root      570 Nov 17  2014 my.cnf
drwxr-xr-x.  2 root root       64 Jan  9  2015 my.cnf.d
```

The preceding code snippet uses `ls` to perform a directory listing and redirects that output to `grep` in order to search the output for the string "my". We can see from the output that there is a `my.cnf` configuration file and a `my.cnf.d` configuration directory. The MySQL processes use these for its configuration. We were able to find these by assuming that anything related to MySQL would have the string "my" in it.

Using the rpm command

If the configuration files were deployed as part of a RPM package, it is possible to use the `rpm` command to identify configuration files. To do this, simply execute the `rpm` command with the `-q` (query) flag, and the `-c` (configfiles) flag, followed by the name of the package:

```
$ rpm -q -c httpd
/etc/httpd/conf.d/autoindex.conf
/etc/httpd/conf.d/userdir.conf
```

```
/etc/httpd/conf.d/welcome.conf
/etc/httpd/conf.modules.d/00-base.conf
/etc/httpd/conf.modules.d/00-dav.conf
/etc/httpd/conf.modules.d/00-lua.conf
/etc/httpd/conf.modules.d/00-mpm.conf
/etc/httpd/conf.modules.d/00-proxy.conf
/etc/httpd/conf.modules.d/00-systemd.conf
/etc/httpd/conf.modules.d/01-cgi.conf
/etc/httpd/conf/httpd.conf
/etc/httpd/conf/magic
/etc/logrotate.d/httpd
/etc/sysconfig/htcacheclean
/etc/sysconfig/httpd
```

The `rpm` command is used to manage RPM packages and is a very useful command when troubleshooting. We will cover this command further in the next section as we explore commands for troubleshooting.

Using the find command

Much like finding log files, to find configuration files on a system, it is possible to utilize the `find` command. When searching for log files, the `find` command was used to search for all files where the name ends in ".log". In the following example, the `find` command is being used to search for all files where the name begins with "http". This `find` command should return at least a few results, which will provide configuration files related to the HTTPD (Apache) service:

```
# find /etc -type f -name "http*"

/etc/httpd/conf/httpd.conf
/etc/sysconfig/httpd
/etc/logrotate.d/httpd
```

The preceding example searches the /etc directory; however, this could also be used to search any application home directory for user configuration files. Similar to searching for log files, using the `find` command to search for configuration files is generally considered a last resort step and should not be the first method used.

The proc filesystem

An extremely useful source of information is the `proc` filesystem. This is a special filesystem that is maintained by the Linux kernel. The `proc` filesystem can be used to find useful information about running processes, as well as other system information. For example, if we wanted to identify the filesystems supported by a system, we could simply read the `/proc/filesystems` file:

```
$ cat /proc/filesystems
nodev   sysfs
nodev   rootfs
nodev   bdev
nodev   proc
nodev   cgroup
nodev   cpuset
nodev   tmpfs
nodev   devtmpfs
nodev   debugfs
nodev   securityfs
nodev   sockfs
nodev   pipefs
nodev   anon_inodefs
nodev   configfs
nodev   devpts
nodev   ramfs
nodev   hugetlbfs
nodev   autofs
nodev   pstore
nodev   mqueue
nodev   selinuxfs
        xfs
nodev   rpc_pipefs
nodev   nfsd
```

This filesystem is extremely useful and contains quite a bit of information about a running system. The `proc filesystem` will be used throughout the troubleshooting steps within this book. It is used in various ways while troubleshooting everything from specific processes to read-only filesystems.

Troubleshooting commands

This section will cover frequently used troubleshooting commands that can be used to gather information from the system or a running service. While it is not feasible to cover every possible command, the commands used do cover fundamental troubleshooting steps for Linux systems.

Command-line basics

The troubleshooting steps used within this book are primarily command-line based. While it is possible to perform many of these things from a graphical desktop environment, the more advanced items are command-line specific. As such, this book assumes that the reader has at least a basic understanding of Linux. To be more specific, this book assumes that the reader has logged into a server via SSH and is familiar with basic commands such as cd, cp, mv, rm, and ls.

For those who might not have much familiarity, I wanted to quickly cover some basic command-line usage that will be required knowledge for this book.

Command flags

Many readers are probably familiar with the following command:

```
$ ls -la
total 588
drwx------. 5 vagrant vagrant   4096 Jul  4 21:26 .
drwxr-xr-x. 3 root    root        20 Jul 22  2014 ..
-rw-rw-r--. 1 vagrant vagrant 153104 Jun 10 17:03 app.c
```

Most should recognize that this is the ls command and it is used to perform a directory listing. What might not be familiar is what exactly the -la part of the command is or does. To understand this better, let's look at the ls command by itself:

```
$ ls
app.c  application  app.py  bomber.py  index.html  lookbusy-1.4
lookbusy-1.4.tar.gz  lotsofiles
```

The previous execution of the ls command looks very different from the previous. The reason for this is because the latter is the default output for ls. The -la portion of the command is what is commonly referred to as command flags or options. The command flags allow a user to change the default behavior of the command providing it with specific options.

In fact, the -la flags are two separate options, -l and -a; they can even be specified separately:

```
$ ls -l -a
total 588
drwx------. 5 vagrant vagrant   4096 Jul  4 21:26 .
drwxr-xr-x. 3 root    root        20 Jul 22  2014 ..
-rw-rw-r--. 1 vagrant vagrant 153104 Jun 10 17:03 app.c
```

We can see from the preceding snippet that the output of ls -la is exactly the same as ls -l -a. For common commands, such as the ls command, it does not matter if the flags are grouped or separated, they will be parsed in the same way. Throughout this book, examples will show both grouped and ungrouped. If grouping or ungrouping is performed for any specific reason it will be called out; otherwise, the grouping or ungrouping used within this book is used for visual appeal and memorization.

In addition to grouping and ungrouping, this book will also show flags in their long format. In the previous examples, we showed the flag -a, this is known as a short flag. This same option can also be provided in the long format --all:

```
$ ls -l --all
total 588
drwx------. 5 vagrant vagrant   4096 Jul  4 21:26 .
drwxr-xr-x. 3 root    root        20 Jul 22  2014 ..
-rw-rw-r--. 1 vagrant vagrant 153104 Jun 10 17:03 app.c
```

The -a and the --all flags are essentially the same option; it can simply be represented in both short and long form.

One important thing to remember is that not every short flag has a long form and vice versa. Each command has its own syntax, some commands only support the short form, others only support the long form, but many support both. In most cases, the long and short flags will both be documented within the command's man page.

The piping command output

Another common command-line practice that will be used several times throughout this book is piping output. Specifically, examples such as the following:

```
$ ls -l --all | grep app
-rw-rw-r--. 1 vagrant vagrant 153104 Jun 10 17:03 app.c
-rwxrwxr-x. 1 vagrant vagrant  29390 May 18 00:47 application
-rw-rw-r--. 1 vagrant vagrant   1198 Jun 10 17:03 app.py
```

In the preceding example, the output of the `ls -l --all` command is piped to the `grep` command. By placing | or the pipe character between the two commands, the output of the first command is "piped" to the input for the second command. The example preceding the `ls` command will be executed; with that, the `grep` command will then search that output for any instance of the pattern "app".

Piping output to `grep` will actually be used quite often throughout this book, as it is a simple way to trim the output into a maintainable size. Many times the examples will also contain multiple levels of piping:

```
$ ls -la | grep app | awk '{print $4,$9}'
vagrant app.c
vagrant application
vagrant app.py
```

In the preceding code the output of `ls -la` is piped to the input of `grep`; however, this time, the output of `grep` is also piped to the input of `awk`.

While many commands can be piped to, not every command supports this. In general, commands that accept user input from files or command-line also accept piped input. As with the flags, a command's man page can be used to identify whether the command accepts piped input or not.

Gathering general information

When managing the same servers for a long time, you start to remember key information about those servers. Such as the amount of physical memory, the size and layout of their filesystems, and what processes should be running. However, when you are not familiar with the server in question it is always a good idea to gather this type of information.

The commands in this section are commands that can be used to gather this type of general information.

w – show who is logged on and what they are doing

Early in my systems administration career, I had a mentor who used to tell me: *I always run w when I log into a server*. This simple tip has actually been very useful over and over again in my career. The w command is simple; when executed it will output information such as system uptime, load average, and who is logged in:

```
# w
 04:07:37 up 14:26,  2 users,  load average: 0.00, 0.01, 0.05
 USER     TTY        LOGIN@   IDLE   JCPU   PCPU WHAT
 root     tty1       Wed13    11:24m 0.13s  0.13s -bash
 root     pts/0      20:47    1.00s  0.21s  0.19s -bash
```

This information can be extremely useful when working with unfamiliar systems. The output can be useful even when you are familiar with the system. With this command, you can see:

- When this system was last rebooted:

  `04:07:37 up 14:26:` This information can be extremely useful; whether it is an alert for a service like Apache being down, or a user calling in because they were locked out of the system. When these issues are caused by an unexpected reboot, the reported issue does not often include this information. By running the w command, it is easy to see the time elapsed since the last reboot.

- The load average of the system:

  `load average: 0.00, 0.01, 0.05:` The load average is a very important measurement of system health. To summarize it, the load average is the average number of processes in a `wait` state over a period of time. The three numbers in the output of w represent different times.

  The numbers are ordered from left to right as 1 minute, 5 minutes, and 15 minutes.

- Who is logged in and what they are running:

	USER	TTY	LOGIN@	IDLE	JCPU	PCPU WHAT
○	root	tty1	Wed13	11:24m	0.13s	0.13s -bash

  The final piece of information that the w command provides is users that are currently logged in and what command they are executing.

This is essentially the same output as the who command, which includes the user logged in, when they logged in, how long they have been idle, and what command their shell is running. The last item in that list is extremely important.

Oftentimes, when working with big teams, it is common for more than one person to respond to an issue or ticket. By running the w command immediately after login, you will see what other users are doing, preventing you from overriding any troubleshooting or corrective steps the other person has taken.

rpm – RPM package manager

The rpm command is used to manage **Red Hat package manager (RPM)**. With this command, you can install and remove RPM packages, as well as search for packages that are already installed.

Earlier in this chapter, we saw how the rpm command can be used to look for configuration files. The following are several additional ways we can use the rpm command to find critical information.

Listing all packages installed

Often when troubleshooting services, a critical step is identifying the version of the service and how it was installed. To list all RPM packages installed on a system, simply execute the rpm command with -q (query) and -a (all):

```
# rpm -q -a
kpatch-0.0-1.el7.noarch
virt-what-1.13-5.el7.x86_64
filesystem-3.2-18.el7.x86_64
gssproxy-0.3.0-9.el7.x86_64
hicolor-icon-theme-0.12-7.el7.noarch
```

The rpm command is a very diverse command with many flags. In the preceding example the -q and -a flags are used. The -q flag tells the rpm command that the action being taken is a query; you can think of this as being put into a "search mode". The -a or --all flag tells the rpm command to list all packages.

A useful feature is to add the --last flag to the preceding command, as this causes the rpm command to list the packages by install time with the latest being first.

Listing all files deployed by a package

Another useful rpm function is to show all of the files deployed by a specific package:

```
# rpm -q --filesbypkg kpatch-0.0-1.el7.noarch
kpatch                          /usr/bin/kpatch
kpatch                          /usr/lib/systemd/system/kpatch.service
```

In the preceding example, we again use the -q flag to specify that we are running a query, along with the --filesbypkg flag. The --filesbypkg flag will cause the rpm command to list all of the files deployed by the specified package.

This example can be very useful when trying to identify a service's configuration file location.

Using package verification

In this third example, we are going to use an extremely useful feature of rpm—verify. The rpm command has the ability to verify whether or not the files deployed by a specified package have been altered from their original contents. To do this, we will use the -V (verify) flag:

```
# rpm -V httpd
S.5....T.  c /etc/httpd/conf/httpd.conf
```

In the preceding example, we simply run the rpm command with the -V flag followed by a package name. As the -q flag is used for querying, the -V flag is for verifying. With this command, we can see that only the /etc/httpd/conf/httpd.conf file was listed; this is because rpm will only output files that have been altered.

In the first column of this output, we can see which verification checks the file failed. While this column is a bit cryptic at first, the rpm man page has a useful table (as shown in the following list) explaining what each character means:

- S: This means that the file size differs
- M: This means that the mode differs (includes permissions and file type)
- 5: This means that the digest (formerly MD5 sum) differs
- D: This means indicates the device major/minor number mismatch
- L: This means indicates the readLink(2) path mismatch
- U: This means that the user ownership differs
- G: This means that the group ownership differs
- T: This means that mTime differs
- P: This means that caPabilities differs

Using this list we can see that the httpd.conf's file size, MD5 sum, and mtime (modify time) are not what was deployed by httpd.rpm. This means that it is highly likely that the httpd.conf file has been modified after installation.

While the rpm command might not seem like a troubleshooting command at first, the preceding examples show just how powerful of a troubleshooting tool it can be. With these examples, it is simple to identify important files and whether or not those files have been modified from the deployed version.

df – report file system space usage

The df command is a very useful command when troubleshooting file system issues.
The df command is used to output space utilization for mounted file systems:

```
# df -h
Filesystem              Size  Used Avail Use% Mounted on
/dev/mapper/rhel-root   6.7G  1.6G  5.2G  24% /
devtmpfs                489M     0  489M   0% /dev
tmpfs                   498M     0  498M   0% /dev/shm
tmpfs                   498M   13M  485M   3% /run
tmpfs                   498M     0  498M   0% /sys/fs/cgroup
/dev/sdb1               212G   58G  144G  29% /repos
/dev/sda1               497M  117M  380M  24% /boot
```

In the preceding example, the df command included the -h flag. This flag causes the
df command to print any size values in a "human readable" format. By default, df
will simply print these values in kilobytes. From the example, we can quickly see
the current usage of all mounted filesystems. Specifically, if we look at the output,
we can see that /filesystem is currently 24 percent used:

```
Filesystem              Size  Used Avail Use% Mounted on
/dev/mapper/rhel-root   6.7G  1.6G  5.2G  24% /
```

This is a very quick and easy way to identify whether any file system is full.
In addition, the df command is also very useful in showing details of what file
systems are mounted and where they are mounted to. From the line containing the
/filesystem, we can see that the underlying device is /dev/mapper/rhel-root.

From this one command, we were able to identify two critical pieces of information.

Showing available inodes

The default behavior for df is to show the amount of used file system space.
However, it can also be used to show the quantity of **inodes** available, used, and
free for each file system. To output the inode utilization, simply add the -i (inode)
flag when executing the df command:

```
# df -i
Filesystem             Inodes IUsed   IFree IUse% Mounted on
/dev/mapper/rhel-root 7032832 44318 6988514    1% /
devtmpfs               125039   347  124692    1% /dev
```

It is still possible to use the –h flag with df to print the output in a human readable format. However, with the –i flag, this abbreviates the output to M for millions, K for thousands, and so on. This output can be easily confused with Megabytes or Kilobytes, so in general, I do not use the human readable inode output when sharing the output with other users/administrators.

free – display memory utilization

When executed, the free command will output statistics about the memory available and in use on the system:

```
$ free
               total        used        free      shared     buffers
cached
Mem:         1018256      789796      228460       13116        3608
543484
-/+ buffers/cache:        242704      775552
Swap:         839676           4      839672
```

From the previous example, we can see that the output of the free command provides the total available memory, amount of memory currently used, and amount of memory free. The free command is a simple and quick way to identify the current state of memory on a system.

However, the output of free can be a bit confusing at first.

What is free, is not always free

Linux utilizes memory differently as compared to other operating systems. In the preceding output, you will see that it has 543,484 KB listed as cached. This memory, while technically used, is actually part of the available memory. The system can reallocate this cached memory as required.

A quick and easy way of seeing what is actually used or free can be seen on the second line of output. The preceding output shows that 775,552 KB of memory is available on the system.

The /proc/meminfo file

In previous RHEL releases, the second line of the free command was the easiest method for identifying how much memory is available. However, with RHEL 7, there have been some improvements to the /proc/meminfo file. One of those improvements is the addition of the **MemAvailable** statistic:

```
$ grep Available /proc/meminfo
MemAvailable:       641056 kB
```

The /proc/meminfo file is one of the many useful files located in the /proc file system. This file is maintained by the kernel and contains the system's current memory statistics. This file can be very useful when troubleshooting memory issues as it contains much more information than the output of the free command.

ps – report a snapshot of current running processes

The ps command is a fundamental command for any troubleshooting activity. This command, when executed, will output a list of running processes:

```
# ps
  PID TTY          TIME CMD
15618 pts/0    00:00:00 ps
17633 pts/0    00:00:00 bash
```

The ps command has many flags and options to show different information about running processes. The following are a few example ps commands that are useful during troubleshooting.

Printing every process in long format

The following ps command uses the -e (everything, all process), -l (long format), and -f (full format) flags. These flags will cause the ps command to not only print every process but will also print them in a format that provides quite a bit of useful information:

```
# ps -elf
F S UID    PID  PPID  C PRI  NI ADDR SZ WCHAN  STIME TTY    TIME CMD
1 S root     2    0    0  80   0 - 0 kthrea Dec24 ?   00:00:00 [kthreadd]
```

In the preceding output of ps -elf, we can see many useful pieces of information for the kthreadd process, information such as the **parent process ID (PPID)**, the **priority (PRI)**, the **niceness value (NI)**, and the **resident memory size (SZ)** of the running processes.

I have found that the preceding example is a very general-purpose ps command and can be used in most situations.

Printing a specific user's processes

The preceding example can get quite large; making it difficult to identify specific processes. This example uses the -U flag to specify a user. This causes the ps command to print all processes running as the specified user; postfix in the following case:

```
ps -U postfix -l
F S   UID   PID  PPID  C PRI  NI ADDR SZ WCHAN   TTY        TIME CMD
```

```
4 S     89  1546  1536  0  80  0 - 23516 ep_pol ?    00:00:00 qmgr
4 S     89 16711  1536  0  80  0 - 23686 ep_pol ?  00:00:00 pickup
```

It is important to note that the –U flag can also be combined with other flags to provide even more information on the running processes. In the preceding example, the -l flag is once again used to print the output in the long format.

Printing a process by process ID

If the process ID or PID is already known, it is possible to narrow down the process listing even further by specifying the process with the –p (process ID) flag:

```
# ps -p 1236 -l
F S    UID    PID  PPID  C PRI  NI ADDR SZ WCHAN   TTY         TIME CMD
4 S      0   1236     1  0  80   0 - 20739 poll_s  ?       00:00:00 sshd
```

This can be especially useful when combined with the –L (show threads with LWP column) or –m (show threads after process) flag, which are used to print process threads. When troubleshooting multithreaded applications the -L and -m flags can be critical.

Printing processes with performance information

The ps command allows the user to customize the columns printed with the -o (user defined format) flag:

```
# ps -U postfix -o pid,user,pcpu,vsz,cmd
  PID USER       %CPU     VSZ CMD
 1546 postfix     0.0   94064 qmgr -l -t unix -u
16711 postfix     0.0   94744 pickup -l -t unix -u
```

The -o option allows for a wide number of custom columns. In the preceding version, I selected options that are similar to those printed in the top command.

The top command is one of the most popular Linux troubleshooting commands. It is used to show the top processes ordered by CPU usage (by default). In this chapter, I have opted to omit the top command, as I feel that the ps command is even more fundamental and flexible than the top command. As one becomes more familiar with the ps command, the top command will be easy to learn and understand.

Networking

Networking is an essential skill for any systems administrator. Without a properly configured network interface, a server serves little purpose. The commands in this section are specifically for looking up network configuration and current status. These commands are essential to learn, as they will not only be useful for troubleshooting but also for day-to-day setup and configuration.

ip – show and manipulate network settings

The ip command is used to manage network settings such as interface configuration, routing and essentially anything network related. While these are not traditionally considered troubleshooting tasks, the ip command can also be used to display a system's network configuration. Without being able to look up networking details such as routing or device configuration, it would be very difficult to troubleshoot network-related issues.

The following examples show various ways to use the ip command to identify critical network configuration settings.

Show IP address configuration for a specific device

One of the core uses of the ip command is to lookup a network interface and display its configuration. To do this, we will use the following command:

```
# ip addr show dev enp0s3
2: enp0s3: <BROADCAST,MULTICAST,UP,LOWER_UP> mtu 1500 qdisc
pfifo_fast state UP qlen 1000
    link/ether 08:00:27:6e:35:18 brd ff:ff:ff:ff:ff:ff
    inet 10.0.2.15/24 brd 10.0.2.255 scope global dynamic enp0s3
        valid_lft 45083sec preferred_lft 45083sec
    inet6 fe80::a00:27ff:fe6e:3518/64 scope link
        valid_lft forever preferred_lft forever
```

In the preceding ip command, the first option provided addr (address) is used to define the type of information we are looking for. The second option show, tells ip to display the configuration of the first option. The third option dev (device) is followed by the network interface device in question; enp0s3. If the third option is omitted the ip command will show the address configuration for all network devices.

The device name enp0s3 might look a bit strange for those who have experience with previous RHEL releases. This device is following a newer network device naming scheme introduced with systemd. As of RHEL 7, network devices will use device names such as the previous, which are based on device driver and BIOS details.

To find out more about RHEL 7's new naming scheme simply reference the following URL:

```
https://access.redhat.com/documentation/en-US/Red_Hat_Enterprise_
Linux/7/html/Networking_Guide/ch-Consistent_Network_Device_Naming.
html
```

Show routing configuration

The `ip` command can also be used to show routing configurations. This information is essential for troubleshooting connectivity issues between servers:

```
# ip route show
default via 10.0.2.2 dev enp0s3  proto static  metric 1024
10.0.2.0/24 dev enp0s3  proto kernel  scope link  src 10.0.2.15
192.168.56.0/24 dev enp0s8  proto kernel  scope link  src
192.168.56.101
```

The preceding `ip` command uses the `route` option followed by the `show` option to display all defined routes for this server. Like the previous example, it is possible to limit this output to a specific device by adding the `dev` (device) option followed by the device name:

```
# ip route show dev enp0s3
default via 10.0.2.2  proto static  metric 1024
10.0.2.0/24  proto kernel  scope link  src 10.0.2.15
```

Show network statistics for a specified device

Where the previous examples showed ways to lookup the current networking configuration, this next command uses the `-s` (statistics) flag to show network statistics for the specified device:

```
# ip -s link show dev enp0s3
2: enp0s3: <BROADCAST,MULTICAST,UP,LOWER_UP> mtu 1500 qdisc
pfifo_fast state UP mode DEFAULT qlen 1000
    link/ether 08:00:27:6e:35:18 brd ff:ff:ff:ff:ff:ff
    RX: bytes  packets  errors  dropped overrun mcast
    109717927 125911   0       0       0       0
    TX: bytes  packets  errors  dropped carrier collsns
    3944294    40127    0       0       0       0
```

In the preceding example, the `link` (network device) option was used to specify that the statistics should be limited to the specified device.

The statistics information shown can be useful when troubleshooting packets that are being dropped or to identify which interface has higher network utilization.

netstat – network statistics

The `netstat` command is an essential tool in any system administrator's tool belt. This can be seen by the fact that the `netstat` command is universally available even to operating systems that do not traditionally utilize command line for administration.

Printing network connections

One of the primary uses of `netstat` is to print the existing established network connections. This can be done by simply executing `netstat`; however, if the `-a` (all) flag is used, the output will also include listening ports:

```
# netstat -na
Active Internet connections (servers and established)
Proto Recv-Q Send-Q Local Address         Foreign Address      State
tcp       0      0 127.0.0.1:25          0.0.0.0:*            LISTEN
tcp       0      0 0.0.0.0:44969         0.0.0.0:*            LISTEN
tcp       0      0 0.0.0.0:111           0.0.0.0:*            LISTEN
tcp       0      0 0.0.0.0:22            0.0.0.0:*            LISTEN
tcp       0      0 192.168.56.101:22     192.168.56.1:50122
ESTABLISHED
tcp6      0      0 ::1:25                :::*                 LISTEN
```

While the `-a` (all) flag used the preceding `netstat` causes to print all listening ports, the `-n` flag is used to force output into a numeric format, such as printing IP addresses rather than DNS host names.

The preceding example will be used heavily during *Chapter 5, Network Troubleshooting,* where we will be troubleshooting network connectivity.

Printing all ports listening for tcp connections

I have seen many instances where a service is running and is visible via the `ps` command; however, the port for clients to connect to was not bound and listening. The following `netstat` command can be very useful when troubleshooting connectivity issues with a service:

```
# netstat -nlp --tcp
Active Internet connections (only servers)
Proto Recv-Q Send-Q Local Address         Foreign Address
State       PID/Program name
tcp       0      0 127.0.0.1:25          0.0.0.0:*
LISTEN      1536/master
tcp       0      0 0.0.0.0:44969         0.0.0.0:*
LISTEN      1270/rpc.statd
tcp       0      0 0.0.0.0:111           0.0.0.0:*
LISTEN      1215/rpcbind
```

```
tcp        0        0 0.0.0.0:22              0.0.0.0:*
LISTEN         1236/sshd
tcp6       0        0 ::1:25                  :::*
LISTEN         1536/master
tcp6       0        0 :::111                  :::*
LISTEN         1215/rpcbind
tcp6       0        0 :::22                   :::*
LISTEN         1236/sshd
tcp6       0        0 :::46072                :::*
LISTEN         1270/rpc.statd
```

The preceding command is very useful as it combines three useful options:

- `-l` (listening), which tells `netstat` to only list listening sockets
- `--tcp`, which tells `netstat` to limit the output to TCP connections
- `-p` (program), which tells `netstat` to list the PID and name of the process listening on that port

Delay

An often overlooked option with `netstat` is to utilize the delay feature. By adding a number at the end of the command, `netstat` will continuously run and will sleep for the specified number of seconds between executions.

If the following command is executed, the `netstat` command will print all listening TCP sockets every five seconds:

```
# netstat -nlp --tcp 5
```

The delay feature can be very useful when investigating network connectivity issues. As it can easily show when an application binds a port for new connections.

Performance

While we touched a bit on troubleshooting performance with commands such as `free` and `ps`, this section will show some very useful commands that answer the age-old question of "Why is it slow?"

iotop – a simple top-like I/O monitor

The `iotop` command is a relatively newer command to Linux. In previous RHEL releases while available it was not installed by default. The `iotop` command provides a top command-like interface but rather than showing which processes are utilizing the most CPU time or memory, it shows processes ordered by I/O utilization:

```
# iotop
Total DISK READ :         0.00 B/s | Total DISK WRITE :         0.00
B/s
Actual DISK READ:         0.00 B/s | Actual DISK WRITE:         0.00
B/s
  TID  PRIO  USER     DISK READ  DISK WRITE  SWAPIN      IO
COMMAND
 1536 be/4 root        0.00 B/s    0.00 B/s  0.00 %  0.00 % master
-w
    1 be/4 root        0.00 B/s    0.00 B/s  0.00 %  0.00 % systemd
--switched-root --system --deserialize 23
```

Unlike some of the previous commands, `iotop` is very specialized to showing processes utilizing I/O. There are however, some very useful flags that can change iotop's default behavior. Flags such as –o (only), which tells `iotop` to only print processes using I/O rather than its default behavior of printing all processes. Another useful set of flags are -q (quiet) and –n (number of iterations).

Together with the -o flag, these flags can be used to tell `iotop` to print only the processes using I/O without clearing the screen for the next iteration:

```
# iotop -o -q -n2
Total DISK READ :         0.00 B/s | Total DISK WRITE :         0.00 B/s
Actual DISK READ:         0.00 B/s | Actual DISK WRITE:         0.00 B/s
  TID  PRIO  USER     DISK READ  DISK WRITE  SWAPIN   IO   COMMAND
Total DISK READ :         0.00 B/s | Total DISK WRITE :         0.00 B/s
Actual DISK READ:         0.00 B/s | Actual DISK WRITE:         0.00 B/s
22965 be/4 root        0.00 B/s    0.00 B/s  0.00 %  0.03 %
[kworker/0:3]
```

If we look at the preceding example output, we can see two independent iterations of the `iotop` command. However, unlike previous examples, the output is continuous allowing us to see which processes were using I/O at each iteration.

By default, the delay between `iotop` iterations is 1 second; however, this can be modified with the -d (delay) flag.

iostat – report I/O and CPU statistics

Where `iotop` shows what processes are utilizing I/O, `iostat` shows what devices are being utilized:

```
# iostat -t 1 2
Linux 3.10.0-123.el7.x86_64 (localhost.localdomain)   12/25/2014
_x86_64_  (1 CPU)


12/25/2014 03:20:10 PM
avg-cpu:  %user   %nice %system %iowait  %steal   %idle
           0.11    0.00    0.17    0.01    0.00   99.72

Device:            tps    kB_read/s    kB_wrtn/s    kB_read
kB_wrtn
sda               0.38         2.84         7.02     261526
646339
sdb               0.01         0.06         0.00       5449
12
dm-0              0.33         2.77         7.00     254948
644275
dm-1              0.00         0.01         0.00        936
4


12/25/2014 03:20:11 PM
avg-cpu:  %user   %nice %system %iowait  %steal   %idle
           0.00    0.00    0.99    0.00    0.00   99.01

Device:            tps    kB_read/s    kB_wrtn/s    kB_read
kB_wrtn
sda               0.00         0.00         0.00          0
0
sdb               0.00         0.00         0.00          0
0
dm-0              0.00         0.00         0.00          0
0
dm-1              0.00         0.00         0.00          0
0
```

The preceding `iostat` command uses the `-t` (timestamp) flag to print a timestamp with each report. The two numbers are interval and count values. In the preceding example, the `iostat` is run with a one second interval for a total count of two iterations.

The `iostat` command can be very useful for diagnosing issues related to I/O. However, the output can often be misleading. When executed, the values provided in the first report are averages since the last reboot of the system. The subsequent reports are since the previous report. In this example, we executed two reports, one second apart. You can see that the numbers in the first report are much higher than the second report.

For this reason, many systems administrators simply ignore the first report but they do not fully understand why. Therefore, it is not uncommon for someone unfamiliar with `iostat` to react to the values in the first report.

The `iostat` command does have a flag `-y` (omit first report), which will actually cause `iostat` to omit the first report. This is a good flag to teach users who may not be very familiar with using `iostat`.

Manipulating the output

The `iostat` command also has quite a few useful flags that allow you to manipulate how it presents data. Flags such as –p (device) allow you to limit statistics to a specified device or –x (extended stats) that will print extended statistics:

```
# iostat -p sda -tx
Linux 3.10.0-123.el7.x86_64 (localhost.localdomain)    12/25/2014
 _x86_64_   (1 CPU)

12/25/2014 03:38:00 PM
avg-cpu:  %user   %nice %system %iowait  %steal   %idle
          0.11    0.00    0.17    0.01    0.00   99.72

Device:           rrqm/s   wrqm/s     r/s     w/s    rkB/s    wkB/s
avgrq-sz avgqu-sz   await r_await w_await   svctm   %util
sda                 0.01     0.02    0.13    0.25     2.81     6.95
51.70     0.00    7.62    1.57   10.79    0.85    0.03
sda1                0.00     0.00    0.02    0.02     0.05     0.02
3.24      0.00    0.24    0.42    0.06    0.23    0.00
sda2                0.01     0.02    0.11    0.19     2.75     6.93
65.47     0.00    9.34    1.82   13.58    0.82    0.02
```

The preceding example uses the `-p` flag to specify the `sda` device, the `-t` flag to print timestamps, and the `-x` flag to print extended statistics. These flags can be very useful when measuring I/O performance for specific devices.

vmstat – report virtual memory statistics

Where `iostat` is used to report statistics about disk I/O performance, `vmstat` is used to report statistics about memory usage and performance:

```
# vmstat 1 3
procs -----------memory---------- ---swap-- -----io---- -system-- ---
---cpu-----
 r  b   swpd   free   buff  cache   si   so    bi    bo   in   cs
us sy id wa st
 2  0      4 225000   3608 544900    0    0     3     7   17   28
 0  0 100  0  0
 0  0      4 224992   3608 544900    0    0     0     0   19   19
 0  0 100  0  0
 0  0      4 224992   3608 544900    0    0     0     0    6    9
 0  0 100  0  0
```

The `vmstat` syntax is very similar to `iostat` where you provide an interval and count of reports as command line arguments. Also, like `iostat`, the first report is actually an average since the last reboot and subsequent reports are since the previous report. Unfortunately, unlike the `iostat` command, the `vmstat` command does not include a flag to omit the first report. As such, in most cases, it is appropriate to simply ignore the first report.

While `vmstat` might not include a flag to omit the first report, it does have some very useful flags; they are flags such as `-m` (slabs), which causes `vmstat` to output the system's `slabinfo` at a defined interval, and `-s` (stats), which prints an extended report of the memory statistics for the system:

```
# vmstat -stats
      1018256 K total memory
       793416 K used memory,
       290372 K active memory
       360660 K inactive memory
       224840 K free memory
         3608 K buffer memory
       544908 K swap cache
       839676 K total swap
            4 K used swap
       839672 K free swap
        10191 non-nice user cpu ticks
           67 nice user cpu ticks
        11353 system cpu ticks
      9389547 idle cpu ticks
          556 IO-wait cpu ticks
           33 IRQ cpu ticks
```

```
      4434 softirq cpu ticks
         0 stolen cpu ticks
    267011 pages paged in
    647220 pages paged out
         0 pages swapped in
         1 pages swapped out
   1619609 interrupts
   2662083 CPU context switches
1419453695 boot time
     59061 forks
```

The preceding code is an example of the -s or --stats flag being used.

sar – collect, report, or save system activity information

One very useful utility is the sar command, sar is a utility that comes with the sysstat package. The sysstat package includes various utilities that collect system metrics such as disk, CPU, memory, and network utilization. By default, this collection will run every 10 minutes and is executed as a cron job within /ettc/cron.d/sysstat.

While the data collected by sysstat can be very useful, this package is sometimes removed in high performance environments. As the collection of the system utilization statistics can add to the system's utilization, causing performance degradation. To see if the sysstat package is installed, simply use the rpm command with the -q (query) flag:

```
# rpm -q sysstat
sysstat-10.1.5-4.el7.x86_64
```

Using the sar command

The sar command allows users to review the information collected by the sysstat utilities. When executed with no flags, the sar command will print the current day's CPU statistics:

```
# sar | head -6
Linux 3.10.0-123.el7.x86_64 (localhost.localdomain)     12/25/2014     _
x86_64_   (1 CPU)

12:00:01 AM     CPU     %user     %nice     %system     %iowait
%steal      %idle
12:10:02 AM     all      0.05      0.00        0.20        0.01
0.00     99.74
```

```
12:20:01 AM     all      0.05      0.00      0.18      0.00
0.00      99.77
12:30:01 AM     all      0.06      0.00      0.25      0.00
0.00      99.69
```

Every day at midnight, the `systat` collector will create a new file to store the collected statistics. To reference the statistics within that file, simply use the `-f` (file) flag to run `sar` against the specified file:

```
# sar -f /var/log/sa/sa13
Linux 3.10.0-123.el7.x86_64 (localhost.localdomain)    12/13/2014
x86_64_    (1 CPU)

10:24:43 AM          LINUX RESTART

10:30:01 AM     CPU   %user    %nice    %system    %iowait
%steal    %idle
10:40:01 AM     all     2.99     0.00      0.96       0.43
0.00      95.62
10:50:01 AM     all     9.70     0.00      2.17       0.00
0.00      88.13
11:00:01 AM     all     0.31     0.00      0.30       0.02
0.00      99.37
11:10:01 AM     all     1.20     0.00      0.41       0.01
0.00      98.38
11:20:01 AM     all     0.01     0.00      0.04       0.01
0.00      99.94
11:30:01 AM     all     0.92     0.07      0.42       0.01
0.00      98.59
11:40:01 AM     all     0.17     0.00      0.08       0.00
0.00      99.74
11:50:02 AM     all     0.01     0.00      0.03       0.00
0.00      99.96
```

In the preceding code, the file specified was /var/log/sa/sa13; this file contains statistics for the 13th day of the current month.

The `sar` command has many useful flags, far too many to list in this chapter. A few extremely useful flags are listed as follows:

- -b: This prints I/O statistics similar to the `iostat` command
- -n ALL: This prints network statistics for all network devices
- -R: This prints memory utilization statistics
- -A: This prints all statistics gathered. It is essentially equivalent to running
  `sar -bBdHqrRSuvwWy -I SUM -I XALL -m ALL -n ALL -u ALL -P ALL`

While the `sar` command shows many statistics, we already covered commands such as `iostat` or `vmstat`. The biggest benefit of the `sar` command is the ability to review statistics in the past. This ability is critical when troubleshooting a performance issue that occurred for a short period of time or was already mitigated.

Summary

In this chapter, you learned that log files, configuration files, and the `/proc` filesystem are key sources of information during troubleshooting. We also covered the basic use of many fundamental troubleshooting commands.

While reading this chapter, you might have noticed that quite a few commands are also used in day-to-day life for non-troubleshooting purposes. If we look back at the troubleshooting process from *Chapter 1, Troubleshooting Best Practices*, the first step included information gathering.

While these commands might not explain the issue themselves, they can help gather information about the issue, which leads to a more accurate and quick resolution. Familiarity with these fundamental commands is critical to your success during troubleshooting.

In the next few chapters, we will use these fundamental commands to troubleshoot real-world scenarios. The next chapter focuses on troubleshooting issues with a web-based application.

3
Troubleshooting a Web Application

In the first and second chapters of this book, we covered the troubleshooting process, common locations for information, and useful troubleshooting commands. In this chapter, we will run through an example problem that has been created in order to demonstrate multiple troubleshooting and remediation steps. In particular, we will look at the steps required to troubleshoot issues with web-based applications.

Throughout this chapter, I will go through each step of the troubleshooting process and explain the reasoning behind each step. While the problem that this chapter covers may not be an extremely common issue, it is important to look at the process and tools used. The process and tools used in this chapter can be applied to most web application issues.

A small back story

Within each chapter of this book, you will find an example issue that covers the common troubleshooting topics. While the focus of this book is to show the commands and concepts necessary to resolve these types of issues, it is also important to show the process around resolving them. To do this, we will explore these issues as if we were a new systems administrator who recently joined a new company.

Each issue will be presented a little differently, but each one will start with an issue being reported.

The reported issue

While starting our new role at a new company, we have been assigned to answer phone calls for the company's **Network Operations Center** (**NOC**). In this role, we will focus on resolving issues within the company's environment and are expected to do so very quickly. For our first issue, we have received a phone call; on the other end of this phone call is a business user who has an issue. *All of a sudden, our blog is showing an installation page and not our posts!*

Now that we have a reported issue, let's start working through the troubleshooting process.

Data gathering

If we look back at *Chapter 1, Troubleshooting Best Practices*, the first step in the troubleshooting process is to understand the problem statement. In this section, we are going to explore how the problem was reported and will try to collect any data that we can to find the root cause of the issue.

For this example, we were notified of the issue via a phone call. This is actually lucky as we have an end user on the phone and can ask questions to get more information from him/her.

Before asking the person reporting the issue for more information, let's first take a look at what was already answered. *All of a sudden, our blog is showing an installation page and not our posts!*

At first, you may feel that this problem statement is vague; this is because it is vague. However, there is still quite a bit of useful information in this single sentence. If we dissect the reported issue, we can gain a better understanding of the problem.

- "Our blog is showing an installation page"
- "All of a sudden"
- "not our posts!"

From these three segments, we can assume the following:

- The blog is showing an unexpected page
- This blog was previously showing posts
- At some point, this changed and it seems that it was somewhat recently

While the above is a pretty good start for determining whether there is an issue and what it is related to, it does not give us enough to create a hypothesis yet.

Asking questions

In order to formulate a hypothesis, we will need more information. One method of getting this information is to ask the person reporting the issue. In order to get more information, we will ask the business user the following questions:

1. When was the last time you saw the blog working?

   Last night.

2. What is the blog's address?

   ```
   http://blog.example.com
   ```

3. Did you receive any other errors?

   No.

While the above questions are not enough to identify the problem, they do give us a starting point of where to start looking.

Duplicating the issue

As previously stated in *Chapter 1, Troubleshooting Best Practices* one of the best methods of finding information is to duplicate the issue. In this case, it seems that we can duplicate the issue by simply going to the address provided.

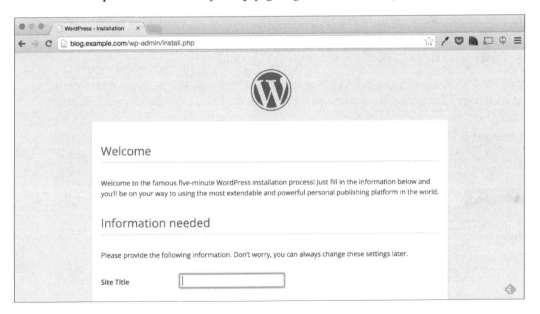

In the previous screenshot, we can see that the blog is performing just as the user described. When we went to the provided URL, we were presented with a default WordPress installation screen.

Does this give us any clue about what the cause of the issue is? No, not really, not unless we have seen this issue before. While this may not tell us the cause of the issue, it does confirm that the issue that the user has reported is reproducible. This step has also told us the name of the software that we are troubleshooting: WordPress.

WordPress is one of the most popular open source blogging platforms. In this chapter, it is assumed that we have no experience managing WordPress and will need to find any information that we need around this web application through online sources.

Understanding the environment

Since we are the new systems administrator, at this point, we know very little about this environment, which means that we have little knowledge of how this blog is deployed. In fact, we do not even know which server it runs from.

Where is this blog hosted?

One thing that we do know, however, is that all servers managed by our company have IPs within the 192.168.0.0/16 subnet. In order to determine whether this is an issue that we can resolve, we first need to determine whether the blog is on a server managed by our company. If this blog doesn't exist on a server managed by this company, our troubleshooting options may be limited.

One way to determine where the blog is hosted is to simply look up the IP address of the blog.example.com address.

Lookup IPs with nslookup

There are many ways to look up the IP address of a DNS name; the command that we will discuss is the nslookup command. To use this command, simply execute nslookup followed by the DNS name to look up: blog.example.com for this example.

```
$ nslookup blog.example.com
Server:     192.0.2.1
Address:    192.0.2.1#53

Non-authoritative answer:
Name:   blog.example.com
Address: 192.168.33.11
```

In the preceding output, the result may be a bit confusing for those unfamiliar with `nslookup`.

```
Non-authoritative answer:
Name:  blog.example.com
Address: 192.168.33.11
```

We know that the preceding information is the result of the `nslookup` query. This block is saying that the `blog.example.com` domain's address is `192.168.33.11`. The first block of output from `nslookup` is simply telling us which DNS server was used to look up this information.

```
Server:    192.0.2.1
Address:   192.0.2.1#53
```

We can see from this block that the DNS server used was `192.0.2.1`.

What about ping, dig, or other tools?

There are many commands that we could have used to look up the IP address of this domain. We could have used `dig`, `host`, or even `ping`. The reason that we chose the `nslookup` command is that for the most part, it is included with most operating systems. So, irrespective of whether you need to look up an IP address from a Windows, Mac, or Linux desktop, you can always use the `nslookup` command.

One caveat with the `nslookup` command, however, is that it specifically uses DNS to look up the address. It does not respect values in `/etc/hosts` or any other name service specified in `/etc/nsswitch.conf`. This is something that we will explore more in the later chapters; for now, we will assume that the IP address of `192.168.33.11` is the correct IP.

Ok, it's within our environment; now what?

Since we are working with a Linux server, the most common way to manage that server is via **Secure Shell (SSH)**. SSH is a secure network service that allows users to remotely access a server's shell. For this book, we are going to assume that you are already familiar with logging into a server via SSH. Whether you use the SSH command-line client or a desktop client like PuTTY, it is assumed that you are able to log into the server with SSH.

In this scenario, we use a laptop that has its own shell environment. To log into our server, we simply execute the `ssh` command from our terminal window.

```
$ ssh vagrant@blog.example.com
vagrant@blog.example.com's password:
```

Once logged in, the first information-gathering command that we execute is the w command.

```
$ w
  18:32:17 up 2 days, 12:05,  1 user,  load average: 0.11, 0.08, 0.07
USER     TTY         LOGIN@   IDLE   JCPU   PCPU WHAT
vagrant  pts/1       00:53    2.00s  0.00s  0.08s sshd: vagrant [priv]
```

In *Chapter 2, Troubleshooting Commands and Sources of Useful Information*, we covered the w command and mentioned that it is the first command executed. We can see quite a bit of useful information in the output of the w command.

From this output, we can determine the following:

- Only 1 user is currently logged in (which is our login session)
- The server in question has been up for 2 days
- The load average is low, which suggests normal

Overall, at the first glance, the server seems to be performing normally. The fact that the issue started last night suggests that the issue did not start after the reboot 2 days ago. With the load average low, it is also safe at this point to assume that the issue is not related to the system load.

What services are installed and running?

Since we have never logged into this server before, and are completely new to this environment, the first thing that we should do is find out what services are running on this server.

Since we know from the install page that the blog is a WordPress blog, we can search Google about the services that it requires. We can do this by using the search term "WordPress install requirements."

This search string returned with the following URL as the first result: https:// wordpress.org/about/requirements/. This page contains the installation requirements for WordPress and lists the following:

- PHP 5.2.4
- MySQL 5.0 or higher
- Either Apache or Nginx web servers

From the fact that we can access the install page, we can assume that a web server and PHP are installed and somewhat working. However, it is always best to validate rather than assume.

Validate the web server

Since WordPress recommends either the **Apache** or the **Nginx** web server, we first need to determine which is installed and, more importantly, identify which is in use for this WordPress application.

The following are a few ways to identify which web servers are installed and running:

- We could use rpm to look at the packages installed
- We could use ps to look at the processes running
- We could simply go to a non-existent page via a browser and see whether the error page says which web server is running
- We can also go to /var/logs and look around to see what log files exist or don't exist

All of these methods are valid and have their own benefits. For this example, we will use a *5th* method (not mentioned earlier), which will answer two questions about the web server configuration on this server.

The first step of this method will be to determine which process is listening on port 80.

```
$ su -
# netstat -nap | grep 80
tcp6      0      0 :::80                    :::*
                  LISTEN         952/httpd
unix  3      [ ]            STREAM      CONNECTED      17280  1521/master
```

As discussed in *Chapter 2, Troubleshooting Commands and Sources of Useful Information*, the netstat command can be used to determine which ports are in use with the -na flags. If we simply add the -p (port) flag to netstat, we can also see which process is listening on each port.

In order to identify which processes are listening on each port, the netstat command must be executed with **super user**-level permissions. As such, we use the su command to switch to the **root** user before executing netstat.

Throughout this book, any command preceded with $ is run as an unprivileged user, while commands preceded with # are executed as the root user.

Port 80 is the default port for HTTP requests; as such, if we look back at the steps performed to duplicate the issue at hand, we can see that the address used was `http://blog.example.com`. Since this is an HTTP address and does not specify a different port, this means that the service that serves the WordPress installation page is listening on port 80.

From the output of the `netstat` command, we can see that process 952 is listening on port 80. The `netstat` output also shows that process 952 is running the `httpd` binary. On RHEL systems, this `httpd` binary is most often Apache.

We can validate whether this is the case with the `ps` command with the `-elf` flags discussed in *Chapter 2, Troubleshooting Commands and Sources of Useful Information*. We will also search the output of the `ps` command with the `grep` command, searching for the string "952":

```
$ ps -elf | grep 952
4 S root       952      1  0  80   0 - 115050 poll_s Jan11 ?
00:00:07 /usr/sbin/httpd -DFOREGROUND
5 S apache    5329    952  0  80   0 - 115050 inet_c 08:54 ?
00:00:00 /usr/sbin/httpd -DFOREGROUND
5 S apache    5330    952  0  80   0 - 115050 inet_c 08:54 ?
00:00:00 /usr/sbin/httpd -DFOREGROUND
5 S apache    5331    952  0  80   0 - 115050 inet_c 08:54 ?
00:00:00 /usr/sbin/httpd -DFOREGROUND
5 S apache    5332    952  0  80   0 - 115050 inet_c 08:54 ?
00:00:00 /usr/sbin/httpd -DFOREGROUND
5 S apache    5333    952  0  80   0 - 119196 inet_c 08:54 ?
00:00:00 /usr/sbin/httpd -DFOREGROUND
```

With the above output, we can see that process 952 and its child processes are running under the **apache** user. This confirms that the software in use is most likely Apache, but to be extra diligent, we can execute the `httpd` binary with the `-version` flag to print the version of the web server software.

```
$ httpd -version
Server version: Apache/2.4.6
Server built:   Jul 23 2014 14:48:00
```

The output of the `httpd` binary shows that it is in fact the Apache web server, which matches the WordPress requirements.

At this point, we have found out the following facts about the web server in use for this server:

- The web server is Apache
- The Apache process is running
- The Apache version is 2.4.6
- The Apache process is listening on port 80

It is possible to identify the same information by using other methods such as rpm. The good part of this method is that if the server has two web server services installed, we know which of these services is listening on port 80. This also tells us which service provides the WordPress install page.

Validating the database service

A common WordPress implementation is to run the Apache, PHP, and MySQL services all on one server. Sometimes, however, the MySQL service will be run from another server or servers. To better understand the environment, we should check whether this environment runs MySQL locally or from another server.

To check this, we will once again use the ps command; this time, however, we will use grep to search for a process that matches the string "mysql":

```
$ ps -elf | grep mysql
4 S mysql      2045     1  0  80   0 - 28836 wait   Jan12 ?
00:00:00 /bin/sh /usr/bin/mysqld_safe --basedir=/usr

0 S mysql      2203  2045  0  80   0 - 226860 poll_s Jan12 ?
00:00:42 /usr/libexec/mysqld --basedir=/usr --datadir=/var/lib/mysql
--plugin-dir=/usr/lib64/mysql/plugin --log-
error=/var/log/mariadb/mariadb.log --pid-
file=/var/run/mariadb/mariadb.pid --
socket=/var/lib/mysql/mysql.sock
```

As you can see from the preceding output, there is in fact a MySQL process currently running. It is also important to note that the ps output shows that the mysqld process is using the following option: -log-error=/var/log/mariadb/mariadb.log.

This is important for two reasons: The first is that this is the location of the log file for the mysqld process, and the second is the fact that this log file is for **MariaDB**, which is different from MySQL.

We can confirm whether MySQL or MariaDB is installed by using the `rpm` and `egrep` commands.

```
$ rpm -qa | egrep "(maria|mysql)"
php-mysql-5.4.16-23.el7_0.3.x86_64
mariadb-5.5.40-2.el7_0.x86_64
mariadb-server-5.5.40-2.el7_0.x86_64
mariadb-libs-5.5.40-2.el7_0.x86_64
```

The `egrep` command is similar to `grep`; however, it accepts search strings in the form of regular expressions. In the above command, we used `egrep` to search for either the string "`mariadb`" or the string "`mysql`." From the preceding output, we can see that this server does in fact have MariaDB installed but not MySQL.

With this information, we can make the assumption that the `mysqld` process that is running is in fact a MariaDB binary. We can verify this by using the `rpm` command with the `-q` (query) and `-l` (list all files) flags.

```
$ rpm -ql mariadb-server | grep "libexec/mysqld"
/usr/libexec/mysqld
```

We can see from the `rpm` command's output that the running `/usr/libexec/mysqld` binary is deployed as part of the **mariadb-server** package. Showing that the running database process is in fact MariaDB and was installed via the mariadb-server package.

At this point, we have found the following facts about the database service running on this server:

- The database service is actually MariaDB
- MariaDB is running
- The log files for this service are at `/var/log/mariadb/`

While MariaDB is a drop-in replacement for MySQL, the requirements for WordPress do not list it as the preferred database service. It is important to make note of this difference as it may determine the root cause of the reported issue.

Validating PHP

Since we know that PHP is required for WordPress, we should also check whether it is installed. We can validate this by again using the `rpm` command.

```
$ rpm -qa | grep php
php-mbstring-5.4.16-23.el7_0.3.x86_64
php-mysql-5.4.16-23.el7_0.3.x86_64
```

```
php-enchant-5.4.16-23.el7_0.3.x86_64

php-process-5.4.16-23.el7_0.3.x86_64

php-xml-5.4.16-23.el7_0.3.x86_64

php-simplepie-1.3.1-4.el7.noarch

php-5.4.16-23.el7_0.3.x86_64

php-gd-5.4.16-23.el7_0.3.x86_64

php-common-5.4.16-23.el7_0.3.x86_64

php-pdo-5.4.16-23.el7_0.3.x86_64

php-PHPMailer-5.2.9-1.el7.noarch

php-cli-5.4.16-23.el7_0.3.x86_64

php-IDNA_Convert-0.8.0-2.el7.noarch

php-getid3-1.9.8-2.el7.noarch
```

PHP by itself is not designed to run as a service such as Apache or MySQL, but rather as a web server module. However, it is possible to use a service such as php-fpm as an application server. This allows PHP to run as a service and to be called by an upstream web server.

To check whether this server runs php-fpm or any other service that frontends PHP, we can again use the ps and grep commands.

```
$ ps -elf | grep php
0 S root       6342  5676  0  80   0 - 28160 pipe_w 17:53 pts/0
00:00:00 grep --color=auto php
```

By using the ps command, we do not see any specific PHP service; however, when going to the blog, we were able to see the install page. This suggests that PHP is configured to run via Apache directly. We can validate this by executing the httpd binary again with the -M (modules) flag.

```
$ httpd -M | grep php
 php5_module (shared)
```

The -M flag will tell the httpd binary to list all of the loaded modules. Included in this list is php5_module, which means that this installation of Apache is able to run PHP applications via php5_module.

A summary of installed and running services

At this point, we have identified the following from our data collection:

- The WordPress requirement of Apache is installed and running
- The WordPress requirement of MySQL appears to be met by MariaDB, which is installed and running
- The WordPress requirement of PHP is installed and appears to be working
- It appears that WordPress is deployed in a single-server setup rather than a multi-server setup

We can assume for now that these facts mean that the issue is not caused by a missing WordPress requirement.

By gathering all of these data points, we have not only learned more about the environment that we are troubleshooting but also eliminated several possible causes of this issue.

Looking for error messages

Now that the installed and configured services have been identified, we know where to start looking for errors or helpful messages. In the next stage of data collection, we are going to look through the various log files of these services to try and to identify any errors that may indicate the cause of this issue.

Apache logs

Since Apache calls PHP when web requests are made, the most likely log file to contain PHP-related errors is the Apache error log. The default log location for RHEL's httpd package is /var/log/httpd/. However, we don't know just yet whether the running httpd service is the RHEL packaged version.

Finding the location of Apache's logs

Since we don't know the location of Apache's logs, we will need to find them. One way to find log files is to simply look in /var/log for any file or folder that matches the name of the service in question. This solution, however, is a bit too simple for our example.

To find the location of the `httpd` log files, we will use a method discussed in *Chapter 2, Troubleshooting Commands and Sources of Useful Information* and search through the service's configuration files. The `/etc` folder is the default folder for system configuration files. It is also the standard location for service configurations. Therefore, it is fairly safe to assume that the `/etc/` folder will contain a configuration file or folder for the `httpd` service.

```
# cd /etc/httpd/
# ls -la
total 20
drwxr-xr-x.  5 root root   86 Jan  7 23:29 .
drwxr-xr-x. 79 root root 8192 Jan 13 16:10 ..
drwxr-xr-x.  2 root root   35 Jan  7 23:29 conf
drwxr-xr-x.  2 root root 4096 Jan  7 23:29 conf.d
drwxr-xr-x.  2 root root 4096 Jan  7 23:29 conf.modules.d
lrwxrwxrwx.  1 root root   19 Jan  7 23:29 logs -> ../../var/log/httpd
lrwxrwxrwx.  1 root root   29 Jan  7 23:29 modules -> ../../usr/lib64/
httpd/modules
lrwxrwxrwx.  1 root root   10 Jan  7 23:29 run -> /run/httpd
```

In the preceding commands, we can see that we can switch to the `/etc/httpd` folder, which contains several configuration files. Since we don't know which configuration file contains the logging configuration, we could spend quite a bit of time reading through each configuration file.

To make this process faster, we can use the `grep` command to search through all of the files for the string "`log`." Since the `/etc/httpd/` folder contains subfolders, we can simply add the `-r` (recursive) flag to cause the `grep` command to search through files contained in these subfolders.

```
# grep -r "log" /etc/httpd/*
./conf/httpd.conf:# with "/", the value of ServerRoot is prepended -- so
'log/access_log'
./conf/httpd.conf:# server as '/www/log/access_log', whereas '/log/
access_log' will be
./conf/httpd.conf:# interpreted as '/log/access_log'.
./conf/httpd.conf:# container, that host's errors will be logged there
and not here.
./conf/httpd.conf:ErrorLog "logs/error_log"
./conf/httpd.conf:# LogLevel: Control the number of messages logged to
the error_log.
```

```
./conf/httpd.conf:<IfModule log_config_module>
./conf/httpd.conf:        <IfModule logio_module>
./conf/httpd.conf:        # define per-<VirtualHost> access log files,
transactions will be
./conf/httpd.conf:        # logged therein and *not* in this file.
./conf/httpd.conf:        #CustomLog "logs/access_log" common
./conf/httpd.conf:        # If you prefer a log file with access, agent, and
referer information
./conf/httpd.conf:        CustomLog "logs/access_log" combined
./conf.modules.d/00-base.conf:LoadModule log_config_module modules/mod_
log_config.so
./conf.modules.d/00-base.conf:LoadModule logio_module modules/mod_logio.
so
./conf.modules.d/00-base.conf:#LoadModule log_debug_module modules/mod_
log_debug.so
```

 The preceding code snippet has been truncated for the sake of brevity, and only the key lines of interest are shown.

While there is quite a bit of output from the preceding grep command, if we review the returned data, we can see that there are actually two log files defined for the httpd service: logs/access_log and logs/error_log.

```
./conf/httpd.conf:ErrorLog "logs/error_log"
./conf/httpd.conf:        CustomLog "logs/access_log" combined
```

The defined logs use the relative path of logs/; this path is relative to the httpd services running folder. In this case, this means that the logs' folder is actually /etc/httpd/logs; however, this may not always be the case. To validate whether this is the case, we can simply perform a folder listing with the ls command in the /etc/httpd folder.

```
# ls -la /etc/httpd | grep logs
lrwxrwxrwx.  1 root root   19 Jan  7 23:29 logs ->
../../var/log/httpd
```

From the ls command, we can see that /etc/httpd/logs exists; however, this is not a folder but a symbolic link to /var/log/httpd/. This means that the two log files, namely access_log and error_log, are actually located within the /var/log/httpd/ folder.

Reviewing the logs

Now that we know where the log files are located, we can search these log files for any useful information. To do this, we will use the `tail` command.

The `tail` command is a useful command that can be used to read the last part of a file or files. By default, when `tail` is executed without any flags, the command will print the last 10 lines of the specified file.

For our troubleshooting, we want to not only see the last 10 lines of data but also watch the file for any new data being appended. To do this, we can use the `-f` (follow) flag, which tells `tail` to follow the specified file or files.

```
# tail -f logs/access_log logs/error_log

==> logs/access_log <==

192.168.33.1 - - [12/Jan/2015:04:39:08 +0000] "GET /wp-includes/js/
wp-util.min.js?ver=4.1 HTTP/1.1" 200 981 "http://blog.example.com/wp-
admin/install.php" "Mozilla/5.0 (Macintosh; Intel Mac OS X 10_10_1)
AppleWebKit/537.36 (KHTML, like Gecko) Chrome/39.0.2171.95 Safari/537.36"

"http://blog.example.com/wp-admin/install.php" "Mozilla/5.0 (Macintosh;
Intel Mac OS X 10_10_1) AppleWebKit/537.36 (KHTML, like Gecko)
Chrome/39.0.2171.95 Safari/537.36"

192.168.33.1 - - [12/Jan/2015:04:39:08 +0000] "GET /wp-admin/js/password-
strength-meter.min.js?ver=4.1 HTTP/1.1" 200 737 "http://blog.example.com/
wp-admin/install.php" "Mozilla/5.0 (Macintosh; Intel Mac OS X 10_10_1)
AppleWebKit/537.36 (KHTML, like Gecko) Chrome/39.0.2171.95 Safari/537.36"

::1 - - [13/Jan/2015:16:08:33 +0000] "GET / HTTP/1.1" 302 - "-"
"curl/7.29.0"

192.168.33.11 - - [13/Jan/2015:16:10:19 +0000] "GET / HTTP/1.1" 302 - "-"
"curl/7.29.0"


==> logs/error_log <==

[Sun Jan 11 06:01:03.679890 2015] [auth_digest:notice] [pid 952] AH01757:
generating secret for digest authentication ...

[Sun Jan 11 06:01:03.680719 2015] [lbmethod_heartbeat:notice] [pid 952]
AH02282: No slotmem from mod_heartmonitor

[Sun Jan 11 06:01:03.705469 2015] [mpm_prefork:notice] [pid 952] AH00163:
Apache/2.4.6 (CentOS) PHP/5.4.16 configured -- resuming normal operations

[Sun Jan 11 06:01:03.705486 2015] [core:notice] [pid 952] AH00094:
Command line: '/usr/sbin/httpd -D FOREGROUND'
```

The RHEL 7 implementation of the `tail` command can actually follow multiple files at the same time. To do this, simply specify all of the files that you wish to read or follow when executing the command. The above is an example of using `tail` to read two files at once.

While there are no immediate PHP errors caused by the last 10 lines of each file, this does not necessarily mean that these files will not show the errors that we need. As this is a web-based application, we may need to load the application in order to trigger any errors.

We could simply open our browser and once again navigate to `http://blog.example.com`. However, for this example, we will utilize a very useful troubleshooting command: `curl`.

Using curl to call our web application

The `curl` command can be used as a client to access many different types of protocols, everything from FTP to SMTP. This command is particularly useful when troubleshooting a web application as it can be used as an HTTP client.

When troubleshooting a web application, you can use the `curl` command to make an HTTP, GET, or POST request to a specified URL, which when placed in the verbose mode with the –v (verbose) flag can produce quite a bit of interesting information.

```
$ curl -v http://blog.example.com
* About to connect() to blog.example.com port 80 (#0)
*   Trying 192.168.33.11...
* Connected to blog.example.com (192.168.33.11) port 80 (#0)
> GET / HTTP/1.1
> User-Agent: curl/7.29.0
> Host: blog.example.com
> Accept: */*
>
< HTTP/1.1 302 Found
< Date: Tue, 13 Jan 2015 21:10:51 GMT
< Server: Apache/2.4.6 PHP/5.4.16
< X-Powered-By: PHP/5.4.16
< Expires: Wed, 11 Jan 1984 05:00:00 GMT
< Cache-Control: no-cache, must-revalidate, max-age=0
< Pragma: no-cache
```

```
< Location: http://blog.example.com/wp-admin/install.php

< Content-Length: 0

< Content-Type: text/html; charset=UTF-8

<

* Connection #0 to host blog.example.com left intact
```

The preceding output shows four key pieces of information that I want to highlight.

```
* Connected to blog.example.com (192.168.33.11) port 80 (#0)
```

The preceding line shows us that when we addressed the page called `blog.example.com`, we did in fact go to the server at `192.168.33.11`. While we already identified that `blog.example.com` resolved to `192.168.33.11`, this line confirms that the output from this command produces data from the expected system.

```
< HTTP/1.1 302 Found
```

The second key piece of information shows the HTTP status code that was provided by the web server.

In this case, the web server replied with a status code of `302`, which is used to indicate a temporary redirect. When a browser requests a page and the web server replies with a 302 status code, the browser knows to redirect the end user to another page.

```
< Location: http://blog.example.com/wp-admin/install.php
```

The next page is determined by the **Location** HTTP header. This header, which is assigned by the web server, along with the HTTP status code of 302 will cause any browser to redirect the end user to the `/wp-admin/install.php` page.

This explains why we see an installation page when we navigate to `blog.example.com` as the web server simply responds with this 302 redirect.

```
< X-Powered-By: PHP/5.4.16
```

The fourth key piece of information is the HTTP header **X-Powered-By**; this is an HTTP header added by PHP. This header is added by PHP when the requested page is processed as by PHP, which means that our curl request was actually processed by PHP.

More importantly, we can see that the version of PHP (5.4.16) meets our minimum requirements as outlined by WordPress.

Requesting a non-PHP page

We can see when requesting a non-PHP page that no **X-Powered-By** header is added in the web server reply. We can do this by requesting an invalid URL.

```
# curl -v http://192.168.33.11/sdfas
* About to connect() to 192.168.33.11 port 80 (#0)
*   Trying 192.168.33.11...
* Connected to 192.168.33.11 (192.168.33.11) port 80 (#0)
> GET /sdfas HTTP/1.1
> User-Agent: curl/7.29.0
> Host: 192.168.33.11
> Accept: */*
>
< HTTP/1.1 404 Not Found
< Date: Tue, 13 Jan 2015 21:18:57 GMT
< Server: Apache/2.4.6 PHP/5.4.16
< Content-Length: 203
< Content-Type: text/html; charset=iso-8859-1
```

As we can see from the output obtained when requesting a non-PHP based page, the X-Powered-By header is not present. This indicates that the web server did not process this page as PHP.

The presence of the X-Powered-By header tells us that when we requested the blog. example.com page, it was processed by PHP. This also means that the HTTP status code of 302 was a response provided by WordPress. This information is important as it means that PHP is most likely processing pages without any issue, thereby eliminating PHP as a possible root cause of the reported issue, at least for now.

We can validate this further by reviewing any log entries generated from the abovementioned web requests.

Reviewing generated log entries

When making the abovementioned requests with curl, we should have caused new log messages to be appended to the two httpd logs. Since we were using the tail command to continuously follow the log files, we can return to our terminal and review the new messages.

```
==> logs/access_log <==
192.168.33.11 - - [13/Jan/2015:23:22:17 +0000] "GET / HTTP/1.1" 302 - "-"
"curl/7.29.0"
```

After our HTTP request to the blog URL, the only entry in either log was the preceding one. However, this is only an informational log message and not an error that would explain the issue. However, the informational log message is also a key data point. If there were an issue with the PHP code or processing, an error message similar to the following would have been generated.

```
[Tue Jan 13 23:24:31.339293 2015] [:error] [pid 5333] [client
192.168.33.11:52102] PHP Parse error:  syntax error, unexpected
'endif' (T_ENDIF) in /var/www/html/wp-includes/functions.php on
line 2574
```

The absence of a PHP error actually confirms that PHP is working as expected. This when combined with the curl results leads us to confidently assume that PHP is not the root cause.

What we learned from httpd logs

While the httpd service logs may not have shown us an error that could answer why this issue is appearing, they have allowed us to eliminate a possible cause. While troubleshooting, you will often find yourself ruling out many possible causes before finding the exact cause of an issue. The troubleshooting steps mentioned earlier are exactly that, thereby eliminating possible causes.

Verifying the database

Earlier while checking what services were running, we found that the MariaDB service was running. We did not, however, validate that we can access the service or that the WordPress application can access this database service.

To validate that we can access the MariaDB service, we can simply use the mysql command.

```
# mysql
Welcome to the MariaDB monitor.  Commands end with ; or \g.
Your MariaDB connection id is 28
Server version: 5.5.40-MariaDB MariaDB Server

Copyright (c) 2000, 2014, Oracle, Monty Program Ab and others.

Type 'help;' or '\h' for help. Type '\c' to clear the current input
statement.

MariaDB [(none)]>
```

The `mysql` command is actually a MariaDB client command. When run from the command line as the **root** user (as shown above), the `mysql` command by default will log into the MariaDB service as the MariaDB root user. While this is the default behavior, it is possible to configure the MariaDB service to disallow direct root login.

The abovementioned results imply that MariaDB allows direct root login, which shows that the MariaDB service itself is up and accepting connections. What they do not reveal is whether or not the WordPress application can access the database.

To determine this, we will need to log into the MariaDB service with the same username and password as the application.

Verifying the WordPress database

In order to connect to the MariaDB service with the same credentials as WordPress, we need to obtain these credentials. We could ask the person who reported the issue for these details, but being a business user, they most likely would not know. Even if they worked with WordPress daily, in general, the database username and password are configured by one person and only used during installation.

This means that we must find this information for ourselves. One way to do this is to look through the configuration for WordPress as every web application that connects to a database has to obtain the login credentials from somewhere, and the most common way to do this is to store them within a configuration file.

An interesting challenge to this approach is the fact that this chapter assumes that we have little-to-no knowledge of WordPress. Finding where WordPress stores its database credentials will be a bit tricky; this is particularly true since we also do not know offhand where the WordPress application is installed either.

Finding the installation path for WordPress

What we do know is that WordPress is a web application served by the `httpd` service. This means that the `httpd` service will have the installation path defined somewhere within its configuration files.

The default configuration for `httpd` is to serve a single domain from a default folder. The default folder can change from distribution to distribution, but in general, for RHEL systems, it is placed under `/var/www/html`.

It is possible to configure `httpd` to serve multiple domains; this is done via a **Virtual Hosts** configuration. At this point, we do not know whether this system is configured to host multiple domains or one single domain.

Checking the default configuration

With the default single-domain configuration, any and all domains pointing to the server's IP would serve the same .html or .php files. With Virtual Hosts, you can configure Apache to serve specific .html or .php files depending on the domain that the request is being made to.

We can determine whether the httpd service is configured for Virtual Hosts or a single domain by executing a simple grep command.

```
# grep -r "DocumentRoot" /etc/httpd/
/etc/httpd/conf/httpd.conf:# DocumentRoot: The folder out of which you
will serve your
/etc/httpd/conf/httpd.conf:DocumentRoot "/var/www/html"
/etc/httpd/conf/httpd.conf:    # access content that does not live under
the DocumentRoot.
```

Since the /etc/httpd folder has a multiple subfolder, we once again used the -r (recursive) flag for grep. The command searched the entire /etc/httpd folder structure for the **DocumentRoot** string.

DocumentRoot is the Apache configuration item that specifies the local folder that contains the .html or .php files for the specified domain. The DocumentRoot setting will be present multiple times for systems that are configured for multiple domains and only one time for single-domain configurations.

From the output above, we can see that on this server, DocumentRoot is only defined once and set to /var/www/html. As this is the default for RHEL systems, it is fairly safe to assume that the httpd service is configured in a single domain-based configuration.

To validate that this is the installation folder of WordPress, we can simply execute the ls command to list the files and folders within this path.

```
# ls -la /var/www/html/
total 156
drwxr-xr-x.  5 root root  4096 Jan  9 22:54 .
drwxr-xr-x.  4 root root    31 Jan  7 23:29 ..
-rw-r--r--.  1 root root   418 Jan  9 21:48 index.php
-rw-r--r--.  1 root root  4951 Jan  9 21:48 wp-activate.php
drwxr-xr-x.  9 root root  4096 Jan  9 21:48 wp-admin
-rw-r--r--.  1 root root   271 Jan  9 21:48 wp-blog-header.php
-rw-r--r--.  1 root root  5008 Jan  9 21:48 wp-comments-post.php
-rw-r--r--.  1 root root  3159 Jan  9 22:01 wp-config.php
```

```
-rw-r--r--.  1 root root  2726 Jan  9 21:48 wp-config-sample.php
drwxr-xr-x.  6 root root    77 Jan  9 21:48 wp-content
-rw-r--r--.  1 root root  2956 Jan  9 21:48 wp-cron.php
drwxr-xr-x. 10 root root  4096 Jan 13 23:25 wp-includes
-rw-r--r--.  1 root root  2380 Jan  9 21:48 wp-links-opml.php
-rw-r--r--.  1 root root  2714 Jan  9 21:48 wp-load.php
-rw-r--r--.  1 root root 33435 Jan  9 21:48 wp-login.php
-rw-r--r--.  1 root root  8252 Jan  9 21:48 wp-mail.php
-rw-r--r--.  1 root root 11115 Jan  9 21:48 wp-settings.php
-rw-r--r--.  1 root root 25152 Jan  9 21:48 wp-signup.php
-rw-r--r--.  1 root root  4035 Jan  9 21:48 wp-trackback.php
-rw-r--r--.  1 root root  3032 Jan  9 21:48 xmlrpc.php
```

From the `ls` command's output, we can see that WordPress is in fact installed in `/var/www/html/`. We can conclude this on the basis of the large number of `.php` files along with the "`wp-`" naming scheme of these files. This will be confirmed, however, by the next steps.

Finding the database credentials

Now that we have identified the installation folder, we simply need to find the database credentials within the WordPress application's configuration files. Unfortunately, we are not very familiar with WordPress and do not know which of these files hold the database credentials.

So, how are we going to find them? By googling it, of course.

As we covered in *Chapter 1, Troubleshooting Best Practices*, Google can be a system administrator's best friend. Since WordPress is a common open source application, it is very likely that there will be online help documentation that covers how to configure or at least recover the database password.

To get started, we will simply search *WordPress database configuration* via Google. While searching Google, we find that one of the first results is linked to the WordPress forum where a user asked where to find the database details in WordPress. (`https://wordpress.org/support/topic/finding-the-database-settings-in-wordpress`)

The first answer was to look through the `wp-config.php` file.

While googling this type of information is easy for popular open source projects, it can also be effective for closed source applications as well, as many times even closed source applications have their documentation online and indexed by Google.

To obtain the database details, we can read the wp-config.php file with the less command. The less command is a simple command that allows users to read files via the command line. This is particularly useful for large files as it buffers the output rather than simply dumping all contents to the screen as in the case of the cat command.

```
# less /var/www/html/wp-config.php


// ** MySQL settings - You can get this information from your web host **
//
/** The name of the database for WordPress */
define('DB_NAME', 'wordpress');


/** MySQL database username */
define('DB_USER', 'wordpress');


/** MySQL database password */
define('DB_PASSWORD', 'password');


/** MySQL hostname */
define('DB_HOST', 'localhost');
```

By reading the configuration file, we can clearly see the database credentials, which are conveniently located towards the top of the file. The following is a list of the details that we could extract from this file:

- NAME (wordpress) of the database that WordPress is trying to use

  define('DB_NAME', 'wordpress');

- HOST (localhost) that WordPress is attempting to connect to

  define('DB_HOST', 'localhost');

- The USER (wordpress) database that WordPress is trying to authenticate with

  define('DB_USER', 'wordpress');

- PASSWORD (password) that it is using for authentication

  define('DB_PASSWORD', 'password');

With the above details, we can connect to the MariaDB services in the same way that the WordPress application does. This will be a critical step in our troubleshooting process.

Connecting as the WordPress user

Now that we have the database credentials, we can test the connectivity again with the mysql command. To connect to MariaDB with a specific username and password, we will need to use the -u (user) and -p (password) flags with the mysql command.

```
# mysql -uwordpress -p
Enter password:
Welcome to the MariaDB monitor.  Commands end with ; or \g.

Your MariaDB connection id is 30

Server version: 5.5.40-MariaDB MariaDB Server

MariaDB [(none)]>
```

In the preceding command, we can see that we added the username after the -u flag but did not include the password after-p. Since we did not include the password, the mysql client simply asked for the password after we hit enter. While it is possible to include the password after-p, this is considered a bad practice from a security perspective. It is always better to let the mysql client ask for the password to reduce the chances of the password being compromised by those looking through the command history.

From the mysql client connection, we can see that by using the same credentials as WordPress, we were able to log into the MariaDB service. This is important as the inability to connect to the database service would impact the WordPress application and could have been a possible cause of the reported issue.

Validating the database structure

Since we can connect to the MariaDB service by using the WordPress credentials, we should next validate whether the database structure exists and is intact.

In this section, we will be executing **Structured Query Language** (SQL) statements from the MariaDB command-line interface. These statements are not shell commands but SQL queries.

SQL is the standard language for interacting with relational databases such as MySQL, MariaDB, Postgres, and Oracle. While SQL is not necessarily a language that every administrator needs to know, it is my advice that any systems administrator that supports a significant number of databases should at least know the basics of SQL.

This is particularly true if the environment you support does not have specific database administrators that manage the database and the database services.

The first item to validate is that the database itself is created and accessible. We can do this by using the show databases query.

```
MariaDB [(none)]> show databases;
+--------------------+
| Database           |
+--------------------+
| information_schema |
| test               |
| wordpress          |
+--------------------+
3 rows in set (0.00 sec)
```

We can see that the WordPress database is in fact listed in this output, meaning that it exists. To validate that the WordPress database is accessible, we will use the use SQL statement.

```
MariaDB [(none)]> use wordpress;
Database changed
```

With the Database changed result, it seems that we have confirmed that the database itself is created and accessible. Now, what about the tables within this database? We can validate that the database tables have been created by using the show tables query.

```
MariaDB [wordpress]> show tables;
+-----------------------+
| Tables_in_wordpress   |
```

```
+-----------------------+
| wp_commentmeta        |
| wp_comments           |
| wp_links              |
| wp_options            |
| wp_postmeta           |
| wp_posts              |
| wp_term_relationships |
| wp_term_taxonomy      |
| wp_terms              |
| wp_usermeta           |
| wp_users              |
+-----------------------+
11 rows in set (0.00 sec)
```

From the results, it appears that quite a few tables exist.

Since we are new to WordPress, it is possible that we may be missing a table and not even know it. As WordPress is documented online quite extensively, we are likely to find a list of tables by googling *WordPress list of database tables*, which returns a very useful database description from the WordPress documentation pages: (https://codex.wordpress.org/Database_Description)

After comparing the output of the show tables query and the Database Description page, we find that no tables are missing.

Since we know which tables exist, we should check whether these tables are accessible; we can do this by running a select query.

```
MariaDB [wordpress]> select count(*) from wp_users;
ERROR 1017 (HY000): Can't find file: './wordpress/wp_users.frm'
(errno: 13)
```

At long last, we have found an error!

The error that we have found, however, is quite interesting as it is not an error that you would typically see from an SQL query. In fact, this error seems to indicate that there is an issue with a file that contains the table data.

What we learned from the database validation

At this point, after validating the database, we have learnt the following:

- MariaDB is accessible by both the root user and the WordPress application
- The database being accessed is created and accessible by the WordPress user
- An error is shown when querying one of the database tables

With this information, we can move to the next step of the troubleshooting process by establishing a hypothesis.

Establishing a hypothesis

At this stage of the troubleshooting process, we will take all of the information that we have gathered and use it to establish an idea as to why the issue occurred and what can be done to resolve it.

To start, let's first review what we have learnt from the Data Gathering steps.

- An established blog site is currently showing a page that is designed to only be shown during initial installation of the blog software
- The blog is using the open source software WordPress
- WordPress is written in PHP and utilizes both Apache and MariaDB services
- Apache and PHP are working correctly and showing no errors
- The WordPress installation is located at /var/www/html
- The MariaDB service is up and accepting connections
- The WordPress application is able to connect to the database service
- When reading from the database tables, we receive an error that indicates an issue with the files that contain the database data

The hypothesis that we can formulate from all of these data points is as follows:

At some point, the data files for MariaDB, and more specifically the WordPress database, are inaccessible to the MariaDB service. It appears that when WordPress connects to the database, it cannot query the tables; thus, it believes that the application has not been installed. Since WordPress does not believe that the application has been installed, it presents an installation page.

We can formulate this hypothesis on the basis of the following key points of information:

1. The only error we have seen is the error from MariaDB.
2. The error is not a typical SQL error, and the message itself indicates an issue with accessing the database files.
3. There are no PHP errors in the Apache logs.
4. Everything else about the WordPress environment seems to be correct.

Now that we have formed a hypothesis, we need to validate that this is true by attempting to resolve the issue. This brings us to the third stage of the troubleshooting process: *Trial and Error*.

Resolving the issue

In this stage, we will attempt to resolve the issue. To do this, let's take a look at what these data files are and what they are used for.

Understanding database data files

Most databases with the exception of in-memory-only databases have some sort of file that is used to store the data on a file system; this is often referred to as persistent storage. MariaDB and MySQL are no exception to this rule.

Depending on the database storage engine in use, there may be one big file or multiple files with different file extensions. Irrespective of the file type or where/how the files are stored, at the end of the day, if these files are not accessible, the database will have issues.

Finding the MariaDB data folder

Since we are new to this environment, we currently do not know where the MariaDB data files are stored. Identifying the location of these files will be the first step in correcting the issue. One way to identify the data folder is to look through the database services' configuration file.

Since the /etc folder is home to most (but not all) configuration files, this is the first place we should look.

```
# ls -la /etc/ | grep -i maria
```

To identify the proper configuration file, we can use the `ls` command to list the `/etc` folder and the `grep` command to search the results for anything with the string "maria." The abovementioned `grep` command uses the `-i` (insensitive) flag, which causes `grep` to search for both uppercase and lowercase strings. This can be helpful if the folder or file has a mixed case name.

Since our command printed no output, there is no folder or file with the string "maria" in its name. This means that the MariaDB services' configuration either is named something that we are not expecting or is not within the `/etc/` folder.

Since MariaDB is supposed to be a drop-in replacement for MySQL, we should also check whether there is a `mysql`-named folder or file.

```
# ls -la /etc/ | grep -i mysql
```

It appears that there is no folder or file matching this name either.

We could easily spend several hours trying to find configuration files for MariaDB by using the `ls` command. Fortunately, there is a faster way to find the configuration files.

Since MariaDB was installed via an RPM package, we can use the `rpm` command to list all files and folders deployed by the package. Earlier when checking how MariaDB was installed, the `rpm` command shows multiple packages for MariaDB. The package that we are interested in is the `mariadb-server` package. This package installs the MariaDB service as well as the default configuration files.

Earlier we used the `-q` and `-l` flags of `rpm` to list all files deployed by this package. If we wanted to limit our query to only configuration files, we could use the `-q` and `-c` flags.

```
$ rpm -qc mariadb-server
/etc/logrotate.d/mariadb
/etc/my.cnf.d/server.cnf
/var/log/mariadb/mariadb.log
```

From the above, we can see that the `mariadb-server` package deploys three configuration files. The `mariadb.log` and `logrotate.d` files are not likely to contain the information that we are looking for as they are related to the logging process.

This leaves the `/etc/my.cnf.d/server.cnf` file. We can read this file by using the `cat` command.

```
# cat /etc/my.cnf.d/server.cnf
#
# These groups are read by the MariaDB server.
```

```
# Use it for options that only the server (but not clients) should see
#
# See the examples of server my.cnf files in /usr/share/mysql/
#

# this is read by the standalone daemon and embedded servers
[server]

# this is only for the mysqld standalone daemon
[mysqld]

# this is only for embedded server
[embedded]

# This group is only read by MariaDB-5.5 servers.
# If you use the same .cnf file for MariaDB of different versions,
# use this group for options that older servers don't understand
[mysqld-5.5]

# These two groups are only read by MariaDB servers, not by MySQL.
# If you use the same .cnf file for MySQL and MariaDB,
# you can put MariaDB-only options here
[mariadb]

[mariadb-5.5]
```

Unfortunately, this file also does not contain the data folder details as we had hoped. This file does, however, give us a clue as to where to look next.

The parent folder of the `server.conf` file is the `/etc/my.cnf.d` folder. The `.d` at the end of the folder name is important, as this naming convention has a special purpose in Linux. The `.d` (dot D) folder types are designed to allow users to simply add a file or many files with custom configurations for the service. When the service is started, all files within this folder are read and the configurations are applied.

This allows users to configure a service without editing the default configuration files; they can simply drop in the configurations that they want to add by creating a new file in the `.d` folder.

It's important to note that this is a configuration scheme and not every service supports this scheme. It seems, however, that the MariaDB service does in fact support this scheme.

What is interesting, however, is the name of this `.d` folder. Typically, the naming convention for a `.d` configuration folder is the service name or folder purpose followed by `.d`. You can see this in practice with the `/etc/cron.d` or `/etc/http/conf.d` folder. The name of the MariaDB `.d` folder suggests that the main configuration file may be named `my.cnf`.

If we check whether such a file exists or not, we will see that it does.

```
# ls -la /etc/ | grep my.cnf
-rw-r--r--.  1 root root       570 Nov 17 12:28 my.cnf
drwxr-xr-x.  2 root root        64 Jan  9 18:20 my.cnf.d
```

This file appears to be the main MariaDB configuration file, which will hopefully contain the data folder configuration. To find out, we can read this file with the `cat` command.

```
# cat /etc/my.cnf
[mysqld]
datadir=/var/lib/mysql
socket=/var/lib/mysql/mysql.sock
# Disabling symbolic-links is recommended to prevent assorted security
risks
symbolic-links=0
# Settings user and group are ignored when systemd is used.
# If you need to run mysqld under a different user or group,
# customize your systemd unit file for mariadb according to the
# instructions in http://fedoraproject.org/wiki/Systemd


[mysqld_safe]
log-error=/var/log/mariadb/mariadb.log
pid-file=/var/run/mariadb/mariadb.pid


#
# include all files from the config folder
#
!includedir /etc/my.cnf.d
```

As anticipated, this file does actually contain the data folder configuration.

```
datadir=/var/lib/mysql
```

Armed with this information, we can now troubleshoot the current state of the WordPress database's data files.

Resolving data file issues

If we change to the `/var/lib/mysql` folder and use the `ls` command to list the folder contents, we can see quite a few database data files/folders.

```
# cd /var/lib/mysql/
# ls -la
total 28712
drwxr-xr-x.  6 mysql mysql      4096 Jan 15 00:20 .
drwxr-xr-x. 29 root  root       4096 Jan 15 05:40 ..
-rw-rw----.  1 mysql mysql     16384 Jan 15 00:20 aria_log.00000001
-rw-rw----.  1 mysql mysql        52 Jan 15 00:20 aria_log_control
-rw-rw----.  1 mysql mysql  18874368 Jan 15 00:20 ibdata1
-rw-rw----.  1 mysql mysql   5242880 Jan 15 00:20 ib_logfile0
-rw-rw----.  1 mysql mysql   5242880 Jan  9 21:39 ib_logfile1
drwx------.  2 mysql mysql      4096 Jan  9 21:39 mysql
srwxrwxrwx.  1 mysql mysql         0 Jan 15 00:20 mysql.sock
drwx------.  2 mysql mysql      4096 Jan  9 21:39 performance_schema
drwx------.  2 mysql mysql         6 Jan  9 21:39 test
drwx------.  2 mysql mysql      4096 Jan  9 22:55 wordpress
```

It appears that each database created on this server exists as a folder under `/var/lib/mysql/`. It also appears from the `ls` output that the folders are in a normal state. Since the issue is with the WordPress database, we will focus on this database by switching to the `wordpress` folder.

```
# cd wordpress/
# ls -la
total 156
drwx------. 2 mysql mysql 4096 Jan  9 22:55 .
drwxr-xr-x. 6 mysql mysql 4096 Jan 15 00:20 ..
-rw-rw----. 1 mysql mysql   65 Jan  9 21:45 db.opt
----------. 1 root  root  8688 Jan  9 22:55 wp_commentmeta.frm
```

```
----------. 1 root    root    13380 Jan  9 22:55 wp_comments.frm
----------. 1 root    root    13176 Jan  9 22:55 wp_links.frm
----------. 1 root    root     8698 Jan  9 22:55 wp_options.frm
----------. 1 root    root     8682 Jan  9 22:55 wp_postmeta.frm
----------. 1 root    root    13684 Jan  9 22:55 wp_posts.frm
----------. 1 root    root     8666 Jan  9 22:55 wp_term_relationships.frm
----------. 1 root    root     8668 Jan  9 22:55 wp_terms.frm
----------. 1 root    root     8768 Jan  9 22:55 wp_term_taxonomy.frm
----------. 1 root    root     8684 Jan  9 22:55 wp_usermeta.frm
----------. 1 root    root     8968 Jan  9 22:55 wp_users.frm
```

Right after executing the `ls` command, we can see that there is something unusual with the files within this folder.

The item that stands out is simply the fact that all the `.frm` files have a file mode of `000`. This means that neither the owner nor the group or other Linux users can read or write these files. This includes the user that MariaDB runs as.

If we look back at the error that we received from MariaDB, we find that the error seems to support the supposition that the invalid permissions are in fact causing an issue. To correct this error, we simply need to reset the permissions to the correct values.

Since we are new to MariaDB, we currently do not know exactly what these values should be.

Luckily, there is an easy way to figure out what the permissions should be: simply look at another database's file permissions.

If we look back at the output of the folder listing for `/var/lib/mysql`, we find that there were several folders. At least one of these other folders should also be a database's data folder. To determine what permissions our `.frm` files should have, we simply need to find other `.frm` files.

```
# find /var/lib/mysql -name "*.frm" -ls
134481927    12 -rw-rw----   1 mysql     mysql          9582 Jan  9 21:39 /
var/lib/mysql/mysql/db.frm
134481930    12 -rw-rw----   1 mysql     mysql          9510 Jan  9 21:39 /
var/lib/mysql/mysql/host.frm
134481933    12 -rw-rw----   1 mysql     mysql         10630 Jan  9 21:39 /
var/lib/mysql/mysql/user.frm
134481936    12 -rw-rw----   1 mysql     mysql          8665 Jan  9 21:39 /
var/lib/mysql/mysql/func.frm
```

```
134481939   12 -rw-rw----    1 mysql     mysql       8586 Jan  9 21:39 /
var/lib/mysql/mysql/plugin.frm

134481942   12 -rw-rw----    1 mysql     mysql       8838 Jan  9 21:39 /
var/lib/mysql/mysql/servers.frm

134481945   12 -rw-rw----    1 mysql     mysql       8955 Jan  9 21:39 /
var/lib/mysql/mysql/tables_priv.frm

134481948   12 -rw-rw----    1 mysql     mysql       8820 Jan  9 21:39 /
var/lib/mysql/mysql/columns_priv.frm

134481951   12 -rw-rw----    1 mysql     mysql       8770 Jan  9 21:39 /
var/lib/mysql/mysql/help_topic.frm

134309941   12 -rw-rw----    1 mysql     mysql       8700 Jan  9 21:39 /
var/lib/mysql/mysql/help_category.frm
```

The find command is a very useful command for troubleshooting and can be used in many different situations. In our example, we use the find command to search for any file in the /var/lib/mysql folder that has a filename that ends with ".frm" via the -name flag. The -ls (folder listing) flag tells the find command to print any files that it finds in a long list format, which will show each file's permissions without having to run a second command.

From the find command's output, we can see that the permissions on the .frm files are set to -rw-rw----; the numeric representation of this is 660. These permissions seem appropriate for our database table and allow the owner and group to read and write these files.

To reset the permissions on our WordPress data files, we will use the chmod command.

```
# chmod -v 660 /var/lib/mysql/wordpress/*.frm

mode of '/var/lib/mysql/wordpress/wp_commentmeta.frm' changed from 0000
(---------) to 0660 (rw-rw----)

mode of '/var/lib/mysql/wordpress/wp_comments.frm' changed from 0000 (---
------) to 0660 (rw-rw----)

mode of '/var/lib/mysql/wordpress/wp_links.frm' changed from 0000 (------
---) to 0660 (rw-rw----)

mode of '/var/lib/mysql/wordpress/wp_options.frm' changed from 0000 (----
-----) to 0660 (rw-rw----)

mode of '/var/lib/mysql/wordpress/wp_postmeta.frm' changed from 0000 (---
------) to 0660 (rw-rw----)

mode of '/var/lib/mysql/wordpress/wp_posts.frm' changed from 0000 (------
---) to 0660 (rw-rw----)

mode of '/var/lib/mysql/wordpress/wp_term_relationships.frm' changed from
0000 (---------) to 0660 (rw-rw----)
```

```
mode of '/var/lib/mysql/wordpress/wp_terms.frm' changed from 0000 (------
---) to 0660 (rw-rw----)
mode of '/var/lib/mysql/wordpress/wp_term_taxonomy.frm' changed from 0000
(---------) to 0660 (rw-rw----)
mode of '/var/lib/mysql/wordpress/wp_usermeta.frm' changed from 0000 (---
------) to 0660 (rw-rw----)
mode of '/var/lib/mysql/wordpress/wp_users.frm' changed from 0000 (------
---) to 0660 (rw-rw----)
```

In the preceding command, the –v (verbose) flag was used with chmod so that we could see the changes in each file's permissions as the command executed.

Validating

Now that the permissions have been set, we can yet again validate with an SQL select query.

```
MariaDB [wordpress]> select count(*) from wp_users;
ERROR 1017 (HY000): Can't find file: './wordpress/wp_users.frm' (errno:
13)
```

From the above query, we can see there is still an error with MariaDB accessing these files. This means that we must not have corrected all of the issues with the data files.

```
# ls -la
total 156
drwx------. 2 mysql mysql  4096 Jan  9 22:55 .
drwxr-xr-x. 6 mysql mysql  4096 Jan 15 00:20 ..
-rw-rw----. 1 mysql mysql    65 Jan  9 21:45 db.opt
-rw-rw----. 1 root  root   8688 Jan  9 22:55 wp_commentmeta.frm
-rw-rw----. 1 root  root  13380 Jan  9 22:55 wp_comments.frm
-rw-rw----. 1 root  root  13176 Jan  9 22:55 wp_links.frm
-rw-rw----. 1 root  root   8698 Jan  9 22:55 wp_options.frm
-rw-rw----. 1 root  root   8682 Jan  9 22:55 wp_postmeta.frm
-rw-rw----. 1 root  root  13684 Jan  9 22:55 wp_posts.frm
-rw-rw----. 1 root  root   8666 Jan  9 22:55 wp_term_relationships.frm
-rw-rw----. 1 root  root   8668 Jan  9 22:55 wp_terms.frm
-rw-rw----. 1 root  root   8768 Jan  9 22:55 wp_term_taxonomy.frm
-rw-rw----. 1 root  root   8684 Jan  9 22:55 wp_usermeta.frm
-rw-rw----. 1 root  root   8968 Jan  9 22:55 wp_users.frm
```

By reviewing the `ls` command's output, we can see one more difference from the example `.frm` files.

```
134481927   12 -rw-rw----    1 mysql     mysql        9582 Jan
9 21:39 /var/lib/mysql/mysql/db.frm
```

The owner and group permissions for the files in the `wordpress` folder are set to `root`, whereas the other `.frm` files are owned and grouped as the `mysql` user.

The permissions of `660` mean that only the owner and group members of the file can access it. In the case of our WordPress files, this means that only the root user and any member of the root group can access these files.

Since MariaDB runs as the `mysql` user, the MariaDB service still cannot access these files. We can reset the ownership and group membership with the `chown` command.

```
# chown -v mysql.mysql ./*.frm
changed ownership of './wp_commentmeta.frm' from root:root to mysql:mysql
changed ownership of './wp_comments.frm' from root:root to mysql:mysql
changed ownership of './wp_links.frm' from root:root to mysql:mysql
changed ownership of './wp_options.frm' from root:root to mysql:mysql
changed ownership of './wp_postmeta.frm' from root:root to mysql:mysql
changed ownership of './wp_posts.frm' from root:root to mysql:mysql
changed ownership of './wp_term_relationships.frm' from root:root to
mysql:mysql
changed ownership of './wp_terms.frm' from root:root to mysql:mysql
changed ownership of './wp_term_taxonomy.frm' from root:root to
mysql:mysql
changed ownership of './wp_usermeta.frm' from root:root to mysql:mysql
changed ownership of './wp_users.frm' from root:root to mysql:mysql
```

Now that the ownership and the group membership of the files are `mysql`, we can rerun our query to see whether the issue is resolved.

```
MariaDB [wordpress]> select count(*) from wp_users;
count(*)
1
```

At long last, we have resolved the error by querying the WordPress database tables.

Final validation

Since we have resolved the database error, and we did not find any other errors while troubleshooting, the next validation step is to see whether the blog is still showing the installation screen.

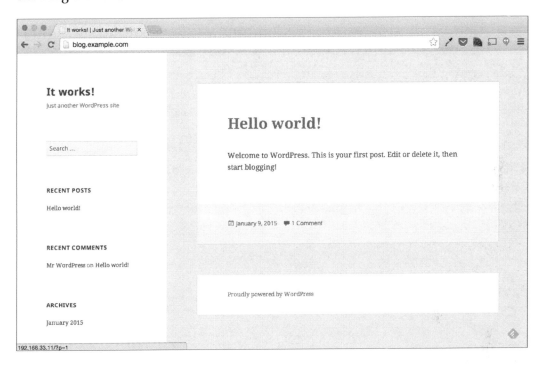

By navigating to `http://blog.example.com` from our browser, we can now see that we no longer receive the installation page, but rather the blog's front page. At this point, it seems that the issue has been resolved.

In general, when working on an issue reported by a person, it is a best practice to have the person who initially reported the problem to validate that everything has been restored to an expected state. I have seen many instances where an incident is caused by more than one issue, and while the more apparent issue is resolved quickly, the other issue(s) is(are) often overlooked. Having the user verify that we have fixed the entire problem will help to ensure that everything has been truly resolved.

For this scenario, when we asked the business user who reported the issue to check whether the issue has been resolved, he/she replied with *Everything looks fixed. Thank you!*

Summary

In this chapter, we walked through the troubleshooting process by using an issue that can easily occur in the real world. We iterated through Steps 1, 2, and 3 of the troubleshooting process to collect data, establish a hypothesis, and resolve the issue; these steps were covered in detail in *Chapter 1, Troubleshooting Best Practices*. We then used several commands and log files that we learned about in *Chapter 2, Troubleshooting Commands and Sources of Useful Information* as well as a few new ones.

While learning the commands used in this chapter is important for any systems administrator working with web applications, it is more important to look at the process that we followed. We started working on the problem with no prior knowledge of the environment or application, but with some basic data collection and trial and error, we could resolve the problem.

In the next chapter, we will use this same troubleshooting process and similar tools for troubleshooting performance issues.

4
Troubleshooting Performance Issues

In *Chapter 3, Troubleshooting a Web Application* we walked through troubleshooting a web application problem by using the troubleshooting methodology covered in *Chapter 1, Troubleshooting Best Practices*. We also used several of the fundamental troubleshooting commands and resources found in *Chapter 2, Troubleshooting Commands and Sources of Useful Information*.

Performance issues

For this chapter, we will continue the scenario that we covered in *Chapter 3, Troubleshooting a Web Application*, where we are a new systems administrator at a new company. As we arrive to start our day, a fellow systems administrator asks us to look into a server being "slow."

When asked for details, the only information our colleague could provide was the hostname and the IP of the server deemed "slow." Our peer mentioned that a user reported it and that the user did not provide many details.

In this scenario, unlike in the scenario discussed in *Chapter 3, Troubleshooting a Web Application* we don't have much information to begin with. It also seems that we are not able to ask the user troubleshooting questions. It is not uncommon as a systems administrator to be required to troubleshoot an issue with very little information. In fact, this type of scenario is quite common.

It's slow

"It's slow" is problematic to troubleshoot. The biggest problem with a complaint about a server or service being slow is that "slow" is relative to the user experiencing the issue.

An important distinction to understand when dealing with any complaint about performance is the benchmark that the environment has been designed for. In some environments, a system running at 30% CPU utilization could be a business-as-usual activity, whereas the other environments may keep their systems running at 10% CPU utilization and a spike of 30% utilization would signal an issue.

While troubleshooting and investigating performance issues, it is important to look back at the historical performance metrics of the system to ensure that you have context around the measurements being collected. This will assist in determining whether the current system utilization is expected or abnormal.

Performance

In general, performance issues can be categorized into five areas:

- Application
- CPU
- Memory
- Disk
- Network

A bottleneck in any one area can often affect other areas as well; therefore, it is a good idea to understand each of these topics. By understanding how each of these resources is accessed and interacts, you will be able to find the root cause of issues that consume multiple resources.

Since the issue being reported did not include any details of the performance issue, we will explore and learn about each of these areas. Once complete, we will look at the data collected and look at historical statistics to determine whether the performance is as expected or whether the system performance really is degraded.

Application

While creating a list of performance categories, I ordered them by areas that I see most often. Every environment is different, but in my experience, the application can often be a primary source of performance issues.

While this chapter is designed to cover performance issues, *Chapter 9, Using System Tools to Troubleshoot Applications* is dedicated to using system tools for troubleshooting application issues, including performance issues. For this chapter, we will assume that our issue is not application related and focus specifically on system performance.

CPU

CPU is a very common performance bottleneck. Sometimes, issues are strictly CPU-based, and at other times, there are instances where an increase in CPU usage is a symptom of another issue.

The most common command to investigate CPU utilization is the top command. The primary role of this command is to identify the CPU utilization of the processes. In *Chapter 2, Troubleshooting Commands and Sources of Useful Information* we discussed utilizing the ps command for this type of activity. In this section, we are going to investigate our slowness complaint by using both top and ps to investigate our CPU utilization.

Top – a single command to look at everything

The **top** command is one of the first commands that both systems administrators and users run to look at the overall system performance. The reason for this is that top shows not only a breakdown of Load Average, CPU, and memory, but it also shows a sorted list of processes utilizing these resources.

The best part of top is the fact that when run without any flags, these details are updated every 3 seconds.

The following is an example of the top output when run without any flags.

```
top - 17:40:43 up  4:07,  2 users,  load average: 0.32, 0.43, 0.44
Tasks: 100 total,   2 running,  98 sleeping,   0 stopped,   0 zombie
%Cpu(s): 37.3 us,  0.7 sy,  0.0 ni, 62.0 id,  0.0 wa,  0.0 hi,  0.0 si,
0.0 st
KiB Mem:    469408 total,   228112 used,   241296 free,     764 buffers
KiB Swap:  1081340 total,        0 used,  1081340 free.   95332 cached
Mem

  PID USER      PR  NI    VIRT    RES    SHR S %CPU %MEM     TIME+
COMMAND
 3023 vagrant   20   0    7396    720    504 S 37.6  0.2  91:08.04
lookbusy
```

```
   11 root      20   0        0        0     0 R   0.3  0.0   0:13.28
rcuos/0

  682 root      20   0   322752     1072   772 S   0.3  0.2   0:05.60
VBoxService

    1 root      20   0    50784     7256  2500 S   0.0  1.5   0:01.39
systemd

    2 root      20   0        0        0     0 S   0.0  0.0   0:00.00
kthreadd

    3 root      20   0        0        0     0 S   0.0  0.0   0:00.24
ksoftirqd/0

    5 root       0 -20        0        0     0 S   0.0  0.0   0:00.00
kworker/0:0H

    6 root      20   0        0        0     0 S   0.0  0.0   0:00.04
kworker/u2:0

    7 root      rt   0        0        0     0 S   0.0  0.0   0:00.00
migration/0

    8 root      20   0        0        0     0 S   0.0  0.0   0:00.00
rcu_bh

    9 root      20   0        0        0     0 S   0.0  0.0   0:00.00
rcuob/0

   10 root      20   0        0        0     0 S   0.0  0.0   0:05.44
rcu_sched
```

There is quite a bit of information displayed with just the default output of `top`. For this section, we will focus solely on the CPU utilization information.

```
%Cpu(s): 37.3 us,  0.7 sy,  0.0 ni, 62.0 id,  0.0 wa,  0.0 hi,  0.0
si,  0.0 st
```

In the first section of the `top` command's output, there is a single line that shows a breakdown of the current CPU utilization. Each item in this list represents a different way in which the CPU is being used. To understand the output better, let's take a look at what each of these values mean:

- **us – User**: This number is the percentage of CPU being consumed by the processes in the user mode. In this mode, applications are not able to access the underlying hardware and are required to use system APIs (a.k.a system calls) to perform privileged executions. When executing these system calls, the execution will be part of the system CPU utilization.

- **sy – System**: This number is the percentage of CPU being consumed by kernel mode execution. In this mode, systems can directly access the underlying hardware; this mode is generally reserved for trusted OS processes.

- **ni – Nice user processes**: This number is the percentage of CPU time being consumed by user processes that have had a nice value set. The us% value is specifically for processes that have not had their niceness values modified from the original value.

- **id – Idle**: This number is the percentage of CPU time spent being idle. Essentially, it is the amount of CPU time spent not being utilized.

- **wa – Wait**: This number is the percentage of CPU time spent waiting. This is typically high when many processes are waiting for I/O devices. I/O wait states do not just refer to hard disks, but rather to all I/O devices including hard disks.

- **hi – Hardware interrupts**: This number is the percentage of CPU time being consumed by hardware interrupts. Hardware interrupts are signals from system hardware, such as hard drives or network devices, that are sent to the CPU. These interrupts signal that there are events that require CPU time.

- **si – Software interrupts**: This number is the percentage of CPU time being consumed by software interrupts. Software interrupts are similar to hardware interrupts; however, they are triggered by a signal sent by the running processes to the kernel.

- **st – Stolen**: This number specifically applies to Linux systems running as a virtual machine. This number is the percentage of CPU time stolen from this machine by the host. This number is usually present when the host machine itself is running into CPU contention. This can also happen in some cloud environments as a method of enforcing resource limitations.

Earlier I mentioned that the output from `top` is refreshed every 3 seconds by default. The CPU percentage line is also refreshed every 3 seconds; `top` will display the percentage of CPU time in each state since the last refresh interval.

What does this output tell us about our issue?

If we review the previous `top` command's output, we can determine quite a bit about this system.

```
%Cpu(s): 37.3 us,  0.7 sy,  0.0 ni, 62.0 id,  0.0 wa,  0.0 hi,  0.0
si,  0.0 st
```

From the preceding output, we can see that 37.3% of the CPU time was being consumed by processes in the user mode. Another 0.7% of the CPU time was used by processes in the kernel execution mode; this is based on the us and sy values. The id value tells us that the rest of the CPU was not utilized, meaning that overall, there is ample CPU available on this server.

Another fact that the top command shows is the lack of CPU time being spent waiting for I/O. We can see this from the wa value being 0.0. This is important as it tells us the performance issue that was reported is not likely due to high I/O. Later in this chapter, as we start exploring disk performance, we will explore I/O wait in depth.

Individual processes from top

The CPU line in top commands output is a summary for the server as a whole, but top also includes CPU utilization for individual processes. To get a clearer focus, we can execute top again, but this time, let's focus on the top running processes.

```
$ top -n 1

top - 15:46:52 up  3:21,  2 users,  load average: 1.03, 1.11, 1.06

Tasks: 108 total,   3 running, 105 sleeping,   0 stopped,   0 zombie

%Cpu(s): 34.1 us,  0.7 sy,  0.0 ni, 65.1 id,  0.0 wa,  0.0 hi,  0.1
si,  0.0 st

KiB Mem:    502060 total,   220284 used,   281776 free,       764
buffers

KiB Swap:  1081340 total,        0 used,  1081340 free.    92940
cached Mem
```

PID	USER	PR	NI	VIRT	RES	SHR	S	%CPU	%MEM	TIME+ COMMAND
3001	vagrant	20	0	7396	720	504	R	98.4	0.1	121:08.67 lookbusy
3002	vagrant	20	0	7396	720	504	S	6.6	0.1	19:05.12 lookbusy
1	root	20	0	50780	7264	2508	S	0.0	1.4	0:01.69 systemd
2	root	20	0	0	0	0	S	0.0	0.0	0:00.01 kthreadd
3	root	20	0	0	0	0	S	0.0	0.0	0:00.97 ksoftirqd/0
5	root	0	-20	0	0	0	S	0.0	0.0	0:00.00 kworker/0:0H
6	root	20	0	0	0	0	S	0.0	0.0	0:00.00 kworker/u4:0
7	root	rt	0	0	0	0	S	0.0	0.0	0:00.67 migration/0

This time when executing the `top` command, the `-n` (number) flag was used. This flag tells `top` to only refresh for a specified number of times, in this case 1 time. This trick can be helpful when trying to capture the output of `top`.

If we review the output of the above `top` command, we can see something quite interesting.

```
 PID USER      PR  NI    VIRT    RES    SHR S  %CPU %MEM     TIME+
COMMAND
 3001 vagrant   20   0    7396    720    504 R  98.4  0.1 121:08.67
lookbusy
```

By default, the `top` command orders the processes by the percentage of CPU utilized by the processes. This means that the first process in the list is the process consuming the most amount of CPU in that interval.

If we look at the top process running under the process id of `3001`, we find that it is using `98.4%` of the CPU time. However, according to the top commands system-wide CPU statistics, `65.1%` of the CPU time is spent in an idle state. This type of scenario is actually a common source of confusion for many systems administrators.

```
%Cpu(s): 34.1 us,  0.7 sy,  0.0 ni, 65.1 id,  0.0 wa,  0.0 hi,  0.1
si,  0.0 st
```

How can a single process be utilizing almost 100% of the CPU time, while the system itself is showing 65% of the CPU time is spent idle? The answer turns out to be simple; when `top` displays the CPU utilization in its header, the scale is based on the system as a whole. With individual processes, however, the CPU utilization scale is for one CPU. This means that our process 3001 is actually utilizing almost one full CPU and that our system most likely has multiple CPUs.

It is quite common to see processes that are able to utilize multiple CPUs show a percentage higher than 100%. For example, a process that is fully utilizing three CPUs would show 300%. This can also cause quite a bit of confusion for users unfamiliar with the difference of `top` commands server total and per-process output.

Determining the number of CPUs available

Previously, we determined that this system must have multiple CPUs available. What we did not determine is how many. The easiest method to determine the number of CPUs available is to simply read the `/proc/cpuinfo` file.

```
# cat /proc/cpuinfo
processor   : 0
vendor_id   : GenuineIntel
```

```
cpu family  : 6
model     : 58
model name  : Intel(R) Core(TM) i7-3615QM CPU @ 2.30GHz
stepping  : 9
microcode  : 0x19
cpu MHz    : 2348.850
cache size  : 6144 KB
physical id  : 0
siblings  : 2
core id    : 0
cpu cores  : 2
apicid    : 0
initial apicid  : 0
fpu    : yes
fpu_exception  : yes
cpuid level  : 5
wp    : yes
flags    : fpu vme de pse tsc msr pae mce cx8 apic sep mtrr pge mca
cmov pat pse36 clflush mmx fxsr sse sse2 ht syscall nx rdtscp lm
constant_tsc rep_good nopl pni ssse3 lahf_lm
bogomips  : 4697.70
clflush size  : 64
cache_alignment  : 64
address sizes  : 36 bits physical, 48 bits virtual
power management:

processor  : 1
vendor_id  : GenuineIntel
cpu family  : 6
model     : 58
model name  : Intel(R) Core(TM) i7-3615QM CPU @ 2.30GHz
stepping  : 9
microcode  : 0x19
cpu MHz    : 2348.850
```

```
cache size   : 6144 KB
physical id  : 0
siblings     : 2
core id      : 1
cpu cores    : 2
apicid       : 1
initial apicid  : 1
fpu      : yes
fpu_exception  : yes
cpuid level  : 5
wp       : yes
flags    : fpu vme de pse tsc msr pae mce cx8 apic sep mtrr pge mca
cmov pat pse36 clflush mmx fxsr sse sse2 ht syscall nx rdtscp lm
constant_tsc rep_good nopl pni ssse3 lahf_lm
bogomips   : 4697.70
clflush size  : 64
cache_alignment  : 64
address sizes  : 36 bits physical, 48 bits virtual
power management:
```

The /proc/cpuinfo file contains quite a bit of useful information about the CPUs available to our system. It shows the type of CPU down to the model, what flags are available, the speed of the CPU, and, most importantly, the number of CPUs available.

Every CPU available to the system will be listed in the cpuinfo file. This means that you can simply count the number of processors available in the cpuinfo file to determine the number of CPUs available to a server.

From the above example, we can determine that this server has 2 CPUs available.

Threads and Cores

An interesting caveat with using cpuinfo to determine whether the number of CPUs available is that the details are a bit misleading when working with CPUs that have multiple cores and are hyper-threaded. The cpuinfo file reports both a core and a thread on the CPU as a processor that it can utilize. This means that even though you may have one physical chip installed on your system, if that chip was a four-core hyper-threaded CPU, the cpuinfo file would display eight processors.

lscpu – Another way to look at CPU info

While `/proc/cpuinfo` is a method that many admins and users use to determine CPU information; on RHEL-based distributions, there is another command that will display this info as well.

```
$ lscpu
Architecture:          x86_64
CPU op-mode(s):        32-bit, 64-bit
Byte Order:            Little Endian
CPU(s):                2
On-line CPU(s) list:   0,1
Thread(s) per core:    1
Core(s) per socket:    2
Socket(s):             1
NUMA node(s):          1
Vendor ID:             GenuineIntel
CPU family:            6
Model:                 58
Model name:            Intel(R) Core(TM) i7-3615QM CPU @ 2.30GHz
Stepping:              9
CPU MHz:               2348.850
BogoMIPS:              4697.70
L1d cache:             32K
L1d cache:             32K
L2d cache:             6144K
NUMA node0 CPU(s):     0,1
```

A difference between the contents of `/proc/cpuinfo` and the `lscpu` command is that `lscpu` makes it very easy to identify the number of cores, sockets, and threads. It can often be a bit difficult to identify this same information from the `/proc/cpuinfo` file.

ps – Drill down deeper on individual processes with ps

While the `top` command can be used to look at individual processes, I personally feel that the `ps` command is better-suited for investigating running processes. In *Chapter 2, Troubleshooting Commands and Sources of Useful Information* we covered the `ps` command and how it can be used to look at many different aspects of a running process.

In this chapter, we will use the ps command to take a deeper look at process 3001 that we identified with the top command as the process utilizing the most CPU time.

```
$ ps -lf 3001
F S UID         PID  PPID  C PRI  NI ADDR SZ WCHAN   STIME TTY
TIME CMD
1 S vagrant   3001  3000 73  80   0 -  1849 hrtime 01:34 pts/1
892:23 lookbusy --cpu-mode curve --cpu-curve-peak 14h -c 20-80
```

In *Chapter 2*, *Troubleshooting Commands and Sources of Useful Information* we discussed using the ps command to display running processes. In the preceding example, we specified two flags that were shown in *Chapter 2*, *Troubleshooting Commands and Sources of Useful Information*, -l (long listing) and -f (full format). In this chapter, we discussed how these flags provide additional details for the processes displayed.

To better understand the above process, let's break down the additional details that these two flags provide.

- Current State: S (interruptible sleep)
- User: vagrant
- Process ID: 3001
- Parent Process ID: 3000
- Priority Value: 80
- Niceness Level: 0
- Command being executed: lookbusy –cpu-mode-curve –cpu-curve-peak 14h -c 20-80

Earlier with the top command, this process was utilizing almost a full CPU, which means that this process is a suspect for the reported slowness. By looking at the above details, we can determine a few things about this process.

First, it is a sub process of process 3000; something we determined by the parent process ID. The second being that, when we ran the ps command, it was waiting for a task to finish; we can determine this by the interruptible sleep state that the process is currently in.

In addition to these two items, we can tell that the process does not have a high scheduling priority. We can determine this by looking at the priority value, which in this case is 80. The scheduling priority system works as follows: the higher the number, the lower the priority that the process has with the system scheduler.

We can also see that the niceness level is set to 0, the default. This means that a user has not adjusted the niceness level to a higher (or lower) priority.

These are all important data points to collect about the process, but by themselves, they do not answer whether or not this process is the cause of the reported slowness.

Using ps to determine process CPU utilization

Since we know that process 3001 is a child of process 3000, we should not only look at the same information for process 3000 but also use ps to identify how much CPU process 3000 is utilizing. We can do this all in one command by using the -o (options) flag with ps. This flag allows you to specify your own output format; it also allows you to see fields that are not always visible via common ps flags.

In the following command, the -o flag is used to format the ps command's output with the key fields from our previous run and include the %cpu field. This additional field will show the CPU utilization of the process. The command will also use the -p flag to specify both process 3000 and process 3001.

```
$ ps -o state,user,pid,ppid,nice,%cpu,cmd -p 3000,3001
S USER        PID  PPID  NI %CPU CMD
S vagrant    3000  2980   0  0.0 lookbusy --cpu-mode curve --cpu-
curve-peak 14h -c 20-80
R vagrant    3001  3000   0 71.5 lookbusy --cpu-mode curve --cpu-
curve-peak 14h -c 20-80
```

While the above command is quite long, it shows just how useful the -o flag can be. Given the right options, it is possible to find out a great deal of information about processes with just the ps command.

From the above command's output, we can see that process 3000 is yet another instance of the lookbusy command. We can also see that process 3000 is a child process of process 2980. Before going much further, we should try to identify all of the processes associated with process 3001.

We can do this by using the ps command with the --forest flag, which tells ps to print the parent and child processes in a tree format. When provided the -e (everything) flag, the ps command will print all processes in this tree format.

By default, the ps command will only print processes related to the user who executed the command. The -e flag changes this behavior to print all possible processes.

The below output is truncated to specifically identify the lookbusy process.

```
$ ps --forest -eo user,pid,ppid,%cpu,cmd
root         1007       1   0.0 /usr/sbin/sshd -D
root         2976    1007   0.0  \_ sshd: vagrant [priv]
vagrant      2979    2976   0.0      \_ sshd: vagrant@pts/1
vagrant      2980    2979   0.0          \_ -bash
vagrant      3000    2980   0.0              \_ lookbusy --cpu-mode curve -
-cpu-curve-peak 14h -c 20-80
vagrant      3001    3000  70.4                  \_ lookbusy --cpu-mode
curve --cpu-curve-peak 14h -c 20-80
vagrant      3002    3000  14.6                  \_ lookbusy --cpu-mode
curve --cpu-curve-peak 14h -c 20-80
```

From the ps output above, we can see that the lookbusy process with the ID 3000 has spawned two processes, namely 3001 and 3002. We can also see that the vagrant user, who is currently logged in via SSH started the lookbusy processes.

Since we also used the −o flag with ps to show CPU utilization, we can see that process 3002 is utilizing 14.6% of a single CPU.

> It is important to note that the ps command also displays the percentage of CPU time for a single processor, meaning that a process that utilizes more than one processor could have a value higher than 100%.

Putting it all together

Now that we have gone through the commands to identify the system's CPU utilization, let's put it together to summarize what has been found.

A quick look with top

Our first step to identifying issues related to CPU performance is to execute the top command.

```
$ top


top - 01:50:36 up 23:41,  2 users,  load average: 0.68, 0.56, 0.48
Tasks: 107 total,   4 running, 103 sleeping,   0 stopped,   0 zombie
%Cpu(s): 34.5 us,  0.7 sy,  0.0 ni, 64.9 id,  0.0 wa,  0.0 hi,  0.0
si,  0.0 st
```

```
KiB Mem:    502060 total,    231168 used,    270892 free,        764
buffers

KiB Swap: 1081340 total,          0 used,  1081340 free.      94628
cached Mem


  PID USER      PR  NI    VIRT    RES    SHR S  %CPU %MEM      TIME+
COMMAND

 3001 vagrant   20   0    7396    724    508 R  68.8  0.1 993:06.80
lookbusy

 3002 vagrant   20   0    7396    724    508 S   1.0  0.1 198:58.16
lookbusy

   12 root      20   0       0      0      0 S   0.3  0.0   3:47.55
rcuos/0

   13 root      20   0       0      0      0 R   0.3  0.0   3:38.85
rcuos/1

 2718 vagrant   20   0  131524   2536   1344 R   0.3  0.5   0:02.28
sshd
```

From the output of `top`, we can identify the following:

- Overall, the system is around 60%–70% idle
- There are two processes running the `lookbusy` command/program, one of which appears to be using 70% of a single CPU
  - Given the CPU utilization on this individual process and the system CPU utilization, the server in question most likely has multiple CPUs
  - We can confirm the presence of multiple CPUs with the `lscpu` command
- Processes 3001 and 3002 are the top two processes utilizing CPU on this system
- The CPU wait state percentage is 0, which means that the issue is not likely to be disk I/O related

Digging deeper with ps

Since we identified processes `3001` and `3002` as suspicious from the `top` command's output, we can investigate these processes further with the `ps` command. To keep our investigation quick, we will use the `ps` command with the `-o` and `--forest` flags to identify the maximum possible information with one command.

```
$ ps --forest -eo user,pid,ppid,%cpu,cmd
root      1007      1  0.0 /usr/sbin/sshd -D
root      2976   1007  0.0  \_ sshd: vagrant [priv]
```

```
vagrant    2979   2976   0.0          \_ sshd: vagrant@pts/1
vagrant    2980   2979   0.0             \_ -bash
vagrant    3000   2980   0.0                \_ lookbusy --cpu-mode curve
--cpu-curve-peak 14h -c 20-80
vagrant    3001   3000 69.8                   \_ lookbusy --cpu-mode
curve --cpu-curve-peak 14h -c 20-80
vagrant    3002   3000 13.9                   \_ lookbusy --cpu-mode
curve --cpu-curve-peak 14h -c 20-80
```

From this output, we can determine the following:

- Processes 3001 and 3002 are child processes of process 3000
- Process 3000 was started by the vagrant user
- The lookbusy command seems to be a command that utilizes a significant amount of CPU
- The method used to launch lookbusy is not indicative of a system process but rather a user running an ad-hoc command

Given the above information, there is a possibility that the lookbusy process launched by the vagrant user is the source of the performance issue. This is a reasonable hypothesis of the root cause if this system normally operates with a lower CPU utilization. However, considering that we are not very familiar with this system, it is also possible that the lookbusy process using almost a full CPU is normal.

Considering that we are not familiar with the system's normal running conditions, we should continue to investigate the other possible sources for performance issues before reaching a conclusion.

Memory

After application and CPU utilization, memory utilization is a very common source of performance degradation. In the CPU section, we utilized top quite extensively, and while top can also be used to identify system and process memory utilization, in this section, we will be using other commands.

free – Looking at free and used memory

As discussed in *Chapter 2, Troubleshooting Commands and Sources of Useful Information* the free command simply prints the current memory availability and usage for the system.

When executed with no flags, the `free` command will output its values in kilobytes. To have the output in megabytes, we can simply execute the `free` command with the -m (megabytes) flag.

```
$ free -m
          total       used       free     shared    buffers     cached
Mem:        490         92        397          1          0         17
-/+ buffers/cache:       74        415
Swap:      1055         57        998
```

The `free` command shows quite a bit of information about this system and how much memory is being used. In order to gain a better understanding of this command, let's break down the output a bit.

Since there are multiple lines in the output, we will start with the first line after the output header:

```
Mem:        490         92        397          1          0         17
```

The first value in this line is the total amount of **physical memory** available to the system. In our case, this is 490 MB. The second value is the amount of **memory used** by the system. The third value is the amount of memory on the system that is **unused**; note that I used the term "unused" rather than "available." The fourth value is the amount of memory used for **shared memory**; unless your system uses shared memory often, this is typically a low number.

The fifth value is the amount of memory used for **buffers**. Linux will often try to speed up disk access by putting frequently used disk information into physical memory. The buffer memory is typically file system metadata. The **Cached memory**, which happens to be the sixth value, is the contents of frequently accessed files.

Linux memory buffers and caches

Linux will typically try to use "unused" memory for buffers and caches. This means that in order to gain efficiencies, the Linux kernel will store frequently accessed file data and filesystem metadata in the unused memory. This allows the system to utilize memory that otherwise would not have been used to enhance disk access which is often slower than system memory.

This is why the third value "unused" memory is typically a lower number than expected.

When a system is running low on unused memory, however, the Linux kernel will release the buffers and cached memory, as it needs. This means that even though technically, the memory used for buffers and caches is used, it is technically available to the system when required.

This brings us to the second line in the output of free.

```
-/+ buffers/cache:        74         415
```

The second line has two values, the first being a part of the **Used** column and the second being a part of the **Free** or "unused" column. These values are Used or Free memory values after taking into consideration the availability of buffers and cached memory.

To explain in simpler terms, the Used value on the second line is the result of the used memory value from the first line being subtracted by the buffers and cached values. For our example, it is 92 MB (used) minus 17 MB (cached).

The free value in the second line is the result of the Free value on the first line with the buffers and cached memory added. Using the values from our example, this would be 397 MB (free) plus 17 MB (cached).

Swapped memory

The third line in the output of the free command is for swap memory.

```
Swap:        1055        57         998
```

In this line, there are three columns: available, used, and free. The swap memory values are fairly self-explanatory. The available swap value is the amount of swap memory available to the system, the used value is the amount of swap currently allocated, and the free value is essentially the amount of swap available minus the amount of swap allocated.

There are many environments where a significant amount of swap being allocated is frowned upon as this is generally an indicator that the system has run out of memory and used the swap space to compensate.

What free tells us about our system

If we look again at the output of free, we can determine quite a few things about this server.

```
$ free -m
        total        used        free      shared     buffers      cached
Mem:      490         105         385           1           0          25
```

```
-/+ buffers/cache:         79        410
Swap:          1055         56        999
```

We can identify that only a small amount of memory (79 MB) is actually in use. This means that overall, the system should have plenty of memory available for processes.

There is an additional interesting fact, however, on the third line, it shows that **56** MB of memory has been written to swap. Although there is currently plenty of memory available on the system, 56 MB has been written to swap. This means that at some point in the past, this system might have been low on memory, low enough that the system had to swap memory pages from the physical memory to the swap memory.

Checking for oomkill

When a Linux system runs out of physical memory, it first attempts to reuse the memory allocated to buffers and caches. If there is no additional memory that can be reclaimed from these sources, then the kernel will take older memory pages from the physical memory and write them to the swap memory. Once both the physical and the swap memory have been allocated, the kernel will launch the **out of memory killer (oomkill)** process. The oomkill process is designed to find processes that utilize large amounts of memory and kill (stop) them.

In general, the oomkill process is unwanted in most environments. When invoked, the oomkill process can kill many different types of processes. Whether processes are part of the system or at the user level, oomkill has the ability to kill them.

With a performance issue that may have affected memory utilization, it is always a good idea to check whether the oomkill process was invoked recently or not. The easiest way to determine whether oomkill was run recently is to simply view the console of the system as the initiation of this process is logged directly to the system console. In the cloud and virtual environments, however, the console may not be available.

Another good way to determine whether oomkill was invoked recently is to search the /var/log/messages log file. We can do this by executing the grep command and searching for the string Out of memory.

```
# grep "Out of memory" /var/log/messages
```

For our example system, there have been no oomkill invocations recently. If our system had invoked the oomkill process, we could expect a message similar to the following:

```
# grep "Out of memory" /var/log/messages
Feb  7 19:38:45 localhost kernel: Out of memory: Kill process 3236
(python) score 838 or sacrifice child
```

In *Chapter 11*, *Recovering from Common Failures* we will once again investigate memory issues and take a deeper look into oomkill and how it works. For this chapter, we can conclude that the system has not completely exhausted its available memory.

ps - Checking individual processes memory utilization

So far, the memory usage on this system seems pretty small, but we know from the CPU validation steps that the processes running lookbusy are suspicious and possibly cause our performance issues. Since we suspect that the lookbusy processes are a problem, we should also look at how much memory these processes are using. To do this, we can once again use the ps command with the -o flag.

```
$ ps -eo user,pid,ppid,%mem,rss,vsize,comm | grep lookbusy
vagrant    3000  2980   0.0      4    7396  lookbusy
vagrant    3001  3000   0.0    296    7396  lookbusy
vagrant    3002  3000   0.0    220    7396  lookbusy
vagrant    5380  2980   0.0      8    7396  lookbusy
vagrant    5381  5380   0.0    268    7396  lookbusy
vagrant    5382  5380   0.0    268    7396  lookbusy
vagrant    5383  5380  40.7 204812  212200  lookbusy
vagrant    5531  2980   0.0     40    7396  lookbusy
vagrant    5532  5531   0.0    288    7396  lookbusy
vagrant    5533  5531   0.0    288    7396  lookbusy
vagrant    5534  5531  34.0 170880  222440  lookbusy
```

This time, however, we ran our ps command a little differently and thus, received different results. This time when executing the ps command, we used the -e (everything) flag to show all processes. The results were then piped to grep in order to narrow filter them to only the processes that match the pattern lookbusy.

This is a very common way of using the ps command; in fact, it is even more common than specifying process ID(s) on the command line. In addition to using grep, this ps command example introduces a few new formatting options.

- **%mem**: This is the percentage of system memory that the process is using
- **rss**: This is the amount of the resident site size of the process, which essentially means the amount of memory used by the process that is not swappable

- **vsize**: This is the amount of virtual memory size; it contains the amount of memory that the process is fully using irrespectively of whether this memory is a part of the physical memory or of the swap memory.

- **comm**: This option is similar to cmd with the exception that it does not display the command-line arguments.

The ps example shows interesting information, particularly the following lines:

```
vagrant    5383  5380 40.7 204812 212200 lookbusy
vagrant    5534  5531 34.0 170880 222440 lookbusy
```

It seems that several additional lookbusy processes have been started and these processes are utilizing 40% and 34% of the system memory (by using the %mem column). From the rss column, we can see that these two processes are using about 374 MB of the total 490 MB of the physical memory.

It also seems that these processes started utilizing a large amount of memory after we started our investigation. Originally, our free output stated that only 70 MB of memory was in use; however, these processes seem to be utilizing much more. We can confirm this by running free again.

```
$ free -m
            total      used      free    shared   buffers    cached
Mem:          490       453        37         0         0         3
-/+ buffers/cache:       449        41
Swap:        1055       310       745
```

Our system is in fact utilizing almost all of its memory now; in fact, we are also using 310 MB of swap space.

vmstat – Monitoring memory allocation and swapping

Since this system seems to have fluctuating memory utilization, there is one very useful command that shows memory allocation and de-allocation along with the number of pages swapped in and out at regular intervals. This command is called vmstat.

```
$ vmstat -n 10 5
procs ----------memory---------- ---swap-- -----io---- -system-- ------cpu-----
 r  b   swpd   free   buff  cache   si   so    bi    bo   in   cs us sy id wa st
```

5	0	204608	31800	0	7676	8	6	12	6	101	131 44
1 55	0	0									
1	0	192704	35816	0	2096	1887	130	4162	130	2080	2538 53
6 39	2	0									
1	0	191340	32324	0	3632	1590	57	3340	57	2097	2533 54
5 41	0	0									
4	0	191272	32260	0	5400	536	2	2150	2	1943	2366 53
4 43	0	0									
3	0	191288	34140	0	4152	392	0	679	0	1896	2366 53
3 44	0	0									

In the above example, the vmstat command was executed with the -n (one-header) flag followed by the delay in seconds (10) and the number of reports to generate (5). These options tell vmstat to only output one header line for this execution rather than a new header line for each report, run the report every 10 seconds, and limit the number of reports to 5. If the limitation on the number of reports is omitted than vmstat will simply run continuously until stopped with *CTRL+C*.

The output of vmstat can be a bit overwhelming at first, but if we break down the output, it will be easier to understand. The output of vmstat has six output categories, namely Procs, Memory, Swap, IO, System, and CPU. In this section, we will focus on two of these categories: Memory and Swap.

- **Memory**
    - ○ swpd: Amount of memory written to swap
    - ○ free: Amount of unused memory
    - ○ buff: Amount of memory used as buffers
    - ○ cache: Amount of memory used as cache
    - ○ inact: Amount of inactive memory
    - ○ active: amount of active memory

- **Swap**
    - ○ si: Amount of memory swapped in from disk
    - ○ so: Amount of memory swapped to disk

Now that we have a definition of these values, let's see what the output of vmstat tells us about this system's memory usage.

```
procs ----------memory---------- ---swap-- -----io---- -system-- ------
cpu-----
 r  b  swpd   free  buff  cache   si  so   bi   bo   in   cs us sy
id wa st
```

```
 5  0 204608   31800        0   7676    8    6    12      6  101  131 44  1
55  0  0
 1  0 192704   35816        0   2096 1887  130  4162    130 2080 2538 53  6
39  2  0
```

If we compare the first and the second line from vmstat's output, we can see a rather large disparity. In particular, we can see that in the first interval, the cache memory was 7676, whereas in the second interval, this value was 2096. We can also see that the si or swapped-in value in the first line is 8 but 1887 in the second line.

The reason for this disparity is that the first report of vmstat is always a summary of statistics since the last reboot, whereas the second report is a summary of statistics since the previous report. Each subsequent report will be a summary of the previous one, meaning that the third report will summarize statistics since the second report. This behavior of vmstat can often cause confusion for new systems administrators and users; therefore, it is often considered an advanced troubleshooting tool.

Because of the method of how vmstat generates the first report, the common practice is to discard it and start from the second report. We will follow this philosophy and specifically look at the second and the third reports.

```
procs -----------memory---------- ---swap-- -----io---- -system-- ------
cpu-----
 r  b   swpd    free   buff  cache   si   so    bi    bo   in   cs us sy
id wa st
 5  0 204608   31800      0   7676    8    6    12     6  101  131 44  1
55  0  0
 1  0 192704   35816      0   2096 1887  130  4162   130 2080 2538 53  6
39  2  0
 1  0 191340   32324      0   3632 1590   57  3340    57 2097 2533 54  5
41  0  0
```

In the second and the third reports, we can see some interesting data.

The first thing that sticks out is the fact that from the first report's generation time to the second report's generation time, there were 1,887 pages swapped in and 130 pages swapped out. The second report also shows that only 35 MB of the memory is free with 0 MB of the memory in buffer and 2 MB of the memory in cache. Based on how Linux utilizes memory, this means that there is effectively only 37 MB of available memory on this system.

This low amount of available memory explains why our system has swapped in a large number of pages. We can see from the third line that the trend is continuing, we continue to swap in quite a few pages and our available memory has reduced to roughly 35 MB.

From this example of vmstat, we can see that our system is now running out of physical memory. Because of this, our system is taking pages of memory from the physical RAM and writing it to our swap device.

Putting it all together

Now that we have explored the tools required for troubleshooting memory utilization, let's put all of them together to troubleshoot the issue of slow system performance.

Taking a look at the system's memory utilization with free

The first command to give us a snapshot of the systems memory utilization is the free command. This command will give us an idea of where to look further for any memory utilization issues.

```
$ free -m
              total       used       free     shared    buffers     cached
Mem:            490        293        196          0          0         18
-/+ buffers/cache:        275        215
Swap:          1055        183        872
```

From the output of free, we can see that there is currently 215 MB of memory available. We can see this via the free column on the second line. We can also see that overall, this system has 183 MB of memory that has been swapped to our swap devices.

Watch what is happening with vmstat

Since the system has swapped (or rather paged) at some point, we can use the vmstat command to see whether the system is swapping right now.

When executing vmstat this time around, we will leave off the number of reports value, which will cause vmstat to continuously report memory statistics, similar to the top command's output.

```
$ vmstat -n 10
procs ----------memory---------- ---swap-- -----io---- -system-- ------cpu-----
 r  b   swpd   free   buff  cache   si   so    bi    bo   in   cs us sy id wa st
 4  0 188008 200320      0 19896   35    8    61     9  156    4 44  1 55  0  0
 4  0 188008 200312      0 19896    0    0     0     0 1361 1314 36  2 62  0  0
```

2	0	188008	200312		0	19896	0	0	0		0	1430	1442	37
2	61	0	0											
0	0	188008	200312		0	19896	0	0	0		0	1431	1418	37
2	61	0	0											
0	0	188008	200280		0	19896	0	0	0		0	1414	1416	37
2	61	0	0											
2	0	188008	200280		0	19896	0	0	0		0	1456	1480	37
2	61	0	0											

This `vmstat` output is different from our earlier execution. From this output, we can see that while there is quite a bit of memory swapped, the system is not currently swapping. We can determine this by the 0 values in both the `si` (swap in) and `so` (swap out) columns.

In fact, the memory utilization seems steady during this `vmstat` run. The `free` memory value is fairly consistent between each `vmstat` report, as well as the cache and buffer memory statistics.

Finding the processes that utilize the most memory with ps

Our system has 490 MB of physical memory, and both `free` and `vmstat` show that roughly, 215 MB of memory available. This means that more than half of our system memory is currently utilized; with this level of use, it is a good idea to find out which processes are utilizing our system's memory. If nothing else, this data will be useful to show what the system's current state is.

To identify the process using the highest amount of memory, we can use the `ps` command along with sort and tail.

```
# ps -eo rss,vsize,user,pid,cmd | sort -nk 1 | tail -n 5
  1004 115452 root       5073 -bash
  1328 123356 root       5953 ps -eo rss,vsize,user,pid,cmd
  2504 525652 root        555 /usr/sbin/NetworkManager --no-daemon
  4124  50780 root          1 /usr/lib/systemd/systemd --switched-root
--system --deserialize 23
204672 212200 vagrant   5383 lookbusy -m 200MB -c 10
```

The above example uses pipes to redirect the output of `ps` to the sort command. The sort command is performing a numeric (`-n`) sort of the first column (`-k 1`). This will have the effect of sorting the output, putting the process with the highest `rss` size at the bottom. After the `sort` command, the output is also piped to the `tail` command, which when specified with the `-n` (number) flag followed by a number will limit the output to only include the specified number of results.

If the concept of chaining commands together with pipes is new,
I highly suggest practicing this as it is extremely useful for day-to-day
sysadmin tasks as well as during troubleshooting. We will discuss
this concept and provide examples several times throughout this book.

```
204672 212200 vagrant  5383 lookbusy -m 200MB -c 10
```

From the output of ps, we can see that process 5383 is using roughly 200 MB of
memory. We can also see that the process is another lookbusy process, which
was again spawned by the vagrant user.

From the output of free, vmstat, and ps, we can determine the following:

- The system currently has roughly 200 MB of available memory
- While the system is not currently swapping, it has in the past, and given
  what we saw earlier from vmstat, we know that it was swapping recently
- We found that process 5383 is utilizing roughly 200 MB of memory
- We also can see that process 5383 was started by the vagrant user and is
  running the lookbusy process
- Using the free command, we can see that this system has 490 MB of
  physical memory

Given the above information, it seems that the lookbusy process executed by the
vagrant user is not only a suspicious user of the CPU but also a suspicious user
of the memory.

Disk

Disk utilization is another common performance bottleneck. In general, performance
issues are rarely due to the amount of disk space. While I have seen performance issues
due to the large number of files or files of a large size, in general, disk performance is
limited by how much is being written to and read from a disk. So, while it is important
to know if a file system is full while troubleshooting performance issues, file system
usage alone does not always indicate whether or not there is an issue.

iostat – CPU and device input/output statistics

The `iostat` command is an essential command for troubleshooting disk performance issues and is similar to vmstat in terms of both the usage and the information that it provides. Like `vmstat`, `iostat` when executed is followed by two numbers, the first being the delay in report generation and the second being the number of reports to generate.

```
$ iostat -x 10 3
Linux 3.10.0-123.el7.x86_64 (blog.example.com)    02/08/2015
 _x86_64_   (2 CPU)
```

avg-cpu:	%user	%nice	%system	%iowait	%steal	%idle
	43.58	0.00	1.07	0.16	0.00	55.19

Device:	rrqm/s	wrqm/s	r/s	w/s	rkB/s	wkB/s
avgrq-sz	avgqu-sz	await	r_await	w_await	svctm	%util
sda	12.63	3.88	8.47	3.47	418.80	347.40
128.27	0.39	32.82	0.80	110.93	0.47	0.56
dm-0	0.00	0.00	16.37	3.96	65.47	15.82
8.00	0.48	23.68	0.48	119.66	0.09	0.19
dm-1	0.00	0.00	4.73	3.21	353.28	331.71
172.51	0.39	48.99	1.07	119.61	0.54	0.43

avg-cpu:	%user	%nice	%system	%iowait	%steal	%idle
	20.22	0.00	20.33	22.14	0.00	37.32

Device:	rrqm/s	wrqm/s	r/s	w/s	rkB/s	wkB/s
avgrq-sz	avgqu-sz	await	r_await	w_await	svctm	%util
sda	0.10	13.67	764.97	808.68	71929.34	78534.73
191.23	62.32	39.75	0.74	76.65	0.42	65.91
dm-0	0.00	0.00	0.00	0.10	0.00	0.40
8.00	0.01	70.00	0.00	70.00	70.00	0.70
dm-1	0.00	0.00	765.27	769.76	71954.89	78713.17
196.31	64.65	42.25	0.74	83.51	0.43	66.46

avg-cpu:	%user	%nice	%system	%iowait	%steal	%idle
	18.23	0.00	15.56	29.26	0.00	36.95

Device:		rrqm/s	wrqm/s	r/s	w/s	rkB/s	wkB/s
avgrq-sz	avgqu-sz	await	r_await	w_await	svctm	%util	
sda		0.10	7.10	697.50	440.10	74747.60	42641.75
206.38	74.13	66.98	0.64	172.13	0.58	66.50	
dm-0		0.00	0.00	0.00	0.00	0.00	0.00
0.00	0.00	0.00	0.00	0.00	0.00	0.00	
dm-1		0.00	0.00	697.40	405.00	74722.00	40888.65
209.74	75.80	70.63	0.66	191.11	0.61	67.24	

In the above example, the −x (extended statistics) flag was provided to print extended statistics. The extended statistics are extremely useful and provide additional information that can be essential for identifying performance bottlenecks.

CPU details

The iostat command will display CPU statistics along with I/O statistics. This is yet another command that can be utilized to troubleshoot CPU utilization. This is particularly useful when the CPU utilization indicates high I/O wait time.

avg-cpu:	%user	%nice	%system	%iowait	%steal	%idle
	20.22	0.00	20.33	22.14	0.00	37.32

The above is the same information displayed from the top command; it is not uncommon with Linux to find multiple commands that output similar information. Since these details have been covered in the CPU troubleshooting section, we will focus on the I/O statistics portion of the iostat command.

Reviewing I/O statistics

To start reviewing the I/O statistics, let's start with the first two reports. I am including the CPU utilization below to help indicate where each report starts as it is the first item in each statistics report.

avg-cpu:	%user	%nice	%system	%iowait	%steal	%idle
	43.58	0.00	1.07	0.16	0.00	55.19

Device:		rrqm/s	wrqm/s	r/s	w/s	rkB/s	wkB/s
avgrq-sz	avgqu-sz	await	r_await	w_await	svctm	%util	
sda		12.63	3.88	8.47	3.47	418.80	347.40
128.27	0.39	32.82	0.80	110.93	0.47	0.56	
dm-0		0.00	0.00	16.37	3.96	65.47	15.82
8.00	0.48	23.68	0.48	119.66	0.09	0.19	
dm-1		0.00	0.00	4.73	3.21	353.28	331.71
172.51	0.39	48.99	1.07	119.61	0.54	0.43	

```
avg-cpu:   %user    %nice %system %iowait   %steal    %idle
           20.22     0.00   20.33   22.14     0.00    37.32


Device:           rrqm/s  wrqm/s      r/s     w/s     rkB/s     wkB/s
avgrq-sz avgqu-sz   await r_await w_await   svctm   %util
sda                 0.10   13.67   764.97  808.68 71929.34 78534.73
191.23    62.32    39.75    0.74   76.65    0.42   65.91

dm-0                0.00    0.00     0.00    0.10     0.00      0.40
8.00      0.01    70.00    0.00   70.00   70.00    0.70

dm-1                0.00    0.00   765.27  769.76 71954.89 78713.17
196.31    64.65    42.25    0.74   83.51    0.43   66.46
```

By comparing the first two reports, we find that there is a large disparity between them. In the first report, the %util value for the sda device is 0.56, and it is 65.91 in the second report.

The reason for this difference is that as in the case of vmstat, the statistics from the first execution of iostat are based on the last time the server rebooted. The second report is based on the time since the first report. This means that the output of the second report is based on the 10 s between the first and the second report generation. This is the same behavior seen in vmstat and is a common behavior for other tools that gather performance statistics.

As with vmstat, we will discard the first report and only look at the second report.

```
avg-cpu:   %user    %nice %system %iowait   %steal    %idle
           20.22     0.00   20.33   22.14     0.00    37.32


Device:           rrqm/s  wrqm/s      r/s     w/s     rkB/s     wkB/s
avgrq-sz avgqu-sz   await r_await w_await   svctm   %util
sda                 0.10   13.67   764.97  808.68 71929.34 78534.73
191.23    62.32    39.75    0.74   76.65    0.42   65.91

dm-0                0.00    0.00     0.00    0.10     0.00      0.40
8.00      0.01    70.00    0.00   70.00   70.00    0.70

dm-1                0.00    0.00   765.27  769.76 71954.89 78713.17
196.31    64.65    42.25    0.74   83.51    0.43   66.46
```

From the above, we can identify several things about this system. The first and most important is the %iowait value in the CPU line.

```
avg-cpu:   %user    %nice %system %iowait   %steal    %idle
           20.22     0.00   20.33   22.14     0.00    37.32
```

Earlier when executing the top command, the percentage of time spent waiting for I/O was quite minimal; however, when running `iostat`, we can see that the CPUs are actually spending a lot of time waiting for I/O. While I/O wait does not necessarily mean waiting for the disk, the rest of this output seems to suggest that there is quite a bit of disk activity.

Device:		rrqm/s	wrqm/s	r/s	w/s	rkB/s	wkB/s
avgrq-sz	avgqu-sz	await	r_await	w_await	svctm	%util	
sda		0.10	13.67	764.97	808.68	71929.34	78534.73
191.23	62.32	39.75	0.74	76.65	0.42	65.91	
dm-0		0.00	0.00	0.00	0.10	0.00	0.40
8.00	0.01	70.00	0.00	70.00	70.00	0.70	
dm-1		0.00	0.00	765.27	769.76	71954.89	78713.17
196.31	64.65	42.25	0.74	83.51	0.43	66.46	

The extended statistics output has many columns, to make this output a little easier to understand, let's break down what these columns tell us.

- **rrqm/s**: Number of read requests per second that are merged and queued
- **wrqm/s**: Number of write requests per second that are merged and queued
- **r/s**: Number of read requests per second completed
- **w/s**: Number of write requests per second completed
- **rkB/s**: Number of reads in kilobytes per second
- **wkB/s**: Number of writes in kilobytes per second
- **avgr-sz**: Average size (in sectors) of requests made to the device
- **avgqu-sz**: Average queue length of requests made to the device
- **await**: Average time in milliseconds that requests wait for to be served
- **r_await**: Average time in milliseconds that read requests wait for to be serviced
- **w_await**: Average time in milliseconds that write requests wait for to be serviced
- **svctm**: This field is invalid and is slated to be removed; it should not be trusted or used
- **%util**: Percentage of CPU time spent while I/O requests are being serviced by this device. A device can only be at most 100% utilized

For our example, we will focus solely on the `r/s`, `w/s`, `await`, and `%util` values, since these values will tell us quite a bit about this system's disk utilization while keeping our example simple.

After reviewing the `iostat` output, we can see that both the `sda` and `dm-1` devices have the highest `%util` value, meaning that they are the closest to being at capacity.

Device:		rrqm/s	wrqm/s	r/s	w/s	rkB/s	wkB/s
avgrq-sz	avgqu-sz	await	r_await	w_await	svctm	%util	
sda		0.10	13.67	764.97	808.68	71929.34	78534.73
191.23	62.32	39.75	0.74	76.65	0.42	65.91	
dm-1		0.00	0.00	765.27	769.76	71954.89	78713.17
196.31	64.65	42.25	0.74	83.51	0.43	66.46	

From this report, we can see that the `sda` device had completed an average of 764 reads (`r/s`) and 808 writes (`w/s`) per second. We can also identify that these requests are taking an average of 39 ms (await) to complete. While these numbers are interesting, they do not necessarily mean that the system is in an abnormal state. Since we are unfamiliar with this system, we do not necessarily know whether the level of reads and writes are unexpected for this system. The information is however important to collect, as these statistics are important pieces of data for the data collection stage of the troubleshooting process.

Another interesting statistic we can see from `iostat` is that the `%util` values for both `sda` and `dm-1` devices are about 66%. This means that during the 10 s between the first report generation and the second, 66% of the CPU time spent was spent waiting for either the `sda` or the `dm-1` device.

Identifying devices

Having 66% utilization for a disk device is generally considered high, while this is quite useful information, it does not tell us who or what is utilizing the disk. To answer these questions, we will need to figure out what exactly `sda` and `dm-1` are being used for.

Since devices from `iostat` commands output are generally disk devices, the first step to identifying these devices is to run the `mount` command.

```
$ mount
proc on /proc type proc (rw,nosuid,nodev,noexec,relatime)
sysfs on /sys type sysfs (rw,nosuid,nodev,noexec,relatime,seclabel)
devtmpfs on /dev type devtmpfs (rw,nosuid,seclabel,size=244828k,nr_
inodes=61207,mode=755)
securityfs on /sys/kernel/security type securityfs (rw,nosuid,nodev,noexe
c,relatime)
tmpfs on /dev/shm type tmpfs (rw,nosuid,nodev,seclabel)
devpts on /dev/pts type devpts (rw,nosuid,noexec,relatime,seclabel,gid=5,
mode=620,ptmxmode=000)
```

```
tmpfs on /run type tmpfs (rw,nosuid,nodev,seclabel,mode=755)

tmpfs on /sys/fs/cgroup type tmpfs (rw,nosuid,nodev,noexec,seclabel,mo
de=755)

configfs on /sys/kernel/config type configfs (rw,relatime)

/dev/mapper/root on / type xfs (rw,relatime,seclabel,attr2,inode64,noquo
ta)

hugetlbfs on /dev/hugepages type hugetlbfs (rw,relatime,seclabel)

mqueue on /dev/mqueue type mqueue (rw,relatime,seclabel)

debugfs on /sys/kernel/debug type debugfs (rw,relatime)

/dev/sda1 on /boot type xfs (rw,relatime,seclabel,attr2,inode64,noquota)
```

The mount command, when run without any options, will display all of the current mounted file systems. The first column in the output of mount is the device that has been mounted. In the output above, we can see that the sda device is in fact a disk device and that it has a partition called sda1 that is mounted as /boot.

What we don't see however is the dm-1 device. Since this device is not listed in the output of the mount command another way, we may identify the dm-1 device by looking within the /dev folder.

All devices on a system are presented as a file within the /dev folder structure. The dm-1 device is no different.

```
$ ls -la /dev/dm-1

brw-rw----. 1 root disk 253, 1 Feb  1 18:47 /dev/dm-1
```

While we have been able to find the location of the dm-1 device, we have yet to identify its use. One thing that does stick out about this device, however, is the name dm-1. When devices start with dm, this is an indication that the device is a logical device created by the device mapper.

Device mapper is a Linux kernel framework that allows the system to create virtual disk devices that "map" back to physical devices. This functionality is used for many features including software raid, disk encryption, and logical volumes.

A common practice within the device mapper framework is to create symlinks for these features that link back to a single logical device. Since we can see with the ls command that dm-1 is a block device via the "b" value in the first column's output (brw-rw----.), we know that dm-1 is not a symlink. We can use this information along with the find command to identify any symlinks that link back to the dm-1 block device.

```
# find -L /dev -samefile /dev/dm-1

/dev/dm-1
```

```
/dev/rhel/root
```

```
/dev/disk/by-uuid/beb5220d-5cab-4c43-85d7-8045f870ba7d
```

```
/dev/disk/by-id/dm-uuid-LVM-qj3iMeektIlL3Z0g4WMPMJRbzacnpS9IVOCzB60GSHCEg
bRKYW9ZKXR5prUPEE1e
```

```
/dev/disk/by-id/dm-name-root
```

```
/dev/block/253:1
```

```
/dev/mapper/root
```

In the earlier chapters, we used the find command to identify configuration and log files. In the above example, we use the -L (follow links) flag, followed by the /dev path and the --samefile flag to tell find to search the /dev folder structure, searching any symlinked folders to identify any file that is the "same file" as /dev/dm-1.

The --samefile flag identifies files that have the same inode number. When the -L flag is included in the command, the output includes symlinks, and it seems that this example has returned several results. The symlink file that sticks out the most is /dev/mapper/root; the reason that this file sticks out is that it was also present in the output of the mount command.

```
/dev/mapper/root on / type xfs
(rw,relatime,seclabel,attr2,inode64,noquota)
```

It seems that /dev/mapper/root appears to be a logical volume. A logical volume within Linux is essentially storage virtualization. This functionality allows you to create pseudo devices (as part of the device mapper), which is mapped to one or more physical devices.

For example, it is possible to take four different hard disks and combine these disks into one logical volume. The logical volume can then be used as the disk for a single file system. It is even possible to add another hard disk at a later time by using logical volumes.

To confirm that the /dev/mapper/root device is in fact a logical volume, we can execute the lvdisplay command, which is used to display the logical volumes on the system.

```
# lvdisplay
  --- Logical volume ---
  LV Path                /dev/rhel/swap
  LV Name                swap
  VG Name                rhel
  LV UUID                y1ICUQ-13uA-Mxfc-JupS-c6PN-7jvw-W8wMV6
```

```
LV Write Access        read/write
LV Creation host, time localhost, 2014-07-21 23:35:55 +0000
LV Status              available
# open                 2
LV Size                1.03 GiB
Current LE             264
Segments               1
Allocation             inherit
Read ahead sectors     auto
- currently set to     256
Block device           253:0


--- Logical volume ---
LV Path                /dev/rhel/root
LV Name                root
VG Name                rhel
LV UUID                VOCzB6-0GSH-CEgb-RKYW-9ZKX-R5pr-UPEE1e
LV Write Access        read/write
LV Creation host, time localhost, 2014-07-21 23:35:55 +0000
LV Status              available
# open                 1
LV Size                38.48 GiB
Current LE             9850
Segments               1
Allocation             inherit
Read ahead sectors     auto
- currently set to     256
Block device           253:1
```

From the output of lvdisplay, we can see an interesting path called /dev/rhel/ root, which also exists with the output of our find command. Let's take a look at this device with the ls command.

```
# ls -la /dev/rhel/root
lrwxrwxrwx. 1 root root 7 Aug  3 16:27 /dev/rhel/root -> ../dm-1
```

Here, we can see that /dev/rhel/root is a symlink to /dev/dm-1; this confirms that /dev/rhel/root is the same as /dev/dm-1 and that these are in fact logical volume devices, which means that these are not really the physical device.

To display the physical device behind these logical volumes, we can use the pvdisplay command.

```
# pvdisplay
   --- Physical volume ---
   PV Name                /dev/sda2
   VG Name                rhel
   PV Size                39.51 GiB / not usable 3.00 MiB
   Allocatable            yes (but full)
   PE Size                4.00 MiB
   Total PE               10114
   Free PE                0
   Allocated PE           10114
   PV UUID                n5xoxm-kvyI-Z7rR-MMcH-1iJI-D68w-NODMaJ
```

We can see from the output of pvdisplay that the dm-1 device actually maps to sda2, which explains why the disk utilizations for dm-1 and sda were extremely close, as any activity on dm-1 is actually being performed on sda.

Who is writing to these devices?

Now that we have found where I/O is being utilized, we need to find out who is utilizing this I/O. The easiest method to find out which processes are writing to disk the most is to use the iotop command. This tool is a relatively new command and is now included by default with Red Hat Enterprise Linux 7. However, this command has not always been available in previous RHEL versions.

Before the adoption of iotop, the method for finding the top processes that are using I/O involved using the ps command and looking through the /proc filesystem.

ps – Using ps to identify processes utilizing I/O

While collecting data related to the CPU, we covered the state field in the output of the ps command. What we didn't cover is the various states that a process can be in. The following list contains the seven possible states that the ps command will show:

- **Uninterruptible sleep** (D): Processes generally in a sleep state when waiting for I/O

- **Running or Runnable** (R): Processes on the run queue
- **Interruptible sleep** (S): Processes waiting for an event to complete but not blocking CPU or I/O
- **Stopped** (T): Processes that are stopped by a job control system such as the jobs command
- **Paging** (P): Processes that are current paging; however, this is less relevant on newer kernels
- **Dead** (X): Processes that are dead, this should never be seen, as dead processes should not show up when running ps
- **Defunct** (Z): Zombie processes that are terminated but left in an undead state

When investigating I/O utilization, it is important to identify with a state listed as D **Uninterruptible Sleep**. As these processes are generally waiting for I/O, they are the most likely processes to be over utilizing disk I/O.

To do this, we will use the ps command with the -e (everything), -l (long format), and -f (full format) flags. We will also use pipes again to redirect the output to the grep command and filter the output to only show processes with a D state.

```
# ps -elf | grep " D "
1 D root      13185      2  2  80   0 -      0 get_re 00:21 ?
00:01:32 [kworker/u4:1]
4 D root      15639 15638 30  80   0 -   4233 balanc 01:26 pts/2
00:00:02 bonnie++ -n 0 -u 0 -r 239 -s 478 -f -b -d /tmp
```

With the above output, we see that there are two processes currently in an uninterruptible sleep state. One process is kworker, which is a kernel system process, and the other is bonnie++, a process launched by the root user. As the kworker process is a generic kernel process, we will focus on the bonnie++ process first.

To better understand this process, we will run the ps command again but this time with the --forest option.

```
# ps -elf -forest
4 S root       1007     1  0  80   0 - 20739 poll_s Feb07 ?
00:00:00 /usr/sbin/sshd -D
4 S root      11239  1007  0  80   0 - 32881 poll_s Feb08 ?
00:00:00  \_ sshd: vagrant [priv]
5 S vagrant   11242 11239  0  80   0 - 32881 poll_s Feb08 ?
00:00:02      \_ sshd: vagrant@pts/2
0 S vagrant   11243 11242  0  80   0 - 28838 wait   Feb08 pts/2
00:00:01          \_ -bash
```

```
4 S root      16052 11243  0  80   0 - 47343 poll_s 01:39 pts/2
00:00:00                  \_ sudo bonnie++ -n 0 -u 0 -r 239 -s 478 -f -b -d /
tmp
4 S root      16053 16052 32  80   0 - 96398 hrtime 01:39 pts/2
00:00:03                  \_ bonnie++ -n 0 -u 0 -r 239 -s 478 -f -b
-d /tmp
```

By reviewing the above output, we can see that the bonnie++ process is actually a child process of process 16052, which is another child process of 11243, which is the bash shell for the vagrant user.

The preceding ps command has shown us that the bonnie++ process with the process id of 16053 is waiting on I/O tasks. However, this does not tell us how much I/O this process is using; to determine this, we can read a special file in the /proc file system called io.

```
# cat /proc/16053/io
rchar: 1002448848
wchar: 1002438751
syscr: 122383
syscw: 122375
read_bytes: 1002704896
write_bytes: 1002438656
cancelled_write_bytes: 0
```

Every running process has a subfolder in /proc with the same name as the process id; for our example, this is /proc/16053. This folder is maintained by the kernel for each running process, and within these folders exist many files that contain information about running processes.

These files are so useful that they are actually the source of the ps command's information. One of these useful files is named io; the io file contains statistics about the number of reads and writes that the process has performed.

From the output of the cat command, we can see that this process has read and written approximately 1 GB of data. While this seems like a lot, it could be over a long period of time. To get a picture of how much this process is writing to disk, we can read this file again to capture the differences.

```
# cat /proc/16053/io
cat: /proc/16053/io: No such file or directory
```

It seems, however, that when we executed the cat command a second time, we received an error that the io file is no longer present. If we run the ps command again and use grep to search the output for the bonnie++ process, we can see that a bonnie++ process is running; however, it is a new process with a new process ID.

```
# ps -elf | grep bonnie
4 S root     17891 11243  0  80   0 - 47343 poll_s 02:34 pts/2
00:00:00 sudo bonnie++ -n 0 -u 0 -r 239 -s 478 -f -b -d /tmp
4 D root     17892 17891 33  80   0 -  4233 sleep_ 02:34 pts/2
00:00:02 bonnie++ -n 0 -u 0 -r 239 -s 478 -f -b -d /tmp
```

As it seems that the child bonnie++ processes are short-lived processes, following the I/O statistics by reading the io file may be quite difficult.

iotop – A top top-like command for disk i/o

Since these processes are starting and stopping so frequently, we can use the iotop command to identify which processes are utilizing I/O the most.

```
# iotop
Total DISK READ :     102.60 M/s | Total DISK WRITE :      26.96 M/s
Actual DISK READ:     102.60 M/s | Actual DISK WRITE:      42.04 M/s
  TID  PRIO  USER     DISK READ  DISK WRITE  SWAPIN      IO>
COMMAND
16395 be/4 root        0.00 B/s    0.00 B/s  0.00 % 45.59 %
[kworker/u4:0]
18250 be/4 root      101.95 M/s   26.96 M/s  0.00 % 42.59 % bonnie++ -n 0
-u 0 -r 239 -s 478 -f -b -d /tmp
```

In the preceding output from iotop, we can see some interesting I/O statistics. With iotop, we can see not only system-wide statistics such as **Total Disk Reads** per second and **Total Disk Writes** per second but also quite a few statistics for single processes.

From the per-process perspective, we can see that the bonnie++ process is reading from disk at a rate of 101.96 MBps and is writing to disk at a rate of 26.96 MBps.

```
16395 be/4 root        0.00 B/s    0.00 B/s  0.00 % 45.59 %
[kworker/u4:0]
18250 be/4 root      101.95 M/s   26.96 M/s  0.00 % 42.59 % bonnie++
-n 0 -u 0 -r 239 -s 478 -f -b -d /tmp
```

The `iotop` command is very similar to the top command in that it will refresh the reported results every few seconds. This has the effect of showing the I/O statistics "live."

 Commands such as `top` and `iotop` are very difficult to show in a book format. I highly suggest executing these commands on a system that has them available to get a feel of how they work.

Putting it all together

Now that we have covered some of the tools for troubleshooting disk performance and utilization, let's put it all together while troubleshooting our reported slowness.

Using iostat to determine whether there is a I/O bandwidth problem

The first command that we will run is `iostat`, as this will first validate for us whether there is in fact an issue or not.

```
# iostat -x 10 3
Linux 3.10.0-123.el7.x86_64 (blog.example.com)    02/09/2015
_x86_64_    (2 CPU)


avg-cpu:  %user   %nice %system %iowait   %steal   %idle
          38.58    0.00    3.22    5.46     0.00    52.75


Device:           rrqm/s   wrqm/s     r/s      w/s     rkB/s     wkB/s
avgrq-sz avgqu-sz    await r_await w_await   svctm   %util
sda               10.86     4.25  122.46   118.15  11968.97  12065.60
199.78    13.27    55.18    0.67  111.67    0.51   12.21
dm-0               0.00     0.00   14.03     3.44     56.14     13.74
8.00     0.42    24.24    0.51  121.15    0.46    0.80
dm-1               0.00     0.00  119.32   112.35  11912.79  12051.98
206.89    13.52    58.33    0.68  119.55    0.52   12.16


avg-cpu:  %user   %nice %system %iowait   %steal   %idle
           7.96    0.00   14.60   29.31     0.00    48.12


Device:           rrqm/s   wrqm/s     r/s      w/s     rkB/s     wkB/s
avgrq-sz avgqu-sz    await r_await w_await   svctm   %util
```

sda		0.70	0.80	804.49	776.85 79041.12 76999.20
197.35	64.26	41.41	0.54	83.73	0.42 66.38
dm-0		0.00	0.00	0.90	0.80 3.59 3.19
8.00	0.08	50.00	0.00	106.25	19.00 3.22
dm-1		0.00	0.00	804.29	726.35 79037.52 76893.81
203.75	64.68	43.03	0.53	90.08	0.44 66.75

avg-cpu:	%user	%nice	%system	%iowait	%steal	%idle
	5.22	0.00	11.21	36.21	0.00	47.36

Device:		rrqm/s	wrqm/s	r/s	w/s	rkB/s	wkB/s
avgrq-sz	avgqu-sz	await	r_await	w_await	svctm	%util	
sda		1.10	0.30	749.40	429.70 84589.20 43619.80		
217.47	76.31	66.49	0.43	181.69	0.58 68.32		
dm-0		0.00	0.00	1.30	0.10 5.20 0.40		
8.00	0.00	2.21	1.00	18.00	1.43 0.20		
dm-1		0.00	0.00	749.00	391.20 84558.40 41891.80		
221.80	76.85	69.23	0.43	200.95	0.60 68.97		

From the output of iostat, we can determine the following:

- The CPU of this system is currently spending quite a bit of time waiting for I/O, 30%–40%
- It appears that the dm-1 and sda devices are the most-utilized devices
- From iostat, it appears that these devices are at 68% utilization, a number that seems is quite high

On the basis of these data points, we can identify that there is a potential I/O utilization issue, unless 68% utilization is expected.

Using iotop to determine which processes are consuming disk bandwidth

Now that we have determined that a sizeable amount of CPU time is being spent waiting for I/O, we should now focus on what processes are utilizing disks the most. To do this, we will use the iotop command.

```
# iotop
Total DISK READ :    100.64 M/s | Total DISK WRITE :     23.91 M/s
Actual DISK READ:    100.67 M/s | Actual DISK WRITE:     38.04 M/s
   TID  PRIO  USER    DISK READ  DISK WRITE  SWAPIN     IO>
COMMAND
```

```
19358 be/4 root          0.00 B/s      0.00 B/s   0.00 % 40.38 %
[kworker/u4:1]

20262 be/4 root        100.35 M/s    23.91 M/s   0.00 % 33.65 % bonnie++
-n 0 -u 0 -r 239 -s 478 -f -b -d /tmp

  363 be/4 root          0.00 B/s      0.00 B/s   0.00 %  2.51 %
[xfsaild/dm-1]

   32 be/4 root          0.00 B/s      0.00 B/s   0.00 %  1.74 % [kswapd0]
```

From the `iotop` command, we can see that process `20262`, which is running the `bonnie++` command, has a high utilization along with large disk read and write values.

From `iotop`, we can determine the following:

- The system's total disk reads per second is 100.64 MBps
- The system's total disk writes per second is 23.91 MBps
- Process `20262` running the `bonnie++` command is reading 100.35 MBps and writing 23.91 MBps
- Comparing the totals, we find that process `20262` is the majority contributor of disk reads and writes

Given the above, it seems that we will need to identify more information about process `20262`.

Using ps to understand more about processes

Now that we have identified a process that is using a significant amount of I/O, we can investigate the details of this process with the `ps` command. We will once again use the `ps` command with the `--forest` flag to show the parent and child process relationship.

```
# ps -elf --forest
1007  0  80   0 - 32881 poll_s Feb08 ?          00:00:00  \_ sshd:
vagrant [priv]

5 S vagrant  11242 11239  0  80   0 - 32881 poll_s Feb08 ?
00:00:05       \_ sshd: vagrant@pts/2

0 S vagrant  11243 11242  0  80   0 - 28838 wait   Feb08 pts/2
00:00:02         \_ -bash

4 S root     20753 11243  0  80   0 - 47343 poll_s 03:52 pts/2
00:00:00           \_ sudo bonnie++ -n 0 -u 0 -r 239 -s 478 -f -b
-d /tmp

4 D root     20754 20753 52  80   0 -  4233 sleep_ 03:52 pts/2
00:00:01             \_ bonnie++ -n 0 -u 0 -r 239 -s 478 -f -b
-d /tmp
```

Using the `ps` command, we can determine the following:

- The `bonnie++` process `20262` identified with `iotop` is absent; however, other `bonnie++` processes are present

- The `vagrant` user has started the parent `bonnie++` processes by using the `sudo` command

- The `vagrant` user is the same user as the user in the earlier observations discussed in the CPU and memory sections

Given the above details, it seems that the vagrant user is a likely suspect for our performance issues.

Network

The final common resource for performance issues is the network. There are many tools to troubleshoot networking issues; however, very few of these commands are geared solely towards network performance. Most of these tools are designed for in-depth network troubleshooting.

Since *Chapter 5, Network Troubleshooting* is dedicated to troubleshooting network issues, this section will focus specifically on performance.

ifstat – Review interface statistics

When it comes to a network, there are about four metrics that can be used to measure throughput.

- **Received Packets**: Number of packets received by the interface
- **Sent Packets**: Number of packets sent out by the interface
- **Received Data**: Amount of data received by the interface
- **Sent Data**: Amount of data sent by the interface

There are many commands that can provide these metrics, everything from `ifconfig` or `ip` to `netstat`. A very useful utility that specifically outputs these metrics is the `ifstat` command.

```
# ifstat
#21506.1804289383 sampling_interval=5 time_const=60
Interface       RX Pkts/Rate    TX Pkts/Rate    RX Data/Rate    TX Data/Rate
                RX Errs/Drop    TX Errs/Drop    RX Over/Rate    TX Coll/Rate
lo                    47 0            47 0          4560 0          4560 0
```

	RX Pkts/Rate	TX Pkts/Rate	RX Data/Rate	TX Data/Rate
	0 0	0 0	0 0	0 0
enp0s3	70579 1	50636 0	17797K 65	5520K 96
	0 0	0 0	0 0	0 0
enp0s8	23034 0	43 0	2951K 18	7035 0
	0 0	0 0	0 0	0 0

Much like `vmstat` or `iostat`, the first report generated by `ifstat` is based on statistics since the server last rebooted. What this means is that the above report indicates that the `enp0s3` interface has received 70,579 packets since the last reboot.

When executing `ifstat` a second time, the results will show a very large disparity from the first report. The reason for this is that the second report is based on the time since the first report.

```
# ifstat
#21506.1804289383 sampling_interval=5 time_const=60
```

Interface	RX Pkts/Rate	TX Pkts/Rate	RX Data/Rate	TX Data/Rate
	RX Errs/Drop	TX Errs/Drop	RX Over/Rate	TX Coll/Rate
lo	0 0	0 0	0 0	0 0
	0 0	0 0	0 0	0 0
enp0s3	23 0	18 0	1530 59	1780 80
	0 0	0 0	0 0	0 0
enp0s8	1 0	0 0	86 10	0 0
	0 0	0 0	0 0	0 0

In the example above, we can see that our system received 23 packets (RX Pkts) and transmitted 18 packets (TX Pkts) over the `enp0s3` interface.

From the `ifstat` command, we can determine the following about our system:

- The network utilization at the moment is fairly small and not likely to cause an impact on this system as a whole
- The processes from the `vagrant` user shown earlier are not likely utilizing a significant amount of network resources

Based on the statistics seen with `ifstat`, there is minimal network traffic on this system, and is not likely causing the perceived slowness.

Quick review of what we have identified

Before going too far ahead, let's review what we have learned from the performance statistics that we have gathered thus far:

- The vagrant user has been launching processes that run the bonnie++ and lookbusy applications

- The lookbusy application seems to either use up to 20%–30% of the overall system CPU.

- This server in question has two CPUs and lookbusy seems to utilize about 60% of one CPU consistently.

- The lookbusy application also seems to use around 200 MB of memory consistently; however, during troubleshooting, we did see these processes using almost all of the system's memory causing the system to swap.

- While the vagrant user was launching the bonnie++ process the system was experiencing a high I/O wait time

- When running, the bonnie++ processes were utilizing approximately 60%–70% of the disk throughput.

- The activity being performed by the vagrant user seems to have little to no effect on network utilization.

Comparing historical metrics

Looking at all of the facts that we learned about this system so far, it seems that our next best course of action would be to recommend contacting the vagrant user to identify whether the lookbusy and bonnie++ applications should be running with such high resource utilization.

While the previous observations show a high resource utilization, this level of utilization may be expected for this environment. Before we start contacting users, we should first review the historical performance metrics of this server. In most environments, there is some sort of server performance monitoring software such as Munin, Cacti, or one of the many cloud SaaS providers in place that collects and stores system statistics.

If your environment utilizes one of these services, you can use the collected performance data to compare previous performance statistics with the information that we just gathered. If for instance over the past 30 days, the CPU performance was never higher than 10%, it stands to reason that the lookbusy processes may not have been running at that time.

Even if your environment does not utilize one of these tools, you still may be able to perform the historical comparisons. To do so, we will use a tool that is installed by default on most Red Hat Enterprise Linux systems; this tool is called sar.

sar – System activity report

In *Chapter 2, Troubleshooting Commands and Sources of Useful Information* we briefly discussed the use of the sar command to review historical performance statistics.

When the sysstat package that deploys the sar utility is installed, it will deploy the /etc/cron.d/sysstat file. Within this file are two cron jobs that run sysstat commands with the sole purpose of collecting system performance statistics and generating reports of the collected information.

```
$ cat /etc/cron.d/sysstat
# Run system activity accounting tool every 10 minutes
*/2 * * * * root /usr/lib64/sa/sa1 1 1
# 0 * * * * root /usr/lib64/sa/sa1 600 6 &
# Generate a daily summary of process accounting at 23:53
53 23 * * * root /usr/lib64/sa/sa2 -A
```

When these commands are executed, the information collected is then stored in the /var/log/sa/ folder.

```
# ls -la /var/log/sa/
total 1280
drwxr-xr-x. 2 root root   4096 Feb  9 00:00 .
drwxr-xr-x. 9 root root   4096 Feb  9 03:17 ..
-rw-r--r--. 1 root root  68508 Feb  1 23:20 sa01
-rw-r--r--. 1 root root  40180 Feb  2 16:00 sa02
-rw-r--r--. 1 root root  28868 Feb  3 05:30 sa03
-rw-r--r--. 1 root root  91084 Feb  4 20:00 sa04
-rw-r--r--. 1 root root  57148 Feb  5 23:50 sa05
-rw-r--r--. 1 root root  34524 Feb  6 23:50 sa06
-rw-r--r--. 1 root root 105224 Feb  7 23:50 sa07
-rw-r--r--. 1 root root 235312 Feb  8 23:50 sa08
-rw-r--r--. 1 root root 105224 Feb  9 06:00 sa09
-rw-r--r--. 1 root root  56616 Jan 23 23:00 sa23
-rw-r--r--. 1 root root  56616 Jan 24 20:10 sa24
-rw-r--r--. 1 root root  24648 Jan 30 23:30 sa30
```

```
-rw-r--r--. 1 root root   11948 Jan 31 23:20 sa31
-rw-r--r--. 1 root root   44476 Feb  5 23:53 sar05
-rw-r--r--. 1 root root   27244 Feb  6 23:53 sar06
-rw-r--r--. 1 root root   81094 Feb  7 23:53 sar07
-rw-r--r--. 1 root root  180299 Feb  8 23:53 sar08
```

The data files that the `sysstat` package generates use a filename that follows the "sa<two digit day>" format. For example, in the above output, we can see that the "sa24" file was generated on January 24th. We can also see that this system has files from January 23rd to February 9th.

The `sar` command is a command that allows us to read these captured performance metrics. This section will show you how to use the `sar` command to review the same statistics that we reviewed earlier with commands such as `iostat`, `top`, and `vmstat`. This time, however, the `sar` command will provide both recent and historical information.

CPU

To look at CPU statistics with the `sar` command, we can simply use the `-u` (CPU Utilization) flag.

```
# sar -u
Linux 3.10.0-123.el7.x86_64 (blog.example.com)    02/09/2015   _x86_64_
(2 CPU)
```

12:00:01 AM %idle	CPU	%user	%nice	%system	%iowait	%steal
12:10:02 AM 41.61	all	7.42	0.00	13.46	37.51	0.00
12:20:01 AM 40.25	all	7.59	0.00	13.61	38.55	0.00
12:30:01 AM 40.60	all	7.44	0.00	13.46	38.50	0.00
12:40:02 AM 44.24	all	8.62	0.00	15.71	31.42	0.00
12:50:02 AM 45.44	all	8.77	0.00	16.13	29.66	0.00
01:00:01 AM 45.49	all	8.88	0.00	16.20	29.43	0.00
01:10:01 AM 41.61	all	7.46	0.00	13.64	37.29	0.00

01:20:02 AM 41.34	all	7.35	0.00	13.52	37.79	0.00
01:30:01 AM 40.64	all	7.40	0.00	13.36	38.60	0.00
01:40:01 AM 41.19	all	7.42	0.00	13.53	37.86	0.00
01:50:01 AM 40.60	all	7.44	0.00	13.58	38.38	0.00
04:20:02 AM 41.22	all	7.51	0.00	13.72	37.56	0.00
04:30:01 AM 40.74	all	7.34	0.00	13.36	38.56	0.00
04:40:02 AM 41.25	all	7.40	0.00	13.41	37.94	0.00
04:50:01 AM 41.01	all	7.45	0.00	13.81	37.73	0.00
05:00:02 AM 41.04	all	7.49	0.00	13.75	37.72	0.00
05:10:01 AM 39.99	all	7.43	0.00	13.30	39.28	0.00
05:20:02 AM 41.07	all	7.24	0.00	13.17	38.52	0.00
05:30:02 AM 44.30	all	13.47	0.00	11.10	31.12	0.00
05:40:01 AM 31.03	all	67.05	0.00	1.92	0.00	0.00
05:50:01 AM 29.82	all	68.32	0.00	1.85	0.00	0.00
06:00:01 AM 28.88	all	69.36	0.00	1.76	0.01	0.00
06:10:01 AM 27.76	all	70.53	0.00	1.71	0.01	0.00
Average: 40.07	all	14.43	0.00	12.36	33.14	0.00

If we look at the header information from above, we can see that the sar command with the -u flag matches the iostat and top CPU details.

12:00:01 AM %idle	CPU	%user	%nice	%system	%iowait	%steal

From the `sar -u` output, we can identify an interesting trend: from 00:00 to 05:30, there was a constant CPU I/O wait time of 30%–40%. However, as of 05:40, the I/O wait decreased, but the user-level CPU utilization increased to 65%–70% utilization.

While these two measurements don't specifically point to any one process, they do show that the I/O wait time has decreased recently while the user CPU time has increased.

To get a better picture of historical statistics, we will need to look at the previous day's CPU utilization. Luckily, we can do just that with the −f (filename) flag. The −f flag will allow us to specify a historical file for the `sar` command. This will allow us to selectively view statistics from the previous day.

```
# sar -f /var/log/sa/sa07 -u
Linux 3.10.0-123.el7.x86_64 (blog.example.com)    02/07/2015
 _x86_64_   (2 CPU)
```

12:00:01 AM	CPU	%user	%nice	%system	%iowait	%steal	%idle
12:10:01 AM	all	24.63	0.00	0.71	0.00	0.00	74.66
12:20:01 AM	all	25.31	0.00	0.70	0.00	0.00	73.99
01:00:01 AM	all	27.59	0.00	0.68	0.00	0.00	71.73
01:10:01 AM	all	29.64	0.00	0.71	0.00	0.00	69.65
05:10:01 AM	all	44.09	0.00	0.63	0.00	0.00	55.28
05:20:01 AM	all	60.94	0.00	0.58	0.00	0.00	38.48
05:30:01 AM	all	62.32	0.00	0.56	0.00	0.00	37.12
05:40:01 AM	all	63.74	0.00	0.56	0.00	0.00	35.70
05:50:01 AM	all	65.08	0.00	0.56	0.00	0.00	34.35
0.00	76.07						
Average:	all	37.98	0.00	0.65	0.00	0.00	61.38

In the report from February 7th, we can see a drastic difference in CPU utilization than what was identified during our previous troubleshooting. One item that stands out is that in the report from the 7th, no CPU time was spent in the I/O wait state.

However, we do see that the user CPU time fluctuated from 20% to 65% depending on the time of day. This may indicate that a higher user CPU time utilization is expected.

Memory

To display memory statistics, we can execute the `sar` command with the `-r` (memory) flag.

```
# sar -r
```

```
Linux 3.10.0-123.el7.x86_64 (blog.example.com)    02/09/2015
_x86_64_   (2 CPU)
```

12:00:01 AM	kbmemfree	kbmemused	%memused	kbbuffers	kbcached
kbcommit	%commit	kbactive	kbinact	kbdirty	
12:10:02 AM	38228	463832	92.39	0	387152
446108	28.17	196156	201128	0	
12:20:01 AM	38724	463336	92.29	0	378440
405128	25.59	194336	193216	73360	
12:30:01 AM	38212	463848	92.39	0	377848
405128	25.59	9108	379348	58996	
12:40:02 AM	37748	464312	92.48	0	387500
446108	28.17	196252	201684	0	
12:50:02 AM	33028	469032	93.42	0	392240
446108	28.17	196872	205884	0	
01:00:01 AM	34716	467344	93.09	0	380616
405128	25.59	195900	195676	69332	
01:10:01 AM	31452	470608	93.74	0	384092
396660	25.05	199100	196928	74372	
05:20:02 AM	38756	463304	92.28	0	387120
399996	25.26	197184	198456	4	
05:30:02 AM	187652	314408	62.62	0	19988
617000	38.97	222900	22524	0	
05:40:01 AM	186896	315164	62.77	0	20116
617064	38.97	223512	22300	0	
05:50:01 AM	186824	315236	62.79	0	20148
617064	38.97	223788	22220	0	
06:00:01 AM	182956	319104	63.56	0	24652
615888	38.90	226744	23288	0	

```
06:10:01 AM    176992    325068    64.75         0    29232
615880    38.90    229356    26500         0

06:20:01 AM    176756    325304    64.79         0    29480
615884    38.90    229448    26588         0

06:30:01 AM    176636    325424    64.82         0    29616
615888    38.90    229516    26820         0

Average:        77860    424200    84.49         0    303730
450102    28.43    170545    182617    29888
```

Again, if we look at the header from the memory report of `sar`, we can see some familiar values.

```
12:00:01 AM kbmemfree kbmemused  %memused kbbuffers   kbcached
kbcommit    %commit   kbactive    kbinact    kbdirty
```

From this report, we can see from the **kbmemused** column that as of 05:40, the system suddenly freed up 150 MB of physical memory. It appears from the `kbcached` column that this 150 MB of memory was allocated to the disk cache. This is based on the fact that at 05:40, the cached memory went from 196 MB to 22 MB.

What is interesting is that this aligns with the CPU utilization change that also occurred at 05:40. If we wished to review historical memory utilization, we could also use the -f (filename) flag with the -r (memory) flag. However, since we can see a rather obvious trend at 05:40, we will focus on this time for now.

Disk

To show disk statistics for today, we can use the -d (block device) flag.

```
# sar -d
Linux 3.10.0-123.el7.x86_64 (blog.example.com)    02/09/2015
  _x86_64_   (2 CPU)


12:00:01 AM        DEV       tps  rd_sec/s  wr_sec/s  avgrq-sz  avgqu-sz
await     svctm    %util

12:10:02 AM    dev8-0   1442.64 150584.15 146120.49    205.67
82.17    56.98     0.51     74.17

12:10:02 AM  dev253-0     1.63     11.11      1.96      8.00
0.06    34.87    19.72      3.22

12:10:02 AM  dev253-1   1402.67 150572.19 146051.96    211.47
82.73    58.98     0.53     74.68

04:20:02 AM    dev8-0   1479.72 152799.09 150240.77    204.80
81.27    54.89     0.50     73.86
```

```
04:20:02 AM  dev253-0      1.74     10.98      2.96      8.00
0.06     31.81     14.60      2.54

04:20:02 AM  dev253-1   1438.57 152788.11 150298.01    210.69
81.84     56.83      0.52     74.38

05:30:02 AM  dev253-0      1.00      7.83      0.17      8.00
0.00      3.81      2.76      0.28

05:30:02 AM  dev253-1   1170.61 123647.27 122655.72    210.41
69.12     59.04      0.53     62.20

05:40:01 AM    dev8-0      0.08      1.00      0.34     16.10
0.00      1.88      1.00      0.01

05:40:01 AM  dev253-0      0.11      0.89      0.00      8.00
0.00      1.57      0.25      0.00

05:40:01 AM  dev253-1      0.05      0.11      0.34      8.97
0.00      2.77      1.17      0.01

05:50:01 AM    dev8-0      0.07      0.49      0.28     11.10
0.00      1.71      1.02      0.01

05:50:01 AM  dev253-0      0.06      0.49      0.00      8.00
0.00      2.54      0.46      0.00

05:50:01 AM  dev253-1      0.05      0.00      0.28      6.07
0.00      1.96      0.96      0.00


Average:          DEV       tps   rd_sec/s  wr_sec/s  avgrq-sz
   avgqu-sz      await     svctm    %util

Average:       dev8-0   1215.88 125807.06 123583.62    205.11
66.86     55.01      0.50     60.82

Average:     dev253-0      2.13     12.48      4.53      8.00
0.10     44.92     17.18      3.65

Average:     dev253-1   1181.94 125794.56 123577.42    210.99
67.31     56.94      0.52     61.17
```

By default, the sar command will print the device name as "dev<major>-<minor>,"
which can be a bit confusing. If the -p (persistent names) flag is added, the device
names will use persistent names, which match the devices from the mount command.

```
# sar -d -p
Linux 3.10.0-123.el7.x86_64 (blog.example.com)    08/16/2015
 _x86_64_   (4 CPU)


01:46:42 AM          DEV       tps   rd_sec/s  wr_sec/s  avgrq-sz
avgqu-sz      await     svctm    %util
01:48:01 AM          sda      0.37      0.00      3.50      9.55
     0.00      1.86      0.48      0.02
```

```
01:48:01 AM rhel-swap      0.00       0.00       0.00       0.00
     0.00       0.00     0.00       0.00
01:48:01 AM rhel-root      0.37       0.00       3.50       9.55
     0.00       2.07     0.48       0.02
```

Even with the names in an unrecognizable format, we can see that dev253-1 seems to have had quite a bit of activity up to 05:40, where the disk tps (transactions per seconds) decreases from 1170 to 0.11. This large drop in disk I/O utilization seems to indicate that a rather large change occurred at 05:40 today.

Network

To show network statistics, we will need to execute the sar command with the -n DEV flag.

```
# sar -n DEV
Linux 3.10.0-123.el7.x86_64 (blog.example.com)    02/09/2015
_x86_64_    (2 CPU)


12:00:01 AM      IFACE   rxpck/s    txpck/s    rxkB/s    txkB/s
rxcmp/s    txcmp/s   rxmcst/s
12:10:02 AM     enp0s3      1.51       1.18      0.10      0.12
0.00       0.00       0.00
12:10:02 AM     enp0s8      0.14       0.00      0.02      0.00
0.00       0.00       0.07
12:10:02 AM         lo      0.00       0.00      0.00      0.00
0.00       0.00       0.00
12:20:01 AM     enp0s3      0.85       0.85      0.05      0.08
0.00       0.00       0.00
12:20:01 AM     enp0s8      0.18       0.00      0.02      0.00
0.00       0.00       0.08
12:20:01 AM         lo      0.00       0.00      0.00      0.00
0.00       0.00       0.00
12:30:01 AM     enp0s3      1.45       1.16      0.10      0.11
0.00       0.00       0.00
12:30:01 AM     enp0s8      0.18       0.00      0.03      0.00
0.00       0.00       0.08
12:30:01 AM         lo      0.00       0.00      0.00      0.00
0.00       0.00       0.00
05:20:02 AM         lo      0.00       0.00      0.00      0.00
0.00       0.00       0.00
05:30:02 AM     enp0s3      1.23       1.02      0.08      0.11
0.00       0.00       0.00
```

05:30:02 AM	enp0s8	0.15	0.00	0.02	0.00
0.00	0.00	0.04			
05:30:02 AM	lo	0.00	0.00	0.00	0.00
0.00	0.00	0.00			
05:40:01 AM	enp0s3	0.79	0.78	0.05	0.14
0.00	0.00	0.00			
05:40:01 AM	enp0s8	0.18	0.00	0.02	0.00
0.00	0.00	0.08			
05:40:01 AM	lo	0.00	0.00	0.00	0.00
0.00	0.00	0.00			
05:50:01 AM	enp0s3	0.76	0.75	0.05	0.13
0.00	0.00	0.00			
05:50:01 AM	enp0s8	0.16	0.00	0.02	0.00
0.00	0.00	0.07			
05:50:01 AM	lo	0.00	0.00	0.00	0.00
0.00	0.00	0.00			
06:00:01 AM	enp0s3	0.67	0.60	0.04	0.10
0.00	0.00	0.00			

In the network statistics report, we see no change throughout the day. This suggests that, overall, there has never been any network performance bottlenecks associated with this server.

Review what we learned by comparing historical statistics

After looking through historical statistics with `sar` and recent statistics using commands such as `ps`, `iostat`, `vmstat`, and `top`, we can come to the following conclusions regarding our "slow performance."

Since we were asked by one of our peers to investigate the issue, our conclusions will be formatted in the form of an e-mail reply to this peer.

Hi Bob!

I looked into that one server where the user said the server was "slow." It seems that the user called vagrant has been running multiple instances of two main programs. The first being the lookbusy application, which seems to use roughly 20%–40% CPU at all times. However, in at least one instance, the lookbusy application also used a great deal of memory, exhausting the system of physical memory and forcing the system to swap heavily. However, this process did not last very long.

The second program was the bonnie++ application, which seems to utilize a lot of disk I/O resources. While the vagrant user was running the bonnie++ application, it utilized approximately 60% of the dm-1 and sda disk bandwidths, causing a high I/O wait of around 30%. Typically, this system has an I/O wait of 0% (confirmed via sar).

It seems that the vagrant user may be running applications that are using resources beyond the expected levels, causing performance degradation for the other users.

Summary

In this chapter, we started to use some advanced Linux commands that we explored in *Chapter 2, Troubleshooting Commands and Sources of Useful Information* such as `iostat` and `vmstat`. We also became very familiar with a fundamental utility within Linux, the `ps` command, while troubleshooting a vague performance issue.

While in *Chapter 3, Troubleshooting a Web Application* we were able to follow the full troubleshooting process from Data Collection to Trial and Error, in this chapter, our actions were primarily focused on the Data Collection and Establishing a Hypothesis stages. It is quite common to find yourself only troubleshooting an issue and not performing corrective actions. There are many issues that should be resolved by a user of the system and not the systems administrator, but it is still the administrator's role to identify the source of the issue.

In *Chapter 5, Network Troubleshooting* we will be troubleshooting some very interesting network issues. Networking is critical to any system; issues can sometimes be simple, and at other times, they are very complex. In the next chapter, we will explore networking and how to troubleshoot network issues by using tools such as `netstat` and `tcpdump`.

5
Network Troubleshooting

In *Chapter 3, Troubleshooting a Web Application*, we took an in-depth look at troubleshooting web applications; while we walked through a complex application error, we completely skipped the networking aspect of web applications. In this chapter, we will investigate a reported issue that will walk us through concepts such as DNS, routing, and of course network configuration for RHEL systems.

Networking is an essential skill for any Linux systems administrator. To quote a past instructor:

> *A server without a network is useless to everyone.*

As a systems administrator, every server or desktop that you manage will have some sort of network connection. Whether this network connection is within a segregated corporate network or directly connected to the Internet, a network is involved.

Since networking is such a critical topic, this chapter will cover many aspects of networking and network connectivity; however, it will not cover firewalls. Firewall troubleshooting and configuration will actually be covered in *Chapter 6, Diagnosing and Correcting Firewall Issues*.

Database connectivity issues

In *Chapter 3, Troubleshooting a Web Application*, we were troubleshooting a problem with the company blog. In this chapter, we will once again troubleshoot this blog; however, today's issue is a bit different.

After arriving for the day, we receive a call from a developer stating: *The WordPress blog is returning an error that it cannot connect to the database.*

Data collection

According to the troubleshooting process that we have been following, the next step is to gather as much data as possible around the issue. One of the best sources of information is the person reporting the issue; for this situation, we will ask two basic questions:

- How can I duplicate the issue and see the error?
- Has anything changed recently with the WordPress application?

When asked, the developer states that we can see the error simply by going to the blog in the web browser. On the second question, the developer informs us that the database service was recently moved from the webserver to a new dedicated database server. He also mentions that the move happened several days ago and that the application was working until today.

Since the database service was moved several days ago and the application was working up until this morning, it is not likely that this change caused the issue. However, we should not discount this as a possibility.

Duplicating the issue

As discussed in the previous chapters, a key data collection task is to duplicate the issue. We do this to not only verify that the issue being reported is the issue occurring but also to find any additional errors that may not have been reported.

Since the developer stated that we could duplicate this by going to the blog directly, we will do that from our web browser.

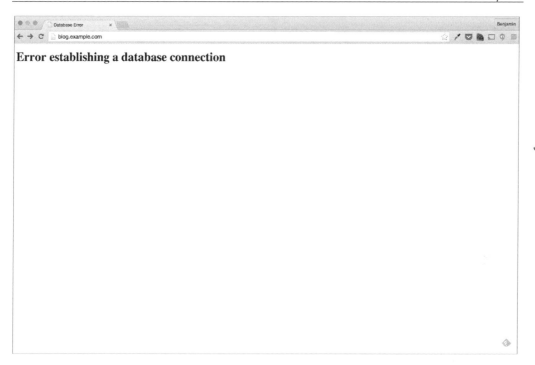

It seems that we can duplicate the issue pretty easily. On the basis of this error, it appears that the application is simply saying that it is having issues establishing a database connection. While this in itself does not mean that the issue is network-related, it could be. The issue could also simply be an issue with the database service itself.

To determine whether the issue is a network issue or a database service issue, we will first need to find which server the application is configured to connect to.

Finding the database server

As with the previous chapter, we will determine which server the application is using by looking through the application configuration files. From our previous troubleshooting in *Chapter 3, Troubleshooting a Web Application*, we know that the WordPress application is hosted on blog.example.com. To get started, we will first log into the blog's webserver and look through the WordPress configuration files.

```
$ ssh blog.example.com -l vagrant
vagrant@blog.example.com's password:
Last login: Sat Feb 28 18:49:40 2015 from 10.0.2.2
[blog]$
```

As we will be executing commands against multiple systems, the examples in this chapter will include a hostname such as blog or db in the command-line prompt.

We learned in *Chapter 3, Troubleshooting a Web Application*, that the WordPress database configuration is stored within the /var/www/html/wp-config.php file. To quickly search this file for database information, we can use the grep command to search for the string DB as this string was present for the database configuration in our previous incident.

```
[blog]$ grep DB wp-config.php
define('DB_NAME', 'wordpress');
define('DB_USER', 'wordpress');
define('DB_PASSWORD', 'password');
define('DB_HOST', 'db.example.com');
define('DB_CHARSET', 'utf8');
define('DB_COLLATE', '');
```

With the above, we can see that the application is currently configured to connect to db.example.com. A simple first troubleshooting step is to simply attempt to connect to the database manually. A simple way to test the database connectivity manually is to use the telnet command.

Testing connectivity

The telnet command is a very useful network and network service troubleshooting tool as it is designed to simply establish a TCP-based network connection to the specified host and port. For our example, we will attempt to connect to the host db.example.com on port 3306.

Port 3306 is the default port for MySQL and MariaDB; in the previous chapter, we already established that this web application requires one of these two database services. As we do not see a specific port listed in the wp-config.php file's configuration, we will assume that the database service is running on this default port.

Telnet from blog.example.com

To get started, we will execute the telnet command from the blog server itself. The fact that we are testing from the same server that the application runs on is important, as this allows us to test under the same network conditions as the application receiving the error.

To use telnet to connect to our database server, we will execute the `telnet` command followed by the hostname (`db.example.com`) and port (`3306`) that we wish to connect to.

```
[blog]$ telnet db.example.com 3306
Trying 192.168.33.12...
telnet: connect to address 192.168.33.12: No route to host
```

It seems that the telnet connection failed. What is interesting is the error being provided; the **No route to host** error seems to clearly indicate a potential network issue.

Telnet from our laptop

Since the connection attempt from the blog server failed with an error indicating there was a network-related issue, we can attempt the same connectivity from our laptop to determine whether the issue is on the blog server's side or the `db` server's side.

To test this connectivity from our laptop, we can once again use the `telnet` command. We can use this command even though our laptop is not necessarily running a Linux operating system. The reason for this is that the `telnet` command is a cross-platform utility; in this chapter, we will utilize several commands that are cross-platform. While there may not be many of them, in general, there are several commands that work on most operating systems, including those that do not traditionally have extensive command line functionality.

While some operating systems have been removing the `telnet` client from default installations, the software can still be installed. For our example, the laptop is running OS X, which currently deploys the `telnet` client.

```
[laptop]$ telnet db.example.com 3306
Trying 10.0.0.50...
Connected to 10.0.0.50.
Escape character is '^]'.
Connection closed by foreign host.
```

It seems that our laptop is also unable to connect to the database service; however, the error is different this time. This time it seems to suggest that the connection attempt was closed by the remote service. We also do not see a message from the remote service, which would indicate that the connection was never fully established.

One caveat to using the `telnet` command to establish port availability is that the `telnet` command will show a connection as **Connected**; however, the connection may not necessarily be established at this point. The general rule when working with telnet is to not assume that the connection was successful until a message from the remote service is received. In our example, we did not receive a message from the remote service.

Ping

Since `telnet` from both the blog server and our laptop failed, we should check whether the issue is isolated to just the database service or connectivity to the server as a whole. One tool to test server-to-server connectivity is the `ping` command, which like the `telnet` command is a cross-platform utility.

To test connectivity with the `ping` command, we can simply execute the command followed by the host that we wish to `ping`.

```
[blog]$ ping db.example.com
PING db.example.com (192.168.33.12) 56(84) bytes of data.
From blog.example.com (192.168.33.11) icmp_seq=1 Destination Host
Unreachable
From blog.example.com (192.168.33.11) icmp_seq=2 Destination Host
Unreachable
From blog.example.com (192.168.33.11) icmp_seq=3 Destination Host
Unreachable
From blog.example.com (192.168.33.11) icmp_seq=4 Destination Host
Unreachable
^C
--- db.example.com ping statistics ---
6 packets transmitted, 0 received, +4 errors, 100% packet loss, time
5008ms
```

The error from the `ping` command seems to be very similar to the error from the `telnet` command. To understand this error better, let's first get a better understanding of how the `ping` command works.

First, before any other action, the `ping` command will try to resolve the hostname provided. What this means is that before doing anything else, our ping execution tried to identify the IP address of db.example.com.

```
PING db.example.com (192.168.33.12) 56(84) bytes of data.
```

From the results, we can see that the `ping` command identified this host as resolving to 192.168.33.12. Once ping has the IP address, it will send an ICMP echo request network packet to that IP. In this case, this means that it is sending an ICMP echo request to 192.168.33.12.

ICMP is a networking protocol that is used as a control system. When the remote host, such as 192.168.33.12 receives an ICMP echo request network packet, it is supposed to send an ICMP echo reply network packet back to the requesting host. This activity allows two hosts to validate network connectivity by performing a simple networking version of *ping pong*.

```
From blog.example.com (192.168.33.11) icmp_seq=1 Destination Host
Unreachable
```

If our ICMP echo request packet had never made it to the 192.168.33.12 server, we simply would have had no output from the `ping` command. However, we received an error; this means that the system on the other side is up, but there is an error with the connectivity between the two hosts that is preventing a full two-way discussion.

One question that arises around this issue is whether the error is true for all network connectivity from the blog server or isolated to the communication between the `blog` and the `db` server. We can test this by performing a `ping` request to another generic address. Since our system is connected to the Internet, we can simply use a common Internet domain.

```
# ping google.com
PING google.com (216.58.216.46) 56(84) bytes of data.
64 bytes from lax02s22-in-f14.1e100.net (216.58.216.46): icmp_seq=1
ttl=63 time=23.5 ms
64 bytes from lax02s22-in-f14.1e100.net (216.58.216.46): icmp_seq=2
ttl=63 time=102 ms
64 bytes from lax02s22-in-f14.1e100.net (216.58.216.46): icmp_seq=3
ttl=63 time=26.9 ms
64 bytes from lax02s22-in-f14.1e100.net (216.58.216.46): icmp_seq=4
ttl=63 time=25.6 ms
64 bytes from lax02s22-in-f14.1e100.net (216.58.216.46): icmp_seq=5
ttl=63 time=25.6 ms
^C
--- google.com ping statistics ---
5 packets transmitted, 5 received, 0% packet loss, time 4106ms
rtt min/avg/max/mdev = 23.598/40.799/102.156/30.697 ms
```

The preceding example is an example of a working `ping` request and reply. Here, we can see not only the IP that `Google.com` resolves to but also the returned `ping` requests. This means that, as our blog server sends an `ICMP echo request`, the remote server `216.58.216.46` sends an `ICMP echo reply`.

Troubleshooting DNS

Something interesting that both the `ping` and the `telnet` commands told us beyond network connectivity is the IP address of the `db.example.com` hostname. However, it seems that our results are different when performing these actions from our laptop as opposed to from the blog server.

From the blog server, our `telnet` tried to connect to `192.168.33.12`, the same address as our `ping` command.

```
[blog]$ telnet db.example.com 3306
Trying 192.168.33.12...
```

However, from the laptop, our telnet tried to connect to 10.0.0.50, a completely different IP address.

```
[laptop]$ telnet db.example.com 3306
Trying 10.0.0.50...
```

The reason for this is simple; it seems that our laptop is getting a different DNS result as our blog server. If that is the case however, it could mean that our issue may simply be related to a DNS issue.

Checking DNS with dig

DNS is an important aspect of modern-day networks. Our current issue is a perfect example of its importance. In the WordPress configuration file, our database server is set to `db.example.com`. This means that before the application server can establish a database connection, it must first look up the IP address.

In many cases, it is fairly safe to assume that the IP address identified by `ping` is likely to be the IP address presented by DNS. However, this is not always the case as we may soon find out with our specific issue.

The `dig` command is a very useful DNS troubleshooting command; it is very flexible and can be used to perform many different types of DNS requests. To validate the DNS for `db.example.com`, we can simply execute the `dig` command followed by the hostname that we wish to query: `db.example.com`.

```
[blog]$ dig db.example.com

; <<>> DiG 9.9.4-RedHat-9.9.4-14.el7_0.1 <<>> db.example.com
;; global options: +cmd
;; Got answer:
;; ->>HEADER<<- opcode: QUERY, status: NOERROR, id: 15857
;; flags: qr rd ra; QUERY: 1, ANSWER: 1, AUTHORITY: 0, ADDITIONAL: 1

;; OPT PSEUDOSECTION:
; EDNS: version: 0, flags:; udp: 4096
;; QUESTION SECTION:
;db.example.com.        IN   A

;; ANSWER SECTION:
db.example.com.    15   IN   A   10.0.0.50

;; Query time: 39 msec
;; SERVER: 10.0.2.3#53(10.0.2.3)
;; WHEN: Sun Mar 01 20:51:22 UTC 2015
;; MSG SIZE  rcvd: 59
```

If we look at the returned data from `dig`, we can see that the DNS name `db.example.com` does not resolve to `192.168.33.12`, but rather to `10.0.0.50`. We can see this in the ANSWER SECTION of the `dig` command's output.

```
;; ANSWER SECTION:
db.example.com.    15   IN   A   10.0.0.50
```

One very useful option with `dig` is the option to specify a server to query. In the previous execution of `dig`, we could see that server `10.0.2.3` was the server that provided the `10.0.0.50` address.

```
;; Query time: 39 msec
;; SERVER: 10.0.2.3#53(10.0.2.3)
```

Since we are unfamiliar with this DNS server, we can validate the returned results further by querying Google's public DNS servers. We can do this by adding @ followed by the DNS server IP or hostname that we wish to use. In the following example, we are requesting 8.8.8.8 a DNS server that is part of Google's public DNS infrastructure.

```
[blog]$ dig @8.8.8.8 db.example.com


; <<>> DiG 9.9.4-RedHat-9.9.4-14.el7_0.1 <<>> @8.8.8.8 example.com
; (1 server found)
;; global options: +cmd
;; Got answer:
;; ->>HEADER<<- opcode: QUERY, status: NOERROR, id: 42743
;; flags: qr rd ra ad; QUERY: 1, ANSWER: 1, AUTHORITY: 0, ADDITIONAL: 1

;; OPT PSEUDOSECTION:
; EDNS: version: 0, flags:; udp: 512
;; QUESTION SECTION:
;db.example.com.        IN   A

;; ANSWER SECTION:
db.example.com.    18639  IN  A  10.0.0.50

;; Query time: 39 msec
;; SERVER: 8.8.8.8#53(8.8.8.8)
;; WHEN: Sun Mar 01 22:14:53 UTC 2015
;; MSG SIZE  rcvd: 56
```
It seems that Google's public DNS has the same results as 10.0.2.3.

Looking up DNS with nslookup

Another great tool for troubleshooting DNS is nslookup. The nslookup command is a command that has been around for quite a while. In fact, it is yet another cross-platform command that exists on practically all major operating systems.

To perform a simple DNS lookup with `nslookup`, we can simply run the command followed by the DNS name to query, similar to `dig`.

```
[blog]$ nslookup db.example.com
Server:     10.0.2.3
Address:    10.0.2.3#53


Non-authoritative answer:
Name:   db.example.com
Address: 10.0.0.50
```

Like `dig`, the `nslookup` command can be used to query a specific DNS server as well. This can be done via two methods. The first is by adding the server address at the end of the command.

```
[blog]$ nslookup db.example.com 8.8.8.8
Server:     8.8.8.8
Address:    8.8.8.8#53


Non-authoritative answer:
Name:   db.example.com
Address: 10.0.0.50
```

The second method is to use `nslookup` in the interactive mode. To go into the interactive mode, simply execute `nslookup` with no other options.

```
# nslookup
>
```

Once in the interactive mode, specify the server to use by entering `server <dns server>`.

```
# nslookup
> server 8.8.8.8
Default server: 8.8.8.8
Address: 8.8.8.8#53
>
```

Finally, to lookup the DNS name, we just type the domain to query.

```
# nslookup
> server 8.8.8.8
Default server: 8.8.8.8
Address: 8.8.8.8#53
> db.example.com
Server:     8.8.8.8
Address:    8.8.8.8#53

Non-authoritative answer:
Name:   db.example.com
Address: 10.0.0.50
>
```

To leave the interactive mode, simply type exit.

```
> exit
```

So why use nslookup rather than dig? While the dig command is very useful, it is not a cross-platform command and has only traditionally existed on Unix and Linux systems. The nslookup command on the other hand is cross-platform and can be found in most environments where the dig command may be unavailable. It is important as a systems administrator to be familiar with many commands, and it is very useful to be able to perform a task using whichever command is available.

What did dig and nslookup tell us?

Now that we have used dig and nslookup to query the DNS name db.example.com, let's review what we have found.

- The domain db.example.com actually resolves to 10.0.0.50
- The ping command returned 192.168.33.12 for the domain db.example.com

How is the ping command returning one address while DNS returns another? One possibility is a configuration in the /etc/hosts file. This is something that we can validate very quickly with a simple grep command.

```
[blog]$ grep example.com /etc/hosts
192.168.33.11 blog.example.com
192.168.33.12 db.example.com
```

A bit about /etc/hosts

Before DNS servers such as **Bind** were created, local hosts files were used to manage the domain-to-IP mappings. This file contained a list of every domain address that the system needed to connect to. However, over time, this method became complicated as networks grew from a few hosts to thousands and millions of hosts.

On Linux and most Unix distributions, the hosts file is located at /etc/hosts. By default, any entry in the /etc/hosts file will supersede DNS requests. This means that, by default, if there is a domain-to-IP mapping in the /etc/hosts file, this mapping will be used and the system will not pull the same domain from another DNS system.

This is the default behavior for Linux; however, we can check whether this server is using this default configuration by reading the /etc/nsswitch.conf file.

```
[blog]$ grep hosts /etc/nsswitch.conf
hosts:      files dns
```

The nsswitch.conf file is a configuration that allows administrators to configure which backend systems to use in order to look up items such as users, groups, netgroups, hostnames, and services. For example, if we wanted to configure a system to use ldap to look up user groups, we could do that by changing the values in the /etc/nsswitch.conf file.

```
[blog]$ grep group /etc/nsswitch.conf
group:      files sss
```

Based on the output of the preceding grep command, the blog system is configured to use local group files and then the SSSD service to look up user groups. To add ldap to this configuration, simply add it to the list in the order desired (that is, ldap files sss).

For the DNS that is specified by the hosts configuration, it appears that our server is configured to look up hosts first on the basis of files and then the DNS. This means that our system will honor the /etc/hosts file before looking up a domain via DNS.

DNS summary

Now that we have confirmed both DNS and the /etc/hosts file, we know that someone has configured this application server to think db.example.com resolves to 192.168.33.12. Was this a mistake or is this a way to connect to the database server without using DNS?

At this point, it is a bit too early to tell, but we do know that the host 192.168.33.12 did not send an ICMP echo reply to our ICMP echo request from the blog server.

Pinging from another location

Whenever dealing with network issues, it is always best to try the connection from multiple locations or servers. This may seem like something obvious to the data collector type of troubleshooter, but the educated guesser troubleshooter may overlook this extremely helpful step.

For our example, we will run a test ping from our laptop to 192.168.33.12.

```
[laptop]$ ping 192.168.33.12
PING 192.168.33.12 (192.168.33.12): 56 data bytes
64 bytes from 192.168.33.12: icmp_seq=0 ttl=64 time=0.573 ms
64 bytes from 192.168.33.12: icmp_seq=1 ttl=64 time=0.425 ms
64 bytes from 192.168.33.12: icmp_seq=2 ttl=64 time=0.461 ms
^C
--- 192.168.33.12 ping statistics ---
3 packets transmitted, 3 packets received, 0.0% packet loss
round-trip min/avg/max/stddev = 0.425/0.486/0.573/0.063 ms
```

From the results of the ping request, it seems that our laptop is able to connect to 192.168.33.12 without any issue.

What does this tell us? Quite a bit actually! It tells us that the server in question is up; it also confirms that there is a connectivity issue, specifically between blog. example.com and db.example.com. If the issue were due to the db.example.com server being down or misconfigured, our laptop would also be impacted.

However that is not the case. It is actually quite the opposite; it seems that connectivity from our laptop to the server works as expected.

Testing port connectivity with cURL

Earlier when testing the MariaDB port from our laptop with telnet, the telnet command was testing the server 10.0.0.50. However, based on the /etc/hosts configuration, it seems that the desired database server is 192.168.33.12.

To verify that the database service is actually up, we should perform the same telnet test with the 192.168.33.12 address. However, this time rather than using telnet, we will perform this test with curl.

I have seen many environments (especially lately) where installing the telnet client is forbidden or not performed by default. For environments such as these, it is important to have some tool that can test port connectivity. If telnet is not available, the curl command can be used as an alternative.

In *Chapter 3, Troubleshooting a Web Application*, we used the `curl` command to request a web page. The `curl` command can actually be used with many different protocols; the protocol that we are interested in for this case is the Telnet protocol.

The following is an example of using `curl` from our laptop to establish a connection to the `db.example.com` server over port `3306`.

```
[laptop]$ curl -v telnet://192.168.33.12:3306
* Rebuilt URL to: telnet://192.168.33.12:3306/
* Hostname was NOT found in DNS cache
*   Trying 192.168.33.12...
* Connected to 192.168.33.12 (192.168.33.12) port 3306 (#0)
* RCVD IAC 106
^C
```

From the example, it seems that not only was the laptop able to connect to the server on port `3306`, but the `curl` command also received a message from the `RCVD IAC 106` service.

When using `curl` for Telnet tests, it is necessary to use the –v (verbose) flag to put curl into the verbose mode. Without the verbose flag, `curl` will simply hide the connectivity details, and the connectivity details are exactly what we are looking for.

In the previous example, we can see that the connection from our laptop was successful; for comparison, we can use this same command to test connectivity from the blog server.

```
[blog]$ curl -v telnet://192.168.33.12:3306
* About to connect() to 192.168.33.12 port 3306 (#0)
*   Trying 192.168.33.12...
* No route to host
* Failed connect to 192.168.33.12:3306; No route to host
* Closing connection 0
curl: (7) Failed connect to 192.168.33.12:3306; No route to host
```

As expected, the connection attempt failed.

From the above tests with `curl`, we can determine that the database server is listening and accepting connections on port `3306`; however, the blog server cannot connect to the database server. What we don't know is if the issue is on the blog server's side or on the database server's side. To identify which side of the connection is having an issue, we will need to look at the details of the network connections. To do this, we will use two commands, the first being `netstat` and the second being `tcpdump`.

Showing current network connections with netstat

The `netstat` command is a very extensive tool and can be used to troubleshoot many aspects of network issues. In this case, we will use two of the basic flags to print the existing network connections.

```
[blog]# netstat -na
Active Internet connections (servers and established)
Proto Recv-Q Send-Q Local Address          Foreign Address
State
tcp        0      0 127.0.0.1:25           0.0.0.0:*
LISTEN
tcp        0      0 0.0.0.0:52903          0.0.0.0:*
LISTEN
tcp        0      0 0.0.0.0:3306           0.0.0.0:*
LISTEN
tcp        0      0 0.0.0.0:111            0.0.0.0:*
LISTEN
tcp        0      0 0.0.0.0:22             0.0.0.0:*
LISTEN
tcp        0      0 10.0.2.16:22           10.0.2.2:50322
ESTABLISHED
tcp        0      0 192.168.33.11:22       192.168.33.1:53359
ESTABLISHED
tcp6       0      0 ::1:25                 :::*
LISTEN
tcp6       0      0 :::57504               :::*
LISTEN
tcp6       0      0 :::111                 :::*
LISTEN
tcp6       0      0 :::80                  :::*
LISTEN
tcp6       0      0 :::22                  :::*
LISTEN
udp        0      0 0.0.0.0:5353           0.0.0.0:*
udp        0      0 0.0.0.0:68             0.0.0.0:*
udp        0      0 0.0.0.0:111            0.0.0.0:*
udp        0      0 0.0.0.0:52594          0.0.0.0:*
udp        0      0 127.0.0.1:904          0.0.0.0:*
udp        0      0 0.0.0.0:49853          0.0.0.0:*
```

udp	0	0 0.0.0.0:53449	0.0.0.0:*
udp	0	0 0.0.0.0:719	0.0.0.0:*
udp6	0	0 :::54762	:::*
udp6	0	0 :::58674	:::*
udp6	0	0 :::111	:::*
udp6	0	0 :::719	:::*
raw6	0	0 :::58	:::*

In the preceding example, we executed the `netstat` command with the –n (no dns) flag, which tells `netstat` to not look up the DNS hostname of the IPs or translate port numbers to service names, and the –a (all) flag that tells `netstat` to print both listening and non-listening sockets.

These flags have the effect of `netstat`, showing all network connections and ports that are bound by applications.

The example `netstat` command shows quite a bit of information. To get a better understanding of this information, let's examine the output a little better.

Proto	Recv-Q	Send-Q	Local Address	Foreign Address	State
tcp	0	0	127.0.0.1:25	0.0.0.0:*	LISTEN

The output of `netstat` is split into six columns, the first being **Proto**, which shows the sockets protocol. In the snippet above, the socket is using the TCP protocol.

The second column **Recv-Q** is a count of bytes received but not copied by the application by using this socket. This is basically the number of bytes waiting between the kernel receiving the data from the network and the application accepting it.

The third column **Send-Q** is a count of bytes sent but not acknowledged by the remote host. Basically, the data has been sent to a remote host, but the local host has not received the remote host's acceptance of this data.

The fourth column is **Local Address**, which is the local server's address used for the socket. Our snippet shows the local host address as 127.0.0.1 and the port as 25.

The fifth column is the **Foreign Address** or remote address. This column lists the remote server's IP and port. Because of the type of example that we used earlier, this is listed as IP 0.0.0.0 and port *, which is a wildcard, meaning anything.

The sixth column, our final column, is the **State** socket. With TCP connections, the state will tell us the current state of the TCP connection. For our preceding example, the state is listed as LISTEN; this tells us that the listed socket is used for accepting TCP connections.

If we put all of the columns together, this single line tells us that our server is listening for new connections on port 25 via the IP 127.0.0.1 and that it is for TCP-based connections.

Using netstat to watch for new connections

Now that we understand the output of netstat a bit more, we can use it to look for new connections from our application server to our database server. To use netstat to watch for new connections, we will use an often overlooked feature of netstat.

Similar to the vmstat command, it is possible to put netstat into a continuous mode, which prints the same output every few seconds. To do this, simply put the interval at the end of the command.

In the following example, we will use the same netstat flags with an interval of 5 s; however, we will also pipe the output to grep and use grep to filter for port 3306.

```
[blog]# netstat -na 5 | grep 3306
tcp        0        1 192.168.33.11:59492        192.168.33.12:3306
SYN_SENT
tcp        0        1 192.168.33.11:59493        192.168.33.12:3306
SYN_SENT
tcp        0        1 192.168.33.11:59494        192.168.33.12:3306
SYN_SENT
```

In addition to running the netstat command, we also can navigate to the blog.example.com address in our browser. We can do this to force the web application to attempt a connection to the database.

In general, web applications have two types of connections to a database, either persistent connections where they always stay connected to the database or non-persistent connections where they are established only when required. Since we don't know which type this WordPress installation uses, it is safer for this type of troubleshooting to assume they are non-persistent. This means that, in order to trigger database connections, there must be traffic to the WordPress application.

From the output of netstat, we can see connection attempts to the database, and not just any database but the database service at 192.168.33.12. This information confirms that, when the web application is attempting to establish a connection, it is using the IP from the hosts file and not from DNS. Up until this point, we suspected that this was the case based on telnet and ping but had no proof of the connection from the application.

An interesting fact however is that the netstat output shows that the TCP connection is in a SYN_SENT state. This SYN_SENT state is the state used when first establishing a network connection. The netstat command can print many different connection states; each one tells us where in the process the connection is in. This information can be key to identifying the root cause of network connectivity issues.

Breakdown of netstat states

Before going too far, we should take a quick look at the different netstat states and what they mean. The following is a full list of states used by netstat:

- ESTABLISHED: The connection has been established and can be used for data transfer
- SYN_SENT: The TCP socket is attempting to establish a connection to the remote host
- SYN_RECV: A TCP connection request has been received from the remote host
- FIN_WAIT1: The TCP connection is closing
- FIN_WAIT2: The TCP connection is waiting for the remote host to close the connection
- TIME_WAIT: The socket is waiting after being closed for any outstanding network packets
- CLOSE: The socket is no longer being used
- CLOSE_WAIT: The remote end has closed its connection, and the local socket is being closed
- LAST_ACK: The remote end has initiated closing the connection, and the local system is waiting for a final acknowledgement
- LISTEN: The socket is being used to listen for incoming connections
- CLOSING: Both the local and the remote sockets are closed, but not all data has been sent
- UNKNOWN: Used for sockets in an unknown state

From the above list, we can determine that the connections to the database from the application never become ESTABLISHED. This means that the application server starts the connection in the SYN_SENT state, but it never transitions to the next state.

Capturing network traffic with tcpdump

To get a better understanding of the network traffic, we will use a second command that allows us to look at the network traffic details—tcpdump. Here, the netstat command is used to print the status of sockets; the tcpdump command is used to create "dumps" or "traces" of network traffic. These dumps allow users to see all aspects of the network traffic captured.

With tcpdump, it is possible to look at the full TCP packet details, from the packet headers to the actual data being transmitted. Not only can it capture this data, but tcpdump can also write the captured data to a file. After the data is written to the file, it can be saved or moved and later read with the tcpdump command or other network packet analysis tools (for example, wireshark).

The following is a simple example of running tcpdump to capture the network traffic.

```
[blog]# tcpdump -nvvv
tcpdump: listening on enp0s3, link-type EN10MB (Ethernet), capture size
65535 bytes
16:18:04.125881 IP (tos 0x10, ttl 64, id 20361, offset 0, flags [DF],
proto TCP (6), length 156)
    10.0.2.16.ssh > 10.0.2.2.52618: Flags [P.], cksum 0x189f (incorrect
-> 0x62a4), seq 3643405490:3643405606, ack 245510335, win 26280, length
116
16:18:04.126203 IP (tos 0x0, ttl 64, id 9942, offset 0, flags [none],
proto TCP (6), length 40)
    10.0.2.2.52618 > 10.0.2.16.ssh: Flags [.], cksum 0xbc71 (correct),
seq 1, ack 116, win 65535, length 0
16:18:05.128497 IP (tos 0x10, ttl 64, id 20362, offset 0, flags [DF],
proto TCP (6), length 332)
    10.0.2.16.ssh > 10.0.2.2.52618: Flags [P.], cksum 0x194f (incorrect
-> 0xecc9), seq 116:408, ack 1, win 26280, length 292
16:18:05.128784 IP (tos 0x0, ttl 64, id 9943, offset 0, flags [none],
proto TCP (6), length 40)
    10.0.2.2.52618 > 10.0.2.16.ssh: Flags [.], cksum 0xbb4d (correct),
seq 1, ack 408, win 65535, length 0
16:18:06.129934 IP (tos 0x10, ttl 64, id 20363, offset 0, flags [DF],
proto TCP (6), length 156)
    10.0.2.16.ssh > 10.0.2.2.52618: Flags [P.], cksum 0x189f (incorrect
-> 0x41d5), seq 408:524, ack 1, win 26280, length 116
16:18:06.130441 IP (tos 0x0, ttl 64, id 9944, offset 0, flags [none],
proto TCP (6), length 40)
```

```
    10.0.2.2.52618 > 10.0.2.16.ssh: Flags [.], cksum 0xbad9 (correct),
seq 1, ack 524, win 65535, length 0
16:18:07.131131 IP (tos 0x10, ttl 64, id 20364, offset 0, flags [DF],
proto TCP (6), length 140)
```

In the preceding example, I have provided several flags to the tcpdump command. The first flag –n (no dns) tells tcpdump to not look up the hostname of any IPs that it finds. The rest of the flags –vvv (verbose) tell tcpdump to be very "very" verbose. The tcpdump command has three levels of verbosity; each –v that is added to the command line increases the verbosity level used. In the preceding example, tcpdump is in its most verbose mode.

The preceding example is one of the simplest ways to run tcpdump; however, it does not capture the traffic that we require.

Taking a look at the server's network interfaces

When tcpdump is executed on systems with multiple network interfaces, unless an interface is defined the command will pick the lowest numbered interface to attach to. In the preceding example, the interface chosen was enp0s3; however, this may not be the interface used for database connectivity.

Before using tcpdump to investigate our network connectivity issue, we first need to identify which network interface is used for this connectivity; to do this, we will use the ip command.

```
[blog]# ip link show
1: lo: <LOOPBACK,UP,LOWER_UP> mtu 65536 qdisc noqueue state UNKNOWN mode
DEFAULT
    link/loopback 00:00:00:00:00:00 brd 00:00:00:00:00:00
2: enp0s3: <BROADCAST,MULTICAST,UP,LOWER_UP> mtu 1500 qdisc pfifo_fast
state UP mode DEFAULT qlen 1000
    link/ether 08:00:27:20:5d:4b brd ff:ff:ff:ff:ff:ff
3: enp0s8: <BROADCAST,MULTICAST,UP,LOWER_UP> mtu 1500 qdisc pfifo_fast
state UP mode DEFAULT qlen 1000
    link/ether 08:00:27:7f:fd:54 brd ff:ff:ff:ff:ff:ff
```

At a high level, the ip command allows users to print, modify, and add network configurations. In the example above, we are telling the ip command to "show" us all of the available "links" by using the show links parameters. The links being shown are actually the defined network interfaces for this server.

What is a network interface?

When talking about a physical server, the network interface is generally a representation of a physical Ethernet port. If we assume that the machine used in the preceding example is a physical machine, we can assume that the enp0s3 and enp0s8 links are physical devices. In reality, however, the abovementioned machine is a virtual machine. This means that the devices are logically attached to this virtual machine; the kernel of this machine however does not know or even need to know the difference.

For example, in this book most interfaces, with the exception of the "lo" or loopback interface, are directly related to physical (or virtually physical) network devices. It is possible, however, to create virtual interfaces, which allows you to create multiple interfaces that link back to a single physical interface. In general, these interfaces are seen with a ":" or "." as a separator from the original device name. If we were to make a virtual interface for enp0s8, it would look something along the lines of enp0s8:1.

Viewing device configuration

From the ip command's output, we can see that there are three network interfaces defined. Before knowing which one is used for our database connectivity, we will first need to understand these interfaces better.

```
1: lo: <LOOPBACK,UP,LOWER_UP> mtu 65536 qdisc noqueue state UNKNOWN mode
DEFAULT
```

The lo or loopback interface is the first one in the list. Anyone who has worked on Linux or Unix long enough will be very familiar with loopback interfaces. The loopback interface is designed to give users of the system a local network address that can only be used to connect back to the local system.

This special interface allows applications located on the same server to interact via TCP/IP without having to expose their connectivity externally to the wider network. It also allows these applications to interact without a network packet leaving the local server, thus making it a very fast networking connection.

Traditionally, the loopback interface IP is well known as 127.0.0.1. However, just like everything else in this book, we will first validate this information before assuming it to be true. We can do this by using the ip command to show the loopback interface's defined address.

```
[blog]# ip addr show lo
1: lo: <LOOPBACK,UP,LOWER_UP> mtu 65536 qdisc noqueue state UNKNOWN
    link/loopback 00:00:00:00:00:00 brd 00:00:00:00:00:00
    inet 127.0.0.1/8 scope host lo
```

```
    valid_lft forever preferred_lft forever
inet6 ::1/128 scope host
    valid_lft forever preferred_lft forever
```

In the previous example that shows available interfaces, the "link show" options were used; in order to show IP addresses, the "addr show" options can be used. The syntax for the ip command to print items follows this same scheme throughout.

The preceding example also specifies the name of the device we are interested in; this limits the output to the specified device. If we were to omit the device name from the preceding command, it would simply print the IP addresses for all devices.

So, what does the above tell us about the lo interface? Well one thing that it tells us is that the lo interface is listening on the IPv4 address of 127.0.0.1; we can see this on the following line.

```
inet 127.0.0.1/8 scope host lo
```

This means that, if we want to connect to this host via the loopback interface, we can do so by targeting 127.0.0.1. The ip command, however, also shows a second IP defined on this interface.

```
inet6 ::1/128 scope host
```

This shows us that the IPv6 address of ::1 is also bound to the lo interface. This address serves the same purpose as 127.0.0.1, but it is designed for IPv6 communication.

With the above information from the ip command, we can see that the lo or loopback interface is defined as expected.

The second interface defined on this server is enp0s3; this device, unlike lo, is either a physical device or a virtualized physical interface. The ip link show command executed earlier has already told us quite a bit about this interface.

```
2: enp0s3: <BROADCAST,MULTICAST,UP,LOWER_UP> mtu 1500 qdisc pfifo_fast
state UP mode DEFAULT qlen 1000
    link/ether 08:00:27:20:5d:4b brd ff:ff:ff:ff:ff:ff
```

From the preceding snippet, we can identify the following:

- The device is in an **up** state: state UP
- The MTU size is **1500**: mtu 1500
- The MAC address is **08:00:27:20:5d:4b**: link/ether 08:00:27:20:5d:4b

From this information, we know that the interface is up and able to be utilized. We also know that the MTU size is set to the default of 1500, and we can easily identify the MAC address. While the MTU size and the MAC address may not be extremely pertinent to this issue, they can be very useful in other situations.

However, for our current task of identifying which interface is used for database connectivity, we will need to identify which IPs are bound to this interface.

```
[blog]# ip addr show enp0s3
2: enp0s3: <BROADCAST,MULTICAST,UP,LOWER_UP> mtu 1500 qdisc pfifo_fast
state UP qlen 1000
    link/ether 08:00:27:20:5d:4b brd ff:ff:ff:ff:ff:ff
    inet 10.0.2.15/24 brd 10.0.2.255 scope global dynamic enp0s3
       valid_lft 49655sec preferred_lft 49655sec
    inet6 fe80::a00:27ff:fe20:5d4b/64 scope link
       valid_lft forever preferred_lft forever
```

From the preceding output, we can see that the `enp0s3` interface is listening to the IPv4 IP of `10.0.2.15` (`inet 10.0.2.15/24`) as well as the IPv6 IP of `f380::a00:27ff:fe20:5d4b` (`inet6 fe80::a00:27ff:fe20:5d4b/64`). Does this tell us that connections to `192.168.33.12` go through this interface? No, but it also doesn't mean that they don't.

What this does tell us is that the `enp0s3` interface is used to connect to the `10.0.2.15/24` network. This network may or may not be able to route to the address of `192.168.33.12`; before making this determination, we should first review the next interface's configuration.

The third interface on this system is `enp0s8`; it is also a physical or virtual network device, and from the information provided by the `ip link show` command, we can see that it has a similar configuration to `enp0s3`.

```
3: enp0s8: <BROADCAST,MULTICAST,UP,LOWER_UP> mtu 1500 qdisc pfifo_fast
state UP mode DEFAULT qlen 1000
    link/ether 08:00:27:7f:fd:54 brd ff:ff:ff:ff:ff:ff
```

From this output, we can see that the interface of `enp0s8` is also in an "UP" state and has the default MTU size of 1500. We can also determine the MAC address of this interface, which at this time is not specifically required; however, it may become useful later.

If we look at the IPs defined on this server, however, there is a significant difference from those of the enp0s3 device.

```
[blog]# ip addr show enp0s8
3: enp0s8: <BROADCAST,MULTICAST,UP,LOWER_UP> mtu 1500 qdisc pfifo_fast
state UP qlen 1000
    link/ether 08:00:27:7f:fd:54 brd ff:ff:ff:ff:ff:ff
    inet 192.168.33.11/24 brd 192.168.33.255 scope global enp0s8
       valid_lft forever preferred_lft forever
    inet6 fe80::a00:27ff:fe7f:fd54/64 scope link
       valid_lft forever preferred_lft forever
```

We can see that the enp0s8 interface is listening on the IPv4 address of 192.168.33.11 (inet 192.168.33.11/24) and the IPv6 address of fe80::a00:27ff:fe7f:fd54 (inet6 fe80::a00:27ff:fe7f:fd54/64).

Does this mean that the enp0s8 interface is used to connect to 192.168.33.12? Well, actually, it may.

The subnet defined for enp0s8 is 192.168.33.11/24, which means that this interface is connected to a network of devices that span the IP range of 192.168.33.0 to 192.168.33.255. Since the database server's IP 192.168.33.12 is within this range, it is very likely that the communication to this address is over the enp0s8 interface.

At this point, we can "suspect" that the interface of enp0s8 is used for communication to the database server. While this interface may be configured to talk to the subnet that contains 192.168.33.12, it is entirely possible to force communication through another interface by using defined routes.

To check whether there is a route defined and forcing communication out through another interface, we will again use the ip command. For this task, however, we will use the "route get" options for the ip command.

```
[blog]# ip route get 192.168.33.12
192.168.33.12 dev enp0s8   src 192.168.33.11
    cache
```

When executed with the "route get" arguments, the ip command will specifically output which interface is used to route to the specified IP.

From the preceding output, we can see that the blog.example.com server is in fact using the enp0s8 interface to route to the 192.168.33.12 address, the IP of db.example.com.

At this point, not only have we used the `ip` command to determine what network interfaces exist on this server, but we have also used it to determine which interface a network packet would take to get to our target host.

The `ip` command is a very useful tool and has recently been slated to replace older commands such as `ifconfig` and `route`. If you are generally familiar with using commands such as `ifconfig` but not as familiar with the `ip` command, it is a good idea to review the usage covered above, as eventually, the `ifconfig` command will be deprecated.

Specifying the interface with tcpdump

Now that we have identified the interface used for communication with `db.example.com` we can start our network trace by using `tcpdump`. As mentioned earlier, we will use the -nvvv flags to put `tcpdump` in the very "very" verbose mode without hostname resolution. This time, however, we will specify that `tcpdump` captures network traffic from the `enp0s8` interface; we can do this with the -i (interface) flag. We will also use the -w (write) flag to write the captured data to a file.

```
[blog]# tcpdump -nvvv -i enp0s8 -w /var/tmp/chapter5.pcap
tcpdump: listening on enp0s8, link-type EN10MB (Ethernet), capture size
65535 bytes

48 packets captured
```

When we first executed the `tcpdump` command, we received quite a bit of output to the screen. When told to save its output to a file, `tcpdump` will not output the captured data to the screen but rather continuously show a counter of captured packets.

Once we have `tcpdump` saving its captured data to a file, we need to duplicate the issue to try to generate database traffic. We will do this by using the same method as we did with the `netstat` command: by simply navigating to `blog.example.com` in a web browser.

As we navigate to the WordPress site, we should see the `packets captured` counter increasing; this indicates that `tcpdump` has seen traffic and has captured it. Once the counter reaches a reasonable number, we can stop the `tcpdump` capture. To do this, simply press *Ctrl + C* on the command line; once stopped, we should see a message similar to the following:

```
^C48 packets captured

48 packets received by filter

0 packets dropped by kernel
```

Reading the captured data

Now that we have the captured the `network trace` saved to a file, we can use this file to investigate the database traffic. The benefit of having this data saved within a file is that we can read this data multiple times and iterate through filters to reduce the output. Further, when running `tcpdump` against the live network stream, we may catch traffic once but never again.

In order to read the saved data, we can run `tcpdump` with the `-r` (read) flag followed by the filename to read.

We could start by using the following command to print the packet header information for all `48` packets that we captured.

```
[blog]# tcpdump -nvvv -r /var/tmp/chapter5.pcap
```

The output of this command, however, can be quite overwhelming; to get to the heart of the issue, we will need to narrow down the output of `tcpdump`. To do this, we will use tcpdump's ability to apply filters to the captured data. In particular, we will be filtering the output to a specific IP address by using the "`host`" filter.

```
[blog]# tcpdump -nvvv -r /var/tmp/chapter5.pcap host 192.168.33.12
reading from file /var/tmp/chapter5.pcap, link-type EN10MB (Ethernet)
03:33:05.569739 IP (tos 0x0, ttl 64, id 26591, offset 0, flags [DF],
proto TCP (6), length 60)
    192.168.33.11.37785 > 192.168.33.12.mysql: Flags [S], cksum
0xc396 (incorrect -> 0x3543), seq 3937874058, win 14600, options [mss
1460,sackOK,TS val 53696341 ecr 0,nop,wscale 6], length 0
03:33:06.573145 IP (tos 0x0, ttl 64, id 26592, offset 0, flags [DF],
proto TCP (6), length 60)
    192.168.33.11.37785 > 192.168.33.12.mysql: Flags [S], cksum
0xc396 (incorrect -> 0x3157), seq 3937874058, win 14600, options [mss
1460,sackOK,TS val 53697345 ecr 0,nop,wscale 6], length 0
03:33:08.580122 IP (tos 0x0, ttl 64, id 26593, offset 0, flags [DF],
proto TCP (6), length 60)
    192.168.33.11.37785 > 192.168.33.12.mysql: Flags [S], cksum
0xc396 (incorrect -> 0x2980), seq 3937874058, win 14600, options [mss
1460,sackOK,TS val 53699352 ecr 0,nop,wscale 6], length 0
```

By adding `host 192.168.33.12` to the end of the `tcpdump` command, the output is filtered to traffic that only relates to the host 192.168.33.12. This is made possible by the `host` filter. The `tcpdump` command has many available filters; however, in this chapter, we will mainly utilize the host filter. I would strongly suggest becoming familiar with `tcpdump` filters for anyone troubleshooting network issues regularly.

When running `tcpdump` (in the same fashion as above), it is important to know that each line is a packet being either sent or received through the specified interface. The below example is one complete `tcpdump` line, which is essentially one packet that has passed through the `enp0s8` interface.

```
03:33:05.569739 IP (tos 0x0, ttl 64, id 26591, offset 0, flags [DF],
proto TCP (6), length 60)
    192.168.33.11.37785 > 192.168.33.12.mysql: Flags [S], cksum
0xc396 (incorrect -> 0x3543), seq 3937874058, win 14600, options [mss
1460,sackOK,TS val 53696341 ecr 0,nop,wscale 6], length 0
```

If we take a look at the preceding line, we can see that this packet is being sent from `192.168.33.11` to `192.168.33.12`. We can see this from the following section:

```
192.168.33.11.37785 > 192.168.33.12.mysql: Flags [S]
```

In fact, out of the whole line, the details in the above snippet are everything we need to start understanding the issue. We can identify from the preceding snippet that this particular packet was sent from `192.168.33.11` to `192.168.33.12`. We can identify this by the first and the second IPs in this snippet. Since `192.168.33.11` is the first IP, it is the source of the packet, and the second IP (`192.168.33.12`) is then the destination.

```
192.168.33.11.37785 > 192.168.33.12.mysql
```

We can also see from this snippet that the connection from `192.168.33.11` was from the local port `37785` to a remote port of `3306`. We can infer this as the fifth dot in the source address is `37785` and "`mysql`" is in the target address. The reason that `tcpdump` has printed "`mysql`" is that by default it will map common service ports to their common name. In this case, it mapped port `3306` to `mysql` and simply printed `mysql`. This can be turned off on the command line by using two –n flags (i.e. `-nn`) to the `tcpdump` command.

The third important item that this section tells us is that the packet being sent is a `SYN` packet. We can identify this via the `Flags [S]` section of the snippet. Each line in `tcpdump` output will have a section for `flags`. When the flags set on a packet are only `S`, this means that the packet is the initial `SYN` packet.

The fact that this packet is a `SYN` packet actually tells us quite a bit about the packet.

A quick primer on TCP

Transmission Control Protocol (TCP) is one of the most utilized protocols for Internet-based communications. It is the protocol of choice for many of the services that we rely on every day. From the HTTP protocol for loading web pages to the favorite of all Linux systems administrators, SSH, these protocols are implemented on top of the TCP protocol.

While TCP is highly used, it is also a rather advanced topic, a topic that every systems administrator should have at least a basic understanding of. In this section, we are going to quickly cover some TCP basics; this will by no means be an extensive guide but is just enough to understand the root of our issue.

To understand our issue, we must first understand how TCP connections are established. With TCP communications, there are generally two important parties, namely the client and the server. The client is the initiator of the connection and will send a SYN packet as the first step to establishing a TCP connection.

When the server receives a SYN packet and is willing to accept the connection, it will send a **Synchronize Acknowledgement (SYN-ACK)** packet back to the client. This is designed for the server to acknowledge that it has received the original SYN packet.

When the client receives this SYN-ACK packet, it then replies to the server with an ACK, sometimes referred to as a SYN-ACK-ACK. The idea behind this packet is for the client to acknowledge that it has received the server's acknowledgement.

This process is known as the *Three-Way Handshake* and is the foundation of TCP. The benefit of this method is that, with each system acknowledging the packets that it receives, there is no question as to whether the client and the server are able to communicate back and forth. Once a three-way handshake has been performed, the connection is moved to an established state. This is where other types of packets can be used, such as **Push (PSH)** packets, which are used to transfer information from the client to the server or vice versa.

Types of TCP packet

Speaking of additional types of packets, it is important to know that the component that defines whether a packet is a SYN packet or an ACK packet is simply a flag being set in the packet header.

On the first packet from our captured data, only the SYN flag is set; this is why we will see output such as Flags [S]. This is an example of the first packet being sent and that packet having only the SYN flag set.

An SYN-ACK packet is a packet where the SYN and the ACK flags are set. This is commonly seen as [S.] in tcpdump.

The following is a table of packet flags commonly seen during troubleshooting activities with tcpdump. This is by no means a full list, but it does give a general idea of the common packet types.

- SYN- [S]: This is a Synchronize packet, the first packet sent from the client to the server.

- SYN-ACK- [S.]: This is a Synchronize Acknowledgement packet; these packet flags are used to indicate that the server received the client's SYN requests.

- ACK- [.]: The Acknowledgement packet is used by both the server and the client to acknowledge the received packets. After the initial SYN packet is sent, all subsequent packets should have the acknowledgement flag set.

- PSH- [P]: This is a Push packet. It is designed to push the buffered network data to the receiver. This is the type of packet where data is actually transferred.

- PSH-ACK- [P.]: The Push Acknowledgement packet is used to both acknowledge a previous packet and send data to the recipient.

- FIN- [F]: The FIN or Finish packet is used to tell the server that there is no more data and that it can close the established connection.

- FIN-ACK- [F.]: The Finish Acknowledgement packet is used to acknowledge that the previous Finish packet was received.

- RST- [R]: The Reset packet is used when the source system wishes to Reset the connection. In general, this is due to an error or the target port is not actually in the listening status.

- RST-ACK -[R.]: The Reset Acknowledgement packet is used to acknowledge that the previous Reset packet was received.

Now that we have explored the different types of packets, let's tie it all together and take a quick look back at the data captured earlier.

```
[blog]# tcpdump -nvvv -r /var/tmp/chapter5.pcap host 192.168.33.12
reading from file /var/tmp/chapter5.pcap, link-type EN10MB (Ethernet)
03:33:05.569739 IP (tos 0x0, ttl 64, id 26591, offset 0, flags [DF],
proto TCP (6), length 60)
    192.168.33.11.37785 > 192.168.33.12.mysql: Flags [S], cksum
0xc396 (incorrect -> 0x3543), seq 3937874058, win 14600, options [mss
1460,sackOK,TS val 53696341 ecr 0,nop,wscale 6], length 0
```

```
03:33:06.573145 IP (tos 0x0, ttl 64, id 26592, offset 0, flags [DF],
proto TCP (6), length 60)

    192.168.33.11.37785 > 192.168.33.12.mysql: Flags [S], cksum
0xc396 (incorrect -> 0x3157), seq 3937874058, win 14600, options [mss
1460,sackOK,TS val 53697345 ecr 0,nop,wscale 6], length 0

03:33:08.580122 IP (tos 0x0, ttl 64, id 26593, offset 0, flags [DF],
proto TCP (6), length 60)

    192.168.33.11.37785 > 192.168.33.12.mysql: Flags [S], cksum
0xc396 (incorrect -> 0x2980), seq 3937874058, win 14600, options [mss
1460,sackOK,TS val 53699352 ecr 0,nop,wscale 6], length 0
```

If we look at just the IP addresses and the flags from the captured data, from each line, it becomes very clear what the issue is.

```
192.168.33.11.37785 > 192.168.33.12.mysql: Flags [S],

192.168.33.11.37785 > 192.168.33.12.mysql: Flags [S],

192.168.33.11.37785 > 192.168.33.12.mysql: Flags [S],
```

If we break down these three packets, we can see that all three of them are from the source port of 37785, targeting the destination port of 3306. We can also see that these packets are SYN packets. What this means is that our system sent 3 SYN packets and never received an SYN-ACK from the destination, in this case 192.168.33.12.

What does this tell us about our network connectivity to the host 192.168.33.12? It tells us that either the remote server 192.168.33.12 is never receiving our packets or it is receiving them and we are never able to receive the SYN-ACK replies. If the issue were due to the database server not accepting our packet, we would expect to see an RST or Reset packet.

Reviewing collected data

At this point, it is a good time to take an inventory of what information we have collected and what we know so far.

The first bit of key information that we have identified is that the blog server (blog.example.com) is unable to connect to the database server (db.example.com). The second bit of key information that we have identified is that the DNS name db.example.com resolves to 10.0.0.50. However, there is also an /etc/hosts file entry overriding DNS on the blog.example.com server. Because of the hosts file, when the web application tries to connect to db.example.com, it is connecting to 192.168.33.12.

We have also identified that the host `192.168.33.11` (`blog.example.com`) is sending the initial SYN packets to `192.168.33.12` when the WordPress application is accessed. However, the server `192.168.33.12` is either not receiving or not replying to these packets.

Throughout our investigation, we reviewed the blog server's network configuration and we determined that it appears to be set up correctly. We can perform additional validation of this by simply using the ping command to send an ICMP echo to an IP within each network interface's subnet.

```
[blog]# ip addr show enp0s3
2: enp0s3: <BROADCAST,MULTICAST,UP,LOWER_UP> mtu 1500 qdisc pfifo_fast
state UP qlen 1000
    link/ether 08:00:27:20:5d:4b brd ff:ff:ff:ff:ff:ff
    inet 10.0.2.16/24 brd 10.0.2.255 scope global dynamic enp0s3
       valid_lft 62208sec preferred_lft 62208sec
    inet6 fe80::a00:27ff:fe20:5d4b/64 scope link
       valid_lft forever preferred_lft forever
```

For the enp0s3 interface, we can see that the IP address bound is `10.0.2.16` with a subnet of `/24` or `255.255.255.0`. With this setup, we should be able to communicate with another IP within this subnet. The following is the output of using the ping command to test connectivity to `10.0.2.2`.

```
[blog]# ping 10.0.2.2
PING 10.0.2.2 (10.0.2.2) 56(84) bytes of data.
64 bytes from 10.0.2.2: icmp_seq=1 ttl=63 time=0.250 ms
64 bytes from 10.0.2.2: icmp_seq=2 ttl=63 time=0.196 ms
64 bytes from 10.0.2.2: icmp_seq=3 ttl=63 time=0.197 ms
^C
--- 10.0.2.2 ping statistics ---
3 packets transmitted, 3 received, 0% packet loss, time 2001ms
rtt min/avg/max/mdev = 0.196/0.214/0.250/0.027 ms
```

This shows that the enp0s3 interface can at least connect to other IPs within its subnet. With enp0s8, we can perform the same test with another IP.

```
[blog]# ip addr show enp0s8
3: enp0s8: <BROADCAST,MULTICAST,UP,LOWER_UP> mtu 1500 qdisc pfifo_fast
state UP qlen 1000
    link/ether 08:00:27:7f:fd:54 brd ff:ff:ff:ff:ff:ff
```

```
    inet 192.168.33.11/24 brd 192.168.33.255 scope global enp0s8
       valid_lft forever preferred_lft forever
    inet6 fe80::a00:27ff:fe7f:fd54/64 scope link
       valid_lft forever preferred_lft forever
```

From the preceding command, we can see that `enp0s8` has the IP `192.168.33.11` bound to it with a subnet of `/24` or `255.255.255.0`. If we can use the ping command to communicate with any other IP in the `192.168.33.11/24` subnet, then we can validate that this interface is also configured correctly.

```
# ping 192.168.33.1
PING 192.168.33.1 (192.168.33.1) 56(84) bytes of data.
64 bytes from 192.168.33.1: icmp_seq=1 ttl=64 time=0.287 ms
64 bytes from 192.168.33.1: icmp_seq=2 ttl=64 time=0.249 ms
64 bytes from 192.168.33.1: icmp_seq=3 ttl=64 time=0.260 ms
64 bytes from 192.168.33.1: icmp_seq=4 ttl=64 time=0.192 ms
^C
--- 192.168.33.1 ping statistics ---
4 packets transmitted, 4 received, 0% packet loss, time 3028ms
rtt min/avg/max/mdev = 0.192/0.247/0.287/0.034 ms
```

From the results, we can see that connectivity to the IP `192.168.33.1` is working as expected. Therefore, this means that, in at least a basic manner, the `enp0s8` interface is configured correctly.

With all of this information, we can assume that the `blog.example.com` server is configured correctly and can connect to the networks that it is configured for. From this point forward, if we want any more information about our issue, we will need to obtain it from the `db.example.com` (`192.168.33.12`) server.

Taking a look on the other side

While it may not always be possible, when dealing with networking issues it is always best to troubleshoot from both sides of the conversation. In our earlier examples, we had two systems that make up our network conversation, namely the client and the server. So far we have looked at everything from the client's perspective; in this section, we are going to take a look at the other side of this conversation, from the server's perspective.

Identifying the network configuration

In the previous section, we went through several steps before looking at the blog server's network configuration. In the case of the database server, we already know that the issue is related to networking and specifically the IP of 192.168.33.12. Since we already know which IP the issue is related to, the first thing that we should do is identify which interface this IP is bound to.

One again, we will do this by using the `ip` command with the `addr show` options.

```
[db]# ip addr show
1: lo: <LOOPBACK,UP,LOWER_UP> mtu 65536 qdisc noqueue state UNKNOWN
    link/loopback 00:00:00:00:00:00 brd 00:00:00:00:00:00
    inet 127.0.0.1/8 scope host lo
       valid_lft forever preferred_lft forever
    inet6 ::1/128 scope host
       valid_lft forever preferred_lft forever
2: enp0s3: <BROADCAST,MULTICAST,UP,LOWER_UP> mtu 1500 qdisc pfifo_fast
state UP qlen 1000
    link/ether 08:00:27:20:5d:4b brd ff:ff:ff:ff:ff:ff
    inet 10.0.2.16/24 brd 10.0.2.255 scope global dynamic enp0s3
       valid_lft 86304sec preferred_lft 86304sec
    inet6 fe80::a00:27ff:fe20:5d4b/64 scope link
       valid_lft forever preferred_lft forever
3: enp0s8: <BROADCAST,MULTICAST,UP,LOWER_UP> mtu 1500 qdisc pfifo_fast
state UP qlen 1000
    link/ether 08:00:27:c9:d3:65 brd ff:ff:ff:ff:ff:ff
    inet 192.168.33.12/24 brd 192.168.33.255 scope global enp0s8
       valid_lft forever preferred_lft forever
    inet6 fe80::a00:27ff:fec9:d365/64 scope link
       valid_lft forever preferred_lft forever
```

In the earlier example, we used the `addr show` options to show the IPs associated with a single interface. This time, however, by omitting the interface name, the `ip` command shows all IPs and the interface that these IPs are bound to. This is a quick and simple way to show both the IP addresses and the interfaces associated with this server.

We can see from the preceding command that the database server has a similar configuration to the application server in that it has three interfaces. Before going too far, let's understand the server's interfaces better and see what information we can identify from them.

```
1: lo: <LOOPBACK,UP,LOWER_UP> mtu 65536 qdisc noqueue state UNKNOWN
    link/loopback 00:00:00:00:00:00 brd 00:00:00:00:00:00
    inet 127.0.0.1/8 scope host lo
       valid_lft forever preferred_lft forever
    inet6 ::1/128 scope host
       valid_lft forever preferred_lft forever
```

The first interface on this server is the loopback interface lo. As discussed previously, this interface is common for every server and is only used for the local network traffic. This interface is not likely to be related to our issue.

```
2: enp0s3: <BROADCAST,MULTICAST,UP,LOWER_UP> mtu 1500 qdisc pfifo_fast
state UP qlen 1000
    link/ether 08:00:27:20:5d:4b brd ff:ff:ff:ff:ff:ff
    inet 10.0.2.16/24 brd 10.0.2.255 scope global dynamic enp0s3
       valid_lft 86304sec preferred_lft 86304sec
    inet6 fe80::a00:27ff:fe20:5d4b/64 scope link
       valid_lft forever preferred_lft forever
```

It seems that, for the second interface, enp0s3, the database server's configuration is very similar to the blog server's. On the web application server, we also had an interface named enp0s3 and this interface was also on the 10.0.2.0/24 network.

Since the connectivity between the blog and database servers seems to be targeting the IP of 192.168.33.12, it seems that enp0s3 is not an interface to focus on as the enp0s3 interface has the IP 10.0.2.16 bound to it.

```
3: enp0s8: <BROADCAST,MULTICAST,UP,LOWER_UP> mtu 1500 qdisc pfifo_fast
state UP qlen 1000
    link/ether 08:00:27:c9:d3:65 brd ff:ff:ff:ff:ff:ff
    inet 192.168.33.12/24 brd 192.168.33.255 scope global enp0s8
       valid_lft forever preferred_lft forever
    inet6 fe80::a00:27ff:fec9:d365/64 scope link
       valid_lft forever preferred_lft forever
```

The third network device enp0s8, on the other hand, does have the IP 192.168.33.12 bound to it. The enp0s8 device is also set up similar to the enp0s8 device on the blog server, as it seems that the two devices are both on the 192.168.33.0/24 network.

From the previous troubleshooting, we know that the IP that our web application's targeting is IP 192.168.33.12. With the ip command, we have confirmed that 192.168.33.12 is bound to this server via the enp0s8 interface.

Testing connectivity from db.example.com

Now that we know that the database server has an expected network configuration, we need to establish whether this server is correctly connected to the 192.168.33.0/24 network. The simplest way is to perform a task that we performed earlier on the blog server; using ping to connect to another IP on that subnet.

```
[db]# ping 192.168.33.1
PING 192.168.33.1 (192.168.33.1) 56(84) bytes of data.
64 bytes from 192.168.33.1: icmp_seq=1 ttl=64 time=0.438 ms
64 bytes from 192.168.33.1: icmp_seq=2 ttl=64 time=0.208 ms
64 bytes from 192.168.33.1: icmp_seq=3 ttl=64 time=0.209 ms
^C
--- 192.168.33.1 ping statistics ---
3 packets transmitted, 3 received, 0% packet loss, time 2001ms
rtt min/avg/max/mdev = 0.208/0.285/0.438/0.108 ms
```

With the above output, we can see that the database server is able to contact another IP on the 192.168.33.0/24 subnet. Earlier while troubleshooting, we tried to connect to the database server from the blog server and that test failed. An interesting test would be to validate that the connectivity fails the other way around as well when the database server initiates a connection to the blog server.

```
[db]# ping 192.168.33.11
PING 192.168.33.11 (192.168.33.11) 56(84) bytes of data.
From 10.0.2.16 icmp_seq=1 Destination Host Unreachable
From 10.0.2.16 icmp_seq=2 Destination Host Unreachable
From 10.0.2.16 icmp_seq=3 Destination Host Unreachable
From 10.0.2.16 icmp_seq=4 Destination Host Unreachable
^C
--- 192.168.33.11 ping statistics ---
6 packets transmitted, 0 received, +4 errors, 100% packet loss, time
5005ms
```

When running the `ping` command from the database server to the IP of the blog server (192.168.33.11), we can see that ping has replied with **Destination Host Unreachable**. This TCP is the same error that we saw when attempting connectivity from the blog server as well.

As mentioned earlier, there are a number of reasons other than network connectivity issues that a ping will fail; to ensure that there is a connectivity issue, we should also test connectivity with `telnet`. We know that the blog server is accepting connections to the web server, so a simple `telnet` to the webserver's port should tell us definitively if there is any connectivity from the database server to the web server.

When running `telnet`, we need to specify a port to connect to. We know that the web server is running and, when we navigate to `http://blog.example.com`, we get a web page. On the basis of this information, we can determine that the default HTTP port is used and is listening. With this information, we also know that we can simply use telnet to connect to port 80, the default port for HTTP communication.

```
[db]# telnet 192.168.33.11 80
-bash: telnet: command not found
```

However, on this server, `telnet` is not installed. That's OK because we can use the `curl` command as we did in our previous examples.

```
[db]# curl telnet://192.168.33.11:80 -v
* About to connect() to 192.168.33.11 port 80 (#0)
*   Trying 192.168.33.11...
* No route to host
* Failed connect to 192.168.33.11:80; No route to host
* Closing connection 0
curl: (7) Failed connect to 192.168.33.11:80; No route to host
```

From the `curl` command's output, we can see that the communication issue is present irrespective of whether the blog or the database server initiates the connection.

Looking for connections with netstat

In the previous section, when troubleshooting from the blog server we used `netstat` to view the open TCP connections to the database server. Now that we are logged into the database server, we can use the same command to see the status of the connections from the database server's perspective. To do this, we will run `netstat` with an interval specified; this causes `netstat` to print network connection statistics every 5 s similar to the `vmstat` or `top` commands.

While the `netstat` command is running, we will simply refresh our browser to cause the WordPress application to attempt a database connection again.

```
[db]# netstat -na 5 | grep 192.168.33.11
```

After running `netstat` in what I like to call the `continuous mode`, and using `grep` to filter for the blog server's IP (192.168.33.11), we could not see any TCP connections or connection attempts.

In many cases, this would seem to indicate that the database server is never receiving a TCP packet from the blog server. We can confirm whether this is the case by using the `tcpdump` command to capture all network traffic on the `enp0s8` interface.

Tracing network connections with tcpdump

Earlier when learning about `tcpdump`, we learned that it defaults to the interface with the lowest number. This means that, in order to capture the connection attempts, we must use the `-i` (interface) flag to trace the correct interface, `enp0s8`. In addition to telling `tcpdump` to watch the `enp0s8` interface, we are also going to have `tcpdump` write its output into a file. We will do this so that we can capture as much data as possible and later use the `tcpdump` command to analyze the data as many times as we need to.

```
[db]# tcpdump -i enp0s8 -w /var/tmp/db-capture.pcap
tcpdump: listening on enp0s8, link-type EN10MB (Ethernet), capture size
65535 bytes
```

Now that `tcpdump` is running, we simply need to refresh our browser again.

```
^C110 packets captured
110 packets received by filter
0 packets dropped by kernel
```

After refreshing the browser and seeing the `packets captured` counter increase, we can stop `tcpdump` by pressing *Ctrl + C* on the keyboard.

Once `tcpdump` has stopped, we can read the captured data with the `-r` (read) flag; however, this will print all of the packets that `tcpdump` captured. In some environments, this may be quite a lot of data. So, to trim the output to only the data that is useful, we will use the `port` filter to tell `tcpdump` to only output the captured traffic that is initiated from or targeting port 3306, the default MySQL port.

We can do this by adding `port 3306` to the end of the `tcpdump` command.

```
[db]# tcpdump -nnvvv -r /var/tmp/db-capture.pcap port 3306
reading from file /var/tmp/db-capture.pcap, link-type EN10MB (Ethernet)
03:11:03.697543 IP (tos 0x10, ttl 64, id 43196, offset 0, flags [DF],
proto TCP (6), length 64)
    192.168.33.1.59510 > 192.168.33.12.3306: Flags [S], cksum 0xc125
(correct), seq 2335155468, win 65535, options [mss 1460,nop,wscale
5,nop,nop,TS val 1314733695 ecr 0,sackOK,eol], length 0
03:11:03.697576 IP (tos 0x0, ttl 64, id 0, offset 0, flags [DF], proto
TCP (6), length 60)
    192.168.33.12.3306 > 192.168.33.1.59510: Flags [S.], cksum 0xc38c
(incorrect -> 0x5d87), seq 2658328059, ack 2335155469, win 14480, options
[mss 1460,sackOK,TS val 1884022 ecr 1314733695,nop,wscale 6], length 0
03:11:03.697712 IP (tos 0x10, ttl 64, id 61120, offset 0, flags [DF],
proto TCP (6), length 52)
    192.168.33.1.59510 > 192.168.33.12.3306: Flags [.], cksum 0xb4cd
(correct), seq 1, ack 1, win 4117, options [nop,nop,TS val 1314733695 ecr
1884022], length 0
03:11:03.712018 IP (tos 0x8, ttl 64, id 25226, offset 0, flags [DF],
proto TCP (6), length 127)
```

While using the preceding filter, however, it seems that this database server is used by more than just the WordPress application. From the `tcpdump` output, we can see more traffic on port `3306` than just the blog server.

To clean up this output further, we can add the host filter to the `tcpdump` command to filter out only the traffic that we are interested in: traffic from the host `192.168.33.11`.

```
[db]# tcpdump -nnvvv -r /var/tmp/db-capture.pcap port 3306 and host
192.168.33.11
reading from file /var/tmp/db-capture.pcap, link-type EN10MB (Ethernet)
04:04:09.167121 IP (tos 0x0, ttl 64, id 60173, offset 0, flags [DF],
proto TCP (6), length 60)
    192.168.33.11.51149 > 192.168.33.12.3306: Flags [S], cksum 0x4111
(correct), seq 558685560, win 14600, options [mss 1460,sackOK,TS val
9320053 ecr 0,nop,wscale 6], length 0
04:04:10.171104 IP (tos 0x0, ttl 64, id 60174, offset 0, flags [DF],
proto TCP (6), length 60)
    192.168.33.11.51149 > 192.168.33.12.3306: Flags [S], cksum 0x3d26
(correct), seq 558685560, win 14600, options [mss 1460,sackOK,TS val
9321056 ecr 0,nop,wscale 6], length 0
```

```
04:04:12.175107 IP (tos 0x0, ttl 64, id 60175, offset 0, flags [DF],
proto TCP (6), length 60)
    192.168.33.11.51149 > 192.168.33.12.3306: Flags [S], cksum 0x3552
(correct), seq 558685560, win 14600, options [mss 1460,sackOK,TS val
9323060 ecr 0,nop,wscale 6], length 0
04:04:16.187731 IP (tos 0x0, ttl 64, id 60176, offset 0, flags [DF],
proto TCP (6), length 60)
    192.168.33.11.51149 > 192.168.33.12.3306: Flags [S], cksum 0x25a5
(correct), seq 558685560, win 14600, options [mss 1460,sackOK,TS val
9327073 ecr 0,nop,wscale 6], length 0
```

Here, we used the "and" operator to tell `tcpdump` to only print traffic that is to/from port `3306` and to/from host `192.168.33.11`.

The `tcpdump` command has many possible filters and operators; however, out of all of them, I would recommend becoming familiar with filtering based on port and host as these will suffice for most occasions.

If we break down the preceding captured network trace, we can see some interesting information; to make it a bit easier to spot, let's trim the output down to show just the IPs and flags being used.

```
04:04:09.167121 IP
    192.168.33.11.51149 > 192.168.33.12.3306: Flags [S],
04:04:10.171104 IP
    192.168.33.11.51149 > 192.168.33.12.3306: Flags [S],
04:04:12.175107 IP
    192.168.33.11.51149 > 192.168.33.12.3306: Flags [S],
04:04:16.187731 IP
    192.168.33.11.51149 > 192.168.33.12.3306: Flags [S],
```

From this information, we can see the SYN packets being sent from `blog.example.com` (`192.168.33.11`) and arriving on `db.example.com` (`192.168.33.12`). What we don't see, however, are the returned SYN-ACKS.

This tells us that we have at least found the source of the networking issue; the server `db.example.com` is not correctly replying to packets received from the blog server.

Now the question is: What can cause this type of problem? There are many reasons for this issue to occur; in general, however, such an issue is due to a misconfiguration in the network configuration settings. Given the information that we have gathered, we can hypothesize that the database server is simply misconfigured.

There are, however, several ways to cause this type of problem with misconfigurations. In order to identify the possible misconfigurations, we can use the tcpdump command to capture all the network traffic on this server.

In the previous examples of tcpdump, we always specified a single interface to watch. In most cases, this is appropriate for the issue as it reduces the volume of data being captured by tcpdump. On very active servers, a few minutes of tcpdump data can be very large, so it is always best to reduce the data to only what is required.

In some occasions, however, such as this issue, it is useful to tell tcpdump to capture the network traffic from all interfaces. To do this, we simply specify any as the interface to watch.

```
[db]# tcpdump -i any -w /var/tmp/alltraffic.pcap
tcpdump: listening on any, link-type LINUX_SLL (Linux cooked), capture
size 65535 bytes
```

Now that we have tcpdump capturing and saving all traffic on all interfaces, we will need to refresh our browser again to force the WordPress application to attempt database connections.

```
^C440 packets captured
443 packets received by filter
0 packets dropped by kernel
```

After a few tries, we can stop the tcpdump again by pressing *Ctrl + C*. With the captured network data saved to a file, we can start to investigate what is happening with these connection attempts.

Since the tcpdump captured a large number of packets, we will once again use the host filter to limit results to the network traffic to and from 192.168.33.11.

```
[db]# tcpdump -nnvvv -r /var/tmp/alltraffic.pcap host 192.168.33.11
reading from file /var/tmp/alltraffic.pcap, link-type LINUX_SLL (Linux
cooked)
15:37:51.616621 IP (tos 0x0, ttl 64, id 8389, offset 0, flags [DF], proto
TCP (6), length 60)
    192.168.33.11.47339 > 192.168.33.12.3306: Flags [S], cksum 0x34dd
(correct), seq 4225047048, win 14600, options [mss 1460,sackOK,TS val
3357389 ecr 0,nop,wscale 6], length 0
15:37:51.616665 IP (tos 0x0, ttl 64, id 0, offset 0, flags [DF], proto
TCP (6), length 60)
    192.168.33.12.3306 > 192.168.33.11.47339: Flags [S.], cksum 0xc396
(incorrect -> 0x3609), seq 1637731271, ack 4225047049, win 14480, options
[mss 1460,sackOK,TS val 3330467 ecr 3357389,nop,wscale 6], length 0
```

```
15:37:51.616891 IP (tos 0x0, ttl 255, id 2947, offset 0, flags [none],
proto TCP (6), length 40)
    192.168.33.11.47339 > 192.168.33.12.3306: Flags [R], cksum 0x10c4
(correct), seq 4225047049, win 0, length 0
15:37:52.619386 IP (tos 0x0, ttl 64, id 8390, offset 0, flags [DF], proto
TCP (6), length 60)
    192.168.33.11.47339 > 192.168.33.12.3306: Flags [S], cksum 0x30f2
(correct), seq 4225047048, win 14600, options [mss 1460,sackOK,TS val
3358392 ecr 0,nop,wscale 6], length 0
15:37:52.619428 IP (tos 0x0, ttl 64, id 0, offset 0, flags [DF], proto
TCP (6), length 60)
    192.168.33.12.3306 > 192.168.33.11.47339: Flags [S.], cksum 0xc396
(incorrect -> 0x1987), seq 1653399428, ack 4225047049, win 14480, options
[mss 1460,sackOK,TS val 3331470 ecr 3358392,nop,wscale 6], length 0
15:37:52.619600 IP (tos 0x0, ttl 255, id 2948, offset 0, flags [none],
proto TCP (6), length 40)
    192.168.33.11.47339 > 192.168.33.12.3306: Flags [R], cksum 0x10c4
(correct), seq 4225047049, win 0, length 0
```

With the captured data, it seems that we have found the expected SYN-ACK. To show
this in a clearer fashion, let's trim the output to just the IPs and flags in use.

```
15:37:51.616621 IP
    192.168.33.11.47339 > 192.168.33.12.3306: Flags [S],
15:37:51.616665 IP
    192.168.33.12.3306 > 192.168.33.11.47339: Flags [S.],
15:37:51.616891 IP
    192.168.33.11.47339 > 192.168.33.12.3306: Flags [R],
15:37:52.619386 IP
    192.168.33.11.47339 > 192.168.33.12.3306: Flags [S],
15:37:52.619428 IP
    192.168.33.12.3306 > 192.168.33.11.47339: Flags [S.],
15:37:52.619600 IP
    192.168.33.11.47339 > 192.168.33.12.3306: Flags [R],
```

With a clearer picture, we can see an interesting series of network packets
being transmitted.

```
15:37:51.616621 IP
    192.168.33.11.47339 > 192.168.33.12.3306: Flags [S],
```

The first packet is an SYN packet from 192.168.33.11 to 192.168.33.12 on port 3306. This is the same type of packet that we have captured with the earlier tcpdump executions.

```
15:37:51.616665 IP
    192.168.33.12.3306 > 192.168.33.11.47339: Flags [S.],
```

However, we have not seen the second packet before. In the second packet, we see that it is an SYN-ACK (identified by Flags [S.]). The SYN-ACK is being sent from 192.168.33.12 on port 3306 to 192.168.33.11 on port 47339 (the port that sent the original SYN packet).

At the first glance, this seems to be a normal SYN and SYN-ACK handshake.

```
15:37:51.616891 IP
    192.168.33.11.47339 > 192.168.33.12.3306: Flags [R],
```

The third packet, however, is interesting as it is a clear indication of an issue. The third packet is a RESET packet (identified by Flags [R]) sent from 192.168.33.11, the blog server. The interesting thing about this is that, when executing tcpdump on the blog server, we never captured a RESET packet. If we execute tcpdump again on the blog server, we can see this one more time.

```
[blog]# tcpdump -i any port 3306

tcpdump: verbose output suppressed, use -v or -vv for full protocol
decode

listening on any, link-type LINUX_SLL (Linux cooked), capture size 65535
bytes

15:24:25.646731 IP blog.example.com.47336 > db.example.com.mysql: Flags
[S], seq 3286710391, win 14600, options [mss 1460,sackOK,TS val 2551514
ecr 0,nop,wscale 6], length 0

15:24:26.648706 IP blog.example.com.47336 > db.example.com.mysql: Flags
[S], seq 3286710391, win 14600, options [mss 1460,sackOK,TS val 2552516
ecr 0,nop,wscale 6], length 0

15:24:28.652763 IP blog.example.com.47336 > db.example.com.mysql: Flags
[S], seq 3286710391, win 14600, options [mss 1460,sackOK,TS val 2554520
ecr 0,nop,wscale 6], length 0

15:24:32.660123 IP blog.example.com.47336 > db.example.com.mysql: Flags
[S], seq 3286710391, win 14600, options [mss 1460,sackOK,TS val 2558528
ecr 0,nop,wscale 6], length 0

15:24:40.676112 IP blog.example.com.47336 > db.example.com.mysql: Flags
[S], seq 3286710391, win 14600, options [mss 1460,sackOK,TS val 2566544
ecr 0,nop,wscale 6], length 0

15:24:56.724102 IP blog.example.com.47336 > db.example.com.mysql: Flags
[S], seq 3286710391, win 14600, options [mss 1460,sackOK,TS val 2582592
ecr 0,nop,wscale 6], length 0
```

From the preceding tcpdump output, we never see either the SYN-ACK or the RESET packets on the blog server. This either means that the RESET is being sent by another system or the SYN-ACK packet is being rejected by the blog server's kernel before tcpdump can capture it.

When the tcpdump command captures network traffic, it does so after the kernel has processed this network traffic. This means that if, for any reason, the kernel is rejecting the packet, it will not be seen via the tcpdump command. Thus, it is possible that the blog server's kernel is rejecting the return packets from the database server before tcpdump is able to capture them.

An additional interesting point revealed by performing a tcpdump on the database is that, if we look at the tcpdump performed on enp0s8, we do not see the SYN-ACK packet. However, if we tell tcpdump to look at all the interfaces we use, tcpdump also shows the SYN-ACK packet to be coming from 192.168.33.12. This suggests that the SYN-ACK is being sent from another interface.

To confirm this, we can run a tcpdump again, limiting the capture to packets that traverse the enp0s8 interface.

```
[db]# tcpdump -nnvvv -i enp0s8 port 3306 and host 192.168.33.11
04:04:09.167121 IP (tos 0x0, ttl 64, id 60173, offset 0, flags [DF],
proto TCP (6), length 60)
    192.168.33.11.51149 > 192.168.33.12.3306: Flags [S], cksum 0x4111
(correct), seq 558685560, win 14600, options [mss 1460,sackOK,TS val
9320053 ecr 0,nop,wscale 6], length 0
04:04:10.171104 IP (tos 0x0, ttl 64, id 60174, offset 0, flags [DF],
proto TCP (6), length 60)
    192.168.33.11.51149 > 192.168.33.12.3306: Flags [S], cksum 0x3d26
(correct), seq 558685560, win 14600, options [mss 1460,sackOK,TS val
9321056 ecr 0,nop,wscale 6], length 0
```

From this execution of tcpdump, we can yet again only see the SYN packets from the blog server. However, if we run the same tcpdump against all interfaces, we should see not only the SYN packets but also the SYN-ACK packets.

```
[db]# tcpdump -nnvvv -i any port 3306 and host 192.168.33.11
15:37:51.616621 IP (tos 0x0, ttl 64, id 8389, offset 0, flags [DF], proto
TCP (6), length 60)
    192.168.33.11.47339 > 192.168.33.12.3306: Flags [S], cksum 0x34dd
(correct), seq 4225047048, win 14600, options [mss 1460,sackOK,TS val
3357389 ecr 0,nop,wscale 6], length 0
15:37:51.616665 IP (tos 0x0, ttl 64, id 0, offset 0, flags [DF], proto
TCP (6), length 60)
```

```
    192.168.33.12.3306 > 192.168.33.11.47339: Flags [S.], cksum 0xc396
(incorrect -> 0x3609), seq 1637731271, ack 4225047049, win 14480, options
[mss 1460,sackOK,TS val 3330467 ecr 3357389,nop,wscale 6], length 0
```

The SYN-ACK packet being returned to 192.168.33.11 is sourced from
192.168.33.12. Earlier, we identified that this IP is bound to the network device
enp0s8. However, when we use tcpdump to look at all of the packets being sent, the
SYN-ACK is not captured going out of enp0s8. This means that the SYN-ACK packet is
being sent from a different interface.

Routing

How does an SYN packet arrive on one interface and an SYN-ACK get returned from
another? One possible answer is that this is due to a misconfiguration in the routing
definitions on the database server.

Every operating system that supports networking maintains something called a
routing table. This routing table is a collection of defined network routes that a
packet should take. To give a bit of context around this concept, let's use the two
interfaces enp0s3 and enp0s8 as examples.

```
# ip addr show enp0s8

3: enp0s8: <BROADCAST,MULTICAST,UP,LOWER_UP> mtu 1500 qdisc pfifo_fast
state UP qlen 1000
    link/ether 08:00:27:c9:d3:65 brd ff:ff:ff:ff:ff:ff
    inet 192.168.33.12/24 brd 192.168.33.255 scope global enp0s8
        valid_lft forever preferred_lft forever
    inet6 fe80::a00:27ff:fec9:d365/64 scope link
        valid_lft forever preferred_lft forever
# ip addr show enp0s3

2: enp0s3: <BROADCAST,MULTICAST,UP,LOWER_UP> mtu 1500 qdisc pfifo_fast
state UP qlen 1000
    link/ether 08:00:27:20:5d:4b brd ff:ff:ff:ff:ff:ff
    inet 10.0.2.16/24 brd 10.0.2.255 scope global dynamic enp0s3
        valid_lft 65115sec preferred_lft 65115sec
    inet6 fe80::a00:27ff:fe20:5d4b/64 scope link
        valid_lft forever preferred_lft forever
```

If we look at these two interfaces, we know that the enp0s8 interface is connected to
the 192.168.33.0/24 (inet 192.168.33.12/24) network and the enp0s3 interface
is connected to the 10.0.2.0/24 (inet 10.0.2.16/24) network.

If we were to connect to the IP 10.0.2.19, the packets should not go out of the enp0s8 interface, as the optimal route for these packets would be to route through the enp0s3 interface. The reason that this is the most optimal route is that the enp0s3 interface is already part of the 10.0.2.0/24 network, which contains the IP 10.0.2.19.

The enp0s8 interface is part of a different network (192.168.33.0/24) and therefore, is the less optimal route. In fact, the enp0s8 interface may not even be able to route to the 10.0.2.0/24 network.

Even though enp0s8 may be a less optimal route, the kernel does not know this without a corresponding entry in the routing table. To dig deeper into our issue, we will need to view the routing table on this database server.

Viewing the routing table

In Linux, there are a few ways to see the current routing table; in this section, I am going to cover two. The first method will utilize the netstat command.

To use the netstat command to view the routing table, simply run it with the -r (route) or --route flag. In the following example, we will also use the -n flag to prevent netstat from performing DNS lookups.

```
[db]# netstat -rn
Kernel IP routing table
```

Destination irtt Iface	Gateway	Genmask	Flags	MSS Window
0.0.0.0 0 enp0s3	10.0.2.2	0.0.0.0	UG	0 0
10.0.2.0 0 enp0s3	0.0.0.0	255.255.255.0	U	0 0
169.254.0.0 0 enp0s8	0.0.0.0	255.255.0.0	U	0 0
192.168.33.0 0 enp0s8	0.0.0.0	255.255.255.0	U	0 0
192.168.33.11 0 enp0s3	10.0.2.1	255.255.255.255	UGH	0 0

While netstat might not be the best Linux command to print the routing table, there is a very specific reason for using it in this example. As I mentioned earlier in this chapter and book, the netstat command is a universal tool that exists on almost every modern server, router, or desktop. By knowing how to look at the routing table with netstat, you can perform basic network troubleshooting on any operating system that has netstat installed.

In general, it is a safe bet that the netstat command would be available and can provide you with at least the basic details of the system's networking status and configurations.

The format of netstat can be a bit cryptic compared with the other utilities such as the ip command. However, the preceding routing table shows us quite a bit of information. To get a better understanding, let's break down the output route by route.

```
Destination      Gateway         Genmask         Flags   MSS Window
irtt Iface
0.0.0.0          10.0.2.2        0.0.0.0         UG        0 0
0 enp0s3
```

As you can see, the output of the netstat command has multiple columns, eight to be precise. The first column is the Destination column. This is used to define what destination address is in scope for the route. In the preceding example, the destination is 0.0.0.0, which is essentially a wildcard value meaning that any and everything should be routed via this table entry.

The second column is Gateway. The gateway address is the next hop that the network packets utilizing this route should be sent to. For this example, the next hop or gateway address is set to 10.0.2.2; this means that any packets being routed via this table entry will be sent to 10.0.2.2, which should then route the packets to the next system until they reach their destination.

The third column is Genmask, which is essentially a way of stating the "generality" of the route. Another way of thinking about this column is as a netmask; in the preceding example, the "genmask" is set to 0.0.0.0, which is an open scope. This means that packets to anywhere should be routed out of this routing table entry.

The fourth column is the Flag column, which is used to provide specific information about this route. The U value in the example means that the interface to use for this route is in an up state. The G value is used to show that the route utilizes a gateway address. In the preceding example, we can see that our route utilizes a gateway address; however, not all of this system's routes do.

The fifth, sixth, and seventh columns are not frequently used on Linux servers. The MSS column is used to show the **maximum segment size** specified for this route. The value of 0 means that this value is set to the default and not altered.

The Window column is the TCP window size, which denotes the maximum amount of data that will be accepted in a single burst. Again, when the value is set to 0, the default size will be used.

The seventh column is `irtt`, which is used to specify the **Initial Round-trip Time** for this route. The kernel will resend packets that are never responded to by setting an initial round-trip time; you can increase or decrease the time after which the kernel considers packets lost. As in the case of the previous two columns, the value of 0 means that the default value will be used for packets using this route.

The eighth and the last column, the `IFace` column, is the network interface that the packets utilizing this route should use. In the preceding example, this is the `enp0s3` interface.

The default route

The first route in our example is actually a very special route for our system.

Destination	Gateway	Genmask	Flags	MSS Window
irtt Iface				
0.0.0.0	10.0.2.2	0.0.0.0	UG	0 0
0 enp0s3				

If we look at the details of this route and the definition of each column, we can determine that this route is the default route for the server. The default route is a special route that is used "by default" when no other route supersedes it. To put it simply, if we have packets that are to be sent to an address such as `172.0.0.10`, these packets would go through the default route.

The reason for this is that there is no other route in our database server's routing table that specifies the IP `172.0.0.10`. As such, the system simply sends packets to this IP through the default route, a catchall route.

We can identify that the first route is the server's default route because of the destination address of `0.0.0.0`, which essentially means anything. The second indication is the `Genmask` of `0.0.0.0`, which together with the destination means any IPv4 address.

It is also typical of the default route to use a gateway address, so the fact that the gateway is set with wildcards for `destination` and `genmask` is a clear indication that the abovementioned route is the default route.

A non-default route will commonly look like the following:

10.0.2.0	0.0.0.0	255.255.255.0	U	0 0
0 enp0s3				

The abovementioned route has a destination of 10.0.2.0 and a `genmask` of 255.255.255.0; this is essentially saying that anything in the 10.0.2.0/24 network would match this route.

Since the range of this route is `10.0.2.0/24`, it is likely that this route was added by the `enp0s3` interface configuration. We can determine this on the basis of the `enp0s3` interface configuration, as it is attached to the `10.0.2.0/24` network, which is the target of this route. By default, Linux will automatically add routes on the basis of the network interface's configuration.

```
10.0.2.0          0.0.0.0         255.255.255.0   U         0 0
0 enp0s3
```

This route is a way for the kernel to ensure that communication for the `10.0.2.0/24` network goes out of the `enp0s3` interface, as this route will supersede the default route. With network routing, the most specific route will always be used. Since the default route is a wildcard and this route is specific to the `10.0.2.0/24` network, this route will be used for anything within the network.

Utilizing IP to show the routing table

Another tool for reviewing the routing table is the `ip` command. The `ip` command, as we can see from its use within this chapter, is a very extensive utility and can be used for practically everything network-related on a modern Linux system.

One use for the `ip` command is to add, remove, or show network routing configurations. To display the current routing table, simply execute the `ip` command with the `route show` options.

```
[db]# ip route show
default via 10.0.2.2 dev enp0s3  proto static  metric 1024
10.0.2.0/24 dev enp0s3  proto kernel  scope link  src 10.0.2.16
169.254.0.0/16 dev enp0s8  scope link  metric 1003
192.168.33.0/24 dev enp0s8  proto kernel  scope link  src 192.168.33.12
192.168.33.11 via 10.0.2.1 dev enp0s3  proto static  metric 1
```

While learning to use the `netstat` command is important for non-Linux operating systems, the `ip` command is an essential tool for any Linux network troubleshooting or configuration.

As we use the `ip` command for troubleshooting routes, we may even find it easier than the `netstat` command. One example is finding the default route. When the `ip` command displays the default route, it uses the word default as the destination rather than 0.0.0.0, a method that is much easier to understand especially for newer system administrators.

It is also easier to read other routes as well. For instance, earlier while looking at routes via `netstat`, our example route looked like the following:

```
10.0.2.0          0.0.0.0          255.255.255.0    U          0 0
0 enp0s3
```

With the `ip` command, the same route is shown in the following format:

```
10.0.2.0/24 dev enp0s3  proto kernel  scope link  src 10.0.2.16
```

In my opinion, the format of `ip` route show is a much simpler format than the format of the `netstat -rn` command.

Looking for routing misconfigurations

Now that we know how to look at the routing table on the server, we can use the `ip` command to find any routes that may cause issues with our database connectivity.

```
[db]# ip route show
default via 10.0.2.2 dev enp0s3  proto static  metric 1024
10.0.2.0/24 dev enp0s3  proto kernel  scope link  src 10.0.2.16
169.254.0.0/16 dev enp0s8  scope link  metric 1003
192.168.33.0/24 dev enp0s8  proto kernel  scope link  src 192.168.33.12
192.168.33.11 via 10.0.2.1 dev enp0s3  proto static  metric 1
```

Here, we can see five routes defined on our system. Let's break down these routes to get a better understanding of them.

```
default via 10.0.2.2 dev enp0s3  proto static  metric 1024
10.0.2.0/24 dev enp0s3  proto kernel  scope link  src 10.0.2.16
```

The first two routes we have already covered and will not review again.

```
169.254.0.0/16 dev enp0s8  scope link  metric 1003
```

The third route defines that all traffic from `169.254.0.0/16` (`169.254.0.0` to `169.254.255.255`) is sent via the `enp0s8` device. This route is a very broad route but most likely does not impact our routing to the IP `192.168.33.11`.

```
192.168.33.0/24 dev enp0s8  proto kernel  scope link  src 192.168.33.12
192.168.33.11 via 10.0.2.1 dev enp0s3  proto static  metric 1
```

The fourth and fifth route, however, will change how network packets to 192.168.33.11 are routed.

```
192.168.33.0/24 dev enp0s8  proto kernel  scope link  src 192.168.33.12
```

The fourth route defines that all the traffic to the `192.168.33.0/24` (`192.168.33.0` to `192.168.33.255`) network is routed out of the enp0s8 interface and sourced from `192.168.33.12`. This route appears to also be added automatically by the enp0s8 interface's configuration; this is similar to the earlier route added by enp0s3.

Since the enp0s8 device is defined to be a part of the `192.168.33.0/24` network, it only makes sense to route traffic for this network out of this interface.

```
192.168.33.11 via 10.0.2.1 dev enp0s3  proto static  metric 1
```

The fifth route, however, defines that all traffic to the specific IP `192.168.33.11` (the blog server's IP) is sent to the gateway of `10.0.2.1` via the enp0s3 device. This is interesting because the fifth route and the fourth route have a very conflicting configuration, as they both define what to do with IPs in the `192.168.33.0/24` network.

More specific routes win

As mentioned earlier, the *golden rule* of routing network packets is that the more specific route always wins. If we look at the routing configuration, we have one route that says all traffic in the `192.168.33.0/24` subnet should go out the enp0s8 device. There is also a second route that says specifically `192.168.33.11` should go out through the enp0s3 device. The IP `192.168.33.11` applies to both of these rules but which route should the system send packets through?

The answer is always the more specific route.

Since the second route specifically defines that all traffic to `192.168.33.11` goes out of the enp0s3 interface, the kernel will route all return packets through the enp0s3 interface. This is the case irrespective of the route defined for `192.168.33.0/24` or even the default route.

We can see all of this in action by using the `ip` command with the `route get` options.

```
[db]# ip route get 192.168.33.11
192.168.33.11 via 10.0.2.1 dev enp0s3  src 10.0.2.16
    cache
```

The `ip` command with the `route get` options will take the IP provided and output which route the packets will take.

When we use this command with `192.168.33.11`, we can see that `ip` specifically shows that the route will be through the `enp0s3` device. If we use the same command with the other IPs, we can see how the default route and the `192.168.33.0/24` routes are used.

```
[db]# ip route get 192.168.33.15
192.168.33.15 dev enp0s8  src 192.168.33.12
    cache
[db]# ip route get 4.4.4.4
4.4.4.4 via 10.0.2.2 dev enp0s3  src 10.0.2.16
    cache
[db]# ip route get 192.168.33.200
192.168.33.200 dev enp0s8  src 192.168.33.12
    cache
[db]# ip route get 169.254.3.5
169.254.3.5 dev enp0s8  src 192.168.33.12
    cache
```

We can see here that when an IP address that is within a subnet with a specific route defined is provided, this specific route is taken. However, when an IP is not defined by a specific route, the default route is taken.

Hypothesis

Now that we understand how packets to `192.168.33.11` are routed, we should adjust our previous hypothesis to reflect that the route of `192.168.33.11` to `enp0s3` is not correct and is causing our issue.

Essentially, what is happening (and we see this via `tcpdump`) is that, when the database server (`192.168.33.12`) receives a network packet from the blog server (`192.168.33.11`), it arrives on the `enp0s8` device. However, when the database server is sending reply packets (`SYN-ACK`) to the web application server, the packets are being sent out via the `enp0s3` interface.

Since the `enp0s3` device is connected to the `10.0.2.0/24` network, it seems that the packet is being rejected (`RESET`) by another system or device on the `10.0.2.0/24` network. Most likely, this is due to the fact that this is a prime example of asynchronous routing.

Asynchronous routing is where a packet arrives on one interface but is replied to on another. In most network configurations, this is denied by default, but in some cases, can be enabled; however, these cases are not extremely common.

In our case, since the enp0s8 interface is part of the 192.168.33.0/24 subnet, it does not make sense to enable asynchronous routing. Our packets to 192.168.33.11 should simply be routed via the enp0s8 interface.

Trial and error

Now that we have identified our issue with data collection and established a possible cause with our hypothesis, we can start our next troubleshooting step: using trial and error to correct the issue.

Removing the invalid route

To correct our issue, we need to remove the invalid route for 192.168.33.11. To do this, we will yet again use the ip command, this time with the route del options.

```
[db]# ip route del 192.168.33.11
[db]# ip route show
default via 10.0.2.2 dev enp0s3  proto static  metric 1024
10.0.2.0/24 dev enp0s3  proto kernel  scope link  src 10.0.2.16
169.254.0.0/16 dev enp0s8  scope link  metric 1003
192.168.33.0/24 dev enp0s8  proto kernel  scope link  src 192.168.33.12
```

In the preceding example, we used the ip command with the route del options to remove a route that targets a single IP. We can use the same command and options to remove routes that are defined for subnets. The following example will remove the route for the 169.254.0.0/16 network:

```
[db]# ip route del 169.254.0.0/16
[db]# ip route show
default via 10.0.2.2 dev enp0s3  proto static  metric 1024
10.0.2.0/24 dev enp0s3  proto kernel  scope link  src 10.0.2.16
192.168.33.0/24 dev enp0s8  proto kernel  scope link  src 192.168.33.12
```

From the `ip` route show execution, we can see that there is no longer a conflicting route for `192.168.33.11`. The question is: Did this fix our issue? The only way to know for sure is to test it and to do this we can simply refresh our browser that has the blog's error page loaded.

It seems that we were successful at correcting the issue. If we perform a `tcpdump` now, we can validate that the blog and database servers are able to communicate.

```
[db]# tcpdump -nnvvv -i enp0s8 port 3306
tcpdump: listening on enp0s8, link-type EN10MB (Ethernet), capture size
65535 bytes
16:14:05.958507 IP (tos 0x0, ttl 64, id 7605, offset 0, flags [DF], proto
TCP (6), length 60)
    192.168.33.11.47350 > 192.168.33.12.3306: Flags [S], cksum 0xa9a7
(correct), seq 4211276877, win 14600, options [mss 1460,sackOK,TS val
46129656 ecr 0,nop,wscale 6], length 0
16:14:05.958603 IP (tos 0x0, ttl 64, id 0, offset 0, flags [DF], proto
TCP (6), length 60)
    192.168.33.12.3306 > 192.168.33.11.47350: Flags [S.], cksum 0xc396
(incorrect -> 0x786b), seq 2378639726, ack 4211276878, win 14480, options
[mss 1460,sackOK,TS val 46102446 ecr 46129656,nop,wscale 6], length 0
```

```
16:14:05.959103 IP (tos 0x0, ttl 64, id 7606, offset 0, flags [DF], proto
TCP (6), length 52)

    192.168.33.11.47350 > 192.168.33.12.3306: Flags [.], cksum 0xdee0
(correct), seq 1, ack 1, win 229, options [nop,nop,TS val 46129657 ecr
46102446], length 0

16:14:05.959336 IP (tos 0x8, ttl 64, id 24256, offset 0, flags [DF],
proto TCP (6), length 138)

    192.168.33.12.3306 > 192.168.33.11.47350: Flags [P.], cksum 0xc3e4
(incorrect -> 0x99c9), seq 1:87, ack 1, win 227, options [nop,nop,TS val
46102447 ecr 46129657], length 86

16:14:05.959663 IP (tos 0x0, ttl 64, id 7607, offset 0, flags [DF], proto
TCP (6), length 52)
```

The preceding output is what we would expect to see from a healthy connection.

Here, we see four packets, the first is an SYN (Flags [S],) from blog.example.com
(192.168.33.11), followed by an SYN-ACK (Flags [S.],) from db.example.com
(192.168.33.12) and an ACK (or SYN-ACK-ACK) (Flags [.],) from blog.example.
com (192.168.33.12). These three packets are the completed TCP three-way
handshake. The fourth packet is a PUSH (Flags [P.],) packet, which is the actual
transfer of data. All of these are signs of a good working network connection.

Configuration files

Now that we have removed the invalid route from the routing table, we can see the
blog is working; this means we have finished, right? No, not yet at least.

When we removed the route by using the ip command, we removed the route from
the active routing table, but we did not remove the route from the system as a whole.
If we were to restart networking, or simply reboot the server, this invalid route
would reappear.

```
[db]# service network restart
Restarting network (via systemctl):                    [  OK  ]
[db]# ip route show
default via 10.0.2.2 dev enp0s3  proto static  metric 1024
10.0.2.0/24 dev enp0s3  proto kernel  scope link  src 10.0.2.16
169.254.0.0/16 dev enp0s8  scope link  metric 1003
192.168.33.0/24 dev enp0s8  proto kernel  scope link  src 192.168.33.12
192.168.33.11 via 10.0.2.1 dev enp0s3  proto static  metric 1
```

This is because, when the system boots, it configures the network on the basis of the configurations within a set of files. The `ip` command is used to manipulate the live network configuration, but not these network configuration files. So, any change made with the `ip` command is not made permanently, but is only temporarily until the next time the system reads and applies the network configuration.

In order to fully remove this route from the network configuration, we will need to modify the networking configuration files.

```
[db]# cd /etc/sysconfig/network-scripts/
```

On Red Hat Enterprise Linux-based systems, the networking configuration files are mostly stored within the `/etc/sysconfig/network-scripts` folder. To get started, we can first switch to this folder and execute ls –la to identify the current network configuration files.

```
[db]# ls -la
total 228
drwxr-xr-x. 2 root root  4096 Mar 14 14:37 .
drwxr-xr-x. 6 root root  4096 Mar 14 23:42 ..
-rw-r--r--. 1 root root   195 Jul 22  2014 ifcfg-enp0s3
-rw-r--r--. 1 root root   217 Mar 14 14:37 ifcfg-enp0s8
-rw-r--r--. 1 root root   254 Apr  2  2014 ifcfg-lo
lrwxrwxrwx. 1 root root    24 Jul 22  2014 ifdown -> ../../../usr/sbin/
ifdown
-rwxr-xr-x. 1 root root   627 Apr  2  2014 ifdown-bnep
-rwxr-xr-x. 1 root root  5553 Apr  2  2014 ifdown-eth
-rwxr-xr-x. 1 root root   781 Apr  2  2014 ifdown-ippp
-rwxr-xr-x. 1 root root  4141 Apr  2  2014 ifdown-ipv6
lrwxrwxrwx. 1 root root    11 Jul 22  2014 ifdown-isdn -> ifdown-ippp
-rwxr-xr-x. 1 root root  1642 Apr  2  2014 ifdown-post
-rwxr-xr-x. 1 root root  1068 Apr  2  2014 ifdown-ppp
-rwxr-xr-x. 1 root root   837 Apr  2  2014 ifdown-routes
-rwxr-xr-x. 1 root root  1444 Apr  2  2014 ifdown-sit
-rwxr-xr-x. 1 root root  1468 Jun  9  2014 ifdown-Team
-rwxr-xr-x. 1 root root  1532 Jun  9  2014 ifdown-TeamPort
-rwxr-xr-x. 1 root root  1462 Apr  2  2014 ifdown-tunnel
lrwxrwxrwx. 1 root root    22 Jul 22  2014 ifup -> ../../../usr/sbin/ifup
-rwxr-xr-x. 1 root root 12449 Apr  2  2014 ifup-aliases
```

```
-rwxr-xr-x. 1 root root   859 Apr  2  2014 ifup-bnep
-rwxr-xr-x. 1 root root 10223 Apr  2  2014 ifup-eth
-rwxr-xr-x. 1 root root 12039 Apr  2  2014 ifup-ippp
-rwxr-xr-x. 1 root root 10430 Apr  2  2014 ifup-ipv6
lrwxrwxrwx. 1 root root     9 Jul 22  2014 ifup-isdn -> ifup-ippp
-rwxr-xr-x. 1 root root   642 Apr  2  2014 ifup-plip
-rwxr-xr-x. 1 root root  1043 Apr  2  2014 ifup-plusb
-rwxr-xr-x. 1 root root  2609 Apr  2  2014 ifup-post
-rwxr-xr-x. 1 root root  4154 Apr  2  2014 ifup-ppp
-rwxr-xr-x. 1 root root  1925 Apr  2  2014 ifup-routes
-rwxr-xr-x. 1 root root  3263 Apr  2  2014 ifup-sit
-rwxr-xr-x. 1 root root  1628 Oct 31  2013 ifup-Team
-rwxr-xr-x. 1 root root  1856 Jun  9  2014 ifup-TeamPort
-rwxr-xr-x. 1 root root  2607 Apr  2  2014 ifup-tunnel
-rwxr-xr-x. 1 root root  1621 Apr  2  2014 ifup-wireless
-rwxr-xr-x. 1 root root  4623 Apr  2  2014 init.ipv6-global
-rw-r--r--. 1 root root 14238 Apr  2  2014 network-functions
-rw-r--r--. 1 root root 26134 Apr  2  2014 network-functions-ipv6
-rw-r--r--. 1 root root    30 Mar 13 02:20 route-enp0s3
```

From the directory listing, we can see several configuration files. In general, however, we will mostly only be interested in files that begin with "ifcfg-" and files that begin with "route-."

The files that begin with "ifcfg-" are used to define network interfaces; the naming convention of these files is "ifcfg-<device name>"; for example, to see enp0s8's configuration, we could read the ifcfg-enp0s8 file.

```
[db]# cat ifcfg-enp0s8
NM_CONTROLLED=no
BOOTPROTO=none
ONBOOT=yes
IPADDR=192.168.33.12
NETMASK=255.255.255.0
DEVICE=enp0s8
PEERDNS=no
```

We can see that this configuration file defines the IP address and `Netmask` used for this interface.

The "`route-`" files are used to define the system's routing configuration. The convention for this file is similar to that of the interface files, "`route-<device name>`." In the folder listing, there was only one route file, `route-enp0s3`. This is the most likely location for the incorrect route to be defined.

```
[db]# cat route-enp0s3
192.168.33.11/32 via 10.0.2.1
```

In general, unless a static route (routes that are statically defined) is defined, the "`route-*`" files do not exist. We can see here that only one route is defined in this file, which means that all the other routes defined in the routing table are dynamically configured on the basis of the interface configurations.

In the preceding example, the route defined in the `route-enp0s3` file does not specify an interface. Because of this, the interface will be defined on the basis of the filename; if this same entry were in the route-enp0s8 file, the network service would attempt to define the route on the `enp0s8` interface.

To ensure that this route no longer appears in the routing table, we need to remove it from this file; alternatively, in this case, since it is the only route, we should remove the file in its entirety.

```
[db]# rm route-enp0s3
rm: remove regular file 'route-enp0s3'? y
```

The decision to remove the file and the route is dependent on the environment being supported; if you are ever unsure if this is the correct action, you should ask someone who can tell you if it is or isn't beforehand. For this example, we will assume that it is OK to remove this network configuration file.

After restarting the network service, we should see the route disappear.

```
[db]# service network restart
Restarting network (via systemctl):                      [  OK  ]
[db]# ip route show
default via 10.0.2.2 dev enp0s3  proto static  metric 1024
10.0.2.0/24 dev enp0s3  proto kernel  scope link  src 10.0.2.16
169.254.0.0/16 dev enp0s8  scope link  metric 1003
192.168.33.0/24 dev enp0s8  proto kernel  scope link  src 192.168.33.12
```

Now that the route is gone and the network configurations have been reloaded, we can safely say that we have corrected the issue. We can validate this by once again loading the webpage to ensure that the blog is working.

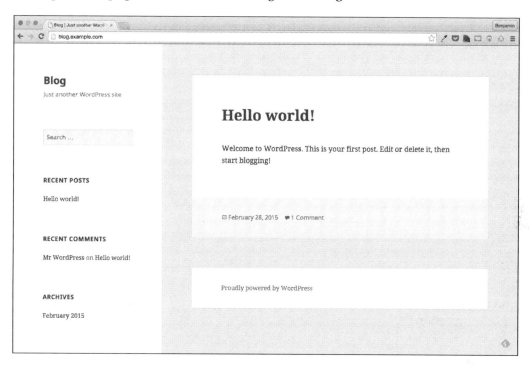

Summary

If we look back at this chapter, we learned quite a bit about troubleshooting network connectivity issues on Linux. We learned how to use the `netstat` and `tcpdump` tools to look at the incoming and outgoing connections. We learned about the TCP three-way handshake and how the `/etc/hosts` file can supersede the DNS settings.

In this chapter, we covered many commands, and while we gave a pretty good overview of each command and what it does, there are some that we barely scratched the surface on.

Commands such as tcpdump are a prime example of this. In this chapter, we used tcpdump quite a bit, but this tool is capable of far more than we used it for. Of all of the commands that we covered in this book, I personally feel that tcpdump is one to spend time learning, as it is a very useful and powerful tool. I have used it to solve many issues, and sometimes, these issues were not network-specific but application-specific.

In this next chapter, we will keep this networking momentum going with troubleshooting firewalls. We will probably see some of the same commands that we used in this chapter reappear in the next chapter, but this is OK; it just shows how important it is to understand networking and the tools to troubleshoot it.

6
Diagnosing and Correcting Firewall Issues

In the previous chapter, we discovered how to troubleshoot networking-related issues with commands such as `telnet`, `ping`, `curl`, `netstat`, `tcpdump`, and `ip`. You also learned how the **TCP protocol** works, as well as how domains are translated to IPs using **DNS**.

In this chapter, we will once again troubleshoot network-related issues; however, this time we will discover how Linux's software firewall `iptables` works and how to troubleshoot network issues generated by a firewall.

Diagnosing firewalls

Chapter 5, *Network Troubleshooting*, was all about networking and how to troubleshoot a misconfigured network. In this chapter, we are going to extend that discussion to firewalls. While troubleshooting firewalls we are likely to use some of the same commands as *Chapter 5*, *Network Troubleshooting*, and repeat a lot of the same process. This is because anytime you are using a firewall to protect a system, you are blocking certain types of network traffic, a misconfiguration of the firewall can impact any network traffic for a system.

We will start this chapter in the same way we did the other chapters, by troubleshooting a reported issue.

Déjà vu

In *Chapter 5, Network Troubleshooting,* our troubleshooting started after a developer called in and reported that the company's blog was reporting a database connectivity error. After troubleshooting, we found that this error was due to a misconfigured static route on the database server. Yet again, today (several days later), we receive a call from the same developer reporting the same issue.

When the developer goes to `http://blog.example.com,` he receives an error stating there is a database connectivity issue. *Not again!*

Since the first step in data collection is to duplicate the issue, the first thing we should do is to pull up the company blog on our own browser.

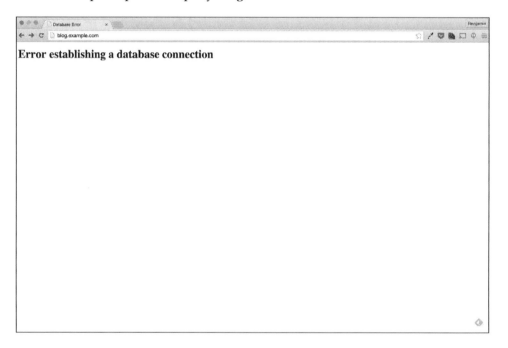

It seems, in fact, that the same error is showing yet again; now to figure out why.

Troubleshooting from historic issues

The first instinct for a **Data Collector** would be to simply run through the same troubleshooting steps from *Chapter 5, Network Troubleshooting.* The **Adaptor** and **Educated Gusser** troubleshooters, however, knowing the issue a few days ago was due to a static route would simply log in to the database server first and check for the same static route.

Maybe someone simply re-added it by mistake, or the route was not fully removed from the system's configuration files:

```
[db]# ip route show
default via 10.0.2.2 dev enp0s3  proto static  metric 1024
10.0.2.0/24 dev enp0s3  proto kernel  scope link  src 10.0.2.15
169.254.0.0/16 dev enp0s8  scope link  metric 1003
192.168.33.0/24 dev enp0s8  proto kernel  scope link  src
192.168.33.12
```

Unfortunately, however, our luck is not that good; from the results of the `ip` command, we can see that the static route from *Chapter 5*, *Network Troubleshooting*, is not present.

Since the route is not present, we will need to start again at step one by checking whether the blog server is able to connect to the database server.

Basic troubleshooting

The first test we should perform is a simple ping from the blog server to the database server. This will quickly answer whether the two servers are able to communicate at all:

```
[blog]$ ping db.example.com
PING db.example.com (192.168.33.12) 56(84) bytes of data.
64 bytes from db.example.com (192.168.33.12): icmp_seq=1 ttl=64
time=0.420 ms
64 bytes from db.example.com (192.168.33.12): icmp_seq=2 ttl=64
time=0.564 ms
64 bytes from db.example.com (192.168.33.12): icmp_seq=3 ttl=64
time=0.562 ms
64 bytes from db.example.com (192.168.33.12): icmp_seq=4 ttl=64
time=0.479 ms
^C
--- db.example.com ping statistics ---
4 packets transmitted, 4 received, 0% packet loss, time 3006ms
rtt min/avg/max/mdev = 0.420/0.506/0.564/0.062 ms
```

From the `ping` command's results we can see that the blog server can communicate with the database server, or rather, the blog server sent an **ICMP echo request** and received an **ICMP echo reply** from the database server. The next connectivity we can test is connectivity to port `3306`, the MySQL port.

We will test this connectivity with the `telnet` command:

```
[blog]$ telnet db.example.com 3306
Trying 192.168.33.12...
telnet: connect to address 192.168.33.12: No route to host
```

The `telnet` however, failed. This shows that there is in fact a problem with the blog server connecting to the database service on the database server.

Validating the MariaDB service

Now that we have established that the blog server cannot communicate with the database server, we need to identify the cause. Before assuming the issue is strictly network-related, we should first validate that the database service is up and running. To do this, we will simply log in to the database server and check for the running database process.

We can use multiple methods to validate that the database processes are running. In the following example, we will use the `ps` command once again:

```
[db]$ ps -elf | grep maria
0 S mysql     1529  1123  0  80   0 - 226863 poll_s 12:21 ?
00:00:04 /usr/libexec/mysqld --basedir=/usr --datadir=/var/lib/mysql
--plugin-dir=/usr/lib64/mysql/plugin --log-error=/var/log/mariadb/
mariadb.log --pid-file=/var/run/mariadb/mariadb.pid --socket=/var/lib/
mysql/mysql.sock
```

With the `ps` command, we are able to see the running **MariaDB** process. In the preceding example, we used the `ps -elf` command to show all processes and the `grep` command to filter that output to find the MariaDB service.

From the results, it appears that the database service is in fact running; but this does not tell us for sure that this process is accepting connections on port `3306`. To validate this, we can use the `netstat` command to identify which ports are listening on this server:

```
[db]$ netstat -na | grep LISTEN
tcp       0     0 127.0.0.1:25          0.0.0.0:*             LISTEN
tcp       0     0 0.0.0.0:46788         0.0.0.0:*             LISTEN
tcp       0     0 0.0.0.0:3306          0.0.0.0:*             LISTEN
tcp       0     0 0.0.0.0:111           0.0.0.0:*             LISTEN
tcp       0     0 0.0.0.0:22            0.0.0.0:*             LISTEN
tcp6      0     0 ::1:25                :::*                  LISTEN
```

```
tcp6      0      0 :::111                    :::*              LISTEN
tcp6      0      0 :::22                     :::*              LISTEN
tcp6      0      0 :::49464                  :::*              LISTEN
```

From the `netstat` command, we can see that there are quite a few ports open on this system and port 3306 is one of them.

Since we know that the blog server is unable to establish a connection to port 3306, we can once again test the connectivity from multiple places. The first place being the database server itself and the second being our laptop just as we did in *Chapter 5, Network Troubleshooting*.

Since the database server does not have the `telnet` client installed, we can use the `curl` command to perform this test:

```
[blog]$ curl -v telnet://localhost:3306
* About to connect() to localhost port 3306 (#0)
*    Trying 127.0.0.1...
* Connected to localhost (127.0.0.1) port 3306 (#0)
R
* RCVD IAC EC
```

> One thing I will say repeatedly in this book is that it is important to know more than one way to perform a task. `telnet` is a very simple example but this concept applies to every task you perform as a system administrator.

Since we have established that the database server is accessible from the local server, we can now test this from our laptop:

```
[laptop]$ telnet 192.168.33.12 3306
Trying 192.168.33.12...
telnet: connect to address 192.168.33.12: Connection refused
telnet: Unable to connect to remote host
```

It seems that from our laptop, the connection to the database service is unavailable, but what happens if we test another port such as 22?

```
[laptop]$ telnet 192.168.33.12 22
Trying 192.168.33.12...
Connected to 192.168.33.12.
```

```
Escape character is '^]'.

SSH-2.0-OpenSSH_6.4

^]

telnet>
```

This is an interesting result; from the laptop, we are able to connect to port 22 but not port 3306. Since port 22 is available on the laptop, what about from the blog server?

```
[blog]$ telnet db.example.com 22

Trying 192.168.33.12...

Connected to db.example.com.

Escape character is '^]'.

SSH-2.0-OpenSSH_6.4

^]
```

These results are quite interesting. In the previous chapter, when our connectivity issue was due to a misconfigured static route, all communication between the blog server and the database server was broken.

In the case of this issue, however, the blog server is unable to connect to port 3306, but it is able to talk to the database server on port 22. What makes this issue more interesting is that locally, on the database server, port 3306 is available and accepting connections.

These key pieces of information are the first signs to indicate that our issue might in fact be due to a firewall. It might be a little early for a Data Collector, but an Adaptor or Educated Guesser troubleshooter might already, at this point, form an hypothesis that this issue is due to a firewall.

Troubleshooting with tcpdump

In *Chapter 5*, *Network Troubleshooting*, we used tcpdump quite extensively to identify our issue; can we tell if the issue is a firewall issue with tcpdump? Maybe, we can certainly use tcpdump to get a better view of the issue.

To start with, we will first capture connectivity to port 22 from the blog server (a connection that we know is working). The tcpdump will run on the database server filtering for port 22; we will also use the -i (interface) flag with the any option to cause tcpdump to capture traffic on all network interfaces:

```
[db]# tcpdump -nnnvvv -i any port 22
tcpdump: listening on any, link-type LINUX_SLL (Linux cooked), capture
size 65535 bytes
```

Once `tcpdump` is running, we can initiate a connection to port 22 from the blog server to see what a full healthy connection looks like:

```
03:03:15.670771 IP (tos 0x10, ttl 64, id 17278, offset 0, flags [DF],
proto TCP (6), length 60)
    192.168.33.11.34133 > 192.168.33.12.22: Flags [S], cksum 0x977b
(correct), seq 2193487479, win 14600, options [mss 1460,sackOK,TS val
7058697 ecr 0,nop,wscale 6], length 0
03:03:15.670847 IP (tos 0x0, ttl 64, id 0, offset 0, flags [DF],
proto TCP (6), length 60)
    192.168.33.12.22 > 192.168.33.11.34133: Flags [S.], cksum 0xc396
(correct), seq 3659372781, ack 2193487480, win 14480, options [mss
1460,sackOK,TS val 7018839 ecr 7058697,nop,wscale 6], length 0
03:03:15.671295 IP (tos 0x10, ttl 64, id 17279, offset 0, flags [DF],
proto TCP (6), length 52)
    192.168.33.11.34133 > 192.168.33.12.22: Flags [.], cksum 0x718b
(correct), seq 1, ack 1, win 229, options [nop,nop,TS val 7058697 ecr
7018839], length 0
```

From the captured data, we can see a standard healthy connection. We can see that the connection is coming from the IP `192.168.33.11`, the blog server's IP. We can also see that the connection arrived on the IP `192.168.33.12` via port 22. We can see all of this from the following line:

```
192.168.33.11.34133 > 192.168.33.12.22: Flags [S], cksum 0x977b
(correct), seq 2193487479, win 14600, options [mss 1460,sackOK,TS val
7058697 ecr 0,nop,wscale 6], length 0
```

From the second captured packet, we can see the **SYN-ACK** reply from the database server to the blog server:

```
    192.168.33.12.22 > 192.168.33.11.34133: Flags [S.], cksum 0x0b15
(correct), seq 3659372781, ack 2193487480, win 14480, options [mss
1460,sackOK,TS val 7018839 ecr 7058697,nop,wscale 6], length 0
```

We can see that the `SYN-ACK` reply was from the `192.168.33.12` IP address to the `192.168.33.11` IP address. So far, the TCP connection seems normal, the third captured packet confirms this for sure:

```
    192.168.33.11.34133 > 192.168.33.12.22: Flags [.], cksum 0x718b
(correct), seq 1, ack 1, win 229, options [nop,nop,TS val 7058697 ecr
7018839], length 0
```

The third packet is a **SYN-ACK-ACK** from the blog server. This means that not only did the blog servers `SYN` packet arrive and get replied to with a `SYN-ACK`, the database servers `SYN-ACK` packet was received by the blog server and replied to with a `SYN-ACK-ACK`. This is a full three-way handshake for port 22.

Now, let's take a look at connectivity to port 3306. To do this, we will use the same tcpdump command, this time changing the port to 3306:

```
[db]# tcpdump -nnnvvv -i any port 3306
tcpdump: listening on any, link-type LINUX_SLL (Linux cooked),
capture size 65535 bytes
```

With tcpdump running, we can use telnet from the blog server to establish a connection:

```
[blog]$ telnet db.example.com 3306
Trying 192.168.33.12...
telnet: connect to address 192.168.33.12: No route to host
```

As expected, the telnet command has failed to connect; let's see if tcpdump captured any packets during this time:

```
06:04:25.488396 IP (tos 0x10, ttl 64, id 44350, offset 0, flags [DF],
proto TCP (6), length 60)
    192.168.33.11.55002 > 192.168.33.12.3306: Flags [S], cksum 0x7699
(correct), seq 3266396266, win 14600, options [mss 1460,sackOK,TS val
12774740 ecr 0,nop,wscale 6], length 0
```

It seems in fact that tcpdump did capture a packet, but only one.

The packet captured was a SYN packet sent from 192.168.33.11 (the blog server) to 192.168.33.12 (the database server). This shows that the packet from the blog server arrives on the database server; but what we don't see is a reply packet.

As you learned in the previous chapter, when we apply filters to tcpdump, we often miss things. In this case, we are filtering tcpdump to look for traffic either from or to port 3306. Since we know that the server in question is the blog server, we can change our filter to capture all traffic from the blog server IP; 192.168.33.11. We can do this by using the host filter of tcpdump:

```
[db]# tcpdump -nnnvvv -i any host 192.168.33.11
tcpdump: listening on any, link-type LINUX_SLL (Linux cooked),
capture size 65535 bytes
```

With tcpdump running again, we can once again initiate a connection with a telnet from the blog server:

```
[blog]$ telnet db.example.com 3306
Trying 192.168.33.12...
telnet: connect to address 192.168.33.12: No route to host
```

Again, the telnet connection was expectedly unsuccessful; however, this time we can see quite a bit more from `tcpdump`:

```
06:16:49.729134 IP (tos 0x10, ttl 64, id 23760, offset 0, flags [DF],
proto TCP (6), length 60)
    192.168.33.11.55003 > 192.168.33.12.3306: Flags [S], cksum 0x9be6
(correct), seq 1849431125, win 14600, options [mss 1460,sackOK,TS val
13518981 ecr 0,nop,wscale 6], length 0
06:16:49.729199 IP (tos 0xd0, ttl 64, id 40207, offset 0, flags
[none], proto ICMP (1), length 88)
    192.168.33.12 > 192.168.33.11: ICMP host 192.168.33.12
unreachable - admin prohibited, length 68
```

This time we can actually see quite a bit of useful information that directly indicates that our issue is due to the system firewall.

It looks like `tcpdump` was able to capture two packets. Let's break down what it was able to capture to get a better understanding of what is going on:

```
06:16:49.729134 IP (tos 0x10, ttl 64, id 23760, offset 0, flags [DF],
proto TCP (6), length 60)
    192.168.33.11.55003 > 192.168.33.12.3306: Flags [S], cksum 0x9be6
(correct), seq 1849431125, win 14600, options [mss 1460,sackOK,TS val
13518981 ecr 0,nop,wscale 6], length 0
```

The first packet is the same as we saw before, a simple `SYN` request from the blog server to the database server on port `3306`. The second packet, however, is quite interesting:

```
06:16:49.729199 IP (tos 0xd0, ttl 64, id 40207, offset 0, flags
[none], proto ICMP (1), length 88)
    192.168.33.12 > 192.168.33.11: ICMP host 192.168.33.12
unreachable - admin prohibited, length 68
```

The second packet isn't even a TCP based packet but rather an **ICMP** packet. Earlier in *Chapter 5, Network Troubleshooting*, we talked about ICMP echo request and reply packets and how they are used by the `ping` command to identify whether a host is available. ICMP, however, is used for more than the `ping` command.

Understanding ICMP

The ICMP protocol is used as a control protocol for sending messages across networks. The echo request and echo reply messages are just one example of this protocol. This protocol is also frequently used to notify other systems of errors.

In this case, the database server is sending an ICMP packet to the blog server, notifying it that the IP host 192.168.33.12 is unreachable:

```
proto ICMP (1), length 88)
    192.168.33.12 > 192.168.33.11: ICMP host 192.168.33.12
unreachable - admin prohibited, length 68
```

Not only is the database server saying it is unreachable, it is also telling the blog server that the reason for the unreachable state is because the connection is administratively prohibited. This type of reply is a telltale sign of a firewall being the source of the connectivity issue, as often administratively prohibited is the type of message firewalls will utilize.

Understanding connection rejections

When a TCP connection is made to a service that is unavailable or to a port that is not being listened to, the Linux kernel will send a reply. The reply, however, is a TCP Reset, which tells the remote system to reset the connection.

We can see this in action by connecting to an invalid port while running tcpdump. On the blog server, port 5000 is not currently being used if we run a tcpdump. Using the port filter, we will see all of the traffic to and from that port:

```
[blog]# tcpdump -vvvnnn -i any port 5000
tcpdump: listening on any, link-type LINUX_SLL (Linux cooked),
capture size 65535 bytes
```

With tcpdump, capturing all traffic on port 5000, we can now use telnet to attempt a connection:

```
[laptop]$ telnet 192.168.33.11 5000
Trying 192.168.33.11...
telnet: connect to address 192.168.33.11: Connection refused
telnet: Unable to connect to remote host
```

We actually can already see something different. Earlier, when we performed a telnet to port 3306 on the database server, the telnet command printed a different message:

```
telnet: connect to address 192.168.33.12: No route to host
```

The reason for this is because previously, when the telnet connection was performed, the server received an ICMP destination unavailable packet.

This time, however, a different reply was sent. We can see this reply in the captured packets by tcpdump:

```
06:57:42.954091 IP (tos 0x10, ttl 64, id 47368, offset 0, flags [DF],
proto TCP (6), length 64)
    192.168.33.1.53198 > 192.168.33.11.5000: Flags [S], cksum 0xca34
(correct), seq 1134882056, win 65535, options [mss 1460,nop,wscale
5,nop,nop,TS val 511014642 ecr 0,sackOK,eol], length 0
06:57:42.954121 IP (tos 0x10, ttl 64, id 0, offset 0, flags [DF],
proto TCP (6), length 40)
    192.168.33.11.5000 > 192.168.33.1.53198: Flags [R.], cksum 0xd86e
(correct), seq 0, ack 1134882057, win 0, length 0
```

This time, the packet being sent back was a TCP Reset:

```
192.168.33.11.5000 > 192.168.33.1.53198: Flags [R.],
```

A **RESET** packet is, typically, what one would expect when the issue is due to simple connectivity errors, as this is the standard TCP response for situations where the client is attempting to connect to a port which is no longer available.

The RESET packet can also be sent by applications that are rejecting a connection. The ICMP destination unreachable, however, is typically the reply you will receive when the packet is being rejected by a firewall; that is, if the firewall service is configured to reply at all.

A quick summary of what you have learned so far

From our troubleshooting so far, we have identified that the blog server is able to establish a connection to the database server over port 22. This connection is actually able to perform a full three-way handshake unlike our previous chapter. However, the blog server is not able to perform a three-way handshake with the database server over port 3306, the database port.

When the blog server attempts to establish a connection to the database server over port 3306, the database server is sending an ICMP destination unreachable packet back to the blog server. This packet is essentially telling the blog server that the connection attempt to the database is being rejected. Yet, the database service is up and listening on port 3306 (verified with netstat). In addition to the port being listened to, if we telnet to port 3306 locally, from the database server itself the connection is established.

Given all of these data points, it is possible that the database server might have the firewall service enabled and blocking connections to port 3306.

Managing the Linux firewall with iptables

When it comes to managing the firewall service within Linux, there are many options, the most popular being `iptables` and `ufw`. For Ubuntu distributions, `ufw` is the default firewall management tool; however, overall, `iptables` is by far the most popular across multiple Linux distributions. Both of these, however, in themselves, are simply user interfaces to **Netfilter**.

Netfilter is a framework within the Linux kernel that allows for packet filtering as well as network and port translation. Tools such as the `iptables` command are simply interacting with the `netfilter` framework to apply these rules.

For this book, we will concentrate on utilizing the `iptables` command and service to manage our firewall rules. Not only is it the most popular firewall tool, it has also been the default firewall service for Red Hat based operating systems for quite a while. Even with the newer `firewalld` service arriving in Red Hat Enterprise Linux 7, this is simply a service to manage `iptables`.

Verify that iptables is running

Since we suspect that our issue is due to the system's firewall configuration, we should first check to see whether the firewall is running and what rules are defined. Since `iptables` runs as a service, the first step is to simply check that service's status:

```
[db]# ps -elf | grep iptables
0 R root      4189  3220  0  80   0 - 28160 -        16:31 pts/0
00:00:00 grep --color=auto iptables
```

Previously, when we went to check whether a service is running, we would simply use the `ps` command. This works great for services such as MariaDB or Apache; `iptables`, however, is different. Since `iptables` is simply a command that interacts with `netfilter`, the `iptables` service is not a daemon process like most other services. In fact, when you start the `iptables` service you are simply applying saved `netfilter` rules, and when you stop the service, you are simply flushing those rules. We will explore this concept a little later in the chapter but for now we will simply check whether the `iptables` service is running using the service command:

```
[db]# service iptables status
Redirecting to /bin/systemctl status  iptables.service
iptables.service - IPv4 firewall with iptables
   Loaded: loaded (/usr/lib/systemd/system/iptables.service; enabled)
   Active: active (exited) since Wed 2015-04-01 16:36:16 UTC; 4min
56s ago
```

```
   Process: 4202 ExecStop=/usr/libexec/iptables/iptables.init stop
(code=exited, status=0/SUCCESS)
   Process: 4332 ExecStart=/usr/libexec/iptables/iptables.init start
(code=exited, status=0/SUCCESS)
 Main PID: 4332 (code=exited, status=0/SUCCESS)


Apr 01 16:36:16 db.example.com systemd[1]: Starting IPv4 firewall
with iptables...
Apr 01 16:36:16 db.example.com iptables.init[4332]: iptables:
Applying firewall rules: [  OK  ]
Apr 01 16:36:16 db.example.com systemd[1]: Started IPv4 firewall with
iptables.
```

With the Red Hat Enterprise Linux 7 release, Red Hat has migrated to systemd, which replaces the standard init system. With this migration, the service command is no longer the preferred command to manage services. This functionality has moved the control command for systemd to the systemctl command.

For RHEL 7, at least the service command is still executable; however, this command is simply a wrapper to systemctl. Here is the command to check the status of the iptables service with the systemctl command. For this book, we will utilize the systemctl commands rather than the legacy service command:

```
[db]# systemctl status iptables.service
iptables.service - IPv4 firewall with iptables
   Loaded: loaded (/usr/lib/systemd/system/iptables.service; enabled)
   Active: active (exited) since Wed 2015-04-01 16:36:16 UTC; 26min
ago
   Process: 4202 ExecStop=/usr/libexec/iptables/iptables.init stop
(code=exited, status=0/SUCCESS)
   Process: 4332 ExecStart=/usr/libexec/iptables/iptables.init start
(code=exited, status=0/SUCCESS)
 Main PID: 4332 (code=exited, status=0/SUCCESS)


Apr 01 16:36:16 db.example.com systemd[1]: Starting IPv4 firewall
with iptables...
Apr 01 16:36:16 db.example.com iptables.init[4332]: iptables:
Applying firewall rules: [  OK  ]
Apr 01 16:36:16 db.example.com systemd[1]: Started IPv4 firewall with
iptables.
```

From the preceding output of `systemctl`, we can see that currently the `iptables` service is active. We can identify this from the 3rd line of the `systemctl` output:

```
    Active: active (exited) since Wed 2015-04-01 16:36:16 UTC; 26min
ago
```

When the `iptables` service is not running, things look quite a bit different:

```
[db]# systemctl status iptables.service

iptables.service - IPv4 firewall with iptables

    Loaded: loaded (/usr/lib/systemd/system/iptables.service; enabled)

    Active: inactive (dead) since Thu 2015-04-02 02:55:26 UTC; 1s ago

   Process: 4489 ExecStop=/usr/libexec/iptables/iptables.init stop
(code=exited, status=0/SUCCESS)

   Process: 4332 ExecStart=/usr/libexec/iptables/iptables.init start
(code=exited, status=0/SUCCESS)

  Main PID: 4332 (code=exited, status=0/SUCCESS)


Apr 01 16:36:16 db.example.com systemd[1]: Starting IPv4 firewall
with iptables...

Apr 01 16:36:16 db.example.com iptables.init[4332]: iptables:
Applying firewall rules: [  OK  ]

Apr 01 16:36:16 db.example.com systemd[1]: Started IPv4 firewall with
iptables.

Apr 02 02:55:26 db.example.com systemd[1]: Stopping IPv4 firewall
with iptables...

Apr 02 02:55:26 db.example.com iptables.init[4489]: iptables: Setting
chains to policy ACCEPT: nat filter [  OK  ]

Apr 02 02:55:26 db.example.com iptables.init[4489]: iptables:
Flushing firewall rules: [  OK  ]

Apr 02 02:55:26 db.example.com iptables.init[4489]: iptables:
Unloading modules: [  OK  ]

Apr 02 02:55:26 db.example.com systemd[1]: Stopped IPv4 firewall with
iptables.
```

From the preceding example, `systemctl` shows the `iptables` service as inactive:

```
    Active: inactive (dead) since Thu 2015-04-02 02:55:26 UTC; 1s ago
```

One of the nice things about `systemctl` is that when running with the status option, the output includes log messages from the service:

```
Apr 02 02:55:26 db.example.com systemd[1]: Stopping IPv4 firewall
with iptables...
```

```
Apr 02 02:55:26 db.example.com iptables.init[4489]: iptables: Setting
chains to policy ACCEPT: nat filter [  OK  ]
Apr 02 02:55:26 db.example.com iptables.init[4489]: iptables:
Flushing firewall rules: [  OK  ]
Apr 02 02:55:26 db.example.com iptables.init[4489]: iptables:
Unloading modules: [  OK  ]
Apr 02 02:55:26 db.example.com systemd[1]: Stopped IPv4 firewall with
iptables.
```

From the preceding code, we can see all of the status messages used by the stop process for the iptables service.

Show iptables rules being enforced

Now that we know that the iptables service is *Active* and running, we should also look at the iptables rules that are defined and being enforced. To do this, we will use the iptables command with the –L (list) and –n (numeric) flags:

```
[db]# iptables -L -n
Chain INPUT (policy ACCEPT)
target      prot opt source               destination
ACCEPT      all  --  0.0.0.0/0            0.0.0.0/0           state
RELATED,ESTABLISHED
ACCEPT      icmp --  0.0.0.0/0            0.0.0.0/0
ACCEPT      all  --  0.0.0.0/0            0.0.0.0/0
ACCEPT      tcp  --  0.0.0.0/0            0.0.0.0/0           state
NEW tcp dpt:22
REJECT      all  --  0.0.0.0/0            0.0.0.0/0           reject-
with icmp-host-prohibited
ACCEPT      tcp  --  192.168.0.0/16       0.0.0.0/0           state
NEW tcp dpt:3306


Chain FORWARD (policy ACCEPT)
target      prot opt source               destination
REJECT      all  --  0.0.0.0/0            0.0.0.0/0           reject-
with icmp-host-prohibited


Chain OUTPUT (policy ACCEPT)
target      prot opt source               destination
```

When executing `iptables`, the flags `-L` and `-n` are not combined. Unlike most other commands, `iptables` has a specific format that requires some flags to be separated from others. In this case, the `-L` flag is separated from the rest of the options. We could add the `-v` (verbose) option to the `-n` but not to the `-L`. The following is an example of executing with the verbose option:

```
[db]# iptables -L -nv
```

It seems from the output of `iptables -L -n` that there are quite a few `iptables` rules in place on this server. Let's break down these rules in order to understand them better.

Understanding iptables rules

Before we get into the individual rules, we should first cover a few general rules of `iptables` and firewalls.

Ordering matters

The first important rule to know is that ordering matters. If we look at the data returned by `iptables -L -n`, we could see that there are multiple rules, the order of which those rules are in determines how that rule is interpreted.

I like to think of `iptables` as a checklist; when a packet is received `iptables` will go through the checklist from top to bottom. When it finds a rule that matches the condition, it applies that rule.

This is one of the most common mistakes people make when using `iptables`, putting rules outside of the top to bottom order.

Default policies

In general, `iptables` is used in two ways, either all traffic unless specifically blocked is allowed, or all traffic unless specifically allowed is blocked. These methodologies are called a **default allow** and **default deny** policy.

It is acceptable to use either policy depending on the desired use of the Linux firewall. In general however, the default deny policy is often considered the more secure approach, as this policy requires a rule to be added for each type of access required for the server in question.

Breaking down the iptables rules

Since `iptables` processes rules from the top down, to better understand the rules in place we are going to take a look at the `iptables` rules from the bottom up:

```
Chain FORWARD (policy ACCEPT)
target     prot opt source              destination
REJECT     all  --  0.0.0.0/0           0.0.0.0/0            reject-
with icmp-host-prohibited
```

The first rule we see says REJECT all protocols from any source to any destination for the FORWARD chain. Does this mean that `iptables` is going to block everything? Yes, but only for packets that are being forwarded.

The `iptables` command categorizes network traffic types into tables and chains. Tables consist of the high-level operations being performed such as filtering, network address translation, or altering packets.

Within each table, there are also several "chains". The chains are used to define the type of traffic to apply the rule to. In the case of the FORWARD chain, this matches traffic that is being forwarded, which is commonly used for routing.

The next chain with rules applied is the INPUT chain:

```
Chain INPUT (policy ACCEPT)
target     prot opt source              destination
ACCEPT     all  --  0.0.0.0/0           0.0.0.0/0            state
RELATED,ESTABLISHED
ACCEPT     icmp --  0.0.0.0/0           0.0.0.0/0
ACCEPT     all  --  0.0.0.0/0           0.0.0.0/0
ACCEPT     tcp  --  0.0.0.0/0           0.0.0.0/0            state
NEW tcp dpt:22
REJECT     all  --  0.0.0.0/0           0.0.0.0/0            reject-
with icmp-host-prohibited
ACCEPT     tcp  --  192.168.0.0/16      0.0.0.0/0            state
NEW tcp dpt:3306
```

This chain applies to traffic that is incoming to the local system; essentially, these rules are only applied to traffic that is arriving on the system:

```
ACCEPT     tcp  --  192.168.0.0/16      0.0.0.0/0            state
NEW tcp dpt:3306
```

If we look at the last rule in the chain, we can see that it specifically defines that the system should ACCEPT TCP traffic with a source IP within the 192.168.0.0/16 network and a destination IP of 0.0.0.0/0, which like with netstat is a wildcard. The last part of this rule defines that this rule applies only to new connections with a destination port of 3306.

To put it simply, this rule would have the effect of allowing any IP within the 192.168.0.0/16 network to access port 3306 on any of the database servers local IPs.

This rule in particular should allow traffic from our blog server (192.168.33.11), but what about the rule above it?

```
REJECT     all  --  0.0.0.0/0              0.0.0.0/0              reject-
with icmp-host-prohibited
```

The preceding rule specifically states that the system should REJECT all protocols from a source IP of 0.0.0.0/0 to a destination IP of 0.0.0.0/0 and reply with an ICMP packet that says the host is prohibited. From our earlier network troubleshooting, we know that the 0.0.0.0/0 network is a wildcard for all networks.

This means that this rule will REJECT all traffic to the system, effectively making our system use a "default deny" policy. However, this isn't really the common method of defining a "default deny" policy.

If we look at the top of this chain's ruleset, we will see the following:

```
Chain INPUT (policy ACCEPT)
```

This is essentially saying that the INPUT chain itself has an ACCEPT policy, which means the chain itself is using a "default allow" policy. However, there is a rule in this chain that will REJECT all traffic.

This means that while the chain's policy is not technically default deny, this rule effectively accomplishes the same thing. Unless traffic is specifically allowed before this rule, the traffic will be denied, effectively making the chain a "default deny" policy.

At this point, we have an interesting problem; the last rule in the INPUT chain specifically allows traffic to port 3306 (the MariaDB port) from the source network of 192.168.0.0/16. However, the rule above that denies all traffic from anywhere to anywhere. If we take a second to remember that iptables is order based, then we can easily see that this might be a problem.

The issue might simply be that the rule to allow port 3306 is defined after a rule that blocks all traffic; essentially, the database traffic is being blocked by the default deny rule.

Before we start acting on this information, however, we should continue looking at the `iptables` rules as there could be another rule defined that counters the two bottom rules:

```
ACCEPT     tcp  --  0.0.0.0/0              0.0.0.0/0              state
NEW tcp dpt:22
```

The third from the last rule in the INPUT chain does explain why SSH traffic is working as expected. This rule specifically states that the system should ACCEPT all TCP protocol traffic from any source to any destination when the connection is a new connection destined for port 22.

This rule essentially defines that all new TCP connections to port 22 are allowed. Since it is before the default deny rule, this means that in no circumstance would new connections to port 22 be blocked by that rule.

If we look at the fourth from the last rule in the INPUT chain, we see a very interesting rule:

```
ACCEPT     all  --  0.0.0.0/0              0.0.0.0/0
```

This rule appears to tell the system to ACCEPT all protocols from any IP (0.0.0.0/0) to any IP (0.0.0.0/0). If we look at this rule and apply the logic that ordering matters; then this rule should allow our database traffic.

Unfortunately, the `iptables` output can sometimes be misleading, as this rule is not showing a critical piece of the rule; the interface:

```
[db]# iptables -L -nv

Chain INPUT (policy ACCEPT 0 packets, 0 bytes)
 pkts bytes target     prot opt in      out     source
destination
   36  2016 ACCEPT     all  --  *       *       0.0.0.0/0
0.0.0.0/0            state RELATED,ESTABLISHED
    0     0 ACCEPT     icmp --  *       *       0.0.0.0/0
0.0.0.0/0
    0     0 ACCEPT     all  --  lo      *       0.0.0.0/0
0.0.0.0/0
    0     0 ACCEPT     tcp  --  *       *       0.0.0.0/0
0.0.0.0/0            state NEW tcp dpt:22
  394 52363 REJECT     all  --  *       *       0.0.0.0/0
0.0.0.0/0            reject-with icmp-host-prohibited
    0     0 ACCEPT     tcp  --  *       *       192.168.0.0/16
0.0.0.0/0            state NEW tcp dpt:3306
```

If we add the –v (verbose) flag to the iptables command, we can see quite a bit more information. In particular, we can see a new column named "in", which stands for interface:

```
    0       0 ACCEPT     all  --  lo      *       0.0.0.0/0
0.0.0.0/0
```

If we take a second look at this same rule, we can see that the interface column shows that this rule only applies to traffic on the loopback interface. Since our database traffic is on the enp0s8 interface, the database traffic does not match this rule:

```
    0       0 ACCEPT     icmp --  *       *       0.0.0.0/0
0.0.0.0/0
```

The fifth from the last rule is very similar, except that it specifically allows all ICMP traffic from any IP to any IP. This explains why our **ping** requests are working as this rule will allow the ICMP echo request and echo reply through the firewall.

The sixth from the last rule, however, is quite a bit different from the others:

```
   36   2016 ACCEPT     all  --  *       *       0.0.0.0/0
0.0.0.0/0              state RELATED,ESTABLISHED
```

This rule does state that the system should ACCEPT all protocols from any IP (0.0.0.0/0) to any IP (0.0.0.0/0); but the rule is limited to only RELATED and ESTABLISHED packets.

Earlier, while reviewing the iptables rule for port 22, we could see that the rule is limited to NEW connections. This essentially means that packets that are used to start a new connection to port 22 such as a SYN and SYN-ACK-ACK are allowed.

When the rule states that the ESTABLISHED state is allowed, iptables will allow packets that are part of an established TCP connection:

This means that new SSH connections are allowed by the rule for port 22.

```
    0       0 ACCEPT     tcp  --  *       *       0.0.0.0/0
0.0.0.0/0              state NEW tcp dpt:22
```

Then, once the TCP connection is established it is allowed by the following rule:

```
   36   2016 ACCEPT     all  --  *       *       0.0.0.0/0
0.0.0.0/0              state RELATED,ESTABLISHED
```

Putting the rules together

Now that we have looked at all of the iptables rules, we can make an educated guess as to why our database traffic is not working.

In the `iptables` ruleset, we can see that the rule to reject all traffic is defined before the rule to allow database connectivity on port 3306:

```
 394 52363 REJECT       all  -- *       *          0.0.0.0/0
0.0.0.0/0              reject-with icmp-host-prohibited
   0     0 ACCEPT       tcp  -- *       *          192.168.0.0/16
0.0.0.0/0              state NEW tcp dpt:3306
```

Since systems are unable to start new connections, they are not able to become established, which would be allowed by the following rule:

```
  36  2016 ACCEPT       all  -- *       *          0.0.0.0/0
0.0.0.0/0              state RELATED,ESTABLISHED
```

We can determine all of this by looking at the rules defined, but this also requires a pretty versed knowledge of `iptables`.

There is another somewhat easier way to determine which rules are blocking or allowing traffic.

Viewing iptables counters

With the verbose output of `iptables`, we not only see the interface the rule applies to, but we also see two additional columns that are very useful. Those two columns are **pkts** and **bytes**:

```
[db]# iptables -L -nv
Chain INPUT (policy ACCEPT 0 packets, 0 bytes)
 pkts bytes target       prot opt in      out     source
destination
   41  2360 ACCEPT       all  -- *       *          0.0.0.0/0
0.0.0.0/0              state RELATED,ESTABLISHED
```

The `pkts` column is the first column in the verbose output of `iptables`, this column contains the number of packets the rule has been applied to. If we look at the preceding rule, we can see that this rule has been applied to 41 packets. The `bytes` column is the second column and is used to denote the number of bytes that the rule has been applied to. For our preceding example, the rule has been applied to 2,360 bytes.

We can use the packet and byte counters in `iptables` to identify which rules are being applied to our database traffic. To do this, we simply need to trigger database activity by refreshing our browser and running `iptables -L -nv` to identify which rules had their counters increased. We can even make this easier by clearing out the current values with the `iptables` command followed by the -z (zero) flag:

```
[db]# iptables -Z
```

If we re-execute the verbose listing for `iptables`, we can see that the counters are 0 for everything except the ESTABLISHED and RELATED rule (a rule that every connection will match, including our SSH session):

```
[db]# iptables -L -nv
Chain INPUT (policy ACCEPT 0 packets, 0 bytes)
 pkts bytes target     prot opt in      out      source
destination
    7   388 ACCEPT     all  -- *        *        0.0.0.0/0
0.0.0.0/0             state RELATED,ESTABLISHED
    0     0 ACCEPT     icmp -- *        *        0.0.0.0/0
0.0.0.0/0
    0     0 ACCEPT     all  -- lo       *        0.0.0.0/0
0.0.0.0/0
    0     0 ACCEPT     tcp  -- *        *        0.0.0.0/0
0.0.0.0/0             state NEW tcp dpt:22
    0     0 REJECT     all  -- *        *        0.0.0.0/0
0.0.0.0/0             reject-with icmp-host-prohibited
    0     0 ACCEPT     tcp  -- *        *        192.168.0.0/16
0.0.0.0/0             state NEW tcp dpt:3306
```

After clearing these values, we can now refresh our web browser and initiate some database traffic:

```
[db]# iptables -L -nv
Chain INPUT (policy ACCEPT 0 packets, 0 bytes)
 pkts bytes target     prot opt in      out      source
destination
   53  3056 ACCEPT     all  -- *        *        0.0.0.0/0
0.0.0.0/0             state RELATED,ESTABLISHED
    0     0 ACCEPT     icmp -- *        *        0.0.0.0/0
0.0.0.0/0
    0     0 ACCEPT     all  -- lo       *        0.0.0.0/0
0.0.0.0/0
    0     0 ACCEPT     tcp  -- *        *        0.0.0.0/0
0.0.0.0/0             state NEW tcp dpt:22
   45  4467 REJECT     all  -- *        *        0.0.0.0/0
0.0.0.0/0             reject-with icmp-host-prohibited
    0     0 ACCEPT     tcp  -- *        *        192.168.0.0/16
0.0.0.0/0             state NEW tcp dpt:3306
```

If we run `iptables -L` in the verbose mode again, we can see that in fact as we suspected the packets are being rejected by the default deny rule. We can see this by the fact that this rule has now rejected 45 packets since we used the `-z` flag to zero the counters.

Using the `-z` flag and counters is a very useful method; however, it might not work in all cases. On busy systems and systems with many rules, it might be difficult to solely use counters to show which rules are being matched. For this reason, it is important to build an experience with `iptables`, understanding its intricacies.

Correcting the iptables rule ordering

Changing `iptables` can be a bit tricky, not because it is difficult to use (though the command syntax is a bit complex), but because there are two steps for modifying `iptables` rules. If one step is forgotten (which it often is), then the issue can persist unexpectedly.

How iptables rules are applied

When the `iptables` service is started, the start script doesn't start a daemon like other services on the system. What the `iptables` service does is simply apply the rules that are defined within a saved rules file (`/etc/sysconfig/iptables`).

These rules are then loaded in the memory, and they become active rules. This means that if we were to simply reorder the rules in memory but not modify the saved file, the next time the server rebooted, our changes would be lost.

On the flip side, if we only modified the saved file but did not reorder the `iptables` rules in memory, our changes will not take effect until the next time the `iptables` service is restarted.

I've seen both of these situations occur somewhat frequently, where someone simply forgot one or the other step. This situation caused even more complication for the issue they were working.

Modifying iptables rules

For this scenario, we will choose a simple method to both execute and remember. We will first edit the `/etc/sysconfig/iptables` file, which holds all of the defined `iptables` rules. Then restart the `iptables` service, which will cause the current rules to be flushed and the new rules in the `/etc/sysconfig/iptables` file to be applied.

To edit the `iptables` file, we can simply use `vi`:

```
[db]# vi /etc/sysconfig/iptables
# Generated by iptables-save v1.4.21 on Mon Mar 30 02:27:35 2015
*nat
:PREROUTING ACCEPT [10:994]
:INPUT ACCEPT [0:0]
:OUTPUT ACCEPT [0:0]
:POSTROUTING ACCEPT [0:0]
COMMIT
# Completed on Mon Mar 30 02:27:35 2015
# Generated by iptables-save v1.4.21 on Mon Mar 30 02:27:35 2015
*filter
:INPUT ACCEPT [0:0]
:FORWARD ACCEPT [0:0]
:OUTPUT ACCEPT [140:11432]
-A INPUT -m state --state RELATED,ESTABLISHED -j ACCEPT
-A INPUT -p icmp -j ACCEPT
-A INPUT -i lo -j ACCEPT
-A INPUT -p tcp -m state --state NEW -m tcp --dport 22 -j ACCEPT
-A INPUT -j REJECT --reject-with icmp-host-prohibited
-A INPUT -p tcp -m state --state NEW -m tcp --src 192.168.0.0/16 --dport 3306 -j ACCEPT
-A FORWARD -j REJECT --reject-with icmp-host-prohibited
COMMIT
# Completed on Mon Mar 30 02:27:35 2015
```

The contents of this file are a bit different than the output of `iptables -L`. The preceding rules are actually just options that can be appended to the `iptables` command. For example, if we wanted to add a rule that allows traffic to port 22, we can simply copy and paste the preceding rule with `-dport 22` with the `iptables` command prepended. The following is an example of what that command would look like:

```
iptables -A INPUT -p tcp -m state --state NEW -m tcp --dport 22 -j ACCEPT
```

When the `iptables` service scripts are adding the `iptables` rules, they also simply append these rules to the `iptables` command.

From the contents of the `iptables` file, we can see the two rules that need to be reordered:

```
-A INPUT -j REJECT --reject-with icmp-host-prohibited
-A INPUT -p tcp -m state --state NEW -m tcp --src 192.168.0.0/16 --
dport 3306 -j ACCEPT
```

In order to resolve our issue, we can simply change these two rules to match the following:

```
-A INPUT -p tcp -m state --state NEW -m tcp --src 192.168.0.0/16 --
dport 3306 -j ACCEPT
-A INPUT -j REJECT --reject-with icmp-host-prohibited
```

Once the change is made, we can **save** and **quit** the file by pressing *Esc* then `:wq` in vi.

Testing our changes

Now that the file is saved, we should be able to simply restart the `iptables` service and the rules will be applied. The only problem is, what if we didn't edit our `iptables` file correctly?

Our current `iptables` configuration has a rule that blocks all traffic except for connections that are allowed by the rules above it. What if we accidently placed that rule before the rule that allows port 22? This would mean that when we restart the `iptables` service, we will no longer be able to establish SSH connections, and since that is our only method for managing this server, that simple mistake could have serious consequences.

Caution should always be exercised when making changes to `iptables`. Even when simply restarting the `iptables` service, it is always best to look through the saved rules in `/etc/sysconfig/iptables` to ensure that there are no unexpected changes that will lock users and yourself out of managing the system.

To help avoid this situation, we can use the `screen` command. The `screen` command is used to open up pseudo terminals that will continue even if our SSH session is disconnected. This is true even if the disconnection is due to firewall changes.

To start the screen, we will simply execute the command `screen`:

```
[db]# screen
```

Once we are within the `screen` session, we are going to do a bit more than simply restart `iptables`. We are actually going to write out a `bash` one-liner that restarts `iptables`, prints the output to the screen to let us know our session still works, waits for two minutes, then finally stops the `iptables` service:

```
[db]# systemctl restart iptables; echo "still here?"; sleep 120;
systemctl stop iptables
```

When we run this command, we will see either one of two things, either our SSH session will close, which likely means we have an error in our `iptables` rules, or we will see a message on our screen that says **still here?**.

If we see the **still here?** message, this means our `iptables` rules did not lock out our SSH session:

```
[db]# systemctl restart iptables.service; echo "still here?"; sleep
120; systemctl stop iptables.service
still here?
```

Since the command finished and our SSH session did not terminate, we can now simply restart `iptables` with the comfort of knowing that we will not be locked out.

 It is always a good idea to establish a new SSH session when the rules are in place without ending the previous SSH session. This verifies that you can initiate new SSH sessions, and if it does not work, you still have the old SSH session alive to resolve the issue.

When we restart `iptables` this time, our new rules will be in place:

```
# systemctl restart iptables.service

# iptables -L -nv

Chain INPUT (policy ACCEPT 0 packets, 0 bytes)
 pkts bytes target       prot opt in      out      source
destination
   15   852 ACCEPT       all  --  *       *        0.0.0.0/0
0.0.0.0/0               state RELATED,ESTABLISHED
    0     0 ACCEPT       icmp --  *       *        0.0.0.0/0
0.0.0.0/0
    0     0 ACCEPT       all  --  lo      *        0.0.0.0/0
0.0.0.0/0
    0     0 ACCEPT       tcp  --  *       *        0.0.0.0/0
0.0.0.0/0               state NEW tcp dpt:22
```

```
     0      0 ACCEPT     tcp  -- *       *       192.168.0.0/16
0.0.0.0/0                  state NEW tcp dpt:3306
     0      0 REJECT     all  -- *       *       0.0.0.0/0
0.0.0.0/0                  reject-with icmp-host-prohibited
```

Now, we can see that the rule to accept port `3306` traffic is in front of the default deny rule. If we refresh our browser, we can also validate that the `iptables` change corrected the issue.

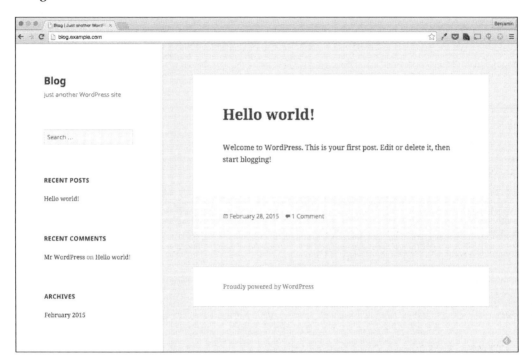

Which it seems, it has!

If we take another look at the `iptables` listing in the verbose mode, we can also see how well our rule is being matched:

```
# iptables -L -nv

Chain INPUT (policy ACCEPT 0 packets, 0 bytes)
 pkts bytes target     prot opt in      out     source
destination
   119 19352 ACCEPT     all  -- *       *       0.0.0.0/0
0.0.0.0/0                  state RELATED,ESTABLISHED
     0      0 ACCEPT     icmp -- *       *       0.0.0.0/0
0.0.0.0/0
```

```
    0      0 ACCEPT     all  --  lo     *        0.0.0.0/0
0.0.0.0/0
    0      0 ACCEPT     tcp  --  *      *        0.0.0.0/0
0.0.0.0/0              state NEW tcp dpt:22
    2    120 ACCEPT     tcp  --  *      *        192.168.0.0/16
0.0.0.0/0              state NEW tcp dpt:3306
   39   4254 REJECT     all  --  *      *        0.0.0.0/0
0.0.0.0/0              reject-with icmp-host-prohibited
```

From the statistics in `iptables`, we can see that two packets have matched our rule now. This combined with the working website means that our minor correction on ordering made a huge difference on what `iptables` allows or denies.

Summary

In this chapter, we experienced what seemed like a simple networking issue with our blog application connecting to its database. In our data collection phase, we used commands such as `netstat` and `tcpdump` to inspect the network packets and quickly discovered that the blog server was receiving an ICMP packet indicating that the database server is rejecting the blog server's TCP packets.

From that point, we suspected the issue was a firewall issue, which after investigating with the `iptables` command we noticed that the firewall rules were out of order.

Afterwards, we were able to use the *trial and error* stage to resolve the issue. This specific issue is a very common issue, something that I personally have seen in many different environments. This is mostly due to lack of knowledge around how `iptables` works and how to define rules properly. While this chapter only covered one type of misconfiguration within `iptables`, the general troubleshooting methods used within this chapter can be applied to most cases.

In *Chapter 7, FileSystem Errors and Recovery*, we will start exploring file system errors and how to recover from them—a tricky topic where one wrong command could mean data loss, something no systems administrator wants to see.

7
Filesystem Errors and Recovery

In *Chapter 5, Network Troubleshooting*, and *Chapter 6, Diagnosing and Correcting Firewall Issues*, we used quite a few tools to troubleshoot network connectivity issues due to misconfigured routes and firewalls. Network related issues are very common and the two example issues are also frequent scenarios. In this chapter, we will be focusing on hardware-related issues and start that with troubleshooting filesystem errors.

Much like the other chapters, we will start with a discovered error and troubleshoot the issue until we find the cause and solution. Along the way, we will discover many of the different commands and logs necessary for troubleshooting filesystem issues.

Diagnosing filesystem errors

Unlike earlier chapters where end users were reporting the issue to us, this time around we have found an issue for ourselves. While performing some daily tasks on the database server we attempted to create a database backup and received the following error:

```
[db]# mysqldump wordpress > /data/backups/wordpress.sql
-bash: /data/backups/wordpress.sql: Read-only file system
```

This error is interesting because it is not necessarily from the `mysqldump` command, but rather from the bash redirect that writes to the `/data/backups/wordpress.sql` file.

If we look at the error it is very specific, the filesystem we were attempting to write the backup to, is `Read-only`. What does `Read-only` mean?

Read-only filesystems

When defining and mounting filesystems on Linux you have many options, but there are two options that define the filesystem's accessibility best. Those two options are rw for read and write, and **ro** for read-only. When a filesystem is mounted with the read and write option, this means that the contents of the filesystem can be read and the users with appropriate permissions can write new files/directories to the filesystem.

When the filesystem is mounted in the read-only mode, it means that while users can read the filesystem, new write requests will be denied.

Using the mount command to list mounted filesystems

Since the error we received specifically states that the filesystem is read-only, our next logical step is to look at the filesystems mounted on this server. To do this, we will use the mount command:

```
[db]# mount
proc on /proc type proc (rw,nosuid,nodev,noexec,relatime)
sysfs on /sys type sysfs (rw,nosuid,nodev,noexec,relatime,seclabel)
devtmpfs on /dev type devtmpfs (rw,nosuid,seclabel,size=228500k,nr_
inodes=57125,mode=755)
securityfs on /sys/kernel/security type securityfs (rw,nosuid,nodev,noexe
c,relatime)
tmpfs on /dev/shm type tmpfs (rw,nosuid,nodev,seclabel)
devpts on /dev/pts type devpts (rw,nosuid,noexec,relatime,seclabel,gid=5,
mode=620,ptmxmode=000)
tmpfs on /run type tmpfs (rw,nosuid,nodev,seclabel,mode=755)
tmpfs on /sys/fs/cgroup type tmpfs (rw,nosuid,nodev,noexec,seclabel,mo
de=755)
selinuxfs on /sys/fs/selinux type selinuxfs (rw,relatime)
systemd-1 on /proc/sys/fs/binfmt_misc type autofs (rw,relatime,fd=33,pgrp
=1,timeout=300,minproto=5,maxproto=5,direct)
mqueue on /dev/mqueue type mqueue (rw,relatime,seclabel)
hugetlbfs on /dev/hugepages type hugetlbfs (rw,relatime,seclabel)
debugfs on /sys/kernel/debug type debugfs (rw,relatime)
sunrpc on /var/lib/nfs/rpc_pipefs type rpc_pipefs (rw,relatime)
nfsd on /proc/fs/nfsd type nfsd (rw,relatime)
```

```
/dev/sda1 on /boot type xfs (rw,relatime,seclabel,attr2,inode64,noquota)
```

```
192.168.33.13:/nfs on /data type nfs4 (rw,relatime,vers=4.0,rsize=65536,w
size=65536,namlen=255,hard,proto=tcp,port=0,timeo=600,retrans=2,sec=sys,c
lientaddr=192.168.33.12,local_lock=none,addr=192.168.33.13)
```

The mount command is a very useful command when dealing with filesystems. Not only can it be used to display the mounted filesystems (as seen in the preceding command), but it can also be used to attach (or mount) and un-attach (unmount) filesystems.

A mounted filesystem

Calling a filesystem a mounted filesystem is a common way of saying that the filesystem is *attached* to the server. With filesystems, they generally have two statuses, either they are attached (mounted) and the contents are accessible to users, or they are un-attached (unmounted) and inaccessible to the users. Later in this chapter, we will cover mounting and unmounting filesystems with the mount command.

The mount command is not the only way to see what filesystems are mounted or not mounted. Another way to do this is to simply read the /proc/mounts file:

```
[db]# cat /proc/mounts

rootfs / rootfs rw 0 0

proc /proc proc rw,nosuid,nodev,noexec,relatime 0 0

sysfs /sys sysfs rw,seclabel,nosuid,nodev,noexec,relatime 0 0

devtmpfs /dev devtmpfs rw,seclabel,nosuid,size=228500k,nr_
inodes=57125,mode=755 0 0

securityfs /sys/kernel/security securityfs
rw,nosuid,nodev,noexec,relatime 0 0

tmpfs /dev/shm tmpfs rw,seclabel,nosuid,nodev 0 0

devpts /dev/pts devpts rw,seclabel,nosuid,noexec,relatime,gid=5,mode=620,
ptmxmode=000 0 0

tmpfs /run tmpfs rw,seclabel,nosuid,nodev,mode=755 0 0

tmpfs /sys/fs/cgroup tmpfs rw,seclabel,nosuid,nodev,noexec,mode=755 0 0

selinuxfs /sys/fs/selinux selinuxfs rw,relatime 0 0

systemd-1 /proc/sys/fs/binfmt_misc autofs rw,relatime,fd=33,pgrp=1,timeou
t=300,minproto=5,maxproto=5,direct 0 0

mqueue /dev/mqueue mqueue rw,seclabel,relatime 0 0

hugetlbfs /dev/hugepages hugetlbfs rw,seclabel,relatime 0 0

debugfs /sys/kernel/debug debugfs rw,relatime 0 0
```

```
sunrpc /var/lib/nfs/rpc_pipefs rpc_pipefs rw,relatime 0 0

nfsd /proc/fs/nfsd nfsd rw,relatime 0 0

/dev/sda1 /boot xfs rw,seclabel,relatime,attr2,inode64,noquota 0 0

192.168.33.13:/nfs /data nfs4 rw,relatime,vers=4.0,rsize=65536,wsize=6553
6,namlen=255,hard,proto=tcp,port=0,timeo=600,retrans=2,sec=sys,clientaddr
=192.168.33.12,local_lock=none,addr=192.168.33.13 0 0
```

In fact, the contents of the /proc/mounts file are extremely close to the output of the mount command, with the main difference being the two numbered columns at the end of each line. To get a better understanding of this file and the output of the mount command, let's take a better look at the /boot filesystem's entry within /proc/mounts:

```
/dev/sda1 /boot xfs rw,seclabel,relatime,attr2,inode64,noquota 0 0
```

The /proc/mounts file has data in six columns—**device**, **mount point**, **filesystem type**, **options**, and two unused columns that exist for backwards compatibility. For a better understanding of these values, let's get a better understanding of the columns.

The first column device, specifies the device to use for the filesystem. In the preceding example, the device that the /boot filesystem lives on is /dev/sda1.

From the name of the device (sda1), we can identify a critical piece of information. This device is a partition of another device, which we can identify by the fact that the device name has a number at the end.

The device, which by the name appears to be a physical drive (assuming it's a hard drive) and is named /dev/sda; this drive has at least one partition, which has a device name of /dev/sda1. Whenever a drive has partitions on it, the partitions are created as their own device, each device getting assigned a number; in this case 1, which means that it is the first partition.

Using fdisk to list available partitions

We can verify this by looking at the /dev/sda device that is using the fdisk command:

```
[db]# fdisk -l /dev/sda


Disk /dev/sda: 42.9 GB, 42949672960 bytes, 83886080 sectors
Units = sectors of 1 * 512 = 512 bytes
Sector size (logical/physical): 512 bytes / 512 bytes
I/O size (minimum/optimal): 512 bytes / 512 bytes
Disk label type: dos
```

```
Disk identifier: 0x0009c844


   Device Boot      Start        End       Blocks   Id  System
/dev/sda1     *      2048    1026047       512000   83  Linux
/dev/sda2          1026048   83886079    41430016   8e  Linux LVM
```

The fdisk command might be familiar because it is a cross-platform command used to create disk partitions. It can however also be used to list partitions.

In the preceding command, we used the -l (list) flag to list the partitions followed by the device we wanted to look at—/dev/sda. However, the fdisk command shows us much more than the partitions available on this drive. It also shows us how large the disk is:

```
Disk /dev/sda: 42.9 GB, 42949672960 bytes, 83886080 sectors
```

We can see this in the first line being printed from the fdisk command, according to this line our device /dev/sda is 42.9 GB in size. If we look towards the bottom of the output, we can also see the partitions created on this disk:

```
   Device Boot      Start        End       Blocks   Id  System
/dev/sda1     *      2048    1026047       512000   83  Linux
/dev/sda2          1026048   83886079    41430016   8e  Linux LVM
```

From the preceding list, it appears that /dev/sda has two partitions, /dev/sda1 and /dev/sda2. Using fdisk, we have been able to identify quite a few details about this filesystem's physical device. If we continue to look at the details from /proc/mounts, we should be able to identify some other very useful information, as follows:

```
/dev/sda1 /boot xfs rw,seclabel,relatime,attr2,inode64,noquota 0 0
```

The second column *mount point* in the preceding line notates the path that this filesystem is mounted to. In this case, the path is /boot; /boot by itself is nothing more than a directory on the / (root) filesystem. However, once the filesystem that exists on the device /dev/sda1 is mounted /boot is now its own filesystem.

To better understand this concept, we will use the mount and umount commands to attach and detach the /boot filesystem:

```
[db]# ls /boot/
config-3.10.0-123.el7.x86_64
grub
grub2
initramfs-0-rescue-dee83c8c69394b688b9c2a55de9e29e4.img
```

```
initramfs-3.10.0-123.el7.x86_64.img
initramfs-3.10.0-123.el7.x86_64kdump.img
initrd-plymouth.img
symvers-3.10.0-123.el7.x86_64.gz
System.map-3.10.0-123.el7.x86_64
vmlinuz-0-rescue-dee83c8c69394b688b9c2a55de9e29e4
vmlinuz-3.10.0-123.el7.x86_64
```

If we perform a simple `ls` command on the `/boot` path, we can see quite a few files within this directory. From the `/proc/mounts` file and the `mount` command, we know that there is a filesystem attached to `/boot`:

```
[db]# mount | grep /boot
/dev/sda1 on /boot type xfs
(rw,relatime,seclabel,attr2,inode64,noquota)
```

In order to un-attach or unmount this filesystem, we can use the `umount` command:

```
[db]# umount /boot
[db]# mount | grep /boot
```

The `umount` command has a pretty simple task, it unmounts mounted filesystems.

> The preceding commands are examples that unmounting a filesystem can be dangerous. In general, you should first verify that the filesystem is not actively being accessed before unmounting it.

Since the `/boot` filesystem is now unmounted, what happens when we perform our `ls` command?

```
# ls /boot
```

The path `/boot` is still valid. However, it is now just an empty directory. This is due to the fact that the filesystem on `/dev/sda1` is not mounted; therefore, any files that existed on that filesystem are not currently accessible on this system.

If we use the `mount` command to remount the filesystem, we will see the files reappear:

```
[db]# mount /boot
[db]# ls /boot
config-3.10.0-123.el7.x86_64
grub
```

```
grub2
initramfs-0-rescue-dee83c8c69394b688b9c2a55de9e29e4.img
initramfs-3.10.0-123.el7.x86_64.img
initramfs-3.10.0-123.el7.x86_64kdump.img
initrd-plymouth.img
symvers-3.10.0-123.el7.x86_64.gz
System.map-3.10.0-123.el7.x86_64
vmlinuz-0-rescue-dee83c8c69394b688b9c2a55de9e29e4
vmlinuz-3.10.0-123.el7.x86_64
```

As we can see, when the mount command is given a path argument, the command will attempt to mount that filesystem. However, when given no arguments the mount command will simply display what filesystems are currently mounted.

Later in this chapter, we will explore using mount and how it understands where and how filesystems should be mounted; for now, let's take a look at the next column in the /proc/mounts output:

```
/dev/sda1 /boot xfs rw,seclabel,relatime,attr2,inode64,noquota 0 0
```

The third column filesystem type denotes the type of filesystem being used. In many operating systems, especially Linux, there is often more than one type of filesystem that can be used. In the preceding case, our boot filesystem is set to xfs, which as of Red Hat Enterprise Linux 7, is the new default file system.

Prior to xfs, older versions of Red Hat defaulted to either the ext3 or ext4 filesystems. The ext3/4 filesystems and others are still supported by Red Hat, so there could be a number of different filesystem types listed in the /proc/mounts file.

For the /boot filesystem, knowing the filesystem type is not immediately useful; however, knowing how to look up the underlying type of filesystem might be required as we dig deeper into this issue:

```
/dev/sda1 /boot xfs rw,seclabel,relatime,attr2,inode64,noquota 0 0
```

The fourth column options shows the options the filesystem has been mounted with.

When a filesystem is mounted, that filesystem can be given specific options in order to change the default behavior of the filesystem. In the preceding example, there are quite a few options provided; let's break down this list to better understand what is being specified:

- **rw**: This mounts the filesystem in the read and write mode
- **seclabel**: This option is added by SELinux to show that this filesystem supports extra attributes for labels
- **relatime**: This tells the filesystem to only modify the access time if it is earlier compared to the modify or change time values of a file/directory
- **attr2**: This enables an improvement in how inline extended attributes are stored on-disk
- **inode64**: This enables the filesystem to create inode numbers greater than 32 bits in length
- **noquota**: This disables disk quotas and enforcement for this filesystem

As we can see from the descriptions, these options can greatly change the way the filesystem behaves. They are also very important to look at when troubleshooting any filesystem issues:

```
/dev/sda1 /boot xfs rw,seclabel,relatime,attr2,inode64,noquota 0 0
```

The last two columns of the /proc/mounts output, which are represented as 0 0 are actually not used in /proc/mounts. These columns are in fact only added for backwards capability with /etc/mtab, which is a similar file, however is not considered up-to-date like /proc/mounts.

The difference between these two files is specifically in their usage. The /etc/mtab file is designed for users or applications to read and utilize where the /proc/mounts file is used by the kernel itself. For this reason, the /proc/mounts file is considered the most authoritative version.

Back to troubleshooting

If we go back to our issue at hand, we received an error when writing a backup to the /data/backups directory. Using the mount command, we can identify which filesystem that directory exists on:

```
# mount | grep "data"
192.168.33.13:/nfs on /data type nfs4 (rw,relatime,vers=4.0,rsize=65536,w
size=65536,namlen=255,hard,proto=tcp,port=0,timeo=600,retrans=2,sec=sys,c
lientaddr=192.168.33.12,local_lock=none,addr=192.168.33.13)
```

Now that we understand the format of the mount command better, we can identify some key information from the preceding command line. We can see that the device for this filesystem is set to (192.168.33.13:/nfs), the mount point (path to attach as) is set to (/data), the filesystem type of is (nfs4), and the filesystem has quite a few options set.

NFS – Network Filesystem

Looking at the /data filesystem we can see that the filesystem type is set to nfs4. This filesystem type means that the filesystem is a **Network Filesystem (NFS)**.

NFS is a service that allows a server to share an exported directory with other remote servers. The nfs4 filesystem type is a special filesystem that allows the remote servers to access this service as if it was a standard filesystem.

The 4 in the filesystem type denotes the version to use, which means the remote server is to use Version 4 of the NFS protocol.

 Currently, the most popular versions for NFS are versions 3 and 4, with 4 being the default for Red Hat Enterprise Linux 6 and 7. There are quite a few differences between version 3 and version 4; however, none of those differences are enough to make a difference in our troubleshooting methodology. If you find yourself running into issues with NFS Version 3, then you can most likely follow the same types of steps that we will follow in this chapter.

Now that we have identified that the filesystem is an NFS filesystem, let's take a look at the options it is mounted with:

```
192.168.33.13:/nfs on /data type nfs4 (rw,relatime,vers=4.0,rsize=65536,w
size=65536,namlen=255,hard,proto=tcp,port=0,timeo=600,retrans=2,sec=sys,c
lientaddr=192.168.33.12,local_lock=none,addr=192.168.33.13)
```

From the error we received, the filesystem appears to be Read-Only, but if we look at the options the first option listed is rw. This means that the NFS filesystem itself has been mounted as Read-Write; which should allow writes to this filesystem.

To test whether the issue is with the path /data/backups or the mounted filesystem /data, we can use the touch command to test creating a file within this filesystem:

```
# touch /data/file.txt
touch: cannot touch '/data/file.txt': Read-only file system
```

Even the `touch` command is not able to create a new file on this filesystem. This is a clear indication that there is a problem with the filesystem; the only question is what is causing the issue.

If we look at the options this filesystem is mounted with, there is nothing that would cause the filesystem to be `Read-Only`; this means that the issue is most likely not with how the filesystem is mounted, but with something else.

Since the issue does not appear to be related to how the NFS filesystem is mounted and this filesystem is network based, a valid next step would be to verify network connectivity to the NFS server.

NFS and network connectivity

Just as with the network troubleshooting, our first test will be to ping the NFS server to see if we get a response; but the question is: *What server should we ping?*

The answer is in the device name that the filesystem is mounted with (`192.168.33.13:/nfs`). When mounting an NFS filesystem, the device is in the format of `<nfs server>:<shared directory>`. For our example, this means that our `/data` filesystem is mounting the `/nfs` directory from the server `192.168.33.13`. To test connectivity, we can simply `ping` the IP `192.168.33.13`:

```
[db]# ping 192.168.33.13
PING 192.168.33.13 (192.168.33.13) 56(84) bytes of data.
64 bytes from 192.168.33.13: icmp_seq=1 ttl=64 time=0.495 ms
64 bytes from 192.168.33.13: icmp_seq=2 ttl=64 time=0.372 ms
64 bytes from 192.168.33.13: icmp_seq=3 ttl=64 time=0.364 ms
64 bytes from 192.168.33.13: icmp_seq=4 ttl=64 time=0.337 ms
^C
--- 192.168.33.13 ping statistics ---
4 packets transmitted, 4 received, 0% packet loss, time 3001ms
rtt min/avg/max/mdev = 0.337/0.392/0.495/0.060 ms
```

From the `ping` results, it appears that the NFS server is up; but what about the NFS service? We can validate connectivity to the NFS service by using the `curl` command to `telnet` to the NFS port. First, however, we need to identify which port we should connect to.

While troubleshooting the database connectivity in earlier chapters, we were mostly using well-known ports; since NFS uses several ports, which are a little less common; we will need to identify which port to connect to:

The easiest way to do this is to search for the ports in the `/etc/services` file:

```
[db]# grep nfs /etc/services
nfs                 2049/tcp        nfsd shilp        # Network File System
nfs                 2049/udp        nfsd shilp        # Network File System
nfs                 2049/sctp       nfsd shilp        # Network File System
netconfsoaphttp 832/tcp                              # NETCONF for SOAP over HTTPS
netconfsoaphttp 832/udp                              # NETCONF for SOAP over HTTPS
netconfsoapbeep 833/tcp                              # NETCONF for SOAP over BEEP
netconfsoapbeep 833/udp                              # NETCONF for SOAP over BEEP
nfsd-keepalive  1110/udp                             # Client status info
picknfs             1598/tcp                         # picknfs
picknfs             1598/udp                         # picknfs
shiva_confsrvr  1651/tcp        shiva-confsrvr   # shiva_confsrvr
shiva_confsrvr  1651/udp        shiva-confsrvr   # shiva_confsrvr
3d-nfsd             2323/tcp                         # 3d-nfsd
3d-nfsd             2323/udp                         # 3d-nfsd
mediacntrlnfsd  2363/tcp                             # Media Central NFSD
mediacntrlnfsd  2363/udp                             # Media Central NFSD
winfs               5009/tcp                         # Microsoft Windows Filesystem
winfs               5009/udp                         # Microsoft Windows Filesystem
enfs                5233/tcp                         # Etinnae Network File Service
nfsrdma             20049/tcp                        # Network File System (NFS) over
RDMA
nfsrdma             20049/udp                        # Network File System (NFS) over
RDMA
nfsrdma             20049/sctp                       # Network File System (NFS) over
RDMA
```

The `/etc/services` file is a static file that is included with many Linux distributions. It is used as a lookup to map network ports to a simple human readable name. From the preceding output, we can see that the `nfs` name is mapped to TCP port `2049`; this is the default port for the NFS service. We can utilize this port to test connectivity, as follows:

```
[db]# curl -vk telnet://192.168.33.13:2049
* About to connect() to 192.168.33.13 port 2049 (#0)
*   Trying 192.168.33.13...
* Connected to 192.168.33.13 (192.168.33.13) port 2049 (#0)
```

Our `telnet` seems successful; we can further validate it by using the `netstat` command:

```
[db]# netstat -na | grep 192.168.33.13
tcp        0        0 192.168.33.12:756        192.168.33.13:2049
ESTABLISHED
```

It seems that connectivity is not an issue, and if our issue is not connectivity related, maybe it is in how the NFS share is configured.

We can actually validate the NFS share's settings and network connectivity in one command — `showmount`.

Using the showmount command

The `showmount` command can be used to display the directories being exported via the `-e` (that shows exports) flag. This command works by querying the NFS service on the specified host.

For our issue, we will be querying the NFS service at `192.168.33.13`:

```
[db]# showmount -e 192.168.33.13
Export list for 192.168.33.13:
/nfs 192.168.33.0/24
```

The format of the `showmount` command uses two columns. The first column is the directory being shared. The second is the network or hostnames the directory is being shared with.

In the preceding example, we can see that the directory being shared from this host is the `/nfs` directory. This matches the directory listed in the device name `192.168.33.13:/nfs` as well.

The network that the `/nfs` directory is being shared with is the `192.166.33.0/24` network, which, as we learned in our networking chapter, is short for `192.168.33.0` through `192.168.33.255`. We already know from previous troubleshooting that the database server we are on is within that network.

We can also see this hasn't changed since the `netstat` command was executed earlier:

```
[db]# netstat -na | grep 192.168.33.13
tcp        0        0 192.168.33.12:756        192.168.33.13:2049
ESTABLISHED
```

The fourth column of the `netstat` command shows the local IP address being used in the ESTABLISHED TCP connection. With the preceding output, we can see the `192.168.33.12` address is the IP of our database server (as seen in previous chapters).

So far everything about this NFS share looks correct, from here we will need to log in to the NFS server to continue troubleshooting.

NFS server configuration

Once logged into the NFS server, the first thing we should check is whether or not the NFS service is running:

```
[db]# systemctl status nfs
nfs-server.service - NFS server and services
   Loaded: loaded (/usr/lib/systemd/system/nfs-server.service; enabled)
   Active: active (exited) since Sat 2015-04-25 14:01:13 MST; 17h ago
  Process: 2226 ExecStart=/usr/sbin/rpc.nfsd $RPCNFSDARGS (code=exited,
status=0/SUCCESS)
  Process: 2225 ExecStartPre=/usr/sbin/exportfs -r (code=exited,
status=0/SUCCESS)
 Main PID: 2226 (code=exited, status=0/SUCCESS)
   CGroup: /system.slice/nfs-server.service
```

Using `systemctl`, we can simply look at the service status; which from the preceding output looks normal. This is to be expected since we were able to both `telnet` to the NFS service and use the `showmount` command to query it.

Exploring /etc/exports

Since the NFS service is running and healthy, the next step is to check the configuration that defines which directories are exported and how they are exported; the `/etc/exports` file:

```
[nfs]# ls -la /etc/exports
-rw-r--r--. 1 root root 40 Apr 26 08:28 /etc/exports
[nfs]# cat /etc/exports
/nfs  192.168.33.0/24(rw,no_root_squash)
```

The format of this file is actually similar to the output of the `showmount` command.

The first column is the directory to be shared and the second column is the network to share it with. However, in this file there is additional information after the network definition.

The network/subnet column is followed by a set of parenthesis with various NFS options within it. These options work very similar to the mount options we saw in the /proc/mounts file.

Could these options be the root cause of our Read-Only file system? Quite possibly. Let's break down these two options to get a better understanding:

- rw: This allows both reads and writes to be performed on the shared directory

- no_root_squash: This disables root_squash; root_squash is a system that maps the root user to an anonymous user

Unfortunately, neither of these options would force the filesystem to be in the Read-Only mode. In fact, based on the description of these options they seem to suggest this NFS share should be in the Read-Write mode.

One interesting fact has surfaced while performing an ls on the /etc/exports file:

```
[nfs]# ls -la /etc/exports
-rw-r--r--. 1 root root 40 Apr 26 08:28 /etc/exports
```

The /etc/exports file has been modified recently. Could it be that our shared filesystem is actually shared as Read-Only but someone has recently changed the /etc/exports file to export the filesystem as Read-Write.

This scenario is entirely possible, and in fact is actually a common issue with NFS. The NFS service is not constantly reading the /etc/exports file looking for changes. In fact, this file is only read when the service is starting.

Any changes to the /etc/exports file will not take effect until after either the service is reloaded or the exported filesystems is refreshed using the exportfs command.

Identifying the current exports

A very common scenario is where someone makes a change to this file and simply forgets to run the commands to refresh the exported filesystems. We can identify whether this is the case by using the exportfs command:

```
[nfs]# exportfs -s
/nfs  192.168.33.0/24(rw,wdelay,no_root_squash,no_subtree_
check,sec=sys,rw,secure,no_root_squash,no_all_squash)
```

When given the -s (show current exports) flag, the exportfs command will simply list the existing shared directories, including the options that the directories are shared with.

Looking at the preceding output, we can see that this filesystem is shared with quite a few options that are not listed in /etc/exports. The reason for this is because all directories shared through NFS have a default list of options that govern how the directory is shared. The options specified in /etc/exports are essentially used to override the default settings.

To get a better understanding of these options, let's break them down:

- rw: This allows both reads and writes to be performed on the shared directory.
- wdelay: This causes NFS to hold a write request if it suspects another write is incoming from another client. This is designed to reduce write conflicts when multiple clients are connected.
- no_root_squash: This disables root_squash, which is a system that maps the root user to an anonymous user.
- no_subtree_check: This disables subtree checking; subtree checking essentially ensures that requests to a directory where a subdirectory is also exported will honor the subdirectory's more restrictive policy.
- sec=sys: This tells NFS to use the user ID and group ID values for permissions and authorization of file access.
- secure: This ensures that NFS only honors requests where the clients port is lower than 1024, essentially requiring it to be from a privileged NFS mount.
- no_all_squash: This disables all_squash, which is used to force all permissions to be mapped to the anonymous user and group.

It seems that these options also do not explain the Read-Only file system. This is an issue that seems to be very tricky to troubleshoot, especially when the NFS service seems to be configured correctly.

Testing NFS from another client

Since the NFS server's configuration seems correct and the client (database server) also appears correct, we will need to narrow down whether the issue is at the client side or the server side.

One way we can do this is by mounting the filesystem on another client and attempting the same write request. From the configuration, it appears we simply need another server in the `192.168.33.0/24` network to perform this test. Perhaps our blog server from earlier chapters is a good client to use?

> In some environments, the answer to this question would be `no`, as a web server is often considered less secure than a database server. However, since this is simply a test environment for this book, it will be OK.

Once we have logged into the blog server, we can test whether or not we can even see the mount with the `showmount` command:

```
[blog]# showmount -e 192.168.33.13
Export list for 192.168.33.13:
/nfs 192.168.33.0/24
```

This answers two questions. The first is whether the NFS client software is installed; since the `showmount` command is present, the answer is likely `yes`.

The second is whether the NFS service is accessible from the blog server, which also appears to be yes.

To test the mount, we will simply use the `mount` command:

```
[blog]# mount -t nfs 192.168.33.13:/nfs /mnt
```

To use the `mount` command to mount a filesystem the syntax is: `mount -t <filesystem type> <device> <mount point>`. In the example above we simply mounted the `192.168.33.13:/nfs` device to the `/mnt` directory with the filesystem type as `nfs`.

While running the command, we did not receive any errors but to ensure that the filesystem is mounted properly, we can use the `mount` command just as we did before:

```
[blog]# mount | grep /mnt
192.168.33.13:/nfs on /mnt type nfs4 (rw,relatime,vers=4.0,rsize=65536,ws
ize=65536,namlen=255,hard,proto=tcp,port=0,timeo=600,retrans=2,sec=sys,cl
ientaddr=192.168.33.11,local_lock=none,addr=192.168.33.13)
```

From the output of the `mount` command, it appears that the `mount` request was successful and in the `Read-Write` mode, which means the `mount` options are similar to the options used on the database server.

Now we can test the filesystem by attempting to create a file with the `touch` command:

```
# touch /mnt/testfile.txt
touch: cannot touch '/mnt/testfile.txt': Read-only file system
```

It appears that the issue is not with the client's configuration, as even our new client is having issues writing to this filesystem.

> As a tip, in the preceding example, I mounted the `/nfs` share to `/mnt`. The `/mnt` directory is used as a generic mount point and is generally considered OK for use. However, it is always a best practice to ensure nothing else is mounted to `/mnt` before hand.

Making mounts permanent

Currently, even though we mounted the NFS share with the `mount` command, this mounted filesystem is not considered persistent. The next time this system reboots, the NFS mount will not be remounted.

That is because as a system boots up, part of the boot process is to read the `/etc/fstab` file and `mount` any filesystems defined within it.

To better understand how this works, let's look at the `/etc/fstab` file on the database server:

```
[db]# cat /etc/fstab

#
# /etc/fstab
# Created by anaconda on Mon Jul 21 23:35:56 2014
#
# Accessible filesystems, by reference, are maintained under '/dev/disk'
# See man pages fstab(5), findfs(8), mount(8) and/or blkid(8) for more
info
#
/dev/mapper/os-root /                           xfs       defaults        1 1
UUID=be76ec1d-686d-44a0-9411-b36931ee239b /boot                           xfs
defaults        1 2
/dev/mapper/os-swap swap                         swap      defaults        0 0
192.168.33.13:/nfs  /data         nfs  defaults  0 0
```

The contents of the /etc/fstab file are actually very similar to the contents of the /proc/mounts file. The first column in the /etc/fstab file is used to specify the device to be mounted, the second column is the path or mount point to mount to, the third column is simply the filesystem type, and the fourth column is the options to mount the filesystem with.

The last two columns, however, are where these files differ, within the /etc/fstab file. These last two columns actually have a meaning. Within the fstab file, the fifth column is used by the dump command.

The dump command is a simple backup utility which reads the /etc/fstab to determine which filesystems to backup. Any filesystem with a 0 value set will not be in scope for a backup, when the dump utility is executed.

While this utility is not heavily used these days, this column in the /etc/fstab file is maintained for backwards capability.

The sixth and final column in the /etc/fstab file is very relevant to today's systems. This column is used to denote the order in which a filesystem check or fsck is performed during the boot process (generally after a failure).

A filesystem check or fsck is a process that runs periodically, checking the filesystem for errors and attempts to correct them. This is a process we will cover a bit further in this chapter.

Unmounting the /mnt filesystem

Since we do not want the NFS shared filesystem to stay mounted on the /mnt path of the blog server, we will need to unmount the filesystem.

We can do this in the same way we did with the /boot filesystem earlier; with the umount command:

```
[blog]# umount /mnt
[blog]# mount | grep /mnt
```

From the blog server, we simply used umount followed by the mount point of /mnt to unmount the NFS mount from the client. Now that we have, we can go back to the NFS server to continue troubleshooting.

Troubleshooting the NFS server, again

Since we identified that even new clients cannot write to the /nfs share, we have at this point narrowed down that the issue is likely on the server side and not the client.

Earlier, while troubleshooting the NFS server, we checked almost everything that there is to check about NFS. We validated that the service is in fact running, accessible by the clients, that the data in /etc/exports is correct, and that the currently exported directories match what is in /etc/exports. At this point, there is only one place left to check: the log files.

By default, the NFS service does not have its own log file like Apache or MariaDB. Instead, this service on the RHEL systems utilizes the syslog facility; which means our logs will be within /var/log/messages.

The messages log is a very frequently used log file for Red Hat Enterprise Linux based Linux distributions. In fact, by default, outside of cron jobs and authentication, every syslog message above the info log level is sent to /var/log/messages on RHEL based systems.

Since the NFS service sends its log messages to the local syslog service, its messages are also included in the messages log.

Finding the NFS log messages

What if we didn't know that NFS logs were sent to the /var/log/messages log file? There is a pretty simple trick to identify which log file contains NFS log messages.

In general, on Linux systems, all system services have their log files located within /var/log. Since we know the default location of majority of logs on the system, we can simply take a quick look through those files to identify which ones might have the NFS log messages:

```
[nfs]# cd /var/log
[nfs]# grep -rc nfs ./*
./anaconda/anaconda.log:14
./anaconda/syslog:44
./anaconda/anaconda.xlog:0
./anaconda/anaconda.program.log:7
./anaconda/anaconda.packaging.log:16
./anaconda/anaconda.storage.log:56
./anaconda/anaconda.ifcfg.log:0
./anaconda/ks-script-Sr69bV.log:0
```

```
./anaconda/ks-script-1fU6U2.log:0
./audit/audit.log:60
./boot.log:4
./btmp:0
./cron:470
./cron-20150420:662
./dmesg:26
./dmesg.old:26
./grubby:0
./lastlog:0
./maillog:112386
./maillog-20150420:17
./messages:3253
./messages-20150420:11804
./sa/sa15:1
./sa/sar15:1
./sa/sa16:1
./sa/sar16:1
./sa/sa17:1
./sa/sa19:1
./sa/sar19:1
./sa/sa20:1
./sa/sa25:1
./sa/sa26:1
./secure:14
./secure-20150420:63
./spooler:0
./tallylog:0
./tuned/tuned.log:0
./wtmp:0
./yum.log:0
```

The `grep` command recursively (`-r`) searches each file for the string "`nfs`" and outputs the filename along with a count (`-c`) of the number of lines where the string is found.

In the preceding output, there are two log files that contain the highest amount of instances of the string "nfs". The first is the `maillog`, which is the system log for e-mail messages; this is not likely related to the NFS service.

The second is the `messages` log file which, as we know, is the system default log file.

Even without prior knowledge of a specific system's logging methods, if you are familiar with Linux in general and tricks as in the preceding example, you can often find which logs contain the data required.

Now that we know the log file we are looking for, let's take a look through the `/var/log/messages` log.

Reading /var/log/messages

Since this `log` file can be quite large, we will use the `tail` command with the `-100` flag, which causes the tail to only display the last `100` lines of the specified file. By limiting the output to `100` lines, we should only see the most relevant data:

```
[nfs]# tail -100 /var/log/messages
Apr 26 10:25:44 nfs kernel: md/raid1:md127: Disk failure on sdb1,
disabling device.
md/raid1:md127: Operation continuing on 1 devices.
Apr 26 10:25:55 nfs kernel: md: unbind<sdb1>
Apr 26 10:25:55 nfs kernel: md: export_rdev(sdb1)
Apr 26 10:27:20 nfs kernel: md: bind<sdb1>
Apr 26 10:27:20 nfs kernel: md: recovery of RAID array md127
Apr 26 10:27:20 nfs kernel: md: minimum _guaranteed_  speed: 1000 KB/sec/
disk.
Apr 26 10:27:20 nfs kernel: md: using maximum available idle IO bandwidth
(but not more than 200000 KB/sec) for recovery.
Apr 26 10:27:20 nfs kernel: md: using 128k window, over a total of
511936k.
Apr 26 10:27:20 nfs kernel: md: md127: recovery done.
Apr 26 10:27:41 nfs nfsdcltrack[4373]: sqlite_remove_client: unexpected
return code from delete: 8
Apr 26 10:27:59 nfs nfsdcltrack[4375]: sqlite_remove_client: unexpected
return code from delete: 8
Apr 26 10:55:06 nfs dhclient[3528]: can't create /var/lib/NetworkManager/
dhclient-05be239d-0ec7-4f2e-a68d-b64eec03fcb2-enp0s3.lease: Read-only
file system
```

```
Apr 26 11:03:43 nfs chronyd[744]: Could not open temporary driftfile /
var/lib/chrony/drift.tmp for writing
```

```
Apr 26 11:55:03 nfs rpc.mountd[4552]: could not open /var/lib/nfs/.xtab.
lock for locking: errno 30 (Read-only file system)
```

```
Apr 26 11:55:03 nfs rpc.mountd[4552]: can't lock /var/lib/nfs/xtab for
writing
```

Since even 100 lines can be quite tedious to go through, I have truncated the output to only the relevant lines. This shows quite a few messages with the string "nfs"; however, not every one of these are messages from the NFS service. Since our NFS server's hostname is set to nfs, each log entry from this system has the string "nfs".

However, even with that, we do still see a few messages related to the NFS service, specifically the following lines:

```
Apr 26 10:27:41 nfs nfsdcltrack[4373]: sqlite_remove_client: unexpected
return code from delete: 8
```

```
Apr 26 10:27:59 nfs nfsdcltrack[4375]: sqlite_remove_client: unexpected
return code from delete: 8
```

```
Apr 26 11:55:03 nfs rpc.mountd[4552]: could not open /var/lib/nfs/.xtab.
lock for locking: errno 30 (Read-only file system)
```

```
Apr 26 11:55:03 nfs rpc.mountd[4552]: can't lock /var/lib/nfs/xtab for
writing
```

The interesting thing about these log entries is that one of them specifically states that the service rpc.mountd was not able to open a file due to the filesystem being Read-only. However, the file it was trying to open /var/lib/nfs/.xtab.lock is not part of our NFS share.

Since this filesystem is not part of our NFS, let's take a quick look at the mounted filesystems on this server. We can do this again, with the mount command:

```
[nfs]# mount
proc on /proc type proc (rw,nosuid,nodev,noexec,relatime)
sysfs on /sys type sysfs (rw,nosuid,nodev,noexec,relatime,seclabel)
devtmpfs on /dev type devtmpfs (rw,nosuid,seclabel,size=241112k,nr_
inodes=60278,mode=755)
securityfs on /sys/kernel/security type securityfs (rw,nosuid,nodev,noexe
c,relatime)
selinuxfs on /sys/fs/selinux type selinuxfs (rw,relatime)
systemd-1 on /proc/sys/fs/binfmt_misc type autofs (rw,relatime,fd=33,pgrp
=1,timeout=300,minproto=5,maxproto=5,direct)
mqueue on /dev/mqueue type mqueue (rw,relatime,seclabel)
debugfs on /sys/kernel/debug type debugfs (rw,relatime)
```

```
hugetlbfs on /dev/hugepages type hugetlbfs (rw,relatime,seclabel)
sunrpc on /var/lib/nfs/rpc_pipefs type rpc_pipefs (rw,relatime)
nfsd on /proc/fs/nfsd type nfsd (rw,relatime)
/dev/mapper/md0-root on / type xfs (ro,relatime,seclabel,attr2,inode64,no
quota)
/dev/md127 on /boot type xfs (ro,relatime,seclabel,attr2,inode64,noquota)
/dev/mapper/md0-nfs on /nfs type xfs (ro,relatime,seclabel,attr2,inode64,
noquota)
```

Like the other server there are quite a bit of mounted filesystems, we however are not interested in all of them; only a small subset.

```
/dev/mapper/md0-root on / type xfs (ro,relatime,seclabel,attr2,inode64,no
quota)
/dev/md127 on /boot type xfs (ro,relatime,seclabel,attr2,inode64,noquota)
/dev/mapper/md0-nfs on /nfs type xfs (ro,relatime,seclabel,attr2,inode64,
noquota)
```

The preceding three lines are the lines that we should be interested in. These three mounted filesystems are persistent filesystems defined for our system. If we look at these three persistent filesystems, we can identify some interesting information.

The / or root filesystem exists on the device /dev/mapper/md0-root. This filesystem is actually incredibly important to our system, as it appears that this server is configured to have the entire operating system installed under the root filesystem (/), a somewhat common setup. This filesystem includes the file in question, the /var/lib/nfs/.xtab.lock file.

The /boot filesystem exists on the device /dev/md127 which judging by the name is most likely a raided device using Linux's software raid system. The /boot filesystem is just as important as the root filesystem as /boot contains all of the necessary files for the server to boot up. Without the /boot filesystem, this system would most likely not restart and would simply kernel panic on the next system restart.

The last filesystem /nfs uses the /dev/mapper/md0-nfs device. From our earlier troubleshooting, we identified this filesystem as an exported filesystem via the NFS service.

Read-only filesystems

If we look back at the error and the output of mount, we will start to identify some interesting errors on this system:

```
Apr 26 11:55:03 nfs rpc.mountd[4552]: could not open /var/lib/nfs/.xtab.
lock for locking: errno 30 (Read-only file system)
```

The error is reporting that the filesystem where the .xtab.lock file is located is Read-Only:

```
/dev/mapper/md0-root on / type xfs (ro,relatime,seclabel,attr2,inode64,no
quota)
```

From the mount command, we can see that the filesystem in question is the / filesystem. After looking at the options for the / or root filesystem we can see that this filesystem is in fact mounted with the ro option.

In fact, if we look at the three filesystems' options, we can see that /, /boot, and /nfs are all mounted with the ro option. Where rw mounts a filesystem as Read-Write, the ro option mounts a filesystem as Read-Only. This means that currently, these filesystems cannot be written to by any user.

For all three of the defined filesystems to be mounted in the Read-Only mode is quite an unusual configuration. To see whether this is the desired configuration, we can check the /etc/fstab file, which is the same file that was used to identify persistent filesystems earlier:

```
[nfs]# cat /etc/fstab
#
# /etc/fstab
# Created by anaconda on Wed Apr 15 09:39:23 2015
#
# Accessible filesystems, by reference, are maintained under '/dev/disk'
# See man pages fstab(5), findfs(8), mount(8) and/or blkid(8) for more
info
#
/dev/mapper/md0-root     /                              xfs     defaults      0
0
UUID=7873e886-78d5-46cc-b4d9-0c385995d915 /boot                    xfs
defaults        0 0
/dev/mapper/md0-nfs      /nfs                           xfs     defaults      0
0
/dev/mapper/md0-swap     swap                           swap    defaults      0
0
```

From the contents of the /etc/fstab file, it appears that these filesystems are not configured to be mounted in the Read-Only mode. Rather, these filesystems are mounted with "default" options.

On Linux, the "default" option for the xfs filesystem mounts the filesystem in the Read-Write mode, not Read-Only. We validate this behavior if we look at the /etc/fstab file on the database server:

```
[db]# cat /etc/fstab
#
# /etc/fstab
# Created by anaconda on Mon Jul 21 23:35:56 2014
#
# Accessible filesystems, by reference, are maintained under '/dev/disk'
# See man pages fstab(5), findfs(8), mount(8) and/or blkid(8) for more
info
#
/dev/mapper/os-root /                      xfs       defaults       1 1
UUID=be76ec1d-686d-44a0-9411-b36931ee239b /boot               xfs
defaults        1 2
/dev/mapper/os-swap swap                     swap      defaults       0 0
192.168.33.13:/nfs   /data        nfs   defaults   0 0
```

On the database server, we can see the / or root filesystem also has the filesystem options set to "defaults". However, when we use the mount command to look at the filesystem options, we can see the rw option as well as some others default options being applied:

```
[db]# mount | grep root
/dev/mapper/os-root on / type xfs (rw,relatime,seclabel,attr2,inode64,noq
uota)
```

This confirms that the Read-Only status of the three persistent filesystems is not the desired configuration.

Identifying disk issues

If the /etc/fstab filesystem is specifically configured so that a filesystem is mounted as Read-Write and the mount command is showing that the filesystem is mounted in Read-Only mode. This is a clear indication that the filesystems in question might have been remounted after they were initially mounted as part of the boot process.

As we discussed earlier, when a Linux system boots, it reads the /etc/fstab file and mounts all of the defined filesystems. However, the process of mounting filesystems stops there. There is no process that continuously monitors the /etc/fstab file for changes and mounts or unmounts the modified filesystems, at least not by default.

In fact it is quite common to see a newly created filesystem not mounted but specified in the /etc/fstab file because someone simply forgot to mount it with the mount command after editing the /etc/fstab file.

It is not very common however to see a filesystem be mounted as Read-Only but for the fstab to be changed afterwards.

In fact for our scenario, that would not be very easy to accomplish as /etc/fstab would not be accessible since the / filesystem is Read-Only:

```
[nfs]# touch /etc/fstab
touch: cannot touch '/etc/fstab': Read-only file system
```

This means that our filesystems being Read-Only, was performed after these filesystems were mounted initially.

The culprit of this state is actually in the log messages that we were looking through earlier:

```
Apr 26 10:25:44 nfs kernel: md/raid1:md127: Disk failure on sdb1,
disabling device.
md/raid1:md127: Operation continuing on 1 devices.
Apr 26 10:25:55 nfs kernel: md: unbind<sdb1>
Apr 26 10:25:55 nfs kernel: md: export_rdev(sdb1)
Apr 26 10:27:20 nfs kernel: md: bind<sdb1>
Apr 26 10:27:20 nfs kernel: md: recovery of RAID array md127
Apr 26 10:27:20 nfs kernel: md: minimum _guaranteed_  speed: 1000 KB/sec/
disk.
Apr 26 10:27:20 nfs kernel: md: using maximum available idle IO bandwidth
(but not more than 200000 KB/sec) for recovery.
Apr 26 10:27:20 nfs kernel: md: using 128k window, over a total of
511936k.
Apr 26 10:27:20 nfs kernel: md: md127: recovery done.
```

From the /var/log/messages log file, we can actually see that at some point, there was an issue with the software raid (md) that marked the disk /dev/sdb1 as failed.

By default with Linux if a physical disk drive fails or otherwise becomes unavailable to the kernel, the Linux kernel will remount the filesystems that live on that physical disk in the Read-Only mode. As in the preceding error message, it seems likely that the failure of the sdb1 physical disk and the md127 raid device are the root cause of the filesystems being Read-Only.

Since software raid and hardware issues are the topic for the next chapter, we will defer troubleshooting the raid and disk issues for *Chapter 8, Hardware Troubleshooting*.

Recovering the filesystem

Now that we know why the filesystem is in the Read-Only mode, we can resolve it. Forcing the filesystem to go from Read-Only to Read-Write is actually pretty easy. However, because we don't know all of the circumstances around the failure that caused the filesystem to go into the Read-Only mode, we must be careful.

Recovering from filesystem errors can be extremely tricky; if not done properly, we could easily find ourselves in a situation where we have corrupted the filesystem or in other ways caused partial or even full data loss.

Since we have multiple filesystems in the Read-Only mode, we will first start with the /boot filesystem. The reason we are starting with the /boot filesystem is because this is technically the best filesystem to experience data loss. Since the /boot filesystem is only used during the server boot process, we can simply ensure that we do not reboot this server before the /boot filesystem can be recovered.

Whenever possible, it is always best to back up the data before taking any action. In the next steps, we are going to assume that the /boot filesystem is backed up periodically.

Unmounting the filesystem

To recover this filesystem, we will perform three steps. In the first step, we will unmount the /boot filesystem. By unmounting the filesystem before taking any additional steps, we will ensure that the filesystem is not being actively written to. This step will greatly reduce the chances of filesystem corruption during this recovery process.

However, before unmounting the filesystem, we need to make sure that no applications or services are trying to write to the filesystem we are attempting to recover.

To ensure this, we can use the `lsof` command. The `lsof` command is used to list open files; we can look through this list to identify if any files in the `/boot` filesystem are open.

If we simply run `lsof` with no options, it will print all of the current open files:

```
[nfs]# lsof
COMMAND       PID TID          USER    FD     TYPE          DEVICE
SIZE/OFF         NODE NAME
systemd       1                root    cwd    DIR           253,1
4096          128 /
```

By adding the `-r` (repeat) flag to `lsof`, we are telling it to run in a repetitive mode. We can then pipe this output to the `grep` command where we can filter the output for files that are open on the `/boot` filesystem:

```
[nfs]# lsof -r | grep /boot
```

If the preceding command does not produce any output for a while, it is safe to proceed with unmounting the filesystem. If the command does print any open files, it is best to find the appropriate processes reading/writing to the filesystem and stop them before unmounting the filesystem.

Since our example has no open files on the `/boot` filesystem, we can proceed with unmounting the `/boot` filesystem. To do this, we will use the `umount` command:

```
[nfs]# umount /boot
```

Luckily the `umount` command finished with no errors. If files were actively being written we might have received an error when unmounting. Generally, this error consists of a message that states that the **device is busy**. To validate that the filesystem was successfully unmounted, we can use the `mount` command again:

```
[nfs]# mount | grep /boot
```

Now that the `/boot` filesystem is unmounted, we can perform the second step in our recovery process. We can now check and repair the filesystem.

Filesystem checks with fsck

Linux has a very useful filesystem check command that can be used to check and repair filesystems. This command is called `fsck`.

The `fsck` command, however, is not actually just one command. Each filesystem type has its own methods of checking consistency and repairing issues. The `fsck` command is simply a wrapper that calls the appropriate commands for the filesystem in question.

For example, when the `fsck` command is run against an `ext4` filesystem, the command being executed is actually `e2fsck`. The `e2fsck` command is used for the `ext2` through `ext4` filesystem types.

We can call `e2fsck` in two ways, either directly or indirectly via the `fsck` command. In this example, we will use the `fsck` method, as this can be used for almost all filesystems supported by Linux.

To use the `fsck` command to simply check the filesystem for consistency, we can run it with no flags and specify the disk device to be checked:

```
[nfs]# fsck /dev/sda1
fsck from util-linux 2.20.1
e2fsck 1.42.9 (4-Feb-2014)
cloudimg-rootfs: clean, 85858/2621440 files, 1976768/10485504 blocks
```

In the preceding example, we can see that the filesystem did not identify any errors. If it did, we would have been asked if we wanted the `e2fsck` utility to correct those errors.

If we wanted to, we could have `fsck` automatically repair the issues found by passing it the `-y` (yes) flag:

```
[nfs]# fsck -y /dev/sda1
fsck from util-linux 2.20.1
e2fsck 1.42 (29-Nov-2011)
/dev/sda1 contains a file system with errors, check forced.
Pass 1: Checking inodes, blocks, and sizes
Inode 2051351 is a unknown file type with mode 0137642 but it looks
like it is really a directory.
Fix? yes


Pass 2: Checking directory structure
Entry 'test' in / (2) has deleted/unused inode 49159.  Clear? yes


Pass 3: Checking directory connectivity
Pass 4: Checking reference counts
Pass 5: Checking group summary information


/dev/sda1: ***** FILE SYSTEM WAS MODIFIED *****
/dev/sda1: 96/2240224 files (7.3% non-contiguous), 3793508/4476416 blocks
```

At this point, the e2fsck command will attempt to correct any errors it finds. Luckily from our example, the errors were able to be corrected; however, there are occasions where this is not the case.

The fsck and xfs filesystems

When the fsck command is run against an xfs filesystem; the outcome is actually quite different:

```
[nfs]# fsck /dev/md127

fsck from util-linux 2.23.2

If you wish to check the consistency of an XFS filesystem or

repair a damaged filesystem, see xfs_repair(8).
```

The xfs filesystem is different from the ext2/3/4 family of filesystems, in that a consistency check is performed each time the filesystem is mounted. This does not mean that you cannot check and repair the filesystem manually. To check an xfs filesystem, we can use the xfs_repair utility:

```
[nfs]# xfs_repair -n /dev/md127

Phase 1 - find and verify superblock...

Phase 2 - using internal log

        - scan filesystem freespace and inode maps...

        - found root inode chunk

Phase 3 - for each AG...

        - scan (but don't clear) agi unlinked lists...

        - process known inodes and perform inode discovery...

        - agno = 0

        - agno = 1

        - agno = 2

        - agno = 3

        - process newly discovered inodes...

Phase 4 - check for duplicate blocks...

        - setting up duplicate extent list...

        - check for inodes claiming duplicate blocks...

        - agno = 0

        - agno = 1

        - agno = 2

        - agno = 3
```

```
No modify flag set, skipping phase 5
Phase 6 - check inode connectivity...
        - traversing filesystem ...
        - traversal finished ...
        - moving disconnected inodes to lost+found ...
Phase 7 - verify link counts...
No modify flag set, skipping filesystem flush and exiting.
```

When executed with the –n (no modify) flag followed by the device to check, the xfs_repair utility will only validate the consistency of the filesystem. When run in this mode it simply will not attempt to repair the filesystem.

To run xfs_repair in a mode that will repair the filesystem simply omit the –n flag, as follows:

```
[nfs]# xfs_repair /dev/md127
Phase 1 - find and verify superblock...
Phase 2 - using internal log
        - zero log...
        - scan filesystem freespace and inode maps...
        - found root inode chunk
Phase 3 - for each AG...
        - scan and clear agi unlinked lists...
        - process known inodes and perform inode discovery...
        - agno = 0
        - agno = 1
        - agno = 2
        - agno = 3
        - process newly discovered inodes...
Phase 4 - check for duplicate blocks...
        - setting up duplicate extent list...
        - check for inodes claiming duplicate blocks...
        - agno = 0
        - agno = 1
        - agno = 2
        - agno = 3
Phase 5 - rebuild AG headers and trees...
        - reset superblock...
```

```
Phase 6 - check inode connectivity...
        - resetting contents of realtime bitmap and summary inodes
        - traversing filesystem ...
        - traversal finished ...
        - moving disconnected inodes to lost+found ...
Phase 7 - verify and correct link counts...
Done
```

From the output of the preceding `xfs_repair` command it seems our /boot filesystem did not require any repair process.

How do these tools repair a filesystem?

You might think that it was quite easy to repair this filesystem with tools such as `fsck` and `xfs_repair`. The reason for that is simply due to the design of filesystems such as `xfs` and `ext2/3/4`. Both `xfs` and the `ext2/3/4` family are journaling filesystems; what this means is that these types of filesystems will keep a log of changes being made to filesystem objects (such as files, directories, and so on).

These changes will be kept in this log until the changes are committed to the main filesystem. The `xfs_repair` utility simply looks through this log and replays the last changes that were not committed to the main filesystem. These filesystem journals allow the filesystem to be very resilient in cases such as unexpected power loss or a reboot of the system.

Unfortunately, sometimes the filesystem's journal and tools such as `xfs_repair` are not enough to correct the situation.

In cases like these, there are some more options such as running the repair in a forceful mode. However, these options should always be reserved for a last ditch effort as they can sometimes in themselves cause filesystem corruption.

If you do find yourself with a corrupted and unrepairable filesystem, it might simply be best to recreate the filesystem and restore backups, if you have backups that is...

Mounting the filesystem

Now that the /boot filesystem has been checked and repaired, we can simply remount it to validate that the data is correct. To do this, we can simply run the `mount` command followed by /boot:

```
[nfs]# mount /boot
[nfs]# mount | grep /boot
/dev/md127 on /boot type xfs (rw,relatime,seclabel,attr2,inode64,noquota)
```

When a filesystem is defined in the `/etc/fstab` file, the `mount` and `umount` commands can be called with just the `mount` point. This will cause these two commands to `mount` or `unmount` the filesystem according to it's definition within the `/etc/fstab` file.

It appears from the output of `mount` that our `/boot` filesystem is now `Read-Write` rather than `Read-Only`. If we perform an `ls` command, we should also still see our original data:

```
[nfs]# ls /boot
config-3.10.0-229.1.2.el7.x86_64                         initrd-plymouth.
img
config-3.10.0-229.el7.x86_64                             symvers-3.10.0-
229.1.2.el7.x86_64.gz
grub
symvers-3.10.0-229.el7.x86_64.gz
grub2                                                    System.map-
3.10.0-229.1.2.el7.x86_64
initramfs-0-rescue-3f370097c831473a8cfec737ff1d6c55.img  System.map-
3.10.0-229.el7.x86_64
initramfs-3.10.0-229.1.2.el7.x86_64.img                  vmlinuz-0-
rescue-3f370097c831473a8cfec737ff1d6c55
initramfs-3.10.0-229.1.2.el7.x86_64kdump.img             vmlinuz-3.10.0-
229.1.2.el7.x86_64
initramfs-3.10.0-229.el7.x86_64.img
vmlinuz-3.10.0-229.el7.x86_64
initramfs-3.10.0-229.el7.x86_64kdump.img
```

It appears that our recovery steps were a success! Now that we have tested them with the `/boot` filesystem, we can move to repairing the `/nfs` filesystem.

Repairing the other filesystems

The steps to repair the `/nfs` filesystem are actually going to be the same as the `/boot` filesystem with only one major difference, as follows:

```
[nfs]# lsof -r | grep /nfs
rpc.statd 1075            rpcuser   cwd     DIR           253,1
40     592302 /var/lib/nfs/statd
rpc.mount 2282            root      cwd     DIR           253,1
4096     9125499 /var/lib/nfs
rpc.mount 2282            root      4u      REG           0,3
0 4026532125 /proc/2280/net/rpc/nfd.export/channel
```

```
rpc.mount 2282              root    5u      REG              0,3
0 4026532129 /proc/2280/net/rpc/nfd.fh/channel
```

When checking for open files on the /nfs filesystem with lsof, we might not see the NFS service processes. However, there is a high likelihood that the NFS service will attempt to access files within this shared filesystem after the lsof command is stopped. To prevent this scenario, it is always best (when possible) to stop the NFS service when performing any changes to a shared filesystem:

```
[nfs]# systemctl stop nfs
```

Once the NFS service is stopped, the rest of the steps are the same:

```
[nfs]# umount /nfs
[nfs]# xfs_repair /dev/md0/nfs
Phase 1 - find and verify superblock...
Phase 2 - using internal log
        - zero log...
        - scan filesystem freespace and inode maps...
        - found root inode chunk
Phase 3 - for each AG...
        - scan and clear agi unlinked lists...
        - process known inodes and perform inode discovery...
        - agno = 0
        - agno = 1
        - agno = 2
        - agno = 3
        - process newly discovered inodes...
Phase 4 - check for duplicate blocks...
        - setting up duplicate extent list...
        - check for inodes claiming duplicate blocks...
        - agno = 0
        - agno = 1
        - agno = 2
        - agno = 3
Phase 5 - rebuild AG headers and trees...
        - reset superblock...
Phase 6 - check inode connectivity...
        - resetting contents of realtime bitmap and summary inodes
```

```
        - traversing filesystem ...

        - traversal finished ...

        - moving disconnected inodes to lost+found ...

Phase 7 - verify and correct link counts...

done
```

Once the filesystem has been repaired, we can simply remount it as follows:

```
[nfs]# mount /nfs

[nfs]# mount | grep /nfs

nfsd on /proc/fs/nfsd type nfsd (rw,relatime)

/dev/mapper/md0-nfs on /nfs type xfs (rw,relatime,seclabel,attr2,inode64,
noquota)
```

After remounting the /nfs filesystem, we can see the options show rw, which means it is Read-Writable.

Recovering the / (root) filesystem

The / or root filesystem is a little different. It is different because it is the top-level filesystem that contains the majority of the Linux packages, binaries, and commands. This means that we cannot simply unmount this filesystem without losing the tools necessary to remount it.

For this reason, we will actually use the mount command to remount the / filesystem without having to unmount it first:

```
[nfs]# mount -o remount /
```

In order to tell the mount command to unmount and then remount the filesystem, we simply need to pass the -o (options) flag followed by the option remount. The -o flag allows you to pass filesystem options such as rw or ro from the command line. When we remount the / filesystem, we are simply passing the remount filesystem option:

```
# mount | grep root

/dev/mapper/md0-root on / type xfs (rw,relatime,seclabel,attr2,inode64,no
quota)
```

If we use the mount command to show the mounted filesystems, we can validate that the / filesystem has been remounted with Read-Write access. Since the filesystem type is xfs, the remount should have caused the filesystem to perform a consistency check and repair. If we have any doubts of the integrity of the / filesystem, our next step should be to simply reboot the NFS server.

If the server is unable to mount the / filesystem, the xfs_repair utility will be called automatically.

Validation

At this point, we can see that the NFS server's filesystems issues have been recovered. We should now validate that our NFS client is able to write to the NFS share. But before we do that, we should also first restart the NFS service we stopped earlier:

```
[nfs]# systemctl start nfs
[nfs]# systemctl status nfs
nfs-server.service - NFS server and services
   Loaded: loaded (/usr/lib/systemd/system/nfs-server.service; enabled)
   Active: active (exited) since Mon 2015-04-27 22:20:46 MST; 6s ago
  Process: 2278 ExecStopPost=/usr/sbin/exportfs -f (code=exited,
status=0/SUCCESS)
  Process: 3098 ExecStopPost=/usr/sbin/exportfs -au (code=exited,
status=1/FAILURE)
  Process: 3095 ExecStop=/usr/sbin/rpc.nfsd 0 (code=exited, status=0/
SUCCESS)
  Process: 3265 ExecStart=/usr/sbin/rpc.nfsd $RPCNFSDARGS (code=exited,
status=0/SUCCESS)
  Process: 3264 ExecStartPre=/usr/sbin/exportfs -r (code=exited,
status=0/SUCCESS)
 Main PID: 3265 (code=exited, status=0/SUCCESS)
   CGroup: /system.slice/nfs-server.service
```

Once the NFS service is started, we can test from the client using the touch command:

```
[db]# touch /data/testfile.txt
[db]# ls -la /data/testfile.txt
-rw-r--r--. 1 root root 0 Apr 28 05:24 /data/testfile.txt
```

It appears that we have successfully corrected our issue.

As a side note, if we noticed that requests to the NFS share were taking a long time, It might be necessary to unmount and mount the NFS share on the client side. This is a common issue if the NFS client has not identified that the NFS server has been restarted.

Summary

In this chapter, we took a rather deep dive into how filesystems are mounted, how NFS is configured and what to do in case of filesystems going into the `Read-Only` mode. We even took that a step further and manually repaired a filesystem where the physical disk device was having issues.

In the next chapter, we will take this same issue further by troubleshooting hardware failures. This means looking at logs for hardware messages, troubleshooting hard drive RAID sets, and many other hardware-related troubleshooting steps.

8
Hardware Troubleshooting

In the last chapter, we identified that the filesystems on our NFS were mounted as **Read-Only**. In order to identify the cause, we performed quite a bit of troubleshooting around NFS and filesystems. We used commands such as showmount to see what NFS shares are available and the mount command to show the mounted filesystems.

Once we identified the issue, we were able to use the fsck command to perform a filesystem check and recover the filesystems.

In this chapter, we will continue down the path from *Chapter 7, FileSystem Errors and Recovery* and investigate a hardware device failure. This chapter will cover many of the log files and tools necessary to determine not only whether a hardware failure has occurred, but why it has occurred as well.

Starting with a log entry

In *Chapter 7, FileSystem Errors and Recovery* while looking through the /var/log/messages log file to identify issues with the NFS servers filesystems, we noticed the following messages:

```
Apr 26 10:25:44 nfs kernel: md/raid1:md127: Disk failure on sdb1,
disabling device.

md/raid1:md127: Operation continuing on 1 devices.

Apr 26 10:25:55 nfs kernel: md: unbind<sdb1>

Apr 26 10:25:55 nfs kernel: md: export_rdev(sdb1)

Apr 26 10:27:20 nfs kernel: md: bind<sdb1>

Apr 26 10:27:20 nfs kernel: md: recovery of RAID array md127

Apr 26 10:27:20 nfs kernel: md: minimum _guaranteed_  speed: 1000 KB/sec/
disk.
```

```
Apr 26 10:27:20 nfs kernel: md: using maximum available idle IO bandwidth
(but not more than 200000 KB/sec) for recovery.

Apr 26 10:27:20 nfs kernel: md: using 128k window, over a total of
511936k.

Apr 26 10:27:20 nfs kernel: md: md127: recovery done.
```

The preceding messages indicate that the RAID device /dev/md127 had a failure. Since the previous chapter was solely focused on the issues with the filesystem itself, we did not investigate the RAID device failure further. In this chapter, we will investigate to determine the cause and resolution.

To start the investigation, we should first review the original log messages as these can tell us quite a bit about the state of the RAID device.

As a start, let's break down the messages into smaller sections as follows:

```
Apr 26 10:25:44 nfs kernel: md/raid1:md127: Disk failure on sdb1,
disabling device.

md/raid1:md127: Operation continuing on 1 devices.
```

The first log message is actually quite telling. The first key piece of information shown is the RAID device that the message is about (md/raid1:md127).

By the name of this device, we already know quite a bit. The first thing we know is that this RAID device is created by Linux's software raid system **multiple device driver (md)**. This system allows Linux to take two independent disks and apply a RAID to them.

Since we will be working primarily with a RAID in this chapter, we should first understand what RAID is and how it works.

What is a RAID?

Redundant Array of Independent Disks (RAID) is often either a software- or hardware-based system that allows users to take multiple disks and use them as one device. The RAID can be configured in multiple ways, allowing for either greater data redundancy or performance.

This configuration is commonly referred to as a RAID level. The different types of RAID levels provide different functionality to get a better idea of the RAID levels. Let's explore a few that are commonly used.

RAID 0 – striping

RAID 0 is one of the simplest RAID levels to understand. The way RAID 0 works is by taking multiple disks and combining them to act as one. When data is written to the RAID device, the data is split and parts are written on each disk. To understand this better, let's put together a simple scenario.

- If we had a simple RAID 0 device that consisted of five 500 GB drives, our RAID device would be the size of all the five drives together—2500 GB or 2.5 TB. If we were to write a 50 MB file to the RAID device, 10 MB of the file's data would be written to each disk at the same time.

This process is commonly referred to as **striping**. In the same context, when that 50 MB file is read from the RAID device, the read request will be processed by each disk at the same time as well.

The ability to split a file and process parts of it to each disk at the same time provides better performance of the write or read requests. In fact, because we have five disks, the requests are faster by a multiple of 5.

A simple analogy to this would be if you had five people building a wall at equal speed, they would be five times faster than a single person building the same wall.

While RAID 0 provides performance, it does not provide any data protection. If a single drive in this RAID fails, the data from that drive is not available and such a failure could result in complete data loss with RAID 0.

RAID 1 – mirroring

RAID 1 is another simple RAID level. Unlike RAID 0 where the drives are combined, in RAID 1 the drives are mirrored. RAID 1 generally consists of two or more drives. When data is written to the RAID device, the data is written to each device in its entirety.

This process is referred to as **mirroring**, since the data is essentially mirrored on all drives:

- Using the same scenario as before, if we had five 500 GB disk drives in a RAID 1 configuration, the total disk size would be 500 GB. When we write the same 50 MB file to the RAID device, each drive will get its own copy of that 50 MB file.

- This also means that the write request will only be as fast as the slowest drive in the RAID. With RAID 1, every drive must complete the write request before it is considered complete.

- Read requests, however, can be served by any one of the RAID 1 drives. Because of this, a RAID 1 can sometimes provide read requests faster, as each request can be performed by a different drive in the RAID.

RAID 1 provides the highest level of data resiliency, as it only requires one disk drive to remain active during failures. Using our five-disk scenario, we could lose four of the five disks and still rebuild and use the RAID. This is the reason why RAID 1 should be used when data protection is more important than disk performance.

RAID 5 – striping with distributed parity

RAID 5 is an example of a difficult-to-understand RAID level. RAID 5 works by striping data across multiple disks such as RAID 0, but it also includes parity. Parity data is special data that is generated by performing an exclusive OR operation on the data written to the RAID device. The resulting data can be used to rebuild the missing data from another drive.

- Using the same example as we did earlier, where we have five 500 GB hard drives in a RAID 5 configuration, if we were to yet again write a 50 MB file, each disk will receive 10 MB of data; this is exactly like RAID 0. However, unlike RAID 0, parity data is also written to each disk. Because of the additional parity data, the total data size available to the RAID is the total of the four drives, with one drive's worth of data allocated to parity. In our case, this would mean 2 TB of available disk space with 500 GB used for parity.

Often, there is a misconception that the parity data is written to a dedicated drive with RAID 5. This is not the case. It is simply that the parity data size is a full disk's worth of space. This data, however, is distributed against all disks.

A reason to use RAID 5 over RAID 0 is the fact that it is possible for the data to be rebuilt if a single drive fails. The only problem with RAID 5 is if two drives fail, the RAID cannot be rebuilt and may result in data loss.

RAID 6 – striping with double distributed parity

RAID 6 is essentially the same type of RAID as RAID 5; however, the parity data is doubled. By doubling the parity data, the RAID can survive up to two disk failures. Since the parity is doubled if we were to take five 500 GB hard drives and place them into a RAID 6 configuration, the available disk space would be 1.5 TB, the sum of 3 drives; the other 1 TB of data space would be occupied by two sets of parity data.

RAID 10 – mirrored and striped

RAID 10 (commonly known as RAID 1 + 0) is another very common RAID level. RAID 10 is essentially a combination of both RAID 1 and RAID 0. With RAID 10 each disk has a mirror and data is striped across all of the mirrored drives. To explain this we will use a similar example as above; however, we will do this with six 500 GB drives.

- If we were to write a 30 MB file, it will be broken into 10 MB chunks and striped to three RAID devices. These RAID devices are RAID 1 mirrors. Essentially, a RAID 10 is numerous RAID 1 devices striped together in a RAID 0 configuration.

The RAID 10 configuration is a good balance between performance and data protection. In order for a complete failure to occur, both sides of a mirror must fail; this means 2 sides of a RAID 1.

Considering the number of disks in the RAID the chances of this are less likely than those of RAID 5. From a performance standpoint, RAID 10 still benefits from the striping methodology and is able to write different chunks of a single file to each disk, by increasing the write speed.

RAID 10 also benefits from having two disks with the same data; as with RAID 1, when a read request is made either disk may serve that request allowing for concurrent read requests to be handled by each disk independently.

The downside to RAID 10 is while it often can meet or exceed the performance of RAID 5 it often takes more hardware to do this as each disk is mirrored and you lose half of the total disk space to the RAID.

With our preceding example, our usable space for six 500 GB drives in a RAID 10 configuration would be 1.5 TB. Simply put, it is 50 percent of our disk capacity. This same capacity is available with 4 drives for RAID 5.

Back to troubleshooting our RAID

Now that we have a better understanding of RAID and the different configurations, let's go back to investigating our errors.

```
Apr 26 10:25:44 nfs kernel: md/raid1:md127: Disk failure on sdb1,
disabling device.
md/raid1:md127: Operation continuing on 1 devices.
```

From the preceding error, we can see that our RAID device is **md127**. We can also see that this device is a RAID 1 device (`md/raid1`). The message stating *Operation continuing on 1 devices* means the second part of the mirror is still operational.

The good thing is that, if both sides of the mirror were unavailable, the RAID would completely fail and result in worse issues.

Since we now know the RAID device affected, the type of RAID used, and even the hard disk that failed, we have quite a bit of information about this failure. If we continue looking at the log entries from `/var/log/messages`, we can find out even more:

```
Apr 26 10:25:55 nfs kernel: md: unbind<sdb1>
Apr 26 10:25:55 nfs kernel: md: export_rdev(sdb1)
Apr 26 10:27:20 nfs kernel: md: bind<sdb1>
Apr 26 10:27:20 nfs kernel: md: recovery of RAID array md127
Apr 26 10:27:20 nfs kernel: md: minimum _guaranteed_  speed: 1000 KB/sec/
disk.
```

The preceding messages are interesting as they indicate that MD the Linux software RAID service attempted to recover the RAID:

```
Apr 26 10:25:55 nfs kernel: md: unbind<sdb1>
```

In the first line of this section of logs, it seems that the device `sdb1` was removed from the RAID:

```
Apr 26 10:27:20 nfs kernel: md: bind<sdb1>
```

The third line, however, is stating that the device `sdb1` has been re-added to the RAID or "**bound**" to the RAID.

The fourth and fifth lines show that the RAID started recovery steps:

```
Apr 26 10:27:20 nfs kernel: md: recovery of RAID array md127
```

```
Apr 26 10:27:20 nfs kernel: md: minimum _guaranteed_  speed: 1000 KB/sec/
disk.
```

How RAID recovery works

Earlier we discussed how various RAID levels are able to rebuild and recover data from lost devices. This happens either via parity data or mirrored data.

When a RAID device loses one of its drives and that drive is either replaced or re-added to the RAID, the RAID manager, whether it is a software or hardware RAID, will start rebuilding the data. The goal of this rebuild is to recreate the data that should be on the missing drive.

If the RAID is a mirrored RAID, the data from the available mirrored disk will be read and written to the replaced disk.

For parity-based RAIDs, the rebuild will be based on the surviving data that has been striped across the RAID and the parity data within the RAID.

During the rebuild process for parity-based RAIDs, any additional failure could result in a failed rebuild. With mirror-based RAIDs, the failure can occur on any disk as long as there is one full copy of the data being used for the rebuild.

At the end of our captured log messages, we can see that the rebuild was successful:

```
Apr 26 10:27:20 nfs kernel: md: md127: recovery done.
```

It appears that the RAID device /dev/md127 is healthy based on the end of the log messages found in the previous chapter.

Checking the current RAID status

While /var/log/messages is a great way to see what has happened on the server, it doesn't necessarily mean that those log messages are accurate with regard to the current state of the RAID.

In order to see the current status of the RAID devices, we can run a few commands.

The first command we will use is the mdadm command:

```
[nfs]# mdadm --detail /dev/md127
/dev/md127:
        Version : 1.0
  Creation Time : Wed Apr 15 09:39:22 2015
     Raid Level : raid1
     Array Size : 511936 (500.02 MiB 524.22 MB)
  Used Dev Size : 511936 (500.02 MiB 524.22 MB)
   Raid Devices : 2
  Total Devices : 1
    Persistence : Superblock is persistent

  Intent Bitmap : Internal

    Update Time : Sun May 10 06:16:10 2015
          State : clean, degraded
```

```
   Active Devices : 1
  Working Devices : 1
   Failed Devices : 0
    Spare Devices : 0


             Name : localhost:boot
             UUID : 7adf0323:b0962394:387e6cd0:b2914469
           Events : 52


    Number   Major   Minor   RaidDevice State
         0       8       1        0      active sync   /dev/sda1
         2       0       0        2      removed
```

The mdadm command is used to manage Linux MD based RAIDs. In the preceding command, we specified the flag --detail followed by a RAID device. This tells mdadm to print the details of the specified RAID device.

The mdadm command can perform more than just printing status; it can also be used to perform RAID activities such as creating, destroying, or modifying a RAID device.

To understand the output of the --detail flag, let's break down the output from above as follows:

```
/dev/md127:
          Version : 1.0
    Creation Time : Wed Apr 15 09:39:22 2015
       Raid Level : raid1
       Array Size : 511936 (500.02 MiB 524.22 MB)
    Used Dev Size : 511936 (500.02 MiB 524.22 MB)
     Raid Devices : 2
    Total Devices : 1
      Persistence : Superblock is persistent
```

The first section tells us quite a bit about the RAID itself. Important items to note are the Creation Time, which in this case is Wed April 15th at 9:39 A.M. This tells us when the RAID was first created.

The Raid Level is also noted, which as we saw in /var/log/messages is RAID 1. We can also see the Array Size, which tells us the total available disk space the RAID device will provide (524 MB) and the number of Raid Devices used in this RAID array, which in this case is two devices.

The number of devices that make up this RAID is important as it can help us understand the state of this RAID.

Since our RAID is made up of a total of two devices, if any one device fails, we know that our RAID will be at risk of a complete failure if the leftover disk is lost. If our RAID consisted of three devices, however, we would know that even the loss of two disks would not cause a complete RAID failure.

Just from the first half of the `mdadm` command, we can see quite a bit of information about this RAID. From the second half, we will find even more key information as follows:

```
    Intent Bitmap : Internal


     Update Time : Sun May 10 06:16:10 2015
           State : clean, degraded
  Active Devices : 1
 Working Devices : 1
  Failed Devices : 0
   Spare Devices : 0


            Name : localhost:boot
            UUID : 7adf0323:b0962394:387e6cd0:b2914469
          Events : 52


   Number   Major   Minor   RaidDevice State
        0       8       1          0     active sync   /dev/sda1
        2       0       0          2     removed
```

The `Update Time` is useful as it shows the last time this RAID changed status, whether that status change was the addition of a disk or a rebuild.

This timestamp can be useful, especially if we are trying to correlate it with log entries in `/var/log/messages` or other system events.

Another key piece of information is the `RAID Device State`, which, for our example, is clean, degraded. The degraded state means that while the RAID has a failed device, the RAID itself is still functional. Degraded simply means functional but suboptimal.

If our RAID device was actively rebuilding or recovering right now, we would also see those statuses listed.

Under the current state output, we can see four device categories that tell us about the hard disks used for this RAID. The first being `Active Devices`; this tells us the number of drives that are currently active in the RAID.

The second is `Working Devices`; this tells us the number of working drives. Often, the number of `Working Devices` and `Active Devices` will be the same.

The fourth item in this list is `Failed Devices`; this is the number of devices currently marked as failed. Even though our RAID currently has a failed device, this number is `0`. There is a valid reason for this, but we will cover that reason in a bit.

The last item in our list is the number of `Spare Devices`. In some RAID systems, you can create spare devices, which are used to rebuild a RAID in events such as drive failure.

These spare devices can come in handy, as the RAID system will usually automatically rebuild the RAID, which reduces the likelihood of complete failure of the RAID.

With the final two lines of the output of `mdadm`, we can see information about the drives that make up the RAID:

```
Number   Major   Minor   RaidDevice State
   0       8       1         0       active sync   /dev/sda1
   2       0       0         2       removed
```

From the output, we can see that we have one disk device /dev/sda1 that is currently in an active sync state. We can also see that another device has been removed from the RAID.

Summarizing the key information

From the output of `mdadm --detail`, we can see that /dev/md127 is a RAID device that has a RAID level of 1 and is currently in a degraded state. We can see from the details that the degraded state is due to the fact that one of the drives that make up the RAID is currently removed.

Looking at md status with /proc/mdstat

Another useful place to look for the current status of MD is /proc/mdstat; this file, like many files in /proc, is constantly updated by the kernel. If we use the cat command to read this file, we can take a quick look at this server's current RAID status:

```
[nfs]# cat /proc/mdstat
Personalities : [raid1]
md126 : active raid1 sda2[0]
      7871488 blocks super 1.2 [2/1] [U_]
      bitmap: 1/1 pages [4KB], 65536KB chunk

md127 : active raid1 sda1[0]
      511936 blocks super 1.0 [2/1] [U_]
      bitmap: 1/1 pages [4KB], 65536KB chunk

unused devices: <none>
```

The contents of /proc/mdstat are somewhat cryptic, but if we break them down it contains quite a lot of information.

```
Personalities : [raid1]
```

The first line Personalities tells us what RAID levels the kernel on this system currently supports. For our example, it is RAID 1:

```
md126 : active raid1 sda2[0]
      7871488 blocks super 1.2 [2/1] [U_]
      bitmap: 1/1 pages [4KB], 65536KB chunk
```

The next set of lines is the current status of /dev/md126, another RAID device on this system that we have not yet looked at. These three lines can actually give us quite a bit of information about md126; in fact, they give us much the same information as mdadm --detail would tell us.

```
md126 : active raid1 sda2[0]
```

Within the first line itself, we can see the device name md126. We can see the current state of the RAID, which is active. We can also see the RAID level of this RAID device RAID 1. Finally, we can also see the disk devices that make up this RAID; which, in our example, is only sda2.

The second line also contains key information as follows:

```
7871488 blocks super 1.2 [2/1] [U_]
```

Specifically, the last two values are the most useful for our current task, [2/1] shows how many disk devices are allocated to this RAID and how many are available. From the value in the example we can see that 2 drives are expected but only 1 drive is available.

The last value [U_] shows the current status of the drives that make up this RAID. The status U is for up and the "_" is for down.

In our example we can see that one disk device is up, and the other is down.

Given the above information, we were able to determine that the RAID device /dev/md126 is currently in an active state; it is using RAID level 1 and currently has one of two disks unavailable.

If we keep looking through the /proc/mdstat file we can see a similar status for md127.

Using both /proc/mdstat and mdadm

After going through /proc/mdstat and mdadm --detail we can see that both provide similar information. From my experience I've found using both mdstat and mdadm can be useful. The /proc/mdstat file is generally where I go for a quick and easy snapshot of all RAID devices on the system, whereas the mdadm command is generally what I use for deeper RAID device details (details such as the number of spare drives, creation time and the last update time).

Identifying a bigger issue

Earlier while using mdadm to look at the current status of md127, we could see that the RAID device md127 had a disk removed from service. While looking through /proc/mdstat we discovered that there is another RAID device /dev/md126, and that too has a disk removed from service.

Another interesting item that we can see is that the RAID device /dev/md126 is a surviving disk: /dev/sda1. This is interesting because the surviving disk for /dev/md127 is /dev/sda2. If we remember from the earlier chapter /dev/sda1 and /dev/sda2 are simply 2 partitions from the same physical disk. Given the fact that both RAID devices have a missing drive and that our logs state that /dev/md127 had /dev/sdb1 removed and re-added. It is likely that both /dev/md127 and /dev/md126 are using partitions from /dev/sdb.

Since /proc/mdstat only has two statuses for RAID devices, up or down, we can confirm whether the second disk has actually been removed from /dev/md126 using the --detail flag:

```
[nfs]# mdadm --detail /dev/md126
/dev/md126:
           Version : 1.2
     Creation Time : Wed Apr 15 09:39:19 2015
        Raid Level : raid1
        Array Size : 7871488 (7.51 GiB 8.06 GB)
     Used Dev Size : 7871488 (7.51 GiB 8.06 GB)
      Raid Devices : 2
     Total Devices : 1
       Persistence : Superblock is persistent

     Intent Bitmap : Internal

       Update Time : Mon May 11 04:03:09 2015
             State : clean, degraded
    Active Devices : 1
   Working Devices : 1
    Failed Devices : 0
     Spare Devices : 0

              Name : localhost:pv00
              UUID : bec13d99:42674929:76663813:f748e7cb
            Events : 5481

    Number   Major   Minor   RaidDevice State
       0       8        2        0       active sync   /dev/sda2
       2       0        0        2       removed
```

From the output, we can see that the current status and configuration for /dev/md126 is exactly the same as /dev/md127. Given this information, we can make an assumption that /dev/md126 once had /dev/sdb2 as part of its RAID.

Since we suspect that the problem may simply be that a single hard drive is having an issue, we need to validate if that is truly the case or not. The first step is to identify whether or not there truly is a /dev/sdb device; the fasted way to do this is to perform a directory listing in /dev with the ls command:

```
[nfs]# ls -la /dev/ | grep sd
brw-rw----.  1 root disk      8,    0 May 10 06:16 sda
brw-rw----.  1 root disk      8,    1 May 10 06:16 sda1
brw-rw----.  1 root disk      8,    2 May 10 06:16 sda2
brw-rw----.  1 root disk      8,   16 May 10 06:16 sdb
brw-rw----.  1 root disk      8,   17 May 10 06:16 sdb1
brw-rw----.  1 root disk      8,   18 May 10 06:16 sdb2
```

We can see from the results of this ls command that there is in fact an sdb, sdb1, and sdb2 device. Before going further, let's get a clearer understanding of /dev.

Understanding /dev

The /dev directory is a special directory where the contents are created by the kernel at installation time. This directory contains special files that allow users or applications to interact with physical and sometimes logical devices.

If we look at the previous ls command's results, we can see that within the /dev directory there are several files that begin with sd.

In the previous chapter, we learned that files that start with sd are actually seen as SCSI or SATA drives. In our case, we have both /dev/sda and /dev/sdb; this means, on this system, there are two physical SCSI or SATA drives.

The additional devices /dev/sda1, /dev/sda2, /dev/sdb1, and /dev/sdb2 are simply partitions of those disks. In fact, with disk drives, a device name that ends with a numeric value is often a partition of another device, just as /dev/sdb1 is a partition of /dev/sdb. While there are of course some exceptions to this rule, it is often safe to make this assumption when troubleshooting disk drives.

More than just disk drives

The /dev/ directory contains far more than just disk drives. If we look in /dev/, we can actually see quite a few common devices.

```
[nfs]# ls -F /dev
autofs            hugepages/        network_throughput  snd/      tty21
tty4    tty58     vcs1
```

block/	initctl|	null	sr0	tty22
tty40	tty59	vcs2		
bsg/	input/	nvram	stderr@	tty23
tty41	tty6	vcs3		
btrfs-control	kmsg	oldmem	stdin@	tty24
tty42	tty60	vcs4		
bus/	log=	port	stdout@	tty25
tty43	tty61	vcs5		
cdrom@	loop-control	ppp	tty	tty26
tty44	tty62	vcs6		
char/	lp0	ptmx	tty0	tty27
tty45	tty63	vcsa		
console	lp1	pts/	tty1	tty28
tty46	tty7	vcsa1		
core@	lp2	random	tty10	tty29
tty47	tty8	vcsa2		
cpu/	lp3	raw/	tty11	tty3
tty48	tty9	vcsa3		
cpu_dma_latency	mapper/	rtc@	tty12	tty30
tty49	ttyS0	vcsa4		
crash	mcelog	rtc0	tty13	tty31
tty5	ttyS1	vcsa5		
disk/	md/	sda	tty14	tty32
tty50	ttyS2	vcsa6		
dm-0	md0/	sda1	tty15	tty33
tty51	ttyS3	vfio/		
dm-1	md126	sda2	tty16	tty34
tty52	uhid	vga_arbiter		
dm-2	md127	sdb	tty17	tty35
tty53	uinput	vhost-net		
fd@	mem	sdb1	tty18	tty36
tty54	urandom	zero		
full	mqueue/	sdb2	tty19	tty37
tty55	usbmon0			
fuse	net/	shm/	tty2	tty38
tty56	usbmon1			
hpet	network_latency	snapshot	tty20	tty39
tty57	vcs			

From the results of this `ls`, we can see that there are numerous files, directories, and symlinks in the /dev directory.

The following is a list of common devices or directories that are useful to know and understand:

- **/dev/cdrom**: This is often a symlink to the cdrom device. The CD-ROM's actual device follows a naming convention similar to hard disks, where it starts with sr and is followed by the number of the device. We can see where the /dev/cdrom symlink points with the ls command:

  ```
  [nfs]# ls -la /dev/cdrom
  lrwxrwxrwx. 1 root root 3 May 10 06:16 /dev/cdrom -> sr0
  ```

- **/dev/console**: This device is not necessarily linked to a specific hardware device like /dev/sda or /dev/sr0. The console device is used for interacting with the systems console, which may or may not be an actual monitor.

- **/dev/cpu**: This is actually a directory that contains additional directories within it for each CPU on the system. Within those directories is a cpuid file used to query information about the CPU:

  ```
  [nfs]# ls -la /dev/cpu/0/cpuid
  crw-------. 1 root root 203, 0 May 10 06:16 /dev/cpu/0/cpuid
  ```

- **/dev/md**: This is another directory that contains symlinks with user-friendly names that link to actual RAID devices. If we use ls, we can see the available RAID devices on this system:

  ```
  [nfs]# ls -la /dev/md/
  total 0
  drwxr-xr-x.  2 root root   80 May 10 06:16 .
  drwxr-xr-x. 20 root root 3180 May 10 06:16 ..
  lrwxrwxrwx.  1 root root    8 May 10 06:16 boot -> ../md127
  lrwxrwxrwx.  1 root root    8 May 10 06:16 pv00 -> ../md126
  ```

- **/dev/random** and **/dev/urandom**: These two devices are used for generating random data. The /dev/random and /dev/urandom devices will both pull random data from the kernel's entropy pool. One difference between these two is that when the system's entropy count is low, the /dev/random device will wait until sufficient entropy has been re-added.

As we learned earlier, the /dev/ directory has quite a few useful files and directories. Getting back to our original issue, however, we have identified that /dev/sdb exists and there are two partitions /dev/sdb1 and /dev/sdb2.

We have not, however, identified whether /dev/sdb was originally part of the two RAID devices currently in a degraded state. To do this, we can utilize the dmesg facility.

Device messages with dmesg

The dmesg command is a great command for troubleshooting hardware issues. When a system initially boots, the kernel will identify the various hardware devices available to that system.

As the kernel identifies these devices, the information is written to the kernel's ring buffer. This ring buffer is essentially an internal log for the kernel. The dmesg command can be used to print this ring buffer.

The following is an example output from the dmesg command; in this example, we will use the head command to shorten the output to only the first 15 lines:

```
[nfs]# dmesg | head -15
[    0.000000] Initializing cgroup subsys cpuset
[    0.000000] Initializing cgroup subsys cpu
[    0.000000] Initializing cgroup subsys cpuacct
[    0.000000] Linux version 3.10.0-229.1.2.el7.x86_64 (builder@kbuilder.
dev.centos.org) (gcc version 4.8.2 20140120 (Red Hat 4.8.2-16) (GCC) ) #1
SMP Fri Mar 27 03:04:26 UTC 2015
[    0.000000] Command line: BOOT_IMAGE=/vmlinuz-3.10.0-229.1.2.el7.
x86_64 root=/dev/mapper/md0-root ro rd.lvm.lv=md0/swap crashkernel=auto
rd.md.uuid=bec13d99:42674929:76663813:f748e7cb rd.lvm.lv=md0/root rd.md.
uuid=7adf0323:b0962394:387e6cd0:b2914469 rhgb quiet LANG=en_US.UTF-8
systemd.debug
[    0.000000] e820: BIOS-provided physical RAM map:
[    0.000000] BIOS-e820: [mem 0x0000000000000000-0x000000000009fbff]
usable
[    0.000000] BIOS-e820: [mem 0x000000000009fc00-0x000000000009ffff]
reserved
[    0.000000] BIOS-e820: [mem 0x00000000000f0000-0x00000000000fffff]
reserved
[    0.000000] BIOS-e820: [mem 0x0000000000100000-0x000000001ffefffff]
usable
[    0.000000] BIOS-e820: [mem 0x000000001fff0000-0x000000001fffffff]
ACPI data
[    0.000000] BIOS-e820: [mem 0x00000000fffc0000-0x00000000ffffffff]
reserved
[    0.000000] NX (Execute Disable) protection: active
[    0.000000] SMBIOS 2.5 present.
[    0.000000] DMI: innotek GmbH VirtualBox/VirtualBox, BIOS VirtualBox
12/01/2006
```

The reason we limited the output to just 15 lines is because the dmesg command will output quite a bit of data. To put it in perspective, we can run the command again, but this time send the output to wc -l, which will count the number of lines printed:

```
[nfs]# dmesg | wc -l
597
```

As we can see, the dmesg command returns 597 lines. Reading all the 597 lines of the kernel's ring buffer is not a quick process.

Since our goal was to find out information about /dev/sdb, we can run the dmesg command again, this time using the grep command to filter the output to /dev/sdb related information:

```
[nfs]# dmesg | grep -C 5 sdb
[    2.176800] scsi 3:0:0:0: CD-ROM            VBOX      CD-ROM
1.0   PQ: 0 ANSI: 5
[    2.194908] sd 0:0:0:0: [sda] 16777216 512-byte logical blocks: (8.58
GB/8.00 GiB)
[    2.194951] sd 0:0:0:0: [sda] Write Protect is off
[    2.194953] sd 0:0:0:0: [sda] Mode Sense: 00 3a 00 00
[    2.194965] sd 0:0:0:0: [sda] Write cache: enabled, read cache:
enabled, doesn't support DPO or FUA
[    2.196250] sd 1:0:0:0: [sdb] 16777216 512-byte logical blocks: (8.58
GB/8.00 GiB)
[    2.196279] sd 1:0:0:0: [sdb] Write Protect is off
[    2.196281] sd 1:0:0:0: [sdb] Mode Sense: 00 3a 00 00
[    2.196294] sd 1:0:0:0: [sdb] Write cache: enabled, read cache:
enabled, doesn't support DPO or FUA
[    2.197471]  sda: sda1 sda2
[    2.197700] sd 0:0:0:0: [sda] Attached SCSI disk
[    2.198139]  sdb: sdb1 sdb2
[    2.198319] sd 1:0:0:0: [sdb] Attached SCSI disk
[    2.200851] sr 3:0:0:0: [sr0] scsi3-mmc drive: 32x/32x xa/form2 tray
[    2.200856] cdrom: Uniform CD-ROM driver Revision: 3.20
[    2.200980] sr 3:0:0:0: Attached scsi CD-ROM sr0
[    2.366634] md: bind<sda1>
[    2.370652] md: raid1 personality registered for level 1
[    2.370820] md/raid1:md127: active with 1 out of 2 mirrors
[    2.371797] created bitmap (1 pages) for device md127
```

```
[    2.372181] md127: bitmap initialized from disk: read 1 pages, set 0
of 8 bits

[    2.373915] md127: detected capacity change from 0 to 524222464

[    2.374767]  md127: unknown partition table

[    2.376065] md: bind<sdb2>

[    2.382976] md: bind<sda2>

[    2.385094] md: kicking non-fresh sdb2 from array!

[    2.385102] md: unbind<sdb2>

[    2.385105] md: export_rdev(sdb2)

[    2.387559] md/raid1:md126: active with 1 out of 2 mirrors

[    2.387874] created bitmap (1 pages) for device md126

[    2.388339] md126: bitmap initialized from disk: read 1 pages, set 19
of 121 bits

[    2.390324] md126: detected capacity change from 0 to 8060403712

[    2.391344]  md126: unknown partition table
```

When executing the preceding example, the -C (context) flag was used to tell grep to include five lines of context to the output. Generally, when grep is run with no flags, only lines that contain the search string ("sdb" , in this case) are printed. With the context flag set to five, the grep command will print 5 lines before and 5 lines after each line that contains the search string.

This use of grep allows us to see not only the lines that include the string sdb, but also the lines before and after, which may contain additional information.

Now that we have this additional information, let's break it down to understand what it is telling us better:

```
[    2.176800] scsi 3:0:0:0: CD-ROM            VBOX      CD-ROM
1.0  PQ: 0 ANSI: 5

[    2.194908] sd 0:0:0:0: [sda] 16777216 512-byte logical blocks: (8.58
GB/8.00 GiB)

[    2.194951] sd 0:0:0:0: [sda] Write Protect is off

[    2.194953] sd 0:0:0:0: [sda] Mode Sense: 00 3a 00 00

[    2.194965] sd 0:0:0:0: [sda] Write cache: enabled, read cache:
enabled, doesn't support DPO or FUA

[    2.196250] sd 1:0:0:0: [sdb] 16777216 512-byte logical blocks: (8.58
GB/8.00 GiB)

[    2.196279] sd 1:0:0:0: [sdb] Write Protect is off

[    2.196281] sd 1:0:0:0: [sdb] Mode Sense: 00 3a 00 00
```

```
[    2.196294] sd 1:0:0:0: [sdb] Write cache: enabled, read cache:
enabled, doesn't support DPO or FUA
[    2.197471]  sda: sda1 sda2
[    2.197700] sd 0:0:0:0: [sda] Attached SCSI disk
[    2.198139]  sdb: sdb1 sdb2
[    2.198319] sd 1:0:0:0: [sdb] Attached SCSI disk
```

The preceding information seems to be standard information about /dev/sdb. We can see some basic information about /dev/sda and /dev/sdb from these messages.

One useful thing we can see from the preceding information is the size of these drives:

```
[    2.194908] sd 0:0:0:0: [sda] 16777216 512-byte logical blocks: (8.58
GB/8.00 GiB)
[    2.196250] sd 1:0:0:0: [sdb] 16777216 512-byte logical blocks: (8.58
GB/8.00 GiB)
```

We can see that each drive is 8.58 GB in size. While the information is useful in general, it is not useful for our current situation. What is useful, however, is the last four lines from the preceding code snippet:

```
[    2.197471]  sda: sda1 sda2
[    2.197700] sd 0:0:0:0: [sda] Attached SCSI disk
[    2.198139]  sdb: sdb1 sdb2
[    2.198319] sd 1:0:0:0: [sdb] Attached SCSI disk
```

These last four lines are showing the available partitions on both /dev/sda and /dev/sdb as well as a message stating that each disk has been Attached.

This information is quite useful as it tells us at the most basic level that these two drives are working. This is something that is in question for /dev/sdb, since we suspect that the RAID system has removed it from service.

So far, the dmesg command has already given us a bit of useful information; let's keep looking through the data to better understand these disks.

```
[    2.200851] sr 3:0:0:0: [sr0] scsi3-mmc drive: 32x/32x xa/form2 tray
[    2.200856] cdrom: Uniform CD-ROM driver Revision: 3.20
[    2.200980] sr 3:0:0:0: Attached scsi CD-ROM sr0
```

The preceding three lines would be useful if we troubleshoot an issue with our CD-ROM device. However, for our disk issue, they are not useful and are only included due to grep's context being set to 5.

The following lines, however, will tell us quite a bit about our disk drives:

```
[    2.366634] md: bind<sda1>
[    2.370652] md: raid1 personality registered for level 1
[    2.370820] md/raid1:md127: active with 1 out of 2 mirrors
[    2.371797] created bitmap (1 pages) for device md127
[    2.372181] md127: bitmap initialized from disk: read 1 pages, set 0
of 8 bits
[    2.373915] md127: detected capacity change from 0 to 524222464
[    2.374767]  md127: unknown partition table
[    2.376065] md: bind<sdb2>
[    2.382976] md: bind<sda2>
[    2.385094] md: kicking non-fresh sdb2 from array!
[    2.385102] md: unbind<sdb2>
[    2.385105] md: export_rdev(sdb2)
[    2.387559] md/raid1:md126: active with 1 out of 2 mirrors
[    2.387874] created bitmap (1 pages) for device md126
[    2.388339] md126: bitmap initialized from disk: read 1 pages, set 19
of 121 bits
[    2.390324] md126: detected capacity change from 0 to 8060403712
[    2.391344]  md126: unknown partition table
```

The last section of dmesg's output tells us quite a bit about the RAID devices and
/dev/sdb. Since there is quite a bit of data, we will need to break this down to really
understand it all:

```
The first few lines show use information about /dev/md127.
[    2.366634] md: bind<sda1>
[    2.370652] md: raid1 personality registered for level 1
[    2.370820] md/raid1:md127: active with 1 out of 2 mirrors
[    2.371797] created bitmap (1 pages) for device md127
[    2.372181] md127: bitmap initialized from disk: read 1 pages, set 0
of 8 bits
[    2.373915] md127: detected capacity change from 0 to 524222464
[    2.374767]  md127: unknown partition table
```

This line appears to be information created during boot, as these messages suggest
the RAID was initializing. It also appears that when the RAID is initialized, it
detected that only one of the two available disks was bound to the RAID.

While this information itself is not new to our troubleshooting, what this tells us is that the system was booted in this state. This means that whatever happened to /dev/sdb may have happened previous to this system's most recent reboot.

It appears from the rest of this snippet that there are similar messages for /dev/md126; however, there is a bit more information included with those messages:

```
[    2.376065] md: bind<sdb2>
[    2.382976] md: bind<sda2>
[    2.385094] md: kicking non-fresh sdb2 from array!
[    2.385102] md: unbind<sdb2>
[    2.385105] md: export_rdev(sdb2)
[    2.387559] md/raid1:md126: active with 1 out of 2 mirrors
[    2.387874] created bitmap (1 pages) for device md126
[    2.388339] md126: bitmap initialized from disk: read 1 pages, set 19
of 121 bits
[    2.390324] md126: detected capacity change from 0 to 8060403712
[    2.391344]  md126: unknown partition table
```

The preceding messages look very similar to the messages from /dev/md127; however, there are a few lines that were not present in the messages at /dev/md127:

```
[    2.376065] md: bind<sdb2>
[    2.382976] md: bind<sda2>
[    2.385094] md: kicking non-fresh sdb2 from array!
[    2.385102] md: unbind<sdb2>
```

If we look at these messages, we can see that /dev/md126 attempted to use /dev/sdb2 in the RAID array; however, it found the drive to be non-fresh. The non-fresh message is interesting as it might explain why /dev/sdb is not being included into the RAID devices.

Summarizing what dmesg has provided

In a RAID set, each disk maintains an event count for every write request. The RAID uses this event count to ensure that each disk has received the appropriate amount of write requests. This allows the RAID to validate the consistency of the entire RAID.

When a RAID is restarting, the RAID manager will check the event count of each disk and ensure that they are consistent.

From the preceding messages, it appears that /dev/sda2 may have a higher event count than /dev/sdb2. This would indicate that some writes occurred on /dev/sda1 that never occurred on /dev/sdb2. This would be abnormal for a mirrored array and would indicate an issue with /dev/sdb2.

How do we check whether the event counts are different? With the mdadm command, we can display the event count for each disk device.

Using mdadm to examine the superblock

To view the event count, we will use the mdadm command with the --examine flag to examine the disk devices:

```
[nfs]# mdadm --examine /dev/sda1
/dev/sda1:
          Magic : a92b4efc
        Version : 1.0
    Feature Map : 0x1
     Array UUID : 7adf0323:b0962394:387e6cd0:b2914469
           Name : localhost:boot
  Creation Time : Wed Apr 15 09:39:22 2015
     Raid Level : raid1
   Raid Devices : 2

 Avail Dev Size : 1023968 (500.07 MiB 524.27 MB)
     Array Size : 511936 (500.02 MiB 524.22 MB)
  Used Dev Size : 1023872 (500.02 MiB 524.22 MB)
   Super Offset : 1023984 sectors
   Unused Space : before=0 sectors, after=96 sectors
          State : clean
    Device UUID : 92d97c32:1f53f59a:14a7deea:34ec8c7c

Internal Bitmap : -16 sectors from superblock
    Update Time : Mon May 11 04:08:10 2015
  Bad Block Log : 512 entries available at offset -8 sectors
       Checksum : bd8c1d5b - correct
         Events : 60


    Device Role : Active device 0
    Array State : A. ('A' == active, '.' == missing, 'R' == replacing)
```

The `--examine` flag is very similar to `--detail` except where `--detail` is used to print the RAID device details. `--examine` is used to print RAID details from the individual disks that make up the RAID. The details that `--examine` prints are actually from the superblock details on the disk.

When the Linux RAID is utilizing a disk as part of a RAID device, the RAID system will reserve some space on the disk for a **superblock**. This superblock is simply used to store metadata about the disk and the RAID.

In the preceding command, we simply printed the RAID superblock information from `/dev/sda1`. To get a better understanding of the RAID superblock, let's take a look at the details the `--examine` flag provides:

```
/dev/sda1:
          Magic : a92b4efc
        Version : 1.0
     Feature Map : 0x1
      Array UUID : 7adf0323:b0962394:387e6cd0:b2914469
           Name : localhost:boot
  Creation Time : Wed Apr 15 09:39:22 2015
      Raid Level : raid1
    Raid Devices : 2
```

The first section of this output provides quite a bit of useful information. The magic number, for instance, is used as a superblock header. This is a value that is used to indicate the beginning of the superblock.

Another useful piece of information is the `Array UUID`. This is a unique identifier for the RAID that this disk belongs to. If we print the details of RAID `md127`, we can see that the Array UUID from `/dev/sda1` and the UUID from `md127` match:

```
[nfs]# mdadm --detail /dev/md127 | grep UUID
           UUID : 7adf0323:b0962394:387e6cd0:b2914469
```

This can be useful when a device name has changed and you need to identify the disks that belong to a specific RAID. An example of this would be if someone accidently put drives into the wrong slot during hardware maintenance. If the drives still contain the UUID, it is possible to identify the RAID the misplaced drives belong to.

The bottom three lines `Creation Time`, `RAID Level`, and `RAID Devices` are also very useful when used with the output of `--detail`.

This second snippet of information is useful for determining information about the disk device:

```
Avail Dev Size : 1023968 (500.07 MiB 524.27 MB)
   Array Size : 511936 (500.02 MiB 524.22 MB)
 Used Dev Size : 1023872 (500.02 MiB 524.22 MB)
  Super Offset : 1023984 sectors
  Unused Space : before=0 sectors, after=96 sectors
         State : clean
   Device UUID : 92d97c32:1f53f59a:14a7deea:34ec8c7c
```

In this snippet, we can see the size of the individual disk and the array in the first three lines. If there was ever a question about the size of each disk in the array, this information could be very useful. In addition to the size, we can also see the current `State` of the RAID. This state matches the state we see from the `--detail` output of `/dev/md127`.

```
[nfs]# mdadm --detail /dev/md127 | grep State
         State : clean, degraded
```

The next section of information from the `--examine` output is very useful for our issue:

```
Internal Bitmap : -16 sectors from superblock
    Update Time : Mon May 11 04:08:10 2015
  Bad Block Log : 512 entries available at offset -8 sectors
       Checksum : bd8c1d5b - correct
         Events : 60


    Device Role : Active device 0
    Array State : A. ('A' == active, '.' == missing, 'R' == replacing)
```

In this section, we can see the `Events` information, which is showing the current event count value on this disk. We can also see the `Array State` value of `/dev/sda1`. The value of `A.` indicates that from the perspective of `/dev/sda1`, its mirrored partner is missing.

As we examine the details of the superblock under /dev/sdb1, we will see an interesting difference in the Array State and Events values:

```
[nfs]# mdadm --examine /dev/sdb1
/dev/sdb1:
          Magic : a92b4efc
        Version : 1.0
     Feature Map : 0x1
      Array UUID : 7adf0323:b0962394:387e6cd0:b2914469
           Name : localhost:boot
   Creation Time : Wed Apr 15 09:39:22 2015
      Raid Level : raid1
    Raid Devices : 2

  Avail Dev Size : 1023968 (500.07 MiB 524.27 MB)
      Array Size : 511936 (500.02 MiB 524.22 MB)
   Used Dev Size : 1023872 (500.02 MiB 524.22 MB)
    Super Offset : 1023984 sectors
    Unused Space : before=0 sectors, after=96 sectors
           State : clean
     Device UUID : 5a9bb172:13102af9:81d761fb:56d83bdd

  Internal Bitmap : -16 sectors from superblock
     Update Time : Mon May  4 21:09:30 2015
    Bad Block Log : 512 entries available at offset -8 sectors
        Checksum : cd226d7b - correct
          Events : 48

     Device Role : Active device 1
     Array State : AA ('A' == active, '.' == missing, 'R' == replacing)
```

From the results, we have answered quite a few questions about /dev/sdb1.

The first question that we had is whether /dev/sdb1 was part of a RAID or not. From the fact that this device has a RAID superblock and that information is printable via mdadm, we can safely say yes.

```
     Array UUID : 7adf0323:b0962394:387e6cd0:b2914469
```

By looking at the `Array UUID`, we can also determine whether this device was a part of `/dev/md127`, as we suspected:

```
[nfs]# mdadm --detail /dev/md127 | grep UUID
         UUID : 7adf0323:b0962394:387e6cd0:b2914469
```

As it appears, `/dev/sdb1` was at some point part of `/dev/md127`.

The final question we need to answer is whether or not the `Events` values differ between `/dev/sda1` and `/dev/sdb1`. From the `--examine` information from `/dev/sda1`, we can see the event count is set to 60. In the preceding code, `--examine` results from `/dev/sdb1`; we can see that the event count is much lower—48:

```
         Events : 48
```

Given the difference, we can safely say that `/dev/sdb1` is 12 events behind `/dev/sda1`. This is a very significant difference and a sensible reason for MD to reject adding `/dev/sdb1` to the RAID array.

As an interesting side note, if we look at the `Array State` of `/dev/sdb1`, we can see that it still believes that it is an active disk in the `/dev/md127` array:

```
   Array State : AA ('A' == active, '.' == missing, 'R' == replacing)
```

This is due to the fact that since the device is no longer part of the RAID, it is not being updated with the current status. We can see this in the update time as well:

```
   Update Time : Mon May  4 21:09:30 2015
```

The `Update Time` for `/dev/sda1` is much more recent; thus, it should be trusted above the disk `/dev/sdb1`.

Checking /dev/sdb2

Now that we know the reasons behind `/dev/sdb1` not being added to `/dev/md127`, we should determine whether the same situation is true for `/dev/sdb2` and `/dev/md126`.

Since we already know that `/dev/sda2` is healthy and part of the `/dev/md126` array, we will focus solely on capturing its `Events` value:

```
[nfs]# mdadm --examine /dev/sda2 | grep Events
         Events : 7517
```

The event count of `/dev/sda2` is quite high in comparison to `/dev/sda1`. From this, we can determine that `/dev/md126` is probably a very active RAID device.

Now that we have the event count, let's take a look at the details of /dev/sdb2:

```
[nfs]# mdadm --examine /dev/sdb2
/dev/sdb2:
          Magic : a92b4efc
        Version : 1.2
    Feature Map : 0x1
     Array UUID : bec13d99:42674929:76663813:f748e7cb
           Name : localhost:pv00
  Creation Time : Wed Apr 15 09:39:19 2015
     Raid Level : raid1
   Raid Devices : 2

 Avail Dev Size : 15742976 (7.51 GiB 8.06 GB)
     Array Size : 7871488 (7.51 GiB 8.06 GB)
    Data Offset : 8192 sectors
   Super Offset : 8 sectors
   Unused Space : before=8104 sectors, after=0 sectors
          State : clean
    Device UUID : 01db1f5f:e8176cad:8ce68d51:deff57f8

Internal Bitmap : 8 sectors from superblock
    Update Time : Mon May  4 21:10:31 2015
  Bad Block Log : 512 entries available at offset 72 sectors
       Checksum : 98a8ace8 - correct
         Events : 541


    Device Role : Active device 1
    Array State : AA ('A' == active, '.' == missing, 'R' == replacing)
```

Again, from the fact that we were able to print superblock information from /dev/sdb2, we have determined that this device is in fact part of a RAID:

```
    Array UUID : bec13d99:42674929:76663813:f748e7cb
```

If we compare the Array UUID of /dev/sdb2 with the UUID of /dev/md126, we will also see that it was in fact part of that RAID array:

```
[nfs]# mdadm --detail /dev/md126 | grep UUID
           UUID : bec13d99:42674929:76663813:f748e7cb
```

This answers our question as to whether /dev/sdb2 was part of the md126 RAID. If we look at the event count of /dev/sdb2, we can also answer the question as to why it is not currently part of that RAID:

```
Events : 541
```

It appears that this device has missed write events that were sent to the md126 RAID, given that the Events count from /dev/sda2 was 7517 and the Events count from /dev/sdb2 is 541.

What we have learned so far

From the troubleshooting steps that we have taken so far, we have collected quite a few key pieces of data. Let's walk through what we have learned and what we can infer from these findings:

- On our system, we have two RAID devices.

  Using the mdadm command and the contents of /proc/mdstat, we were able to determine that this system has two RAID devices–/dev/md126 and /dev/md127.

- Both RAID devices are a RAID 1 and missing a mirrored device.

  With the mdadm command and output of dmesg, we were able to identify that both RAID devices are set up as a RAID 1 device. On top of that, we were also able to see that both RAID devices were missing a disk; both the missing devices were partitions from the /dev/sdb hard disk.

- Both /dev/sdb1 and /dev/sdb2 have mismatched event counts.

  With the mdadm command, we were able to inspect the superblock details of the /dev/sdb1 and /dev/sdb2 devices. During this, we were able to see that the event counts for those devices are not matching the active partitions on /dev/sda.

  For this reason, the RAID will not re-add the /dev/sdb devices to their respective RAID arrays.

- The disk /dev/sdb seems to be functional.

  While the RAID hasn't added /dev/sdb1 or /dev/sdb2 to their respective RAID arrays, it does not mean that the device /dev/sdb is faulty.

From the messages in dmesg, we did not see any errors for the /dev/sdb device itself. We also were able to use mdadm to inspect the partitions on those drives. From everything we have done so far, these drives appear to be functional.

Re-adding the drives to the arrays

The /dev/sdb disk seems to be functional and, outside the event count difference, we cannot see any reason the RAID would reject the devices. Our next step will be an attempt to re-add the removed devices to their RAID arrays.

The first RAID we will attempt this with is /dev/md127:

```
[nfs]# mdadm --detail /dev/md127
/dev/md127:
          Version : 1.0
    Creation Time : Wed Apr 15 09:39:22 2015
       Raid Level : raid1
       Array Size : 511936 (500.02 MiB 524.22 MB)
    Used Dev Size : 511936 (500.02 MiB 524.22 MB)
     Raid Devices : 2
    Total Devices : 1
      Persistence : Superblock is persistent

     Intent Bitmap : Internal

      Update Time : Mon May 11 04:08:10 2015
            State : clean, degraded
   Active Devices : 1
  Working Devices : 1
   Failed Devices : 0
    Spare Devices : 0

             Name : localhost:boot
             UUID : 7adf0323:b0962394:387e6cd0:b2914469
           Events : 60

    Number   Major   Minor   RaidDevice State
       0       8       1        0      active sync   /dev/sda1
       2       0       0        2      removed
```

The simplest way to re-add the drive is to simply use the -a (add) flag with mdadm.

```
[nfs]# mdadm /dev/md127 -a /dev/sdb1
mdadm: re-added /dev/sdb1
```

The preceding command will tell mdadm to add the device /dev/sdb1 to the RAID device /dev/md127. Since /dev/sdb1 was already part of the RAID array, the MD service simply re-adds the disk and re-syncs the missing events from /dev/sda1.

We can see this in action if we look at the RAID details with the --detail flag:

```
[nfs]# mdadm --detail /dev/md127
/dev/md127:
          Version : 1.0
    Creation Time : Wed Apr 15 09:39:22 2015
       Raid Level : raid1
       Array Size : 511936 (500.02 MiB 524.22 MB)
    Used Dev Size : 511936 (500.02 MiB 524.22 MB)
     Raid Devices : 2
    Total Devices : 2
      Persistence : Superblock is persistent

     Intent Bitmap : Internal

      Update Time : Mon May 11 16:47:32 2015
            State : clean, degraded, recovering
   Active Devices : 1
  Working Devices : 2
   Failed Devices : 0
    Spare Devices : 1

   Rebuild Status : 50% complete

             Name : localhost:boot
             UUID : 7adf0323:b0962394:387e6cd0:b2914469
           Events : 66

    Number   Major   Minor   RaidDevice State
       0       8        1        0       active sync   /dev/sda1
       1       8       17        1       spare rebuilding   /dev/sdb1
```

From the preceding output, we can see a few differences from the earlier examples. One very important difference is the Rebuild Status:

```
Rebuild Status : 50% complete
```

With mdadm --detail, we can see the completion status of the drives re-syncing. If there were any errors in this process, we will also be able to see this. If we look at the bottom three lines, we can also see which devices are active and which are being rebuilt.

```
Number    Major    Minor    RaidDevice State
   0        8        1          0       active sync    /dev/sda1
   1        8        17         1       spare rebuilding    /dev/sdb1
```

After a few seconds, if we run mdadm --detail again, we should see that the RAID device has re-synced:

```
[nfs]# mdadm --detail /dev/md127
/dev/md127:
          Version : 1.0
    Creation Time : Wed Apr 15 09:39:22 2015
       Raid Level : raid1
       Array Size : 511936 (500.02 MiB 524.22 MB)
    Used Dev Size : 511936 (500.02 MiB 524.22 MB)
     Raid Devices : 2
    Total Devices : 2
      Persistence : Superblock is persistent

     Intent Bitmap : Internal

      Update Time : Mon May 11 16:47:32 2015
            State : clean
   Active Devices : 2
  Working Devices : 2
   Failed Devices : 0
    Spare Devices : 0

             Name : localhost:boot
             UUID : 7adf0323:b0962394:387e6cd0:b2914469
           Events : 69
```

Number	Major	Minor	RaidDevice	State	
0	8	1	0	active sync	/dev/sda1
1	8	17	1	active sync	/dev/sdb1

Now we can see that both drives are listed as `active sync` state and that the RAID `State` is simply `clean`.

The preceding output is what a functional RAID 1 device should look like. At this point, we can consider the issue with `/dev/md127` resolved.

Adding a new disk device

Sometimes you will find yourself in a situation where your disk drive was actually faulty and the actual physical hardware must be replaced. In situations like this, once the partitions `/dev/sdb1` and `/dev/sdb2` are recreated, the device can simply be added to the RAID using the same steps as we used earlier.

When the command `mdadm <raid device> -a <disk device>` is executed, `mdadm` first checks to see whether the disk device was ever once part of the RAID.

It does this by reading the superblock information on the disk device. If the device was previously part of the RAID, it simply re-adds it and starts a rebuild to re-sync the drives.

If the disk device was never part of the RAID, it will be added as a spare device, and if the RAID is degraded, the spare device will be used to get the RAID back into a clean state.

When disks are not added cleanly

In a previous work environment, when we replaced hard drives the drives were always quality tested before being used to replace faulty drives in production environments. Often, this quality testing involved creating partitions and adding those partitions to an existing RAID.

Because those devices already had a RAID superblock on them, `mdadm` would reject the addition of the devices to the RAID. It is possible to clear an existing RAID `superblock` using the `mdadm` command:

```
[nfs]# mdadm --zero-superblock /dev/sdb2
```

The preceding command will tell `mdadm` to remove the RAID `superblock` information from the specified disk—in this case, `/dev/sdb2`:

```
[nfs]# mdadm --examine /dev/sdb2
mdadm: No md superblock detected on /dev/sdb2.
```

Using --examine, we can see that there is now no superblock on the device that had one before.

The --zero-superblock flag should be used with caution and only when the device data is no longer required. Once this superblock information is removed, the RAID sees this disk as a blank disk, and during any re-sync process, the existing data will be overwritten.

Once the superblock is removed, the same steps can be performed to add it to a RAID array:

```
[nfs]# mdadm /dev/md126 -a /dev/sdb2
mdadm: added /dev/sdb2
```

Another way to watch the rebuild status

Earlier we used mdadm --detail to show the rebuild status of md127. Another way to see this information is via /proc/mdstat:

```
[nfs]# cat /proc/mdstat
Personalities : [raid1]
md126 : active raid1 sdb2[2] sda2[0]
      7871488 blocks super 1.2 [2/1] [U_]
      [>...................]  recovery =  0.0% (1984/7871488)
finish=65.5min speed=1984K/sec
      bitmap: 1/1 pages [4KB], 65536KB chunk

md127 : active raid1 sdb1[1] sda1[0]
      511936 blocks super 1.0 [2/2] [UU]
      bitmap: 0/1 pages [0KB], 65536KB chunk


unused devices: <none>
```

After a bit, the RAID will finish re-syncing; now, both the RAID arrays are in a healthy status:

```
[nfs]# cat /proc/mdstat
Personalities : [raid1]
md126 : active raid1 sdb2[2] sda2[0]
      7871488 blocks super 1.2 [2/2] [UU]
      bitmap: 0/1 pages [0KB], 65536KB chunk
```

```
md127 : active raid1 sdb1[1] sda1[0]
      511936 blocks super 1.0 [2/2] [UU]
      bitmap: 0/1 pages [0KB], 65536KB chunk

unused devices: <none>
```

Summary

In the previous chapter, *Chapter 7, FileSystem Errors and Recovery* we noticed a simple RAID failure message in our /var/log/messages log file. In this chapter, we used a Data Collector approach to investigate the cause of that failure message.

After investigating with the RAID management command mdadm, we found several RAID devices in a degraded state. Using dmesg, we were able to determine which hard drive devices were affected and that the disks at some point were removed from service. We also found that the disk **event counts** were mismatched, preventing the disks from being re-added automatically.

We verified that the devices were not physically faulty with dmesg and choose to re-add them to the RAID array.

While this chapter focused heavily on RAID and disk failures, both /var/log/messages and dmesg can be used to troubleshoot other device failures. For devices other than hard disks, however, the solution is often a simple replacement. Of course, like most things, this depends on the type of failure experienced.

In the next chapter, we will show how to troubleshoot custom user applications and the use of system tools to perform some advanced troubleshooting.

9
Using System Tools to Troubleshoot Applications

In the previous chapter, we covered troubleshooting hardware issues. Specifically, you learned what to do when hard disks have been removed from a RAID and cannot be read.

In this chapter, we will get back to troubleshooting applications, but unlike earlier examples, we will not be troubleshooting a popular open source application such as WordPress. In this chapter, we will focus on a custom application that will be much more difficult to troubleshoot than a well-known one.

Open source versus home-grown applications

Popular open source projects often have an online community or bug/issue tracker. As we experienced in *Chapter 3*, *Troubleshooting a Web Application*, these can be useful resources for troubleshooting application issues. Often, the issue has already been reported or asked about in these communities, with the majority of these posts also containing a solution for the issue.

These solutions are posted on the Internet in open forums; any errors from the application can also simply be searched for on Google. Most of the time, the search will show multiple possible answers. It is a pretty rare occurrence when an error from a popular open source application produces zero search results on Google.

With custom applications, however, application errors might not always be resolved with a quick Google search. Sometimes, an application provides a generic error such as **Permission Denied** or **File not found**. On other occasions, however, they produce no error or application-specific errors such as the issue we will be working with today.

When faced with nondescriptive errors in open source tools, you can always ask for help on an online site of some sort. With custom applications, however, you might not always have the option of asking a developer what the error means.

Sometimes, it is up to the systems administrator to fix the application with little to no help from the developer.

When those situations occur, there are a myriad of tools at the administrator's disposal. In today's chapter, we will be exploring some of these tools while, of course, troubleshooting a custom application.

When the application won't start

For this chapter's problem, we will start as we have with most other problems, except today, rather than receiving an alert or phone call, we are actually asked a question by another systems administrator.

The systems administrator is attempting to start an application on the blog web server. When they attempt to start the application, it appears to be starting; however, at the end, it simply prints an error message and exits.

Our first response to this scenario is of course the first step in the troubleshooting process — duplicate it.

The other systems administrator informs us that they are starting the application by performing the following steps:

1. Logging into the server as the `vagrant` user
2. Moving to the directory `/opt/myapp`
3. Running the script `start.sh`

Before going any further, let's attempt those same steps:

```
$ whoami
vagrant
$ cd /opt/myapp/
$ ls -la
total 8
drwxr-xr-x. 5 vagrant vagrant  69 May 18 03:11 .
drwxr-xr-x. 4 root    root     50 May 18 00:48 ..
drwxrwxr-x. 2 vagrant vagrant  24 May 18 01:14 bin
```

```
drwxrwxr-x. 2 vagrant vagrant  23 May 18 00:51 conf
drwxrwxr-x. 2 vagrant vagrant   6 May 18 00:50 logs
-rwxr-xr-x. 1 vagrant vagrant 101 May 18 03:11 start.sh
$ ./start.sh
Initializing with configuration file /opt/myapp/conf/config.yml
- - - - - - - - - - - - - - - - - - - - - - - - - - - - - -
Starting service: [Failed]
```

In the preceding steps, we follow the same steps as the previous administrator and get the same results. The application appears to have failed to start.

In the preceding example, the whoami command was used to show that we were logged in as the vagrant user. This command is very handy when dealing with applications as it can be used to ensure the proper system user is performing the start process.

We can see from the preceding startup attempt that the application failed to start with the following message:

```
Starting service: [Failed]
```

However, we need to know why it failed to start and whether the process truly failed

To answer the question on whether the process truly failed or not is actually quite simple. To do this, we can simply check the exit code of the application, which is done by printing the $? variable after executing the start.sh script, as follows:

```
$ echo $?
1
```

Exit codes

On Linux and Unix systems, programs have the ability to pass a value to their parent process while they terminate. This value is called an **exit code**. Programs that are terminating or "exiting" use exit codes to tell the process that invoked it whether that program was successful or unsuccessful.

For POSIX systems (such as Red Hat Enterprise Linux), the standard convention is for programs to exit with a 0 status code for success and a non-zero status code for failure. Since our preceding example exited with a status code of 1, this means the application exited with a failure.

To understand exit codes a little better, let's write a quick little script that performs a successful task:

```
$ cat /var/tmp/exitcodes.sh
#!/bin/bash
touch /var/tmp/file.txt
```

This quick little shell script performs one task, it runs the touch command on the file /var/tmp/file.txt. If that file exists, the touch command simply updates the access time on that file. If the file does not exist, the touch command will create it.

Since /var/tmp is a temporary directory with open permissions, this script, when executed as the vagrant user, should be successful:

```
$ /var/tmp/exitcodes.sh
```

After executing the command, we can see the exit code by using the BASH special variable $?. This variable is a special variable in the BASH shell that can only be used to read the exit code of the last program executed. This variable is one of a few special variables in the BASH shell that can only be read and never written.

To see the exit status of our script, we can echo the value of $? to our screen:

```
$ echo $?
0
```

It looks like this script returned a 0 exit status. This means the script executed successfully and most likely updated or created the file /var/tmp/file.txt. We can validate that the file was updated by performing an ls -la on the file itself:

```
$ ls -la /var/tmp/file.txt
-rw-rw-r--. 1 vagrant vagrant 0 May 25 14:25 /var/tmp/file.txt
```

From the output of the ls command, it appears the file was updated or created recently.

The preceding example shows what happens when a script is successful, but what about when the script is unsuccessful? With a modified version of the preceding script, we can easily see what happens when a script fails:

```
$ cat /var/tmp/exitcodes.sh
#!/bin/bash
touch /some/directory/that/doesnt/exist/file.txt
```

The modified version will attempt to create a file in a directory that does not exist. That script will then fail and exit with an exit code that indicates failure:

```
$ /var/tmp/exitcodes.sh
touch: cannot touch '/some/directory/that/doesnt/exist/file.txt': No such
file or directory
```

We can see from the output of the script that the touch command failed, but what about the exit code?

```
$ echo $?
1
```

The exit code also shows that the script has failed. The standard for exit codes is 0 for a success and anything non-zero is a failure. In general, you will see either a 0 or 1 exit code. Some applications, however, will use other exit codes to indicate specific failures:

```
$ somecommand
-bash: somecommand: command not found
$ echo $?
127
```

For example, if we were to execute a command that does not exist from the BASH shell, the exit code provided will be 127. This exit code is a convention used to indicate that the command was not found. The following is a list of exit codes that are used for specific purposes:

- 0: Success
- 1: General failure has occurred
- 2: Misuse of shell built-ins
- 126: Command invoked could not be executed
- 127: Command not found
- 128: Invalid argument passed to the exit command
- 130: Command stopped with *Ctrl* + *C* keys
- 255: Exit code provided is out of the 0 - 255 range

This list is a good general guide for exit codes. However, since each application can provide its own exit codes you might find that a command or application provides an exit code that is not within the preceding list. For open source applications, you can generally look up what the exit code means. For custom applications, however, you may or may not have the ability to look up what the exit codes means.

Is the script failing, or the application?

One interesting thing about shell scripts and exit codes is that when a shell script is executed, the exit code for that script will be the exit code of the last command executed.

To put this in perspective, we can modify our test script again:

```
$ cat /var/tmp/exitcodes.sh
#!/bin/bash
touch /some/directory/that/doesnt/exist/file.txt
echo "It works"
```

The preceding command should produce an interesting result. The `touch` command will fail; however, the echo command will be successful.

What this means is that when executed, even though the `touch` command fails, the `echo` command is successful so the exit code from the command line should show the script as successful:

```
$ /var/tmp/exitcodes.sh
touch: cannot touch '/some/directory/that/doesnt/exist/file.txt': No such file or directory
It works
$ echo $?
0
```

The preceding command is an example of a script that does not handle errors gracefully. If we were to rely on this script to provide us with the correct status of the execution solely by the exit code, we would have incorrect results.

It is always good for a systems administrator to be a bit skeptical of unknown scripts. I have found many occasions (and written a few myself) where scripts have no error checking. For this reason, one of the first steps we should perform with our issue is to validate that the exit code of 1 is actually coming from the application being launched.

To do this, we will need to read the start script:

```
$ cat ./start.sh
#!/bin/bash

HOMEDIR=/opt/myapp

$HOMEDIR/bin/application --deamon --config $HOMEDIR/conf/config.yml
```

From the look of things, the start script is very basic. It looks like the script simply sets the $HOMEDIR variable to /opt/myapp and then runs the application by running the command $HOMEDIR/bin/application.

 After the value of $HOMEDIR is set to /opt/myapp, you can assume that any future reference to $HOMEDIR is actually the value /opt/myapp.

From the preceding script, we can see that the last command executed is the application, meaning the exit code we received was from the application and not another command. This proves that we are receiving the true exit status of this application.

The start script does provide us with a bit more information than just which command provides the exit code. If we take a look at the application's command line parameters, we can understand even more about this application:

$HOMEDIR/bin/application --deamon --config $HOMEDIR/conf/config.yml

This is the command that actually starts the application within the start.sh script. The script is running the command /opt/myapp/bin/application with the arguments --daemon and --config /opt/myapp/conf/config.yml. While we might not know much about this application, we can make some assumptions.

One assumption we can make is that the --daemon flag causes this application to daemonize itself. On Unix and Linux systems, a process that runs continuously as a background process is referred to as a daemon.

Typically, a daemon process is a service that doesn't require user input. A few easily recognizable examples of daemons are Apache or MySQL. These processes run in the background and perform a service rather than running in a user's desktop or shell.

With the preceding flag, we can safely assume that this process is designed to run in the background once it is started successfully.

Another assumption we can make based on the command line parameters is that the file /opt/myapp/conf/config.yml is used as a configuration file for the application. This seems pretty straightforward considering the flag is named --config.

The preceding assumptions are pretty easy to recognize because the flags use the long format --option. However, not all applications or services use the long format for command line flags. Often, these are single character flags.

While every application has its own command line flags and might differ from application to application, common flags such as `--config` and `--deamon` are often shortened to `-c` and `-d` or `-D`. If our application was provided with single character flags, it would have looked more like the following:

```
$HOMEDIR/bin/application -d -c $HOMEDIR/conf/config.yml
```

Even with the shortened options, we can safely identify that `-c` specifies a configuration file.

A wealth of information in the configuration file

We know that this application is using the configuration file `/opt/myapp/conf/config.yml`. If we read this file, we might find information about the application and what task it is trying to perform:

```
$ cat conf/config.yml
port: 25
debug: True
logdir: /opt/myapp/logs
```

The configuration file for this application is quite short, but there is quite a bit of useful information within it. The first configuration item is interesting, as it seems to specify port `25` as a port for the application to use. Without knowing exactly what this application does, this information is not immediately useful but might be useful to us later.

The second item seems to suggest the application is in a debug mode. Often applications or services might have a `debug` mode, which causes them to log or output debugging information for troubleshooting. In our case, it seems the debug option is enabled, as the value of this item is `True`.

The third and final item is what appears to be a directory path for logs. Log files are always useful for troubleshooting applications. Often, you are able to find information about the application issue within log files. This is especially true if the application is in a `debug` state, which appears to be the case for our application.

Since our application seems to be in the `debug` mode and we know the location of the log directory. We can check that log directory for any log files that might have been created during the application's start process:

```
$ ls -la /opt/myapp/logs/
total 4
drwxrwxr-x. 2 vagrant vagrant  22 May 30 03:51 .
```

```
drwxr-xr-x. 5 vagrant vagrant  53 May 30 03:49 ..
-rw-rw-r--. 1 vagrant vagrant 454 May 30 03:54 debug.out
```

If we run an `ls -la` in the log directory, we can see a `debug.out` file. Based on the name, this file is most likely the debug output from the application but not necessarily the application's primary log file. This file, however, might be even more useful than a standard log as it might contain the reason the application startup is failing:

```
$ cat debug.out
Configuration file processed
------------------------
Starting service: [Failed]
Configuration file processed
------------------------
Starting service: [Success]
- - - - - - - - - - - - - - - - - - - - - - - - -
Proccessed 5 messages
Proccessed 5 messages
Configuration file processed
------------------------
Starting service: [Failed]
Configuration file processed
------------------------
Starting service: [Failed]
```

Based on the contents of this file it appears that this file contains logs from multiple executions of this application. We can see this based on a repeated pattern.

```
Configuration file processed
------------------------
```

This seems to be the first item printed each time the application starts. We can see these lines a total of four times; most likely, this means this application has been started at least four times in the past.

Within this file, we can see an important log message:

```
Starting service: [Success]
```

It seems that the second time this application was started the application startup was successful. However, each time it was started afterwards the application failed.

Watching log files during startup

Since the debug file's contents do not include timestamps, it is somewhat difficult to know whether the debug output from this file was written when we started the application or during a previous startup.

Since we don't know which lines were written during our last attempt as compared to other attempts, we will need to try and identify how many log entries are written each time the application is started. To do this, we can use the `tail` command with the `-f` or `--follow` flag:

```
$ tail -f debug.out

- - - - - - - - - - - - - - - - - - - - - - - - - - - - -

Proccessed 5 messages
Proccessed 5 messages
 [Failed]
Configuration file processed
-------------------------
Starting service: [Failed]
Configuration file processed
-------------------------
Starting service: [Failed]
```

When first starting the `tail` command with the `-f` (follow) flag, the last 10 lines of the file are printed. This is also the default behavior of tail if it is run with no flags.

However, the `-f` flag doesn't simply stop at the last 10 lines. When run with the `-f` flag, `tail` will continuously monitor the specified file for new data. Once `tail` sees new data written to the specified file, the data will then be written to the output of `tail`.

By running tail `-f` against the `debug.out` file, we will be able to identify any new debug logs being written by the application. If we once again execute the `start.sh` script we should see any possible debug data being printed by the application during startup:

```
$ ./start.sh
Initializing with configuration file /opt/myapp/conf/config.yml

- - - - - - - - - - - - - - - - - - - - - - - - - - - - -

Starting service: [Failed]
```

The `start.sh` script's output is the same as last time, which is not much of a surprise at this point. However, now that we are watching the `debug.out` file, we might find something useful:

```
Configuration file processed
-------------------------
Starting service: [Failed]
```

From the `tail` command, we can see that the preceding three lines were printed during the execution of `start.sh`. While this in itself does not explain why the application is unable to start, it does tell us something interesting:

```
$ cat debug.out
Configuration file processed
-------------------------
Starting service: [Failed]
Configuration file processed
-------------------------
Starting service: [Success]
- - - - - - - - - - - - - - - - - - - - - - - - -
Processed 5 messages
Processed 5 messages
Configuration file processed
-------------------------
Starting service: [Failed]
Configuration file processed
-------------------------
Starting service: [Failed]
Configuration file processed
-------------------------
Starting service: [Failed]
```

Given that when the application fails to start, "`Failed`" messages from the preceding command are printed, and we can see that the last three times the `start.sh` script was executed, it failed. However, the instance before that was successful.

So far, I executed the start script twice and the other admin executed the script once. This would account for the three failures we see at the end of the `debug.out` file. The interesting thing about this is that the instance before those the application successfully started.

This is interesting because it indicates a strong possibility that a previous instance of the application might be running.

Checking whether the application is already running

One very common cause for this type of problem is simply that the application is already running. Some applications should only be started once, and the application itself will check whether another instance is running before completing a startup.

In general, if this scenario were the case, we would expect the application to print an error to the screen or the `debug.out` file. However, not every application has appropriate error handling or messaging. This is especially true for custom applications, and it seems to be true for the application we are working with as well.

At the moment, we are making the assumption that our issue is caused by another instance of the application. This is an educated guess based on debug messages and previous experience. While we do not have any hard facts (yet) that tell us whether another instance is running or not; this scenario is quite common.

This situation is a perfect example of an **Educated Guesser** using previous experience to build a hypothesis of a root cause. Of course, after forming a hypothesis, our next step is to validate whether or not it is correct. Even if our hypothesis turns out to be incorrect we at least can eliminate a potential cause of our problem.

Since our current hypothesis is that we might already have an instance of the application running, we can validate it by executing the ps command:

```
$ ps -elf | grep application
0 S vagrant   7110  5567  0  80   0 - 28160 pipe_w 15:22 pts/0
00:00:00 grep --color=auto application
```

From this, it appears that our hypothesis might be incorrect. However, the preceding command simply performs a process list and searches that output for any instance of the word application. While this command might be enough, some applications during startup (especially ones that daemonize) will launch another process that might not match the string "`application`".

Since we have been starting the application as the "vagrant" user it seems likely that even if the application daemonized, the processes would be running as the vagrant user. Using the same command we can also search the process list for processes running as the vagrant user:

```
$ ps -elf | grep vagrant
4 S root      4230  984  0 80   0 - 32881 poll_s May30 ?
00:00:00 sshd: vagrant [priv]
5 S vagrant   4233 4230  0 80   0 - 32881 poll_s May30 ?
00:00:00 sshd: vagrant@pts/1
0 S vagrant   4234 4233  0 80   0 - 28838 n_tty_ May30 pts/1
00:00:00 -bash
4 S root      5563  984  0 80   0 - 32881 poll_s May31 ?
00:00:00 sshd: vagrant [priv]
5 S vagrant   5566 5563  0 80   0 - 32881 poll_s May31 ?
00:00:01 sshd: vagrant@pts/0
0 S vagrant   5567 5566  0 80   0 - 28857 wait   May31 pts/0
00:00:00 -bash
0 R vagrant   7333 5567  0 80   0 - 30839 -      14:58 pts/0
00:00:00 ps -elf
0 S vagrant   7334 5567  0 80   0 - 28160 pipe_w 14:58 pts/0
00:00:00 grep --color=auto vagrant
```

This command gave us quite a bit more output, but unfortunately none of these processes are the application we are looking for.

Checking open files

The preceding process list commands did not provide any results that would indicate that an instance of our application is running. However, before assuming that it is in fact not running we should perform one final check.

Since we know that the application we are working with appears to be installed into /opt/myapp and we can see both configuration files and logs within that directory. It is pretty safe to assume that the application in question might open one or more of the files located within /opt/myapp.

One very useful command is the **lsof** command. With this command, we can list all of the open files on the system. While this might not sound very powerful at first, let's take a detailed look at this command to understand how much information it can actually provide.

When running the `lsof` command, permissions become very critical to understand. When executing `lsof` with no parameters, the command will print a list of all open files for every process it can identify. If we run this command as an unprivileged user such as the "vagrant" user, the output will only consist of processes that are running as the vagrant user. If we run the command as the root user, however, this command will print open files for all processes on the system.

To put into perspective just how many files this translates to, we will run the `lsof` command and redirect the output to the `wc -l` command, which will count the number of lines provided in the output:

```
# lsof | wc -l
3840
```

From the `wc` command, we can see that there are currently 3840 files open on this system. Now some of these files might be duplicated, as it is possible for more than one process to open the same file. However, the sheer number of open files on this system is quite large. To put it in further perspective, this system is also a fairly underutilized system and is not running many applications in general. Do not be surprised if after executing the preceding commands on a well-utilized system the number of open files is exponentially higher.

Since looking at 3840 open files is not very practical, let's get a better understanding of `lsof` by taking a look at the first 10 files from the `lsof` output. We can do this by redirecting the command's output to the `head` command, which, like the `tail` command, will print 10 lines by default. However, where the `tail` command prints the last 10 lines, the `head` command prints the first 10:

```
# lsof | head
COMMAND     PID TID     USER   FD     TYPE            DEVICE   SIZE/OFF
NODE NAME
systemd       1          root   cwd    DIR             253,1       4096
128 /
systemd       1          root   rtd    DIR             253,1       4096
128 /
systemd       1          root   txt    REG             253,1    1214408
67629956 /usr/lib/systemd/systemd
systemd       1          root   mem    REG             253,1      58288
134298633 /usr/lib64/libnss_files-2.17.so
systemd       1          root   mem    REG             253,1      90632
134373166 /usr/lib64/libz.so.1.2.7
systemd       1          root   mem    REG             253,1      19888
134393597 /usr/lib64/libattr.so.1.1.0
```

```
systemd        1            root  mem        REG              253,1      113320
134298625 /usr/lib64/libnsl-2.17.so
systemd        1            root  mem        REG              253,1      153184
134801313 /usr/lib64/liblzma.so.5.0.99
systemd        1            root  mem        REG              253,1      398264
134373152 /usr/lib64/libpcre.so.1.2.0
```

As we can see, the lsof command, when executed as the root, is able to provide us with quite a bit of useful information. Let's just look at the first line of output to understand what lsof displays:

```
COMMAND     PID TID    USER    FD      TYPE          DEVICE  SIZE/OFF
NODE NAME
systemd        1        root  cwd      DIR            253,1       4096
128 /
```

The lsof command prints 10 columns with each open file.

The first column is the COMMAND column. This field contains the name of the executable that has the file open. This is very useful when identifying which processes have a specific file open.

For our use case, this will tell us which processes have the files we are interested in open and might tell us the process name of the application we are looking for.

The second column is the PID column. This field is just as useful as the first as this shows the process ID of the application that has opened the files displayed. This value will allow us to narrow down the application to a specific process if it is in fact running.

The third column is the TID column, which in our output is blank. This column contains the thread ID of the process in question. In Linux, multithreaded applications are able to spawn threads, which are also known as lightweight processes. These threads are similar to a regular process but are able to share resources such as file descriptors and memory maps. You might hear these referred to as threads or lightweight processes but these are essentially the same thing.

In order to see the TID field, we can add the -K (show threads) flag to the lsof command. This will cause lsof to print all of the lightweight processes as well as the full processes.

The fourth column of the lsof output is the USER field. This field will print the username or UID (if a username is not found) of the process that has opened the file. It is important to know that this field is the user the process is executing and not the owner of the file itself.

For example, if a process running as `rotot` had opened a file owned by `vagrant`, the USER field in `lsof` will show root. The reason for this is because the `lsof` command is used to show which processes have files open and is utilized to display information about the process, not necessarily the files.

Understanding file descriptors

The fifth column is very interesting as this is the field for **File Descriptor (FD)**; which is a tricky Unix and Linux topic to understand.

File descriptors are part of the POSIX **application programming interface (API)**, which is a standard that all modern Linux and Unix operating systems follow. From a program's perspective, the file descriptor is an object that is represented by a nonnegative number. This number is used as an identifier for a table of open files managed by the kernel on a per-process basis.

Since the kernel maintains this on a per-process level, the data is contained within the `/proc` file system. We can see this open file table by performing an `ls -la` in the `/proc/<process id>/fd` directory:

```
# ls -la /proc/1/fd
total 0
dr-x------. 2 root root  0 May 17 23:07 .
dr-xr-xr-x. 8 root root  0 May 17 23:07 ..
lrwx------. 1 root root 64 May 17 23:07 0 -> /dev/null
lrwx------. 1 root root 64 May 17 23:07 1 -> /dev/null
lrwx------. 1 root root 64 Jun  1 15:08 10 -> socket:[7951]
lr-x------. 1 root root 64 Jun  1 15:08 11 -> /proc/1/mountinfo
lr-x------. 1 root root 64 Jun  1 15:08 12 -> /proc/swaps
lrwx------. 1 root root 64 Jun  1 15:08 13 -> socket:[11438]
lr-x------. 1 root root 64 Jun  1 15:08 14 -> anon_inode:inotify
lrwx------. 1 root root 64 May 17 23:07 2 -> /dev/null
lrwx------. 1 root root 64 Jun  1 15:08 20 -> socket:[7955]
lrwx------. 1 root root 64 Jun  1 15:08 21 -> socket:[13968]
lrwx------. 1 root root 64 Jun  1 15:08 22 -> socket:[13980]
lrwx------. 1 root root 64 May 17 23:07 23 -> socket:[13989]
lrwx------. 1 root root 64 Jun  1 15:08 24 -> socket:[7989]
lrwx------. 1 root root 64 Jun  1 15:08 25 -> /dev/initctl
```

```
lrwx------. 1 root root 64 Jun  1 15:08 26 -> socket:[7999]
lrwx------. 1 root root 64 May 17 23:07 27 -> socket:[6631]
lrwx------. 1 root root 64 May 17 23:07 28 -> socket:[6634]
lrwx------. 1 root root 64 May 17 23:07 29 -> socket:[6636]
lr-x------. 1 root root 64 May 17 23:07 3 -> anon_inode:inotify
lrwx------. 1 root root 64 May 17 23:07 30 -> socket:[8006]
lr-x------. 1 root root 64 Jun  1 15:08 31 -> anon_inode:inotify
lr-x------. 1 root root 64 Jun  1 15:08 32 -> /dev/autofs
lr-x------. 1 root root 64 Jun  1 15:08 33 -> pipe:[10502]
lr-x------. 1 root root 64 Jun  1 15:08 34 -> anon_inode:inotify
lrwx------. 1 root root 64 Jun  1 15:08 35 -> anon_inode:[timerfd]
lrwx------. 1 root root 64 Jun  1 15:08 36 -> socket:[8095]
lrwx------. 1 root root 64 Jun  1 15:08 37 -> /run/dmeventd-server
lrwx------. 1 root root 64 Jun  1 15:08 38 -> /run/dmeventd-client
lrwx------. 1 root root 64 Jun  1 15:08 4 -> anon_inode:[eventpoll]
lrwx------. 1 root root 64 Jun  1 15:08 43 -> socket:[11199]
lrwx------. 1 root root 64 Jun  1 15:08 47 -> socket:[14300]
lrwx------. 1 root root 64 Jun  1 15:08 48 -> socket:[14300]
lrwx------. 1 root root 64 Jun  1 15:08 5 -> anon_inode:[signalfd]
lr-x------. 1 root root 64 Jun  1 15:08 6 -> /sys/fs/cgroup/systemd
lrwx------. 1 root root 64 Jun  1 15:08 7 -> socket:[7917]
lrwx------. 1 root root 64 Jun  1 15:08 8 -> anon_inode:[timerfd]
lrwx------. 1 root root 64 Jun  1 15:08 9 -> socket:[7919]
```

This is a file descriptor table for the systemd process. As you can see, there is a number and that number is linked to a file/object.

What is not easily represented in this output is that this is ever-changing. When a file/object is closed, the file descriptor number then becomes reusable for the kernel to assign it to a new open file/object. Depending on how often a process is opening and closing files, if we were to repeat the same ls, we might see a completely different set of open file in this table.

With this, we would expect the FD field in lsof to always show a number. However, the FD field in the lsof output can actually contain more than just the file descriptor number. This is because lsof actually shows more open items than just files.

When executed, the `lsof` command will print many different types of open objects; not all of these are files. An example of this can be seen in the first line of output from our `lsof` command earlier:

```
COMMAND      PID TID   USER    FD      TYPE            DEVICE  SIZE/OFF
NODE NAME
systemd      1         root   cwd      DIR             253,1     4096
128 /
```

The preceding item is not a file, but rather a directory. Because this is a directory the FD field shows `cwd`, which is used to represent the current working directory of the open item. This is actually a very different output from what would be printed when the open item is a file.

To better show the difference, we can run an `lsof` command against a specific file by providing the file as an argument to `lsof`:

```
# lsof /dev/null | head
COMMAND      PID    USER    FD      TYPE DEVICE SIZE/OFF NODE NAME
systemd      1      root    0u      CHR    1,3     0t0    23 /dev/null
systemd      1      root    1u      CHR    1,3     0t0    23 /dev/null
systemd      1      root    2u      CHR    1,3     0t0    23 /dev/null
systemd-j    436    root    0r      CHR    1,3     0t0    23 /dev/null
systemd-j    436    root    1w      CHR    1,3     0t0    23 /dev/null
systemd-j    436    root    2w      CHR    1,3     0t0    23 /dev/null
lvmetad      469    root    0r      CHR    1,3     0t0    23 /dev/null
systemd-u    476    root    0u      CHR    1,3     0t0    23 /dev/null
systemd-u    476    root    1u      CHR    1,3     0t0    23 /dev/null
```

In the preceding output, we are able to not only see that many processes have `/dev/null` open, but that the FD field is quite different for each line. If we look at the first line, we can see that the `systemd` process has `/dev/null` open and that the FD field has a value of `0u`.

When `lsof` is displaying an open item that is a standard file, the FD field will contain the file descriptor number associated with that open file in the kernels table, `0` in this case.

If we look back at the `/proc/1/fd` directory, we can actually see this represented in the kernels table:

```
# ls -la /proc/1/fd/0
lrwx------. 1 root root 64 May 17 23:07 /proc/1/fd/0 -> /dev/null
```

The file descriptor number can potentially be followed by two more values depending on how the file is opened and whether it is locked.

The first potential value shows the mode that the file is opened in. From our example, this is represented by the u in the 0u value. The lowercase u represents that the file is opened for both read and write access.

The following is a list of potential modes that lsof will display:

- r: The lowercase r represents that the file is opened for read only
- w: The lowercase w represents that the file is opened for writes only
- u: The lowercase u represents that the file is opened for both read and writes
- <space>: The blank space is used to depict that the mode the file is open in is unknown and that there is no lock currently on the file
- -: The hyphen is used to depict that the mode the file is open in is unknown and that there is currently a lock on the file

The last two values are actually quite interesting as they bring us to the second potential value after the file descriptor number.

Processes on Linux and Unix systems are allowed to request files to be locked when they are opened. There are multiple types of locks and this is shown in the lsof output as well:

```
master     1586         root   10uW     REG          253,1        33
135127929 /var/spool/postfix/pid/master.pid
```

In the preceding example, the FD field contained 10uW. From the previous examples we know that 10 is the file descriptor number and that u denotes that this file is open for both read and write but the w is new. This W shows what type of lock the process has on this file; a write lock for this example.

Like the file open mode, there are many different types of locks that can be seen from lsof. This is a list of possible locks shown by lsof:

- N: This is used for Solaris NFS locks of unknown types
- r: This is a read lock on part of a file
- R: This is a read lock on an entire file
- w: This is a write lock on part of a file
- W: This is a write lock on an entire file
- u: This is a read and write lock of any length
- U: This is a read and write lock of unknown type

- x: This is a SCO Openserver Xenix lock of a partial file
- X: This is a SCO Openserver Xenix lock of a full file

You might notice that there are several possible locks that are not Linux-specific. This is because `lsof` is a tool widely used in both Linux and Unix and supports many Unix distributions such as Solaris and SCO.

Now that we have covered how `lsof` displays the FD field for actual files, let's take a look at how it displays open objects that are not necessarily files:

```
iprupdate  595         root  cwd      DIR              253,1      4096
128 /
iprupdate  595         root  rtd      DIR              253,1      4096
128 /
iprupdate  595         root  txt      REG              253,1    114784
135146206 /usr/sbin/iprupdate
iprupdate  595         root  mem      REG              253,1   2107600
134298615 /usr/lib64/libc-2.17.so
```

With this, we can see quite a few different FD values in this list, such as `cwd`, `rtd`, `txt`, and `mem`. We already know from an earlier example that `cwd` is used to show a `Current Working Directory` but the others are quite new. There are actually quite a few possible file types depending on the object that is open. The following list contains all of the possible values that can be displayed if a file descriptor number is not used:

- `cwd`: Current working directory
- `Lnn`: Library reference for AIX systems (`nn` is a number value)
- `err`: File descriptor information error
- `jld`: FreeBSD jailed directory
- `ltx`: Shared library text
- `Mxx`: Hex memory mapped (`xx` is a type number)
- `m86`: DOS merged mapped file
- `mem`: Memory mapped file
- `mmap`: Memory mapped device
- `pd`: Parent directory
- `rtd`: Root directory
- `tr`: Kernel trace file
- `txt`: Program text
- `v86`: VP/ix mapped file

We can see that there are many possible values for the FD field. Now that we have seen the possible values, let's take a look at the preceding example to better understand what types of open items were shown:

```
iprupdate  595        root  cwd       DIR              253,1        4096
128 /
iprupdate  595        root  rtd       DIR              253,1        4096
128 /
iprupdate  595        root  txt       REG              253,1      114784
135146206 /usr/sbin/iprupdate
iprupdate  595        root  mem       REG              253,1     2107600
134298615 /usr/lib64/libc-2.17.so
```

The first two lines are interesting as they are both for the "/" directory. However, the first line shows the "/" directory as cwd, which means it is the current working directory. The second line shows the "/" directory as rtd, which means this is also the root directory for the iprupdate program.

The third line shows that /usr/sbin/iprupdate is the program itself as it has a FD field value of txt. This means the open file is the code of the program. The fourth line for the open item /usr/lib64/libc-2.17.so shows a FD of mem. This means the file /usr/lib64/libc-2.17.so has been read and placed into memory for the iprupdate process. This means that this file can be accessed as a memory object. This is a common practice for library files such as libc-2.17.so.

Getting back to the lsof output

Now that we have thoroughly explored the FD field, let's move to the sixth column of the lsof output, the TYPE field. This field shows the type of file that is being opened. As there are quite a large number of possible types, it would be a bit tricky to list them here; however, you can always find this referenced in the lsof man page, which is accessible online or via the "man lsof" command.

While we will not be listing every possible file type, we can take a quick look at a few file types captured from our example system:

```
systemd      1        root  mem       REG              253,1      160240
134296681 /usr/lib64/ld-2.17.so
systemd      1        root  0u        CHR                1,3         0t0
23 /dev/null
systemd      1        root  6r        DIR               0,20           0
6404 /sys/fs/cgroup/systemd
systemd      1        root  7u        unix 0xffff88001d672580         0t0
7917 @/org/freedesktop/systemd1/notify
```

The first example item shows a TYPE of REG. This TYPE is very common as the item being listed is a Regular file. The second example item shows **Character special file (CHR)**. The CHR denotes special files that present themselves as files but are actually an interface for a device. The item listed /dev/null is a perfect example of a character file as it is used as input to nothing. Anything that is written to /dev/null is nullified and if you were to read this file, you would receive no output.

The third item shows DIR, it should not be a surprise that DIR stands for a directory. This is a very common TYPE as many processes at some level will require a directory to be opened.

The fourth item shows unix, which shows that this open item is a Unix socket file. Unix socket files are special files that are used as input/output devices for process communication. These files should show up quite often in the lsof output.

As we can see from the preceding example, on Linux systems, there are several different types of files.

Now that we have looked at the sixth column of the output in lsof, the TYPE column, let's take a quick look at the seventh, the DEVICE column:

```
COMMAND     PID TID    USER    FD      TYPE            DEVICE  SIZE/OFF
NODE NAME

systemd     1          root    cwd     DIR             253,1   4096
128 /
```

If we look at the preceding item, we can see the DEVICE column has a value of 253,1. These numbers represent the major and minor numbers of the device that this item is on. Major and minor numbers in Linux are used by the system to determine how a device is accessed. The major number, which in this case is 253, is used to determine which driver the system should use. Once the driver is selected, the minor number, 1 in our case, is then used to narrow down how exactly this device should be accessed.

> Major and minor numbers are actually an important part of Linux and how it uses devices. While we will not be covering this topic in depth within this book, it is something I would suggest learning more about as this information is incredibly useful when troubleshooting issues with hardware devices.

```
systemd       1         root    mem     REG             253,1   160240
134296681 /usr/lib64/ld-2.17.so

systemd       1         root    0u      CHR             1,3     0t0
12 /dev/null
```

Now that we have explored the DEVICE column, let's take a look at the eighth column of the lsof output, SIZE/OFF. The SIZE/OFF column is used to display either the size of the open item or the **offset**. Offsets are generally displayed with devices such as socket files and character files. When this column contains an offset, it will be preceded with "0t". In the above example, we can see the character file /dev/null has an offset value of 0t0.

The SIZE value is used when referring to open items such as regular files. This value is actually the size of the file in bytes. For example, we can see that the SIZE column for /usr/lib64/ld-2.17.so is 160240. This means this file is roughly 160 KB in size.

The ninth column in the lsof output is the NODE column:

```
httpd       3205       apache     2w        REG              253,1          497
134812768 /var/log/httpd/error_log
httpd       3205       apache     4u        IPv6             16097          0t0
TCP *:http (LISTEN)
```

For regular files, the NODE column will show the **inode** number of the file. Within a filesystem, every file has an inode, this inode is used as an index that contains all of the individual files' metadata. This metadata consists of items such as the file's location on disk, file permissions, the creation time, and modification time of the file. Like major and minor numbers, I suggest taking a deeper dive into inodes and what they contain, as inodes are a core component to how files exist on a Linux system.

You can see, from the first item in the preceding example, the inode of /var/log/httpd/error_log is 134812768.

The second line, however, shows the NODE as TCP, which is not an inode. The reason it shows TCP is because the open item is a TCP Socket, which is not a file on a filesystem. Like the TYPE column, the NODE column will change based on the open item. However, on most systems, you will generally see an inode number, TCP or UDP (for UDP Sockets).

The tenth and final column in the lsof output is pretty self-explanatory, as we have referenced it several times already. The tenth column is the NAME field, which is as simple as it sounds; it lists the name of the open item:

```
COMMAND     PID TID    USER     FD        TYPE             DEVICE   SIZE/OFF
NODE NAME
systemd      1         root     cwd       DIR              253,1          4096
128 /
```

Using lsof to check whether we have a previously running process

Now that we know a lot more about how `lsof` works and how it can help us, let's use this command to check whether there are any running instances of our application.

If we simply ran the `lsof` command as the root user, we would see all of the open files on this system. However, that output can be quite overwhelming even when we redirect the output to commands such as `less` or `grep`. Luckily, `lsof` will allow us to specify files and directories to look for:

```
# lsof /opt/myapp/conf/config.yml
COMMAND   PID    USER    FD   TYPE DEVICE SIZE/OFF     NODE NAME
less     3494 vagrant    4r    REG  253,1       45 201948450 /opt/myapp/
conf/config.yml
```

As we can see, by specifying a file in the preceding command, we limited the output to processes that have the file open.

If we specify a directory, the output is similar:

```
# lsof /opt/myapp/
COMMAND   PID    USER    FD   TYPE DEVICE SIZE/OFF NODE NAME
bash     3474 vagrant   cwd    DIR  253,1       53 25264 /opt/myapp
less     3509 vagrant   cwd    DIR  253,1       53 25264 /opt/myapp
```

From this, we can see that two processes have the /opt/myapp directory open. Another way we could limit the output of `lsof` is to specify the +D (directory contents) flag, followed by a directory. This flag will tell `lsof` to look for any open items from that directory and below.

For example, we saw that when using `lsof` against the configuration file, the `less` process had it opened. We could also see that when used against the /opt/myapp/ directory, two processes had the directory open.

We can see all of these items with just one command using the +D flag:

```
# lsof +D /opt/myapp/
COMMAND   PID    USER    FD   TYPE DEVICE SIZE/OFF     NODE NAME
bash     3474 vagrant   cwd    DIR  253,1       53    25264 /opt/myapp
less     3509 vagrant   cwd    DIR  253,1       53    25264 /opt/myapp
less     3509 vagrant    4r    REG  253,1       45 201948450 /opt/myapp/
conf/config.yml
```

This would also show us any other items located under the /opt/myapp directory. Since we are looking to check whether another instance of the application is running let's take a look at the preceding lsof output and see what can be learned:

```
COMMAND   PID     USER   FD    TYPE DEVICE SIZE/OFF    NODE NAME
bash     3474 vagrant  cwd     DIR  253,1       53    25264 /opt/myapp
```

The first open item shows a process of bash, running as the vagrant user with a file descriptor of a current working directory. This line is most likely our own bash process that is currently in the /opt/myapp directory, currently executing the less command on the /opt/myapp/conf/config.yml file.

We can check this by using the ps command and grep for the string 3474, the process ID of the bash command:

```
# ps -elf | grep 3474
0 S vagrant    3474  3473  0  80   0 - 28857 wait    20:09 pts/1
00:00:00 -bash
0 S vagrant    3509  3474  0  80   0 - 27562 n_tty_ 20:14 pts/1
00:00:00 less conf/config.yml
0 S root       3576  2978  0  80   0 - 28160 pipe_w 21:08 pts/0
00:00:00 grep --color=auto 3474
```

I opted to use the grep command in this case, as we will also be able to see any child processes that reference process ID 3474. The same thing can be performed without the grep command as well by running the following command:

```
# ps -lp 3474 --ppid 3474
F S   UID   PID  PPID  C PRI  NI ADDR SZ WCHAN   TTY         TIME CMD
0 S  1000  3474  3473  0  80   0 - 28857 wait    pts/1   00:00:00 bash
0 S  1000  3509  3474  0  80   0 - 27562 n_tty_  pts/1   00:00:00 less
```

Overall, both produce the same results; however, the first method is easier to remember.

If we look at the process list output, we can see that the bash command is in fact related to our shell as its child process is the less command that we know we have running in another window.

We can also see the process ID of the less command: 3509. The same process ID is shown in the less command in the lsof output:

```
less     3509 vagrant  cwd     DIR  253,1       53    25264 /opt/myapp
less     3509 vagrant   4r     REG  253,1       45 201948450 /opt/myapp/
conf/config.yml
```

Since the output only shows our own processes, it is safe to assume that there is not a previous application instance running in the background.

Finding out more about the application

We now know that the problem is not that another instance of this application is running. At this point, we should try and identify more about this application and what it is doing.

The first thing to do when trying to find out more information about this application is to see what type of file the application is. We can do this by using the `file` command:

```
$ file bin/application
bin/application: setuid ELF 64-bit LSB executable, x86-64, version 1
(SYSV), dynamically linked (uses shared libs), for GNU/Linux 2.6.32, Buil
dID[sha1]=0xbc4685b44eb120ff2252e21bd735933d51409ffa, not stripped
```

The `file` command is a very useful command to have in your tool belt, as this command will identify the file type of the file being specified. In the preceding example, we can see that the "`application`" file is a compiled binary. We can see that it is compiled by this particular output: `ELF 64-bit LSB executable`.

This line also tells us that the application is compiled as a 64-bit application. This is interesting as there are quite a few differences between 64-bit and 32-bit applications. One very common scenario is due to the amount of resources a 64-bit application can consume; 32-bit applications are often much more limited than a 64-bit version.

Another common issue is when trying to execute a 64-bit application on a 32-bit kernel. We have yet to validate whether we are running on a 64-bit kernel; if we are attempting to run a 64-bit executable with a 32-bit kernel, we are bound to receive some errors.

The types of errors seen by trying to execute a 64-bit application on a 32-bit kernel are pretty specific and not very likely to be the cause of our issue. Even though it is not a likely cause, we can check whether the kernel is a 64-bit kernel or not with the `uname -a` command:

```
$ uname -a
Linux blog.example.com 3.10.0-123.el7.x86_64 #1 SMP Mon Jun 30 12:09:22
UTC 2014 x86_64 x86_64 x86_64 GNU/Linux
```

From the output of the uname -a command, we can see that the kernel is in fact a 64-bit kernel by the presence of this string "`x86_64`".

Tracing an application with strace

Since we know that the application is a compiled binary and we do not have the source code, this makes reading the code within the application fairly difficult. What we can do, however, is trace the system calls that the application is performing to see if we can find any information as to why it is not starting.

What is a system call?

System calls are the primary interface between an application and the kernel. Simply put, a system call is a method of requesting the kernel to perform an action.

Most applications do not need to worry about system calls, as system calls are generally called by low-level libraries, such as the GNU C Library. While the programmer need not worry about system calls, it is important to know that every action performed by an application drills down to some sort of system call.

This is important to know because we can trace these system calls to determine what exactly an application is doing. Much like we use `tcpdump` to trace network traffic on a system, we can use a command called `strace` to trace the system calls of a process.

To get the feel of `strace`, let's use `strace` to perform a system call trace on our `exitcodes.sh` script from earlier. To do this, we will run the `strace` command followed by the `exitcodes.sh` script.

When executed, the `strace` command will start up and then execute the `exitcodes.sh` script. While the `exitcodes.sh` script is running, the `strace` command will print every system call and the arguments provided to them from the `exitcodes.sh` script:

```
$ strace /var/tmp/exitcodes.sh
execve("/var/tmp/exitcodes.sh", ["/var/tmp/exitcodes.sh"], [/* 26 vars
*/]) = 0
brk(0)                                  = 0x261a000
mmap(NULL, 4096, PROT_READ|PROT_WRITE, MAP_PRIVATE|MAP_ANONYMOUS, -1, 0)
= 0x7f890bd12000
access("/etc/ld.so.preload", R_OK)      = -1 ENOENT (No such file or
directory)
open("/etc/ld.so.cache", O_RDONLY|O_CLOEXEC) = 3
fstat(3, {st_mode=S_IFREG|0644, st_size=24646, ...}) = 0
mmap(NULL, 24646, PROT_READ, MAP_PRIVATE, 3, 0) = 0x7f890bd0b000
close(3)                                = 0
open("/lib64/libtinfo.so.5", O_RDONLY|O_CLOEXEC) = 3
```

```
read(3, "\177ELF\2\1\1\0\0\0\0\0\0\0\0\0\3\0>\0\1\0\0\0@\316\0\0\0\0\0\0"
..., 832) = 832
fstat(3, {st_mode=S_IFREG|0755, st_size=174520, ...}) = 0
mmap(NULL, 2268928, PROT_READ|PROT_EXEC, MAP_PRIVATE|MAP_DENYWRITE, 3, 0)
= 0x7f890b8c9000
mprotect(0x7f890b8ee000, 2097152, PROT_NONE) = 0
mmap(0x7f890baee000, 20480, PROT_READ|PROT_WRITE, MAP_PRIVATE|MAP_
FIXED|MAP_DENYWRITE, 3, 0x25000) = 0x7f890baee000
close(3)                                 = 0
open("/lib64/libdl.so.2", O_RDONLY|O_CLOEXEC) = 3
read(3, "\177ELF\2\1\1\0\0\0\0\0\0\0\0\0\3\0>\0\1\0\0\0\320\16\0\0\0\0\0\
0"..., 832) = 832
fstat(3, {st_mode=S_IFREG|0755, st_size=19512, ...}) = 0
```

This is only a small portion of the output from strace. The full output is actually several pages long. However, the exitcodes.sh script isn't very long. In fact, it's a simple three-line script:

```
$ cat /var/tmp/exitcodes.sh
#!/bin/bash
touch /some/directory/that/doesnt/exist/file.txt
echo "It works"
```

This script is a good example as to how much heavy lifting higher-level programming languages, such as bash, provide. Now that we know what the exitcodes.sh script does, let's take a look at some of the system calls it performs.

We will start with the first eight lines:

```
execve("/var/tmp/exitcodes.sh", ["/var/tmp/exitcodes.sh"], [/* 26 vars
*/]) = 0
brk(0)                                   = 0x261a000
mmap(NULL, 4096, PROT_READ|PROT_WRITE, MAP_PRIVATE|MAP_ANONYMOUS, -1, 0)
= 0x7f890bd12000
access("/etc/ld.so.preload", R_OK)       = -1 ENOENT (No such file or
directory)
open("/etc/ld.so.cache", O_RDONLY|O_CLOEXEC) = 3
fstat(3, {st_mode=S_IFREG|0644, st_size=24646, ...}) = 0
mmap(NULL, 24646, PROT_READ, MAP_PRIVATE, 3, 0) = 0x7f890bd0b000
close(3)                                 = 0
```

As system calls are quite extensive and some of them are complicated to understand. We will focus our breakdown on system calls that are common and a bit easier to understand.

The first system call that we will examine is the `access()` system call:

```
access("/etc/ld.so.preload", R_OK)      = -1 ENOENT (No such file or
directory)
```

Most system calls have a name that roughly explains the function it performs. The `access()` system call is no different, as this system call is used to check whether the application calling it has sufficient access to open the file specified. In the preceding example, the file specified is /etc/ld.so.preload.

An interesting thing about `strace` is not only does it show the system call, it also shows the return value. In our preceding example, the `access()` system call received a return value of `-1`, which is the typical value for errors. When the return value is an error, `strace` will also provide the error string. In this case, the `access()` call received the error `-1 ENOENT (No such file or directory)`.

The preceding error is pretty self-explanatory, as it seems the file /etc/ld.so.preload simply does not exist.

The next system call is one that will be seen quite often; it is the `open()` system call:

```
open("/etc/ld.so.cache", O_RDONLY|O_CLOEXEC) = 3
```

The `open()` system call performs just what it says, it is used to open (or create and open) a file or device. From the preceding example, we can see that the file specified is the /etc/ld.so.cache file. We can also see that one of the arguments passed to this system call is "`O_RDONLY`". This argument tells the `open()` call to open the file in the read only mode.

Even if we didn't already know that the `O_RDONLY` argument tells the open command to open the file in read only, the name is almost self-descriptive. For system calls that are not self-descriptive, the information can be found with a fairly quick Google search, as system calls are very well documented:

```
fstat(3, {st_mode=S_IFREG|0644, st_size=24646, ...}) = 0
```

The next system call to look at is the `fstat()` system call. This system call will pull the status of a file. The information this system call provides includes things such as the inode number, user ownership, and size of the file. By itself, the `fstat()` system call might not look very important but when we look at the next system call, `mmap()`, the information it provides can be important.

```
mmap(NULL, 24646, PROT_READ, MAP_PRIVATE, 3, 0) = 0x7f890bd0b000
```

This system call can be used to map or unmap a file into memory. If we look at the `fstat()` line and look at the `mmap()` line, we will see two numbers that coincide. The fstat() line has `st_size=24646`, which is the second argument provided to `mmap()`.

Even without knowing the details of these system calls it is pretty easy to build the assumption that the `mmap()` system call mapped the file from the `fstat()` call into the memory.

The final system call from the preceding example is very simple to understand:

```
close(3)                                = 0
```

The `close()` system call simply closes the open file or device. Given that earlier we opened the file `/etc/ld.so.cache`, it only makes sense that this `close()` system call was used to close that file. Before we get back to debugging our application, let's take a quick look at the last four lines put together:

```
open("/etc/ld.so.cache", O_RDONLY|O_CLOEXEC) = 3
fstat(3, {st_mode=S_IFREG|0644, st_size=24646, ...}) = 0
mmap(NULL, 24646, PROT_READ, MAP_PRIVATE, 3, 0) = 0x7f890bd0b000
close(3)
```

As we look at these four system calls, we can start to see a pattern. The `open()` call is used to open the `/etc/ld.so.cache` file and is given a return value of 3. The `fstat()` command is provided 3 as input and gets `st_size=24646` as output. The `mmap()` function is given 24646 and 3 as input and the `close()` function is provided with 3 as input.

Given that the output of the `open()` call is 3 and the value 3 has been used multiple times in these four system calls, it is safe to conclude that this number 3 is the file descriptor number of the open file `/etc/ld.so.cache`. With that conclusion, it is also pretty safe to assume that the preceding four system calls perform the actions of opening the file `/etc/ld.so.cache`, determining the size of the file, mapping that file into memory, and then closing the file descriptor.

As you can see, this is quite a bit of information from just four simple system calls. Let's put what you just learned into practice and use `strace` to trace the application process.

Using strace to identify why the application will not start

Earlier, when we ran `strace`, we simply provided it with a command to execute. This is one way you can invoke `strace`, but what do you do if the process is already running? Well, `strace` can also trace running processes.

When tracing an existing process, we can start `strace` with the –p (process) flag followed by the process ID to trace. This causes `strace` to bind to that process and start tracing it. For tracing our application startup, we are going to use this method.

To do this, we are going to execute the `start.sh` script in the background and then run `strace` against the process ID of the `start.sh` script:

```
$ ./start.sh &
[1] 3353
```

By adding & to the end of the command line, we are telling the start script to run in the background. The output provides us with the process ID of the running script, 3353. However, in another window as the root user, we can use `strace` to trace this process with the following command:

```
# strace -o /var/tmp/app.out -f -p 3353
Process 3353 attached
Process 3360 attached
```

The preceding command adds a few more options than just –p and the process ID. We also add the –o /var/tmp/app.out arguments. This option will tell `strace` to save the traced data to the output file /var/tmp/app.out. The earlier `strace` that we ran provided quite a bit of output; by specifying that the data should be written to a file, the data will be a bit more manageable to search.

The other new option we added is –f; this argument tells `strace` to follow child processes. Since the start script starts the application, the application itself is considered a child process of the start script. In the preceding example we can see that `strace` was attached to two processes. We can assume that the second process received the process ID of 3360, this is important to know, as we will need to reference that process ID while looking through the trace output:

```
# less /var/tmp/app.out
```

Let's get started reading the `strace` output and attempt to identify what is happening. While going through this output, we will limit it to only sections that are useful for identifying our issue:

```
3360  execve("/opt/myapp/bin/application", ["/opt/myapp/bin/application",
"--deamon", "--config", "/opt/myapp/conf/config.yml"], [/* 28 vars */]) =
0
```

The first system call that appears interesting is the `execve()` system call. This particular call of `execve()` appears to be executing the /opt/myapp/bin/ application binary.

One important item to point out is that, with this output, we can see a number before the system call. This number, 3360, is the process ID of the process that executed the system call. The process ID will only be shown when the strace command is tracing multiple processes.

```
The next group of system calls that seem important are the following:
3360  open("/opt/myapp/conf/config.yml", O_RDONLY) = 3
3360  fstat(3, {st_mode=S_IFREG|0600, st_size=45, ...}) = 0
3360  fstat(3, {st_mode=S_IFREG|0600, st_size=45, ...}) = 0
3360  mmap(NULL, 4096, PROT_READ|PROT_WRITE, MAP_PRIVATE|MAP_ANONYMOUS,
-1, 0) = 0x7fd0528df000
3360  read(3, "port: 25\ndebug: True\nlogdir: /op"..., 4096) = 45
3360  read(3, "", 4096)                = 0
3360  read(3, "", 4096)                = 0
```

From the preceding group, we can see that the application is opening the `config.yml` file in read only and did not receive an error. We can also see that the `read()` system call (which appears to be reading from file descriptor 3) is reading the `config.yml` file.

```
3360  close(3)                         = 0
```

It appears further down the file that this file descriptor is closed using the `close()` system call. This information is useful as it tells us that we are able to read the `config.yml` file and that our issue is not related to permissions on the configuration file:

```
3360  open("/opt/myapp/logs/debug.out", O_WRONLY|O_CREAT|O_APPEND, 0666)
= 3
3360  lseek(3, 0, SEEK_END)            = 1711
3360  fstat(3, {st_mode=S_IFREG|0664, st_size=1711, ...}) = 0
3360  fstat(3, {st_mode=S_IFREG|0664, st_size=1711, ...}) = 0
```

```
3360  mmap(NULL, 4096, PROT_READ|PROT_WRITE, MAP_PRIVATE|MAP_ANONYMOUS,
-1, 0) = 0x7fd0528df000
3360  write(1, "- - - - - - - - - - - - - - - - - "..., 52) = 52
```

If we continue, we can see that our configuration is taking effect as well, as the process has opened the debug.out file for writing using the open() call and written to it with the write() call.

For applications that have many log files, system calls such as the above can be useful for identifying log messages that might not have been obvious.

When looking through system calls, you can roughly understand the context of when the message was generated and possibly why. This context can be extremely useful depending on the issue.

```
3360  socket(PF_INET, SOCK_STREAM, IPPROTO_IP) = 4
3360  bind(4, {sa_family=AF_INET, sin_port=htons(25), sin_addr=inet_
addr("0.0.0.0")}, 16) = -1 EADDRINUSE (Address already in use)
3360  open("/dev/null", O_WRONLY|O_CREAT|O_TRUNC, 0666) = 5
3360  fstat(5, {st_mode=S_IFCHR|0666, st_rdev=makedev(1, 3), ...}) = 0
3360  write(1, "Starting service: [Failed]\n", 27) = 27
3360  write(3, "Configuration file processed\r\n--"..., 86) = 86
3360  close(3)                          = 0
```

Speaking of context, the preceding system calls explain our problem specifically, one system call. While the strace file contained many system calls that returned errors, the majority of them were like the following:

```
3360  stat("/usr/lib64/python2.7/encodings/ascii", 0x7fff8ef0d670) = -1
ENOENT (No such file or directory)
```

This is fairly common, as it simply means the process attempted to access a file that is not present. In the trace file, however, there is one error that sticks out more than the others:

```
3360  bind(4, {sa_family=AF_INET, sin_port=htons(25), sin_addr=inet_
addr("0.0.0.0")}, 16) = -1 EADDRINUSE (Address already in use)
```

The preceding system call bind() is a system call that binds a socket. The preceding example appears to binding a network socket. If we think back to our configuration file, we know that port 25 is specified:

```
# cat /opt/myapp/conf/config.yml
port: 25
```

In the system call, we can see the string `sin_port=htons(25)`, which might mean this bind system call is trying to bind to port 25. From the return value provided, we can see that the `bind()` call received an error. The message of that error suggests "Address is already in use".

Since we know that the application is configured to utilize port 25 in some way and we can see a `bind()` system call, it stands to reason that this application might not be starting simply because port 25 is already being used by another process, which at this point, is our new hypothesis.

Resolving the conflict

As you learned in the networking chapter, we can verify that a process has port 25 in use with a quick `netstat` command:

```
# netstat -nap | grep :25
tcp       0      0 127.0.0.1:25           0.0.0.0:*
LISTEN          1588/master
tcp6      0      0 ::1:25                 :::*
LISTEN          1588/master
```

When we run `netstat` as the root user and add the `-p` flag, the command will include the process ID and name of process for each LISTEN-ing socket. From this, we can see that port 25 is in fact being used and the process 1588 is the one listening.

To get a better understanding of what process this is, we can once again utilize the `ps` command:

```
# ps -elf | grep 1588
5 S root       1588      1  0  80    0 - 22924 ep_pol 13:53 ?
00:00:00 /usr/libexec/postfix/master -w
4 S postfix    1616   1588  0  80    0 - 22967 ep_pol 13:53 ?
00:00:00 qmgr -l -t unix -u
4 S postfix    3504   1588  0  80    0 - 22950 ep_pol 20:36 ?
00:00:00 pickup -l -t unix -u
```

It appears that the `postfix` service is the one listening on port 25, which is not very surprising since this port is generally used for SMTP communication and postfix is an e-mail service.

The question now is, should postfix be listening on this port or should the application? Unfortunately, there is no easy answer to that question, as it truly depends on the systems and what they are doing.

For the sake of this exercise, we will assume the answer is that the custom application should be using port 25, and postfix should not be running.

To stop postfix from listening on port 25, we will first stop postfix using the systemctl commands:

```
# systemctl stop postfix
```

This stops the postfix service where the next command will disable it from starting up again on the next reboot:

```
# systemctl disable postfix
rm '/etc/systemd/system/multi-user.target.wants/postfix.service'
```

Disabling the postfix service is an important step to resolving this issue. Currently, we believe the issue is caused by a port conflict between the custom application and postfix. If we do not disable the postfix service, the next time the system reboots it will be started again. This will then prevent the custom application from being started as well.

While this might seem basic, I want to stress the importance of this step as, on numerous occasions, I've seen an issue happen repeatedly, simply because the person who resolved it the first time didn't disable a service.

If we run the systemctl status command, we can now see that the postfix service is stopped and disabled:

```
# systemctl status postfix
postfix.service - Postfix Mail Transport Agent
   Loaded: loaded (/usr/lib/systemd/system/postfix.service; disabled)
   Active: inactive (dead)


Jun 09 04:05:42 blog.example.com systemd[1]: Starting Postfix Mail
Transport Agent...
Jun 09 04:05:43 blog.example.com postfix/master[1588]: daemon started --
version 2.10.1, configuration /etc/postfix
Jun 09 04:05:43 blog.example.com systemd[1]: Started Postfix Mail
Transport Agent.
Jun 09 21:14:14 blog.example.com systemd[1]: Stopping Postfix Mail
Transport Agent...
Jun 09 21:14:14 blog.example.com systemd[1]: Stopped Postfix Mail
Transport Agent.
```

With the `postfix` service stopped, we can now once again start the application to see if the issue is resolved.

```
$ ./start.sh
Initializing with configuration file /opt/myapp/conf/config.yml
- - - - - - - - - - - - - - - - - - - - - - - - - - - -
Starting service: [Success]
- - - - - - - - - - - - - - - - - - - - - - - - - - - -
Proccessed 5 messages
Proccessed 5 messages
Proccessed 5 messages
```

It appears the issue was in fact resolved by stopping the `postfix` service. We can see this by the "`[Success]`" message printed from the startup process. We can also see this if we run the `lsof` command again:

```
# lsof +D /opt/myapp/
COMMAND      PID     USER   FD    TYPE DEVICE SIZE/OFF      NODE NAME
bash        3332 vagrant   cwd    DIR   253,1       53     25264 /opt/myapp
start.sh    3585 vagrant   cwd    DIR   253,1       53     25264 /opt/myapp
start.sh    3585 vagrant   255r   REG   253,1      111     25304 /opt/myapp/
start.sh
applicati   3588    root   cwd    DIR   253,1       53     25264 /opt/myapp
applicati   3588    root   txt    REG   253,1    36196  68112463 /opt/myapp/
bin/application
applicati   3588    root    3w    REG   253,1     1797 134803515 /opt/myapp/
logs/debug.out
```

Now that the application is running, we can see several processes have open items in the /opt/myapp directory. We can also see that one of those processes is the application command with a process ID of 3588. To get a better look at what the application is doing we can once again run `lsof`, but this time we will search only for files open by the process ID 3588:

```
# lsof -p 3588
COMMAND      PID USER   FD    TYPE DEVICE SIZE/OFF     NODE NAME
applicati   3588 root   cwd    DIR   253,1       53    25264 /opt/myapp
applicati   3588 root   rtd    DIR   253,1     4096      128 /
applicati   3588 root   txt    REG   253,1    36196 68112463 /opt/myapp/
bin/application
```

```
applicati 3588 root    mem    REG  253,1    160240 134296681 /usr/lib64/ld-
2.17.so
applicati 3588 root     0u    CHR  136,2       0t0         5 /dev/pts/2
applicati 3588 root     1u    CHR  136,2       0t0         5 /dev/pts/2
applicati 3588 root     2u    CHR  136,2       0t0         5 /dev/pts/2
applicati 3588 root     3w    REG  253,1      1797 134803515 /opt/myapp/
logs/debug.out
applicati 3588 root     4u    sock   0,6       0t0     38488 protocol: TCP
```

The –p (process) flag will filter the lsof output to a specific process. In this case, we limited the output to the custom application we just started:

```
applicati 3588 root     4u    sock   0,6       0t0     38488 protocol: TCP
```

In the last line, we can see that the application has a TCP socket open. Given the status messages from the application and the results from lsof, it is pretty safe to say the application has started and started correctly.

Summary

We took an application issue and used common Linux tools such as lsof and strace to find the root cause, a port conflict. What is even more important is that we did this with no prior knowledge of the application or the tasks it was attempting to perform.

With the example from this chapter, we can easily see how having access to and knowledge of basic Linux tools, together with an understanding of the troubleshooting process, can enable you to solve almost any issue, whether that issue is an application issue or a systems issue.

In the next chapter, we will examine the Linux user and kernel limits, and how they can sometimes cause issues.

10
Understanding Linux User and Kernel Limits

In the previous chapter, we used tools such as `lsof` and `strace` to identify the root cause of an application issue.

In this chapter, we will once again identify the root cause of an application-related issue. However, we will also focus on learning and understanding Linux user and kernel limitations.

A reported issue

Much like the previous chapter, which focused on an issue with a custom application, today's issue comes from the same custom application.

Today, we will be working on an issue reported by an application support team. However, this time the support team was able to provide us with quite a bit of information.

The application we were working on in *Chapter 9, Using System Tools to Troubleshoot Applications*, now receives messages over `port 25` and stores them in a queue directory. Periodically, a job runs to process those queued messages, but the job *doesn't seem to be working anymore*.

The application support team has noticed quite a large amount of messages backlogged in the queue. However, even though they have been troubleshooting the issue as much as possible, they are stuck and require our assistance.

Why is the job failing?

Since the issue being reported is that a scheduled job is not working, we should first focus on the job itself. In this scenario, we have the application support team available to answer any questions. So, let's get a few more details about this job.

Background questions

The following is a quick list of questions that should help provide you with additional information:

- How is the job run?
- Can we run the job manually if we need to?
- What does this job execute?

These three questions may seem pretty basic, but they are important. Let's first look at the answers the application team provides:

- How is the job run?

  The job is executed as a cron job.

- Can we run the job manually if we need to?

  Yes, it should be okay to execute the job manually as often as needed.

- What does this job execute?

  The job executes the /opt/myapp/bin/processor command as the vagrant user.

The preceding three questions are important because they will save us quite a bit of troubleshooting time. The first question is focused on how the job is executed. Since the reported issue is that the job is not working, we don't know yet if the issue is because the job is not running or if the job is being executed but failing for some reason.

The answer to the first question tells us that the job is executed by `crond`, which is the **cron daemon** that runs on Linux. This is useful as we can use this information to identify whether the job is being executed or not. In general, there are many methods for scheduled jobs to be executed. Sometimes the software that is executing the scheduled job runs on a different system and sometimes it runs on the same local system.

In this case, the job is being executed by `crond` on the same server.

The second question is also important. Just like we had to launch the application manually in the last chapter, we may need to perform this troubleshooting step with this reported issue as well. Based on the answer, it seems we are free to execute this command as many times as needed.

The third question is useful as it tells us not only what command is being executed but also which job to look out for. Cron jobs are a very common method of scheduling tasks. It is common for a system to have many cron jobs scheduled.

Is the cron job even running?

Since we know that the job is being executed by crond, we should first check whether the job is being executed or not. To do this, we can check the cron logs on the server in question. For example, consider the following log:

```
# ls -la /var/log/cron*
-rw-r--r--. 1 root root 30792 Jun 10 18:05 /var/log/cron
-rw-r--r--. 1 root root 28261 May 18 03:41 /var/log/cron-20150518
-rw-r--r--. 1 root root  6152 May 24 21:12 /var/log/cron-20150524
-rw-r--r--. 1 root root 42565 Jun  1 15:50 /var/log/cron-20150601
-rw-r--r--. 1 root root 18286 Jun  7 16:22 /var/log/cron-20150607
```

Specifically, on Red Hat based Linux systems we can check the /var/log/cron log file. I specified "Red Hat based" in the previous sentence because on non-Red-Hat-based systems the cron logs may be located in a different log file. Debian-based systems, for example, default to /var/log/syslog.

If we didn't know which log file contained cron logs, there is a simple trick to find it. Just run the following command line:

```
# grep -ic cron /var/log/* | grep -v :0
/var/log/cron:400
/var/log/cron-20150518:379
/var/log/cron-20150524:86
/var/log/cron-20150601:590
/var/log/cron-20150607:248
/var/log/messages:1
/var/log/secure:1
```

The preceding command will use `grep` to search all of the log files in `/var/log` for the string `cron`. The command will also search for `Cron`, `CRON`, `cRon`, and so on, as we added the `-i` (insensitive) flag to the `grep` command. This tells `grep` to search in case-insensitivity mode. Essentially, this means any match of the word "cron" will be found even if the word is capitalized or mixed case. We also added the `-c` (count) flag to the `grep` command, which causes it to count the number of instances it has found:

```
/var/log/cron:400
```

If we look at the first result, we can see that `grep` has found 400 instances of the word "cron" in `/var/log/cron`.

Finally, we redirect the results to another `grep` command with the `-v` flag followed by `:0`. This `grep` will take the results of the first execution and omit (`-v`) any lines with the string `:0`. This is useful for restricting the results to only files with the `cron` string within them.

From the preceding results, we can see that the file, `/var/log/cron`, has the most instances of the word "cron" within it. This fact alone is a good indication that `/var/log/cron` is the log file for the `crond` daemon.

Now that we know which log file has the log messages we are looking for, we can take a look at the contents of that log file. Since this log file is quite large we will use the `less` command to read this file:

```
# less /var/log/cron
```

Since there is quite a bit of information in this log, we will only focus on log entries that will help explain the issue. The following segment is an interesting group of log messages that should answer whether our job is running or not:

```
Jun 10 18:01:01 localhost CROND[2033]: (root) CMD (run-parts /etc/cron.
hourly)

Jun 10 18:01:01 localhost run-parts(/etc/cron.hourly)[2033]: starting
0anacron

Jun 10 18:01:01 localhost run-parts(/etc/cron.hourly)[2042]: finished
0anacron

Jun 10 18:01:01 localhost run-parts(/etc/cron.hourly)[2033]: starting
0yum-hourly.cron

Jun 10 18:01:01 localhost run-parts(/etc/cron.hourly)[2048]: finished
0yum-hourly.cron

Jun 10 18:05:01 localhost CROND[2053]: (vagrant) CMD (/opt/myapp/bin/
processor --debug --config /opt/myapp/conf/config.yml > /dev/null)
```

```
Jun 10 18:10:01 localhost CROND[2086]: (root) CMD (/usr/lib64/sa/sa1 1 1)

Jun 10 18:10:01 localhost CROND[2087]: (vagrant) CMD (/opt/myapp/bin/
processor --debug --config /opt/myapp/conf/config.yml > /dev/null)

Jun 10 18:15:01 localhost CROND[2137]: (vagrant) CMD (/opt/myapp/bin/
processor --debug --config /opt/myapp/conf/config.yml > /dev/null)

Jun 10 18:20:01 localhost CROND[2147]: (root) CMD (/usr/lib64/sa/sa1 1 1)
```

The preceding log messages show quite a few lines. Let's break down the logs to get a better understanding of what is being executed. Consider the following lines:

```
Jun 10 18:01:01 localhost CROND[2033]: (root) CMD (run-parts /etc/cron.
hourly)

Jun 10 18:01:01 localhost run-parts(/etc/cron.hourly)[2033]: starting
0anacron

Jun 10 18:01:01 localhost run-parts(/etc/cron.hourly)[2042]: finished
0anacron

Jun 10 18:01:01 localhost run-parts(/etc/cron.hourly)[2033]: starting
0yum-hourly.cron

Jun 10 18:01:01 localhost run-parts(/etc/cron.hourly)[2048]: finished
0yum-hourly.cron
```

The first few lines do not seem to be the job we are searching for but rather the cron.
hourly jobs.

On Linux systems, there are multiple ways to specify cron jobs. On RHEL systems, there are several directories within /etc/ that start with the name cron:

```
# ls -laF /etc/ | grep cron
-rw-------.  1 root root      541 Jun  9  2014 anacrontab
drwxr-xr-x.  2 root root       34 Jan 23 15:43 cron.d/
drwxr-xr-x.  2 root root       62 Jul 22  2014 cron.daily/
-rw-------.  1 root root        0 Jun  9  2014 cron.deny
drwxr-xr-x.  2 root root       44 Jul 22  2014 cron.hourly/
drwxr-xr-x.  2 root root        6 Jun  9  2014 cron.monthly/
-rw-r--r--.  1 root root      451 Jun  9  2014 crontab
drwxr-xr-x.  2 root root        6 Jun  9  2014 cron.weekly/
```

The cron.daily, cron.hourly, cron.monthly, and cron.weekly directories are all directories that can contain scripts. These scripts are to be run per the time specified in the directory name.

For example, let's look at `/etc/cron.hourly/0yum-hourly.cron`:

```
# cat /etc/cron.hourly/0yum-hourly.cron
#!/bin/bash


# Only run if this flag is set. The flag is created by the yum-cron init
# script when the service is started -- this allows one to use chkconfig and
# the standard "service stop|start" commands to enable or disable yum-cron.
if [[ ! -f /var/lock/subsys/yum-cron ]]; then
  exit 0
fi


# Action!
exec /usr/sbin/yum-cron /etc/yum/yum-cron-hourly.conf
```

The preceding file is a simple `bash` script that the `crond` daemon will execute every hour, as it is in the `cron.hourly` directory. In general the scripts that are contained within these directories are put there by system services. However, these directories are also open to systems administrators to place their own scripts.

User crontabs

If we continue down the log file, we can see an entry that is relevant to our custom job:

```
Jun 10 18:10:01 localhost CROND[2087]: (vagrant) CMD (/opt/myapp/bin/
processor --debug --config /opt/myapp/conf/config.yml > /dev/null)
```

This line shows the `processor` command that the application support team referenced. This line must be the job the application support team is having issues with. The log entry tells us quite a bit of useful information. For one, it provides us with the command line options being passed to this job:

```
/opt/myapp/bin/processor --debug --config /opt/myapp/conf/config.yml > /
dev/null
```

It also tells us the job is being executed as `vagrant`. The most important thing this log entry tells us though is that the job is being executed.

Since we know the job is being executed, we should then verify if the job is successful. To do this we will take an easy approach and execute the job manually:

```
$ /opt/myapp/bin/processor --debug --config /opt/myapp/conf/config.yml
Initializing with configuration file /opt/myapp/conf/config.yml

- - - - - - - - - - - - - - - - - - - - - - - - - - - -

Starting message processing job
Traceback (most recent call last):
  File "app.py", line 28, in init app (app.c:1488)
IOError: [Errno 24] Too many open files: '/opt/myapp/
queue/1433955823.29_0.txt'
```

We should omit `> /dev/null` from the end of the cron task as this will redirect the output to `/dev/null`. This is a common way of throwing away the output of cron jobs. For this manual execution, we can utilize the output to help troubleshoot the issue.

Once executed, the job seems to fail. Not only does it fail, but it is also producing an error message along with the failure:

```
IOError: [Errno 24] Too many open files: '/opt/myapp/
queue/1433955823.29_0.txt'
```

This error is interesting, as it seems to suggest that the application is opening too many files. *Why would that matter?*

Understanding user limits

On Linux systems, there are limitations that every process is held to. These limits are in place to prevent processes from utilizing too many system resources.

While these limits are enforced on every user, it is possible, however, to set different limits per user. To check what limits are set on the vagrant user by default, we can use the ulimit command:

```
$ ulimit -a
core file size          (blocks, -c) 0
data seg size           (kbytes, -d) unlimited
scheduling priority             (-e) 0
file size               (blocks, -f) unlimited
pending signals                 (-i) 3825
max locked memory       (kbytes, -l) 64
```

```
max memory size           (kbytes, -m) unlimited
open files                         (-n) 1024
pipe size          (512 bytes, -p) 8
POSIX message queues      (bytes, -q) 819200
real-time priority                (-r) 0
stack size              (kbytes, -s) 8192
cpu time              (seconds, -t) unlimited
max user processes                (-u) 3825
virtual memory          (kbytes, -v) unlimited
file locks                         (-x) unlimited
```

When we executed the `ulimit` command, we did so as the vagrant user. This is important as when we run the `ulimit` command as any other user including root, the output will be the limits of that user.

If we look at the output of the `ulimit` command, we can see that there are quite a few limitations that can be set.

The file size limit

Let's take a look and breakdown a few key limits:

```
file size               (blocks, -f) unlimited
```

The first interesting item is the `file size` limit. This limit will restrict how large a file the user can create. The current setting for the vagrant user is `unlimited` but what would happen if we set this value to a smaller number?

We can do this by executing `ulimit -f` followed by the number of blocks to limit the file to. For example, consider the following command line:

```
$ ulimit -f 10
```

After setting the value to `10` we can verify it took effect by running `ulimit -f` again, but this time with no value:

```
$ ulimit -f
10
```

Now that our limit is set to 10 blocks, let's try to create a 500 MB file by using the `dd` command:

```
$ dd if=/dev/zero of=/var/tmp/bigfile bs=1M count=500
File size limit exceeded
```

One nice thing about user limits on Linux is generally the errors provided are self-explanatory. We can see from the preceding output that not only was the dd command unable to create the file it received an error stating that the file, size limit was exceeded.

The max user processes limit

Another interesting limit is the max processes limit:

```
max user processes              (-u) 3825
```

This limit prevents a user from having *too many running processes* at one time. This is a very useful and interesting limitation as it can easily prevent a rogue application from taking over a system.

It can also be a limitation that you will often encounter. This is especially true for applications that launch many sub processes or threads. To see how this limitation works, we can change our setting to 10:

```
$ ulimit -u 10
$ ulimit -u
10
```

Like the file size limit, we can modify the process limit using the ulimit command. This time, however, we use the -u flag. Each user limit has its own unique flag with the ulimit command. We can see these flags in the output of ulimit -a, and of course, each flag is referenced in the man page for ulimit.

Now that we have set our processes to be limited to 10, we can see that limit enforced by running a command:

```
$ man ulimit
man: fork failed: Resource temporarily unavailable
```

By simply being logged into the vagrant user through SSH, we are already utilizing multiple processes. It will be quite easy to run into the limit of 10 processes as any new command we run will put our login over the limitation.

From the preceding example we can see that when the man command was executed, it was not able to start a child process and thus returned an error stating Resource temporarily unavailable.

The open files limit

The final interesting user limit that I want explore is the `open files` limit:

```
open files                     (-n) 1024
```

The `open files` limit will restrict a process from opening more than the defined number of files. This limit can be used to prevent a process from opening too many files at one time. This is something that can come in handy when preventing an application from consuming too many of the system's resources.

Like the other limits, let's see what happens when we reduce this limit to a very unreasonable number:

```
$ ulimit -n 2
$ ls
-bash: start_pipeline: pgrp pipe: Too many open files
ls: error while loading shared libraries: libselinux.so.1: cannot open
shared object file: Error 24
```

As with the other examples, we received an error, `Too many open files`, in this case. However, this error looks quite familiar. If we were to look back at the error received from our scheduled job we will see why.

```
IOError: [Errno 24] Too many open files: '/opt/myapp/
queue/1433955823.29_0.txt'
```

After setting our max number of open files to 2, the `ls` command produced an error; the error has the same exact error message our application received when executed earlier.

Does this mean that our application is trying to open more files than our system is configured to allow? That is a strong possibility.

Changing user limits

Since we suspect the `open files` limit is preventing the application from executing, we can set its limit to a higher value. However, this is not as simple as executing `ulimit -n`; the following output is what we get when it's executed:

```
$ ulimit -n
1024
$ ulimit -n 5000
```

```
-bash: ulimit: open files: cannot modify limit: Operation not permitted
$ ulimit -n 4096
$ ulimit -n
4096
```

By default, on our example system the highest the vagrant user is allowed to raise the `open files` limitation to is `4096`. As we can see from the preceding error, anything higher is denied; but like most things with Linux we can change this.

The limits.conf file

The user limits that we have been using and modifying are part of Linux's PAM system. PAM or Pluggable Authentication Modules is a system that provides a modular authentication system.

For example, if our system was to utilize LDAP for authentication, the `pam_ldap.so` library would be used to provide this functionality. However, since our system uses local users for authentication, the `pam_localuser.so` library handles the user authentication.

We can validate this if we read the `/etc/pam.d/system-auth` file:

```
$ cat /etc/pam.d/system-auth
#%PAM-1.0
# This file is auto-generated.
# User changes will be destroyed the next time authconfig is run.
auth        required        pam_env.so
auth        sufficient      pam_unix.so nullok try_first_pass
auth        requisite       pam_succeed_if.so uid >= 1000 quiet_success
auth        required        pam_deny.so

account     required        pam_unix.so
account     sufficient      pam_localuser.so
account     sufficient      pam_succeed_if.so uid < 1000 quiet
account     required        pam_permit.so

password    requisite       pam_pwquality.so try_first_pass local_users_
only retry=3 authtok_type=
password    sufficient      pam_unix.so sha512 shadow nullok try_first_pass
use_authtok
password    required        pam_deny.so
```

```
session      optional      pam_keyinit.so revoke
session      required      pam_limits.so
-session     optional       pam_systemd.so
session      [success=1 default=ignore] pam_succeed_if.so service in crond
quiet use_uid
session      required      pam_unix.so
```

If we look at the preceding example, we can see that pam_localuser.so is listed with account as the first column:

```
account      sufficient      pam_localuser.so
```

This means the pam_localuser.so module is a sufficient module to allow an account to be utilized, which essentially means that the user is able to log in if they have a correct /etc/passwd and /etc/shadow entry.

```
session      required      pam_limits.so
```

If we look at the preceding line, we can see where user limits are enforced. This line essentially tells the system that the pam_limits.so module is required for all user sessions. This effectively ensures that the user limits, which the pam_limits.so module identifies are enforced on each user session.

The configuration for this PAM module is located in /etc/security/limits.conf and /etc/security/limits.d/:

```
$ cat /etc/security/limits.conf
#This file sets the resource limits for the users logged in via PAM.
#          - core - limits the core file size (KB)
#          - data - max data size (KB)
#          - fsize - maximum filesize (KB)
#          - memlock - max locked-in-memory address space (KB)
#          - nofile - max number of open files
#          - rss - max resident set size (KB)
#          - stack - max stack size (KB)
#          - cpu - max CPU time (MIN)
#          - nproc - max number of processes
#          - as - address space limit (KB)
#          - maxlogins - max number of logins for this user
#          - maxsyslogins - max number of logins on the system
#          - priority - the priority to run user process with
```

```
#              - locks - max number of file locks the user can hold
#              - sigpending - max number of pending signals
#              - msgqueue - max memory used by POSIX message queues (bytes)
#              - nice - max nice priority allowed to raise to values: [-20, 19]
#              - rtprio - max realtime priority
#
#<domain>        <type>   <item>          <value>
#

#*               soft     core            0
#*               hard     rss             10000
#@student        hard     nproc           20
#@faculty        soft     nproc           20
#@faculty        hard     nproc           50
#ftp             hard     nproc           0
#@student        -        maxlogins       4
```

When we read the `limits.conf` file, we can see quite a bit of useful information about user limits.

Within this file, the available limitations are listed along with a description of what that limitation enforces. For example, in the preceding command lines, we can see the following for the number of `open files` limit:

```
#              - nofile - max number of open files
```

From this line we can see that if we want to change the number of open files available to our user, we will need to use the `nofile` type. On top of listing what each limitation does, the `limits.conf` file also contains examples of setting custom limits for users and groups:

```
#ftp             hard     nproc           0
```

Given this example we can see what format we need to use to set the limit; but what should we set the limitation too? If we look back at the error from our job, we can see that the error listed a file in the `/opt/myapp/queue` directory:

```
IOError: [Errno 24] Too many open files: '/opt/myapp/
queue/1433955823.29_0.txt'
```

It is safe to say that the application is trying to open the files within this directory. So, to determine how many files this process needs to have open, let's find out how many files exist in this directory by using the following command line:

```
$ ls -la /opt/myapp/queue/ | wc -l
492304
```

The preceding command uses `ls -la` to list all of the files and directories within the `queue/` directory and redirects that output to `wc -l`. The `wc` command will count the number of lines (`-l`) from the provided output, which essentially means that within the `queue/` directory, there are 492,304 files and/or directories.

Given the large number, we should set the number of `open files` limit to `500000`, enough to process the `queue/` directory with a little extra just in case. We can do this by appending the following line to the `limits.conf` file:

```
# vi /etc/security/limits.conf
```

After adding our line with `vi`, or another text editor, we can verify it is there with the `tail` command:

```
$ tail /etc/security/limits.conf
#@student        hard    nproc        20
#@faculty        soft    nproc        20
#@faculty        hard    nproc        50
#ftp             hard    nproc        0
#@student        -       maxlogins    4

vagrant     soft    nofile    100000
vagrant     hard    nofile    500000


# End of file
```

Changing these settings does not mean our login shell instantly has a limit of `500000`. Our logged in session still has a limitation of `4096` set.

```
$ ulimit -n
4096
```

We also still cannot increase it beyond that value.

```
$ ulimit -n 9000
-bash: ulimit: open files: cannot modify limit: Operation not permitted
```

In order for our change to take effect, we must log in to our user once again.

As we discussed earlier, these limitations are set by PAM, which is applied during the login of our shell session. Since the limitations are set during login, we are still being restricted by the previous values picked up when we last logged in.

To obtain the new limitations, we must log out and log back in (or spawn a new login session). For our examples, we will log out of our shell and log back in.

```
$ ulimit -n
100000
$ ulimit -n 501000
-bash: ulimit: open files: cannot modify limit: Operation not permitted
$ ulimit -n 500000
$ ulimit -n
500000
```

If we look at the preceding command lines, we can see something quite interesting.

When we logged in this time, our number of files limitation was set to `100000`, which just happens to be the same limit we set as the `soft` limit in the `limits.conf` file. This happened because the `soft` limit is the limit set by default for each session.

The `hard` limit is the highest value above the `soft` limit that this user can set. We can see this in action in the preceding example, as we were able to set the `nofile` limit to `500000` but not `501000`.

Future proofing the scheduled job

The reason we set the `soft` limit to `100000` was because we are planning for similar scenarios in the future. With the `soft` limit set at `100000`, the cron job that runs this scheduled job will be limited to 100,000 open files. However, since the `hard` limit is set to `500000`, someone can then manually run the job with a higher limit set on their login session.

As long as the number of files in the `queue` directory does not exceed 500,000, there should no longer be a need for anyone to edit the `/etc/security/limits.conf` file.

Running the job again

Now that our limitations have been increased, we can try to run the job again.

```
$ /opt/myapp/bin/processor --debug --config /opt/myapp/conf/config.yml
Initializing with configuration file /opt/myapp/conf/config.yml
- - - - - - - - - - - - - - - - - - - - - - - - - - - -
Starting message processing job
Traceback (most recent call last):
  File "app.py", line 28, in init app (app.c:1488)
IOError: [Errno 23] Too many open files in system: '/opt/myapp/
queue/1433955989.86_5.txt'
```

Once again we received an error. However, this time the error is just a little bit different.

In the previous run, we received the following error.

```
IOError: [Errno 24] Too many open files: '/opt/myapp/
queue/1433955823.29_0.txt'
```

However, this time we received this error.

```
IOError: [Errno 23] Too many open files in system: '/opt/myapp/
queue/1433955989.86_5.txt'
```

The difference is extremely subtle, but in the second run our error stated **Too many open files in system**, whereas our first run did not include in system. The reason for this is because we hit a different type of limitation, not a **user** limitation, but a **system** limitation.

Kernel tunables

The Linux Kernel itself can set limitations on a system as well. These limits are defined based on kernel parameters. Some of these parameters are static and cannot be changed during runtime; while others can. When a kernel parameter can be changed during runtime this is called a **tunable parameter**.

We can see both static and tunable kernel parameters and their current values by using the sysctl command:

```
# sysctl -a | head
abi.vsyscall32 = 1
crypto.fips_enabled = 0
```

```
debug.exception-trace = 1
debug.kprobes-optimization = 1
dev.hpet.max-user-freq = 64
dev.mac_hid.mouse_button2_keycode = 97
dev.mac_hid.mouse_button3_keycode = 100
dev.mac_hid.mouse_button_emulation = 0
dev.parport.default.spintime = 500
dev.parport.default.timeslice = 200
```

Since there are many parameters available, I used the `head` command to limit the output to the first 10. The error we received earlier mentioned a limitation on the system, this suggests we may be hitting a limit imposed by the kernel itself.

The only problem is how do we know which one? The fastest answer of course is to search Google. Since there are so many kernel parameters (800+ on the system we are working on), it is difficult to simply read the output of `sysctl -a` and find the right one.

A more realistic approach is to simply search for the type of parameter we are looking to modify. An example search for our scenario would be `Linux parameter max open files`. If we were to perform this search we will most likely find the parameter and how to modify it. If Google is not an option however, there is another way.

In general, the kernel parameters have a name that describes what the parameter controls.

For example, if we were to look for the kernel parameter that disables IPv6 we would first start by searching for the `net` string, as in network:

```
# sysctl -a | grep -c net
556
```

However, this still returns a large number of results. Within those results, we can see the string `ipv6` though.

```
# sysctl -a | grep -c ipv6
233
```

Still, quite a few results; however, we get the following output if we add a search for the string `disable`:

```
# sysctl -a | grep ipv6 | grep disable
net.ipv6.conf.all.disable_ipv6 = 0
net.ipv6.conf.default.disable_ipv6 = 0
net.ipv6.conf.enp0s3.disable_ipv6 = 0
net.ipv6.conf.enp0s8.disable_ipv6 = 0
net.ipv6.conf.lo.disable_ipv6 = 0
```

We can finally narrow down the possible parameters. However, we do not fully know what these parameters do. Not yet, at least.

If we perform a quick search through /usr/share/doc, we might find a few documents that explain what these settings do. We can do this quickly by performing a recursive search for -r through this directory using grep. In order to keep the output simple, we can add -l (list file), which causes grep to only list the filenames it finds the desired string within:

```
# grep -rl net.ipv6 /usr/share/doc/
/usr/share/doc/grub2-tools-2.02/grub.html
```

On Red Hat based Linux systems, the /usr/share/doc directory is used for additional documentation outside of the system's man pages. If we were limited to only utilizing the documentation on the system itself, the /usr/share/doc directory is one of the first places to check.

Finding the kernel parameter for open files

Since we like performing tasks the hard way, we will try to identify the kernel parameter that is potentially limiting us without searching for it on Google. The first step to do this will be to search the sysctl output for the string file.

The reason we are searching for file is because we are hitting a limitation on the number of files. While this may not provide the exact parameter we are trying to identify, the search at least is going to get us started:

```
# sysctl -a | grep file
fs.file-max = 48582
fs.file-nr = 1088  0  48582
fs.xfs.filestream_centisecs = 3000
```

Searching for `file` may have actually been a very good choice after all. Simply based on the names of the parameters, the two that may be interesting to us are `fs.file-max` and `fs.file-nr`. At this point, we do not know which one controls the number of open files or if either of these do.

To find out more information we can search through the `doc` directory.

```
# grep -r fs.file- /usr/share/doc/
/usr/share/doc/postfix-2.10.1/README_FILES/TUNING_README:
fs.file-max=16384
```

It seems that a document named TUNING_README, located in the Postfix services documentation, has a reference to at least one of our values. Let's check out the file to see what this document says about this kernel parameter:

```
* Configure the kernel for more open files and sockets. The details are
    extremely system dependent and change with the operating system
version. Be
    sure to verify the following information with your system tuning
guide:


        o Linux kernel parameters can be specified in /etc/sysctl.conf or
changed
        with sysctl commands:

        fs.file-max=16384
        kernel.threads-max=2048
```

If we read the contents of the file around where it lists our kernel parameter, we can see that it specifically calls out parameters to *configure the kernel for more open files and sockets.*

This document calls out two kernel parameters to allow for more open files and sockets. The first is called `fs.file-max`, which is one we also identified with our `sysctl` search. The second is called `kernel.threads-max`, which is fairly new.

Simply based on the names, it seems the tunable parameter we want to modify is the `fs.file-max` parameter. Let's take a look at its current value as follows:

```
# sysctl fs.file-max
fs.file-max = 48582
```

We can list the current value of this parameter by executing `sysctl` followed by the parameter name (as shown in the preceding command lines). This will simply display the value as it is defined currently; which seems to be set at 48582 a number far lower than our current user limits.

> In the preceding example, we found this parameter in a postfix document. While this may be good, it is not exact. If you often find yourself needing to search locally for kernel parameters, it would be a good idea to install the `kernel-doc` package. The `kernel-doc` package contains quite a bit of information, especially about tunables.

Changing kernel tunables

Since we believe the `fs.file-max` parameter controls the maximum number of open files a system can have, we should change this value to allow our job to run.

Like most system configuration items on Linux, there is the option to change this value ad-hoc and on reboot. Earlier we set the `limits.conf` file to allow the vagrant user the ability to open 100,000 files as a `soft` limit and 500,000 as a `hard` limit. The question is do we want this user to be able to open 500,000 files as a normal operation? Or should this be a one-time task to correct the issue we are currently facing?

The answer is simply: *it depends!*

If we look at the situation we are working on currently, the job in question has not been run for quite a while. Because of this there is a large backlog of messages in the queue. However, these are not normal conditions.

Earlier when we set the user limit to 100,000 files, we did so as this is a somewhat appropriate value for this job. With this considered, we should also set the kernel parameter to a value slightly over 100000 but not too far over.

For this scenario and in this environment, we are going to perform two actions. The first is to configure the system to allow for *125,000 open files by default*. The second is to set the current parameter to *525,000 open files* to allow the scheduled job to run successfully.

Permanently changing a tunable

Since we want to change the value of `fs.file-max` to `125000` by default, we will need to edit the `sysctl.conf` file. The `sysctl.conf` file is a system configuration file, which allows you to specify custom values for tunable kernel parameters. During every reboot of the system, this file is read and the values within it are applied.

In order to set our `fs.file-max` value to `125000` we can simply append the following line to this file:

```
# vi /etc/sysctl.conf
fs.file-max=125000
```

Now that we have added our custom value, we will need to tell the system to apply it.

As mentioned earlier, the `sysctl.conf` file is applied on reboot, however we can also apply the settings to this file at any time using the `sysctl` command with the –p flag.

```
# sysctl -p
fs.file-max = 125000
```

When given the –p flag, the `sysctl` command will read and apply the values to the file specified, or if no file is specified `/etc/sysctl.conf`. Since we did not specify a file after the –p flag, the `sysctl` command applied the values added to `/etc/sysctl.conf` and printed the values it modified.

Let's validate it was applied appropriately by executing `sysctl` again.

```
# sysctl fs.file-max
fs.file-max = 125000
```

It appears that in fact the value was applied appropriately, but what about setting it to `525000`?

Temporarily changing a tunable

While it may be simple enough to change the `/etc/sysctl.conf` to a higher value, apply it, and then revert the change. There is a much easier way to change a tunable's value temporarily.

The `sysctl` command, when provided with the `-w` option, will allow modification of tunable values. To see this in action, we will use this to set the `fs.file-max` value to `525000`.

```
# sysctl -w fs.file-max=525000
fs.file-max = 525000
```

Like when we applied the `sysctl.conf` file's values, when we executed `sysctl -w` it printed the values it applied. If we validate them again, we will see the value is set to `525000` files:

```
# sysctl fs.file-max
fs.file-max = 525000
```

Running the job one last time

Now that we have set our `open files` limit to `500000` for the vagrant user and `525000` on the system as a whole. We can execute this job manually one more time, and this time it should be successful:

```
$ /opt/myapp/bin/processor --debug --config /opt/myapp/conf/config.yml
Initializing with configuration file /opt/myapp/conf/config.yml
- - - - - - - - - - - - - - - - - - - - - - - - - - - - -
Starting message processing job
Added 492304 to queue
Processing 492304 messages
Processed 492304 messages
```

This time the job executed without providing any errors! We can see from the output of the job that all of the files in `/opt/myapp/queue` were processed as well.

A look back

Now that we have resolved the issue, let's take a second to look at what we did to resolve the issue.

Too many open files

In order to troubleshoot our issue, we executed a scheduled cron job manually. If we circle back to previous chapters, this is a prime example of duplicating an issue and seeing it for ourselves.

In this case, the job was not performing the tasks it was supposed to. In order to identify the reason, we ran it manually.

During that manual execution, we were able to identify the following error:

```
IOError: [Errno 24] Too many open files: '/opt/myapp/
queue/1433955823.29_0.txt'
```

This error is very common and is caused by the job running into user limits that prevent a single user from opening too many files. To resolve this we added custom settings to the `/etc/security/limits.conf` file.

These changes set the `soft` limitation of `open files` to `100000` for our user by default. We also allowed the user to increase the `open files` limit to `500000` on an ad-hoc basis via the `hard` setting:

```
IOError: [Errno 23] Too many open files in system: '/opt/myapp/
queue/1433955989.86_5.txt'
```

After modifying these limits, we executed the job again and experienced a similar but different error.

This time the `open files` limitation was being imposed on the system itself, which in this case imposed a system-wide limit of 48,000 open files.

To resolve this we set a permanent setting of `125000` in the `/etc/sysctl.conf` file and temporarily changed the value to `525000`.

From that point we were able to execute the job manually. Beyond this instance however, since we changed the default limitations we also gave this job more resources to execute normally. As long as there is not a backlog of greater than 100,000 files this job should execute without issue in the future.

A bit of clean up

Speaking of normal executions, in order to reduce the kernel's limitation of open files we can execute the `sysctl` command again with the `-p` option. This will reset the value to the defined value within the `/etc/sysctl.conf` file.

```
# sysctl -p
fs.file-max = 125000
```

One caveat to this method is that `sysctl -p` will only reset the values specified in `/etc/sysctl.conf`; *which only contains a handful of tunable values by default*. If a value not specified in `/etc/sysctl.conf` is modified, the `sysctl -p` method will not reset this value to default.

Summary

In this chapter, we became very familiar with the kernel and user limitations enforced within Linux. These settings become very useful as any application that utilizes many resources will eventually run into one of these.

In the next chapter, we will be focusing on a very common but very tricky issue. We will focus on troubleshooting and identifying the cause of a system running out of memory. When a system runs out of memory, there are a lot of consequences such as application processes being killed.

11
Recovering from Common Failures

In the previous chapter, we explored the user and system limitations that exist on Linux servers. We looked at what limits are in place and how to change the values for applications that require more than default.

In this chapter, we will put our troubleshooting skills to use with a system that has had its resources exhausted.

The reported problem

Today's chapter, much like the other chapters, will start with someone reporting an issue. The issue being reported is that Apache is no longer running on the server, which serves the company's blog: `blog.example.com`.

A fellow systems administrator who is reporting the issue has explained that someone reported that the blog was down and when he logged into the server he could see Apache was no longer running. At that point, our peer was unsure what to do to continue and asked for our help.

Is Apache really down?

The first thing that we should do when a service is reported as down is to validate that it really is down. This is essentially our *duplicate it for ourselves* step from our troubleshooting process. With a service such as Apache, we should also validate that it is in fact down fairly quickly.

In my experience, I have often been told that a service is down when it really was not. The server may have been having an issue but it was not technically down. The difference between up or down can change the troubleshooting steps that we need to perform to resolve the issue.

This said, the first step that I always perform for issues like this is to validate whether the service really is down or whether the service simply is not responding.

To validate that Apache is really down, we will use the ps command. As we learned earlier, this command will print a list of the currently running processes. We will redirect this output to the grep command to check whether there are any instances of the httpd (Apache) service running:

```
# ps -elf | grep http
0 S root      2645  1974  0  80   0 - 28160 pipe_w 21:45 pts/0
00:00:00 grep --color=auto http
```

From the output of the abovementioned ps command, we can see that there are no processes running with the name httpd. Under normal circumstances, we would expect to see at least a few lines that look similar to the following example:

```
5 D apache    2383     1  0  80   0 - 115279 conges 20:58 ?
00:00:04 /usr/sbin/httpd -DFOREGROUND
```

Since there are no httpd processes found in the process list, we can conclude that Apache is in fact down on this system. The question now is, why?

Why is it down?

Before simply resolving the issue by starting the Apache service, we are going to first figure out why the Apache service is not running. This is a process called **Root Cause Analysis (RCA)**, which is a formal process that is used to understand what first caused the issue.

We will get very familiar with this process in the next chapter. In this chapter, we will keep it simple and focus specifically on why Apache is not running.

One of the first places for us to look is in the Apache logs in /var/log/httpd. We learned of these logs in the previous chapters while troubleshooting other webserver-related issues. As we saw in these earlier chapters, application and service logs can be very helpful in determining what has happened to the service.

Since Apache is no longer running, we are more interested in the last few events that happened. If the service experienced a fatal error or was stopped, there should be a message at the end of the log file showing this.

Because we are only interested in the last few events, we will use the `tail` command to show the last 10 lines of the `error_log` file. The `error_log` file is the first log to check as it is the most likely place for anything unusual:

```
# tail /var/log/httpd/error_log

[Sun Jun 21 20:51:32.889455 2015]  [mpm_prefork:notice]  [pid 2218]
AH00163: Apache/2.4.6  PHP/5.4.16 configured -- resuming normal
operations

[Sun Jun 21 20:51:32.889690 2015]  [core:notice]  [pid 2218]
AH00094: Command line: '/usr/sbin/httpd -D FOREGROUND'

[Sun Jun 21 20:51:33.892170 2015]  [mpm_prefork:error]  [pid 2218]
AH00161: server reached MaxRequestWorkers setting, consider
raising the MaxRequestWorkers setting

[Sun Jun 21 20:53:42.577787 2015]  [mpm_prefork:notice]  [pid 2218]
AH00170: caught SIGWINCH, shutting down gracefully
[Sun Jun 21 20:53:44.677885 2015]  [core:notice]  [pid 2249] SELinux
policy enabled; httpd running as context system_u:system_r:httpd_t:s0

[Sun Jun 21 20:53:44.678919 2015]  [suexec:notice]  [pid 2249] AH01232:
suEXEC mechanism enabled (wrapper: /usr/sbin/suexec)

[Sun Jun 21 20:53:44.703088 2015]  [auth_digest:notice]  [pid 2249]
AH01757: generating secret for digest authentication ...

[Sun Jun 21 20:53:44.704046 2015]  [lbmethod_heartbeat:notice]  [pid 2249]
AH02282: No slotmem from mod_heartmonitor

[Sun Jun 21 20:53:44.732504 2015]  [mpm_prefork:notice]  [pid 2249]
AH00163: Apache/2.4.6  PHP/5.4.16 configured -- resuming normal
operations

[Sun Jun 21 20:53:44.732568 2015]  [core:notice]  [pid 2249] AH00094:
Command line: '/usr/sbin/httpd -D FOREGROUND'
```

From the `error_log` file contents, we can see quite a few interesting messages. Let's take a quick look at some of the more informational log entries.

```
[Sun Jun 21 20:53:42.577787 2015]  [mpm_prefork:notice]  [pid 2218]
AH00170: caught SIGWINCH, shutting down gracefully
```

The preceding line shows that the Apache process was shut down on `Sunday, Jun 21` at `20:53`. We can see this as the error message clearly states `shutting down gracefully`. The next few lines, however, seem to indicate that the Apache service was back up only 2 seconds later:

```
[Sun Jun 21 20:53:44.677885 2015]  [core:notice]  [pid 2249] SELinux policy
enabled; httpd running as context system_u:system_r:httpd_t:s0

[Sun Jun 21 20:53:44.678919 2015]  [suexec:notice]  [pid 2249] AH01232:
suEXEC mechanism enabled (wrapper: /usr/sbin/suexec)
```

```
[Sun Jun 21 20:53:44.703088 2015] [auth_digest:notice] [pid 2249]
AH01757: generating secret for digest authentication ...
```

```
[Sun Jun 21 20:53:44.704046 2015] [lbmethod_heartbeat:notice] [pid 2249]
AH02282: No slotmem from mod_heartmonitor
```

```
[Sun Jun 21 20:53:44.732504 2015] [mpm_prefork:notice] [pid 2249]
AH00163: Apache/2.4.6  PHP/5.4.16 configured -- resuming normal
operations
```

The shutdown log entry shows a process id of `2218`, whereas the preceding five lines show a process id of `2249`. The 5th line also states `resuming normal operations`. These four messages seem to indicate that the Apache process simply restarted. Most likely, this was a graceful restart of Apache.

A graceful restart of Apache is a fairly common task performed during the modification of its configuration. This is a way to restart the Apache process without taking it fully down and impacting the web service.

```
[Sun Jun 21 20:53:44.732568 2015] [core:notice] [pid 2249] AH00094:
Command line: '/usr/sbin/httpd -D FOREGROUND'
```

The most interesting thing that these 10 lines tell us, however, is that the last log Apache printed was nothing more than a notification. When Apache was stopped gracefully, it logged a message in the `error_log` file to show that it was being stopped.

Since the Apache processes are no longer running and there are no log entries showing that it was shut down gracefully or even ungracefully, we conclude that irrespective of the reason why Apache was not running, it did not shut down normally.

If a person shut down the service by using `apachectl` or the `systemctl` command, we would expect to see a message similar to that discussed in the earlier example. Since the last line of the log file shows no shutdown message, we can only assume that this process was killed or terminated under abnormal circumstances.

Now, the question is *What might have caused the Apache process to terminate in an abnormal manner like this?*

One place that may provide a clue as to what happened with Apache is the systemd facility as Red Hat Enterprise Linux 7 services, such as Apache, have been moved to systemd. Upon booting, the `systemd` facility starts up any service that it has been configured to start.

When a process that `systemd` starts is terminated, that activity is captured by `systemd`. Depending on what has happened since the process was terminated, we can see whether `systemd` captured this event by using the `systemctl` command:

```
# systemctl status httpd
httpd.service - The Apache HTTP Server
   Loaded: loaded (/usr/lib/systemd/system/httpd.service; enabled)
   Active: failed (Result: timeout) since Fri 2015-06-26 21:21:38 UTC;
22min ago
  Process: 2521 ExecStop=/bin/kill -WINCH ${MAINPID} (code=exited,
status=0/SUCCESS)
  Process: 2249 ExecStart=/usr/sbin/httpd $OPTIONS -DFOREGROUND
(code=killed, signal=KILL)
 Main PID: 2249 (code=killed, signal=KILL)
   Status: "Total requests: 1649; Current requests/sec: -1.29; Current
traffic:   0 B/sec"


Jun 21 20:53:44 blog.example.com systemd[1]: Started The Apache HTTP
Server.
Jun 26 21:12:55 blog.example.com systemd[1]: httpd.service: main process
exited, code=killed, status=9/KILL
Jun 26 21:21:20 blog.example.com systemd[1]: httpd.service stopping timed
out. Killing.
Jun 26 21:21:38 blog.example.com systemd[1]: Unit httpd.service entered
failed state.
```

The output of the `systemctl status` command shows quite a bit of information. Since we covered this quite a bit in the previous chapters, I am going to skip to just the parts of this output that will tell us what happened to the Apache service.

The first two lines that look interesting are the following:

```
  Process: 2249 ExecStart=/usr/sbin/httpd $OPTIONS -DFOREGROUND
(code=killed, signal=KILL)
 Main PID: 2249 (code=killed, signal=KILL)
```

In these two lines, we can see process id `2249`, which we also saw in the `error_log` file. This is the process id of the Apache instance started on `Sunday, June 21`. We can also see from these lines that process `2249` was killed. This seems to indicate that someone or something killed our Apache service:

```
Jun 21 20:53:44 blog.example.com systemd[1]: Started The Apache HTTP
Server.
Jun 26 21:12:55 blog.example.com systemd[1]: httpd.service: main process
exited, code=killed, status=9/KILL
```

```
Jun 26 21:21:20 blog.example.com systemd[1]: httpd.service stopping timed
out. Killing.
Jun 26 21:21:38 blog.example.com systemd[1]: Unit httpd.service entered
failed state.
```

If we look at the last few lines in the `systemctl` status output, we can see events that the `systemd` facility captured. The first event that we can see is that the Apache service was started on `June 21` at `20:53`. This isn't much of a surprise as it correlates with the information we saw in `error_log`.

The last three lines, however, show that the Apache process was subsequently killed on `June 26` at `21:21`. Unfortunately these events do not show exactly why the Apache process was killed or who killed it. What it does tell us is the exact time that Apache was killed. This also shows that it was not likely that the `systemd` facility stopped the Apache service.

What else was happening at that time?

Since we were not able to determine the cause from the Apache logs or `systemctl status`, we will need to keep digging to understand what else may have killed this service.

```
# date
Sun Jun 28 18:32:33 UTC 2015
```

Since the 26th was several days ago, we have a somewhat limited set of places to look for additional information. One place that we can look is the `/var/log/messages` log file. As we discovered in the earlier chapters, the `messages` log contains quite a lot of diverse information from many of the different facilities within the system. If there were a place that could tell us what was happening with the system at that time, it would be there.

Searching the messages log

The `messages` log is quite large and has many log entries within it:

```
# wc -l /var/log/messages
21683 /var/log/messages
```

Therefore, we need to filter log messages that are either not relevant to our issue or not during the time of our issue. The first thing that we can do is search the log for messages from the day Apache was stopped: `June 26`:

```
# tail -1 /var/log/messages
Jun 28 20:44:01 localhost systemd: Started Session 348 of user vagrant.
```

From the previously mentioned `tail` command, we can see that messages within the `/var/log/messages` file have the format of date, hostname, process, and then message. The date field is a three-letter month followed by the day number and a 24-h timestamp.

Since our issue occurred on June 26th, we can search this log file for any instance of the string "Jun 26". This should provide all messages that were written on the 26th:

```
# grep -c "Jun 26" /var/log/messages
17864
```

This evidently is still quite a few log messages, far too many to read them all. Given this number, we need to filter the messages even more, maybe by the process:

```
# grep "Jun 26" /var/log/messages | cut -d\  -f1,2,5 | sort -n | uniq -c
| sort -nk 1 | tail
     39 Jun 26 journal:
     56 Jun 26 NetworkManager:
     76 Jun 26 NetworkManager[582]:
     76 Jun 26 NetworkManager[588]:
     78 Jun 26 NetworkManager[580]:
     79 Jun 26 systemd-logind:
    110 Jun 26 systemd[1]:
    152 Jun 26 NetworkManager[574]:
   1684 Jun 26 systemd:
  15077 Jun 26 kernel:
```

The preceding code is commonly called a **bash** one-liner. This is often a series of commands that redirect their output to another command to provide a function or output that one command by itself cannot perform or generate. In this case, we have a one-liner that shows us which processes were logging the most on June 26th.

Breaking down this useful one-liner

The above mentioned one-liner is somewhat complicated at first but once we break down this one-liner, it becomes much easier to understand. This is a useful one-liner as it makes identifying trends within log files a lot easier.

Let's break down this one-liner to get a better understanding of what it is doing:

```
# grep "Jun 26" /var/log/messages | cut -d\  -f1,2,5 | sort | uniq -c |
sort -nk 1 | tail
```

We already know what the first command does; it simply searches the /var/log/ messages file for any instance of the string "Jun 26". The other commands are ones that we haven't covered before, but they can be useful commands to know.

The cut command

The cut command in this one-liner is used to read the output of the grep command and print only specific parts of each line. To understand how this works, we should first run the one-liner ending at the cut command:

```
# grep "Jun 26" /var/log/messages | cut -d\ -f1,2,5
Jun 26 systemd:
Jun 26 systemd:
Jun 26 systemd:
Jun 26 systemd:
Jun 26 systemd:
Jun 26 systemd:
Jun 26 systemd:
Jun 26 systemd:
Jun 26 systemd:
Jun 26 systemd:
```

The preceding cut command works by specifying a delimiter and cutting the output by that delimiter.

A delimiter is a character used to break down the line into multiple fields; we can specify it with the –d flag. In the preceding example, the –d flag is followed by "\"; the backslash is an escape character and is followed by a single space. This tells the cut command to use a single space character as the delimiter.

The –f flag is used to specify the fields that should be displayed. These fields are the strings of text between the delimiter.

For example, let's take a look at the following command:

```
$ echo "Apples:Bananas:Carrots:Dried Cherries" | cut -d: -f1,2,4
Apples:Bananas:Dried Cherries
```

Here, we specified that the ":" character is the delimiter for cut. We also specified that it should print the first, second, and fourth fields. This had the effect of printing Apples (the first field), Bananas (the second field), and Dried Cherries (the fourth field). The third field, Carrots, was omitted from the output. This is because we didn't specifically tell the cut command to print the third field.

Now that we know how `cut` works, let's look at how it processes the `messages` log entries.

Here's a sample of a log message:

```
Jun 28 21:50:01 localhost systemd: Created slice user-0.slice.
```

When we executed the `cut` command in our one-liner, we specifically told it to only print the first, second, and fifth fields:

```
# grep "Jun 26" /var/log/messages | cut -d\  -f1,2,5
Jun 26 systemd:
```

By specifying a single space character to be the delimiter in our `cut` command, we can see that this causes `cut` to only print the month, day, and program from each log entry. By itself, this may not seem very useful, but as we continue looking through this one-liner, the functionality provided by cut will be critical.

The sort command

The next command `sort` is actually used twice within this one-liner:

```
# grep "Jun 26" /var/log/messages | cut -d\  -f1,2,5 | sort | head
Jun 26 audispd:
Jun 26 audispd:
Jun 26 audispd:
Jun 26 audispd:
Jun 26 audispd:
Jun 26 auditd[539]:
Jun 26 auditd[539]:
Jun 26 auditd[542]:
Jun 26 auditd[542]:
Jun 26 auditd[548]:
```

This command is actually pretty simple in what it does. The `sort` command in this one-liner takes the output of the `cut` command and orders (sorts) it.

To explain this better, let's look at the following example:

```
# cat /var/tmp/fruits.txt
Apples
Dried Cherries
Carrots
Bananas
```

The above file again has several fruits, and this time, they are not in alphabetical order. If we use the sort command to read this file, however, the order of these fruits will change:

```
# sort /var/tmp/fruits.txt
Apples
Bananas
Carrots
Dried Cherries
```

As we can see, the order is now alphabetical despite how the fruits are listed in the file itself. The nice thing about sort is that it can be used to order text in several different ways. In fact, in the second instance of sort within our one-liner, we use the -n flag to sort the text numerically as well:

```
# cat /var/tmp/numbers.txt
10
23
2312
23292
1212
129191
# sort -n /var/tmp/numbers.txt
10
23
1212
2312
23292
129191
```

The uniq command

The reason that our one-liner contains the sort command is simply to order the input sent to uniq -c:

```
# grep "Jun 26" /var/log/messages | cut -d\  -f1,2,5 | sort | uniq -c |
head
      5 Jun 26 audispd:
      2 Jun 26 auditd[539]:
      2 Jun 26 auditd[542]:
```

```
 3 Jun 26 auditd[548]:
 2 Jun 26 auditd[550]:
 2 Jun 26 auditd[553]:
15 Jun 26 augenrules:
38 Jun 26 avahi-daemon[573]:
19 Jun 26 avahi-daemon[579]:
19 Jun 26 avahi-daemon[581]:
```

The `uniq` command can be used to identify lines that match and display these lines in a single unique line. To understand this better, let's look at the following example:

```
$ cat /var/tmp/duplicates.txt
Apple
Apple
Apple
Apple
Banana
Banana
Banana
Carrot
Carrot
```

Our example file "`duplicates.txt`" contains multiple duplicate lines. When we read this file with `uniq`, we will only see each unique line:

```
$ uniq /var/tmp/duplicates.txt
Apple
Banana
Carrot
```

This can be somewhat useful; however, I find that with the `-c` flag, the output can be even more useful:

```
$ uniq -c /var/tmp/duplicates.txt
      4 Apple
      3 Banana
      2 Carrot
```

With the −c flag, the uniq command will count the number of times that it finds each line. Here, we can see that there are four lines with the word Apple. Therefore, the uniq command printed the number 4 before the word Apple to show that there were four instances of this line:

```
$ cat /var/tmp/duplicates.txt
Apple
Apple
Orange
Apple
Apple
Banana
Banana
Banana
Carrot
Carrot
$ uniq -c /var/tmp/duplicates.txt
      2 Apple
      1 Orange
      2 Apple
      3 Banana
      2 Carrot
```

One caveat to the uniq command is that in order to get an accurate count, each instance needs to be right after the other. You can see what happens when we add the word Orange between the groups of Apple lines.

Tying it all together

If we look at our command again, we can now better understand what it is doing:

```
# grep "Jun 26" /var/log/messages | cut -d\  -f1,2,5 | sort | uniq -c |
sort -n | tail
     39 Jun 26 journal:
     56 Jun 26 NetworkManager:
     76 Jun 26 NetworkManager[582]:
     76 Jun 26 NetworkManager[588]:
     78 Jun 26 NetworkManager[580]:
     79 Jun 26 systemd-logind:
```

```
  110  Jun 26 systemd[1]:
  152  Jun 26 NetworkManager[574]:
 1684  Jun 26 systemd:
15077  Jun 26 kernel:
```

The above command will filter and print all of the log messages in /var/log/ messages that match the string "Jun 26". The output will then be sent to the cut command, which prints the month, day, and process of each line. This output is then sent to the sort command to order the output into groups that match each other. The sorted output is then sent to uniq -c that counts the number of occurrences of each line and prints one unique line with the count.

From there, we add another sort to order the output by the number added by uniq, and add tail to shorten the output to the last 10 lines.

So, what exactly does this fancy one-liner tell us? Well, it tells us that the kernel facility and the systemd process are logging quite a bit. In fact, in comparison to the other items listed, we can see that these two have more log messages than the others.

However, it may not be unusual for systemd and kernel to have more log messages in /var/log/messages. If there was another process that wrote many logs, we would be able to see this in the one-liner's output. However, since our first run did not yield anything useful, we can modify the one-liner to narrow down the output:

```
Jun 26 19:51:10 localhost auditd[550]: Started dispatcher: /sbin/audispd
pid: 562
```

If we look at the format of a messages log entry, we can see that after the process, the log message can be found. To narrow down our search a little bit more, we can add a little bit of the message to our output.

We can do this by changing the cut command's field list to "1,2,5-8". By adding the "-8" after 5, we find that the cut command displays all fields from 5 to 8. This has the effect of including the first three words of each log message in our one-liner:

```
# grep "Jun 26" /var/log/messages | cut -d\  -f1,2,5-8 | sort | uniq -c |
sort -n | tail -30
    64 Jun 26 kernel: 131055 pages RAM
    64 Jun 26 kernel: 5572 pages reserved
    64 Jun 26 kernel: lowmem_reserve[]: 0 462
    77 Jun 26 kernel: [  579]
    79 Jun 26 kernel: Out of memory:
    80 Jun 26 kernel: [<ffffffff810b68f8>] ? ktime_get_ts+0x48/0xe0
```

```
  80 Jun 26 kernel: [<ffffffff81102e03>] ? proc_do_uts_
string+0xe3/0x130
  80 Jun 26 kernel: [<ffffffff8114520e>] oom_kill_process+0x24e/0x3b0
  80 Jun 26 kernel: [<ffffffff81145a36>] out_of_memory+0x4b6/0x4f0
  80 Jun 26 kernel: [<ffffffff8114b579>] __alloc_pages_
nodemask+0xa09/0xb10
  80 Jun 26 kernel: [<ffffffff815dd02d>] dump_header+0x8e/0x214
  80 Jun 26 kernel: [ pid ]
  81 Jun 26 kernel: [<ffffffff8118bc3a>] alloc_pages_vma+0x9a/0x140
  93 Jun 26 kernel: Call Trace:
  93 Jun 26 kernel: [<ffffffff815e19ba>] dump_stack+0x19/0x1b
  93 Jun 26 kernel: [<ffffffff815e97c8>] page_fault+0x28/0x30
  93 Jun 26 kernel: [<ffffffff815ed186>] __do_page_fault+0x156/0x540
  93 Jun 26 kernel: [<ffffffff815ed58a>] do_page_fault+0x1a/0x70
  93 Jun 26 kernel: Free swap
  93 Jun 26 kernel: Hardware name: innotek
  93 Jun 26 kernel: lowmem_reserve[]: 0 0
  93 Jun 26 kernel: Mem-Info:
  93 Jun 26 kernel: Node 0 DMA:
  93 Jun 26 kernel: Node 0 DMA32:
  93 Jun 26 kernel: Node 0 hugepages_total=0
  93 Jun 26 kernel: Swap cache stats:
  93 Jun 26 kernel: Total swap =
 186 Jun 26 kernel: Node 0 DMA
 186 Jun 26 kernel: Node 0 DMA32
 489 Jun 26 kernel: CPU
```

If we also increase the `tail` command to display the last 30 lines, we can see some interesting trends. The first line that is very interesting is the fourth line in the output:

```
  79 Jun 26 kernel: Out of memory:
```

It seems that the `kernel` printed `79` log messages that start with the term "Out of memory". While it may seem a bit obvious to say, it seems that this server may have run out of memory at some point.

The next two interesting lines seem to support this theory as well:

```
  80 Jun 26 kernel: [<ffffffff8114520e>] oom_kill_process+0x24e/0x3b0
  80 Jun 26 kernel: [<ffffffff81145a36>] out_of_memory+0x4b6/0x4f0
```

The first line seems to suggest that the kernel killed a process; the second line once again indicates that there is an *out of memory* situation. Could this system have run out of memory and in doing so killed the Apache process? This seems very likely.

What happens when a Linux system runs out of memory?

On Linux, memory is managed a bit differently from that on other operating systems. When a system is running low on memory, the kernel has a process that is designed to reclaim the used memory; this process is called **out of memory killer (oom-kill)**.

The `oom-kill` process is designed to kill processes that utilize a large amount of memory in order to free this memory for critical system processes. We will cover `oom-kill` in a bit, but first, we should understand how Linux defines out of memory.

Minimum free memory

On Linux, the oom-kill process will be initiated when the amount of free memory is lower than a defined minimum. This minimum is of course a kernel tunable parameter named `vm.min_free_kbytes`. This parameter allows you to set the amount of memory in kilobytes that the system ensures is always available.

When the available memory is below the value of this parameter, the system starts to take action. Before going too far, let's first look at what this value is set at on our system and refresh how memory is managed in Linux.

We can view the current `vm.min_free_kbytes` value with the same `sysctl` command that we used in the previous chapter:

```
# sysctl vm.min_free_kbytes
vm.min_free_kbytes = 11424
```

Currently, the value is `11424` kilobytes or approximately 11 megabytes. This means that our system's free memory must always be greater than 11 megabytes or the system will kick off the oom-kill process. This seems pretty straightforward, but as we know from *Chapter 4, Troubleshooting Performance Issues*, the way Linux manages memory is not necessarily that easy:

```
# free
              total       used       free     shared    buffers cached
Mem:         243788     230012      13776         60          0 2272
-/+ buffers/cache:      227740      16048
Swap:       1081340     231908     849432
```

If we run the `free` command on this system, we can see the current memory usage and how much is available. Before going too far, we will break down this output to refresh our understanding of how Linux uses memory.

```
              total        used        free      shared    buffers   cached
Mem:         243788      230012       13776          60          0 2272
```

In the first line, we can see that the system has a total of 243MB of physical memory. We can see in the second column that 230MB of that is currently used, and the third column shows that 13MB is unused. It is this unused value that the system is measuring in order to determine whether or not the minimum required memory is currently free.

This is important because if we remember from *Chapter 4, Troubleshooting Performance Issues*, there is a second "memory free" value that we use to determine how much memory is available.

```
              total        used        free      shared    buffers cached
Mem:         243788      230012       13776          60          0 2272
-/+ buffers/cache:        227740       16048
```

On the second line of `free`, we can see the amount of used and free memory when the system accounts for the memory used by the cache. As we learned earlier, the Linux system very aggressively caches files and filesystem attributes. All of this cache is stored in memory, and we can see that in the instant when this `free` command was run, we had 2,272 KB of memory used by cache.

When the free memory (not including cache) starts to get close to the `min_free_kbytes` value, the system will start reclaiming some of the memory used for the cache. This is designed to allow the system to cache what it can, but during low memory conditions, this cache becomes disposable in order to prevent the oom-kill process from starting:

```
Swap:       1081340      231908      849432
```

The third line of the `free` command brings us to another important step in Linux's memory management: swapping. As we can see from the preceding line, when this `free` command was executed, the system swapped roughly 231MB of data from the physical memory to the swap device.

This is what we would expect to see on a system that has been running low on available memory. When `free` memory starts to become scarce, the system will start taking memory objects that are in the physical memory and push them to the swap memory.

How aggressively the system starts to perform these swapping activities depends greatly on the value defined in the kernel parameter called `vm.swappiness`:

```
$ sysctl vm.swappiness
vm.swappiness = 30
```

On our system, the `swappiness` value is currently set to `30`. This tunable parameter accepts values between 0 and 100, with 100 allowing for the most aggressive swapping policy.

When the `swappiness` value is lower, the system will prefer to retain memory objects in the physical memory for as long as possible before moving them to the swap device.

A quick recap

Before going into oom-kill, let's recap what happens when the memory starts to get low on a Linux system. The system will first try to free memory objects used for disk cache and move the used memory to the swap device. If the system is unable to free an adequate amount of memory through the two previously mentioned processes, the kernel kicks off the oom-kill process.

How oom-kill works

As mentioned earlier, the oom-kill process is a process launched when free memory is low. This process is designed to identify processes that are utilizing large amounts of memory and are not critical to the system operation.

So, how does oom-kill determine this? Well, it's actually determined by the kernel and is constantly updated.

We discussed in the earlier chapters how every running process on a system has a folder within the `/proc` file system. The `kernel` maintains this folder, and within it, there are many interesting files.

```
# ls -la /proc/6689/oom_*
-rw-r--r--. 1 root root 0 Jun 29 15:23 /proc/6689/oom_adj
-r--r--r--. 1 root root 0 Jun 29 15:23 /proc/6689/oom_score
-rw-r--r--. 1 root root 0 Jun 29 15:23 /proc/6689/oom_score_adj
```

The three previously mentioned files are specifically relevant to the oom-kill process and how likely each process is to be killed. The first file that we are going to look at is the `oom_score` file:

```
# cat /proc/6689/oom_score
40
```

If we `cat` this file, we see that it simply contains a number. However, this number is very important to the oom-kill process as this number is process 6689's OOM Score.

The OOM Score is a value that the `kernel` assigns to a process that determines whether the corresponding process is a high or low priority for oom-kill. The higher the score, the more likely the process is to be killed. When the kernel assigns this process a value, it bases the value on the amount of memory and swap that the process uses as well as its criticality to the system.

You may be asking yourself, *I wonder if there is a way to adjust the oom score for my processes.* The answer to this question is yes, there is! This is where the other two files `oom_adj` and `oom_score_adj` come into play. These two files allow you to adjust the oom score of a process, allowing you to control the likelihood of the process being killed.

Currently, the `oom_adj` file is to be depreciated in lieu of `oom_score_adj`. For this reason, we will simply focus on the `oom_score_adj` file.

Adjusting the oom score

The `oom_score_adj` file supports values from -1000 to 1000, where the higher value will increase the likelihood of oom-kill selecting the process. Let's see what happens to our oom score when we add an adjustment of 800 to our process:

```
# echo "800" > /proc/6689/oom_score_adj
# cat /proc/6689/oom_score
840
```

Simply by changing the contents to 800, the kernel detected this adjustment and added 800 to the oom score for this process. If this system were to run out of memory in the near future, this process would absolutely be killed by oom-kill.

If we were to change this value to -1000, this would essentially exclude the process from oom-kill.

Determining whether our process was killed by oom-kill

Now that we know what happens when a system runs low on memory, let's take a closer look at what exactly happened to our system. To do this, we will use `less` to read the `/var/log/messages` file and look for the first instance of the "`kernel: Out of memory`" message:

```
Jun 26 00:53:39 blog kernel: Out of memory: Kill process 5664
(processor) score 265 or sacrifice child
```

Interestingly enough, the first instance of an "Out of memory" log message is 20 hours before our Apache process was killed. To add to this, the process killed is a very familiar process, the "processor" cronjob from the previous chapter.

This single log entry can actually tell us quite a bit about that process and why oom-kill selected this process. On the first line, we can see that the kernel has given the processor process a score of 265. While not the highest score, we have seen that the score of 265 is very likely to be higher than that of most processes running at this time.

This seems to suggest that the processor job was utilizing quite a bit of memory at this time. Let's keep looking through this file to see what else may have been happening on this system:

```
Jun 26 00:54:31 blog kernel: Out of memory: Kill process 5677
(processor) score 273 or sacrifice child
```

Just a bit further down the log file, we can see yet another instance of the processor process being killed. It seems that every time this job runs, this system is running out of memory.

In the interest of time, let's jump down to the 21st hour to take a closer look at the time that our Apache process being killed:

```
Jun 26 21:12:54 localhost kernel: Out of memory: Kill process 2249
(httpd) score 7 or sacrifice child

Jun 26 21:12:54 localhost kernel: Killed process 2249 (httpd)
total-vm:462648kB, anon-rss:436kB, file-rss:8kB

Jun 26 21:12:54 localhost kernel: httpd invoked oom-killer:
gfp_mask=0x200da, order=0, oom_score_adj=0
```

It seems that the messages log had our answer all along. From the preceding few lines, we can see process 2249, which happens to be our Apache server process id:

```
Jun 26 21:12:55 blog.example.com systemd[1]: httpd.service: main
process exited, code=killed, status=9/KILL
```

Here, we see that systemd detected that the process was killed at 21:12:55. Further, we can see from the messages log that oom-kill targeted this process at 21:12:54. At this point, there is no doubt that the process was killed by oom-kill.

Why did the system run out of memory?

At this point, we were able to determine that the Apache service was killed by the system when it ran out of memory. Unfortunately, oom-kill is not the root cause of the issue, but rather a symptom. While it is the reason that the Apache service is down, if we simply restarted the process and did nothing else, the issue may reoccur.

At this point, we need to identify what caused the system to run out of memory in the first place. To do this, let's take a look at the entire list of Out of memory messages in the messages log file:

```
# grep "Out of memory" /var/log/messages* | cut -d\  -f1,2,10,12 |
uniq -c
    38 /var/log/messages:Jun 28 process (processor)
     1 /var/log/messages:Jun 28 process (application)
    10 /var/log/messages:Jun 28 process (processor)
     1 /var/log/messages-20150615:Jun 10 process (python)
     1 /var/log/messages-20150628:Jun 22 process (processor)
    47 /var/log/messages-20150628:Jun 26 process (processor)
    32 /var/log/messages-20150628:Jun 26 process (httpd)
```

Using the cut and uniq -c commands again, we can see an interesting trend in the messages log. We can see that the kernel has invoked oom-kill quite a few times. We can see that even today the system kicked off the oom-kill process.

The first thing that we should do now is to figure out just how much memory this system has.

```
# free -m
             total       used       free     shared    buffers
cached
Mem:           238        206         32          0          0
2
-/+ buffers/cache:        203         34
Swap:         1055        428        627
```

Using the free command, we can see that the system has 238 MB of physical memory and 1055 MB of swap. However, we can also see that only 34 MB of memory is free and that the system has swapped 428 MB of physical memory.

It's very obvious that for the current workload that this system is under, it simply does not have enough memory allocated.

If we look back at the processes that are targeted by oom-kill, we can see an interesting trend:

```
# grep "Out of memory" /var/log/messages* | cut -d\  -f10,12 |
sort | uniq -c
      1 process (application)
     32 process (httpd)
    118 process (processor)
      1 process (python)
```

Here, it is very obvious that the two processes that were killed the most often were httpd and processor. What we learned earlier is that oom-kill identifies which processes to kill on the basis of the amount of memory that they are using. This means that these two processes are using the most memory on the system, but just how much memory are they using?

```
# ps -eo rss,size,cmd | grep processor
    0    340 /bin/sh -c /opt/myapp/bin/processor --debug --config
/opt/myapp/conf/config.yml > /dev/null
130924 240520 /opt/myapp/bin/processor --debug --config
/opt/myapp/conf/config.yml
  964    336 grep --color=auto processor
```

Using the ps command to specifically display the **rss** and **size** fields, which we learned in *Chapter 4, Troubleshooting Performance Issues*, we can see that the processor job is using 130 MB of resident memory and 240 MB of virtual memory.

If the system only has 238 MB of physical memory and the process is using 240 MB of virtual memory, eventually, this system is going to run low on physical memory.

Resolving the issue in the long-term and short-term

Issues such as the one discussed in this chapter can be a bit tricky, as they generally have two paths to resolution. There is a long-term fix and a short-term fix; both are necessary, but one is only temporary.

Long-term resolution

For the long-term resolution of this issue, we really have two options. We could increase the server's physical memory to provide both Apache and Processor adequate memory for their tasks. Alternatively, we could move the processor to another server.

Since we know that this server has frequently killed the Apache service and the `processor` job, it is likely that the memory on the system is simply too low for it to perform both these roles. By moving the `processor` job (and likely the custom app that it is part of) to another system, we would be moving the workload to a dedicated server.

On the basis of the memory usage of the processor, it may also be worth increasing the memory on the new server as well. As it seems, the `processor` job utilizes enough memory to cause out of memory conditions on a low memory server such as the one that it is on now.

Determining which long-term solution is best frankly depends on the environment and the applications causing the system to run out of memory. In some cases, it may be better to simply increase the server's memory and call it a day.

This task is very easy in virtual and cloud environments, but it may not always be the best answer. Determining which answer is better truly depends on the environment that you are working with.

Short-term resolution

Let's say hypothetically that both the long-term resolutions would take several days to implement. As of right now, the Apache service is still down on our system. This means that our company blog is also still down; to resolve the issue momentarily, we need to bring Apache back up.

However, we shouldn't just simply restart Apache with the `systemctl` command. Before bringing anything up, we should actually first reboot the server.

When most Linux administrators hear the words "let's reboot" they get a sinking feeling in their stomach. This is because, as Linux systems administrators, we very rarely need to reboot our systems. We have been told that rebooting Linux servers outside of updating the kernel is a naughty thing to do.

For the most part, we are correct in believing that rebooting a server is not the right solution. However, I consider the system running out of memory to be a special case.

It is my opinion that when oom-kill is launched the system in question should be rebooted before being fully restored to its normal state.

The reason I say this is that the oom-kill process can kill any process, including critical system processes. While the oom-kill process does log via syslog what processes were killed, the syslog daemon is just another process on the system that can be killed by oom-kill.

Even if oom-kill did not kill the syslog process in situations where oom-kill has killed many different processes, it can be tricky to ensure each one is up and running as it should be. This is particularly true when the person working on the issue is less experienced.

While you can spend time determining what processes are running and ensure that you restart each process, it is much faster and arguably safer to simply reboot the server. As you know that upon booting, every process that is defined to start will be started.

While not every system administrator would agree with this opinion, I believe that it is the best approach to ensure that the system is in a stable state. It's important to remember though that this is only a short-term solution, upon rebooting, unless something changes, the system can simply run out of memory again.

For our situation, it would be best to disable the `processor` job until the server's memory can be increased or the job can be moved to a dedicated system. However, that may not be acceptable in all situations. Like the long-term resolution, preventing this from happening again is situational and depends on the environment that you are managing.

Since we assume that the short-term solution is the right solution for our example, we will proceed to reboot the system:

```
# reboot
Connection to 127.0.0.1 closed by remote host.
```

Once the system is back online, we can validate that Apache is running with the `systemctl` command:

```
# systemctl status httpd
httpd.service - The Apache HTTP Server
   Loaded: loaded (/usr/lib/systemd/system/httpd.service; enabled)
   Active: active (running) since Wed 2015-07-01 15:37:22 UTC; 1min 29s
ago
 Main PID: 1012 (httpd)
   Status: "Total requests: 0; Current requests/sec: 0; Current traffic:
0 B/sec"
   CGroup: /system.slice/httpd.service
           ├─1012 /usr/sbin/httpd -DFOREGROUND
           ├─1439 /usr/sbin/httpd -DFOREGROUND
           ├─1443 /usr/sbin/httpd -DFOREGROUND
           ├─1444 /usr/sbin/httpd -DFOREGROUND
```

```
├─1445 /usr/sbin/httpd -DFOREGROUND
└─1449 /usr/sbin/httpd -DFOREGROUND
```

```
Jul 01 15:37:22 blog.example.com systemd[1]: Started The Apache HTTP
Server.
```

If we run `free` again on this system, we can see that the memory utilization is much lower, at least until now:

```
# free -m
             total       used       free     shared    buffers
cached
Mem:           238        202         35          4          0
86
-/+ buffers/cache:        115        122
Swap:         1055          0       1055
```

Summary

In this chapter, we used our troubleshooting skills to identify both the issue affecting the company blog and the root cause of this issue. We were able to use the skills and techniques that we learned in earlier chapters to determine that the Apache service was down. We also identified that the root cause of this issue was the system running out of memory.

We could see by investigating the log files that the two processes using the most memory on the system were Apache and a custom application named `processor`. Furthermore, by identifying these processes, we were able to make a long-term recommendation to prevent this issue from re-occurring.

On top of all this, we learned quite a bit about what happens when Linux systems run out of memory.

In the next chapter, we will put everything you have learned this far to the test by performing a root cause analysis of an unresponsive system.

12
Root Cause Analysis of an Unexpected Reboot

In this last chapter, we will put the troubleshooting methods and skills that you learned in previous chapters to the test. We will perform a root cause analysis of one of the most difficult real-world scenarios: an unexpected reboot.

As we discussed in *Chapter 1*, *Troubleshooting Best Practices*, a root cause analysis is a bit more involved than simply troubleshooting and resolving an issue. In Enterprise environments, you will find that every issue that causes a significant impact will require a root cause analysis (RCA). The reason for this is because Enterprise environments often have well-established processes of how incidents are supposed to be handled.

In general, when a significant incident occurs, the organization impacted by it wants to avoid it from happening again. You can see this in many industries even outside of technical environments.

As we discussed in *Chapter 1*, *Troubleshooting Best Practices*, a useful RCA has the following characteristics:

- The problem as it was reported
- The actual root cause of the problem
- A timeline of events and actions taken
- Any key data points
- A plan of action to prevent the incident from re-occurring

For today's issue, we will use an incident to build a sample root cause analysis document. To do this, we will use the information gathering and troubleshooting steps you learned in previous chapters. While doing all of this, you will also learn to handle unexpected reboots, one of the worst incidents to identify the root cause for.

The reason unexpected reboots are difficult is that when the system reboots you often lose the information you need to identify the root cause of the issue. As we have seen in previous chapters, the more data we can collect during an issue, the more likely we are to identify the cause of the issue.

The information lost during reboots can often be the difference between identifying the root cause and not identifying the root cause.

A late night alert

As we have been progressing through the chapters and solving many issues for our recent employer, we have also been gaining their confidence in our abilities. Recently, we were even placed on the **on call** rotation, which means that if issues occur after hours an alert will be sent to our phone by SMS.

Of course, the first night of being on call we get an alert; the alert is not a good one.

ALERT: blog.example.com is no longer responding to ICMP Pings

When we were added to the on call rotation, our team lead informed us that any major incident that occurs after hours must also have an RCA performed. The reason for this is so that others in our group can learn and understand what we did to resolve the issue and how to prevent it from happening again.

As we discussed earlier one of the key components to a useful RCA is listing when things happen. A major event in our timeline is when we received the alert; based on our SMS message we can see that we received the alert on July 05th, 2015 at 01:52 or rather; 1:52 A.M. on the fifth of July (welcome to on call!).

Identifying the issue

From the alert, we can see that our monitoring system was unable to perform ICMP pings to our company blog server. The first thing we should do is determine whether or not we can ping the server:

```
$ ping blog.example.com
PING blog.example.com (192.168.33.11): 56 data bytes
64 bytes from 192.168.33.11: icmp_seq=0 ttl=64 time=0.832 ms
64 bytes from 192.168.33.11: icmp_seq=1 ttl=64 time=0.382 ms
64 bytes from 192.168.33.11: icmp_seq=2 ttl=64 time=0.240 ms
64 bytes from 192.168.33.11: icmp_seq=3 ttl=64 time=0.234 ms
^C
```

```
--- blog.example.com ping statistics ---
4 packets transmitted, 4 packets received, 0.0% packet loss
round-trip min/avg/max/stddev = 0.234/0.422/0.832/0.244 ms
```

It seems that we are able to ping the server in question, so maybe this is a false alert? Just in case, let's attempt to log in to the system:

```
$ ssh 192.168.33.11 -l vagrant
vagrant@192.168.33.11's password:
$
```

Looks like we were able to log in and the system is up and running; let's start taking a look around to check whether we can identify any issues.

As covered in a previous chapter, the first command we always run is w:

```
$ w
01:59:46 up 9 min,  1 user,   load average: 0.00, 0.01, 0.02
USER     TTY         LOGIN@   IDLE   JCPU   PCPU WHAT
vagrant  pts/0       01:59    2.00s  0.03s  0.01s w
```

In this instance, this little habit has actually paid off quite well. With the output of the w command, we can see that this server has only been up for 9 minutes. It seems our monitoring system could not ping our server because it was rebooting.

 We should take note that we were able to identify that the server was rebooted after logging in; this will be a critical event in our timeline.

Did someone reboot this server?

While we have just identified the root cause of the alert, this is not the root cause of the issue. We need to identify why the server rebooted. It's not often (at least shouldn't be) that servers reboot themselves; sometimes it can simply be someone performing maintenance on this server without letting others know. We can see if anyone has been logged into this server recently using the last command:

```
$ last
vagrant  pts/0          192.168.33.1    Sun Jul  5 01:59   still logged in
joe  pts/1          192.168.33.1    Sat Jun  6 18:49 - 21:37  (02:48)
bob  pts/0          10.0.2.2         Sat Jun  6 18:16 - 21:37  (03:21)
billy  pts/0          10.0.2.2         Sat Jun  6 17:09 - 18:14  (01:05)
doug  pts/0          10.0.2.2         Sat Jun  6 15:26 - 17:08  (01:42)
```

The last command's output starts with the latest logins at the top. This data is pulled from /var/log/wtmp, which is used to store login details. At the end of the last command's output, we see the following line:

wtmp begins Mon Jun 21 23:39:24 2014

This tells us how far back the wtmp log file goes; a pretty useful piece of information. If we want to see a specific number of logins, we could simply add the −n flag followed by the number of logins we wish to see.

This can be pretty useful in general; however, since we don't know how many logins there have been lately on this machine we will just use the default.

From the output we received, we can see that there haven't been any logins on this server recently. Outside of someone physically pressing the power button or unplugging this system, we can assume that a person did not reboot the server.

[This is another fact/event that we should use in our timeline.]

What do the logs tell us?

Since a person didn't reboot this server, our next hypothesis is that this server was rebooted by either a software or hardware problem. The next logical step for us is to look through the system log files to determine what happened:

01:59:46 up 9 min, 1 user, load average: 0.00, 0.01, 0.02

In the output of w, we see that the server has been up for 9 minutes and that the time of that command execution was 01:59. Since we are going to look through the logs on this system, we should start looking at a time window of 01:45 to 01:52.

The first log we should look through is the /var/log/messages log. By default, on Red Hat based systems this log file contains all the info and higher log messages. This means that if we want to find information about why we rebooted, then this is the prime location.

The following snippet was grabbed using the less command to read /var/log/ messages:

Jul 5 01:48:01 localhost auditd[560]: Audit daemon is low on disk space for logging

Jul 5 01:48:01 localhost auditd[560]: Audit daemon is suspending logging due to low disk space.

Jul 5 01:50:02 localhost watchdog[608]: loadavg 25 9 3 is higher than the given threshold 24 18 12!

Jul 5 01:50:02 localhost watchdog[608]: shutting down the system because of error -3

Jul 5 01:50:12 localhost rsyslogd: [origin software="rsyslogd" swVersion="7.4.7" x-pid="593" x-info="http://www.rsyslog.com"] exiting on signal 15.

Jul 5 01:50:32 localhost systemd: Time has been changed

Jul 5 01:50:32 localhost NetworkManager[594]: <info> dhclient started with pid 722

Jul 5 01:50:32 localhost NetworkManager[594]: <info> Activation (enp0s3) Stage 3 of 5 (IP Configure Start) complete.

Jul 5 01:50:32 localhost vboxadd-service: Starting VirtualBox Guest Addition service [OK]

Jul 5 01:50:32 localhost systemd: Started LSB: VirtualBox Additions service.

Jul 5 01:50:32 localhost dhclient[722]: Internet Systems Consortium DHCP Client 4.2.5

Jul 5 01:50:32 localhost dhclient[722]: Copyright 2004-2013 Internet Systems Consortium.

Jul 5 01:50:32 localhost dhclient[722]: All rights reserved.

Jul 5 01:50:32 localhost dhclient[722]: For info, please visit https://www.isc.org/software/dhcp/

Jul 5 01:50:32 localhost dhclient[722]:

Jul 5 01:50:32 localhost NetworkManager: Internet Systems Consortium DHCP Client 4.2.5

Jul 5 01:50:32 localhost NetworkManager: Copyright 2004-2013 Internet Systems Consortium.

Jul 5 01:50:32 localhost NetworkManager: All rights reserved.

Jul 5 01:50:32 localhost NetworkManager: For info, please visit https://www.isc.org/software/dhcp/

Jul 5 01:50:32 localhost NetworkManager[594]: <info> (enp0s3): DHCPv4 state changed nbi -> preinit

Jul 5 01:50:32 localhost dhclient[722]: Listening on LPF/enp0s3/08:00:27:20:5d:4b

Jul 5 01:50:32 localhost dhclient[722]: Sending on   LPF/enp0s3/08:00:27:20:5d:4b

Jul 5 01:50:32 localhost dhclient[722]: Sending on   Socket/fallback

Jul 5 01:50:32 localhost dhclient[722]: DHCPREQUEST on enp0s3 to 255.255.255.255 port 67 (xid=0x3ae55b57)

Since there is quite a bit of information here, let's break down what we see a little bit.

The first task is finding a log message that is clearly written on boot. By identifying a log message that is written on boot, we will be able to identify which logs were written prior to and after the reboot. We will also be able to identify a boot time for our root cause documentation:

```
Jul  5 01:50:12 localhost rsyslogd: [origin software="rsyslogd"
swVersion="7.4.7" x-pid="593" x-info="http://www.rsyslog.com"] exiting on
signal 15.
Jul  5 01:50:32 localhost systemd: Time has been changed
Jul  5 01:50:32 localhost NetworkManager[594]: <info> dhclient started
with pid 722
Jul  5 01:50:32 localhost NetworkManager[594]: <info> Activation (enp0s3)
Stage 3 of 5 (IP Configure Start) complete.
```

The first log entry that looks promising is the message from `NetworkManager` at `01:50:32`. This message is stating that the `NetworkManager` service has started `dhclient`.

The `dhclient` process is used to make DHCP requests and configure network settings based on the reply. This process is generally only called when the network is being reconfigured or at boot time:

```
Jul  5 01:50:12 localhost rsyslogd: [origin software="rsyslogd"
swVersion="7.4.7" x-pid="593" x-info="http://www.rsyslog.com"] exiting on
signal 15.
```

If we look at the preceding line, we can see that at 01:50:12, the `rsyslogd` process is `exiting on signal 15`. This means, the `rsyslogd` process was sent a signal to terminate, a pretty standard process during shutdown.

We can determine that at 01:50:12 the server was in the shutdown process and at 01:50:32 the server was in the boot process. This means, we should be looking at everything before 01:50:12 to determine why the system rebooted.

 The shutdown time and boot time will also be needed for our root cause timelines.

From the preceding captured logs, we can see two processes wrote to `/var/log/messages` before 01:50; the `auditd` and watchdog processes.

```
Jul  5 01:48:01 localhost auditd[560]: Audit daemon is low on disk space
for logging
Jul  5 01:48:01 localhost auditd[560]: Audit daemon is suspending logging
due to low disk space.
```

Let's first take a look at the `auditd` process. We can see a "low on disk space" message in the first line. Could our system have run into an issue due to low disk space? It's possible, and it is something we can check right now:

```
# df -h
Filesystem               Size  Used Avail Use% Mounted on
/dev/mapper/centos-root   39G   39G   32M 100% /
devtmpfs                 491M     0  491M   0% /dev
tmpfs                    498M     0  498M   0% /dev/shm
tmpfs                    498M  6.5M  491M   2% /run
tmpfs                    498M     0  498M   0% /sys/fs/cgroup
/dev/sda1                497M  104M  394M  21% /boot
```

It does seem like the filesystem is at 100 percent but something like that in itself would not typically cause a reboot. Considering the second `auditd` message displays **the daemon is suspending logging**; this would also not seem like a reboot procedure. Let's keep looking and see what else we can identify:

```
Jul  5 01:50:02 localhost watchdog[608]: loadavg 25 9 3 is higher than
the given threshold 24 18 12!
Jul  5 01:50:02 localhost watchdog[608]: shutting down the system because
of error -3
```

The next two messages from the `watchdog` process are interesting. The first one states that the `loadavg` for the server is higher than a specified threshold. The second message is very interesting as it specifically states, "shutting down the system".

Could the `watchdog` process have rebooted this server? Maybe, but the first question is, what is the `watchdog` process?

Learning about new processes and services

It's not uncommon when digging through the `messages` log to find a process you have never used or seen before:

```
# ps -eo cmd | sort | uniq | wc -l
115
```

Even on our basic example system, there are 115 unique commands in the process list. This is especially true when you add in a newer release such as Red Hat Enterprise Linux 7 (newer at the time of writing this). Each new release brings in new functionality, which might even mean new processes running by default. It's very hard to keep up with it all.

For the sake of our example, watchdog is one of those cases. At this point, outside of inferring from the name that it watches things, we have no idea what this process does. So how do we learn more about it? Well, we either Google it, or man it:

```
$ man watchdog

NAME

        watchdog - a software watchdog daemon


SYNOPSIS

        watchdog [-F|--foreground] [-f|--force] [-c filename|--config-file
filename] [-v|--verbose] [-s|--sync] [-b|--softboot] [-q|--no-action]


DESCRIPTION

        The  Linux  kernel  can  reset  the system if serious problems
are detected.  This can be implemented via special watchdog hardware, or
via a slightly less reliable software-only watchdog inside the kernel.
Either way, there needs to be a daemon that tells the kernel the system
is working fine. If the daemon stops doing that, the system is reset.


        watchdog is such a daemon. It opens /dev/watchdog, and keeps
writing to it often enough to keep the kernel from resetting, at least
once per minute. Each write delays the reboot time another minute. After
a minute  of  inactivity the watchdog hardware will cause the reset. In
the case of the software watchdog the ability to reboot will depend on
the state of the machines and interrupts.


        The watchdog daemon can be stopped without causing a reboot if the
device /dev/watchdog is closed correctly, unless your kernel is compiled
with the CONFIG_WATCHDOG_NOWAYOUT option enabled.
```

Based on the man page, we have identified that the watchdog service is actually used to determine whether the server is healthy. If the watchdog is unable to do this, it might reboot the server:

```
Jul  5 01:50:02 localhost watchdog[608]: shutting down the system because
of error -3
```

It seems from this log message that the watchdog software is the one that caused the reboot. Could it be that watchdog rebooted the system because the filesystems are full?

If we go further down the man page, we will see another piece of useful information, as follows:

```
TESTS
        The watchdog daemon does several tests to check the system status:

        ·   Is the process table full?

        ·   Is there enough free memory?

        ·   Are some files accessible?

        ·   Have some files changed within a given interval?

        ·   Is the average work load too high?
```

On the last "test" in this list, it states that the watchdog daemon can check whether the average work load is too high:

```
Jul  5 01:50:02 localhost watchdog[608]: loadavg 25 9 3 is higher than
the given threshold 24 18 12!
```

Given the man page and the preceding log message, it seems that watchdog didn't reboot the server because of the filesystem, but rather due to the load average of the server.

[Before going further, let's note that at 01:50:02 the watchdog process kicked off the reboot.]

What caused the high load average?

While we have identified what rebooted the server, we still have not gotten to the root cause of the issue. We still need to figure out what caused the high load average. Unfortunately, this would classify as information that is lost during a reboot.

If the system was still experiencing a high load average, we would simply be able to use top or ps to figure out which processes are using the most CPU time. Once the system was rebooted however, any process that was causing a high load average would have been restarted.

Unless these processes started causing a high load average again, we have no way of identifying the source.

```
$ w
 02:13:07 up  23 min,  1 user,  load average: 0.00, 0.01, 0.05
USER     TTY          LOGIN@   IDLE   JCPU   PCPU WHAT
vagrant  pts/0        01:59    3.00s  0.26s  0.10s sshd: vagrant [priv]
```

However, we are able to identify when the load average started to increase and how high it went. This information might be useful as we investigate further, as we can use it to identify what time things started to go wrong.

To look at a historical view of the load average, we can use the `sar` command:

```
$ sar
```

Lucky for us, it seems the `sar` commands collection interval is set to every 2 minutes. The default is 10 minutes, which means we would normally see a line for every 10 minutes:

```
01:42:01 AM    all    0.01    0.00    0.06    0.00    0.00   99.92
01:44:01 AM    all    0.01    0.00    0.06    0.00    0.00   99.93
01:46:01 AM    all    0.01    0.00    0.06    0.00    0.00   99.93
01:48:01 AM    all   33.49    0.00    2.14    0.00    0.00   64.37
01:50:05 AM    all   87.80    0.00   12.19    0.00    0.00    0.01
Average:       all    3.31    0.00    0.45    0.00    0.00   96.24


01:50:23 AM         LINUX RESTART


01:52:01 AM    CPU   %user   %nice  %system  %iowait  %steal  %idle
01:54:01 AM    all    0.01    0.00    0.06    0.00    0.00   99.93
01:56:01 AM    all    0.01    0.00    0.05    0.00    0.00   99.94
01:58:01 AM    all    0.01    0.00    0.05    0.00    0.00   99.94
02:00:01 AM    all    0.03    0.00    0.10    0.00    0.00   99.87
```

Looking at the output, we can see that at 01:46, this system has hardly any CPU usage. However, starting at 01:48, there was a 33 percent utilization of the CPU in the user space.

It also seems that at 01:50, sar was able to capture the CPU utilization that was being used at 99.99 percent, with 87.8 percent being used by the user, and 12.19 percent being used by the system.

The above are all good facts to use during our root
cause summary.

With this, we now know that our issue started sometime between `01:44` and `01:46`,
we can see this from the CPU usage.

Let's take a look at the load average with the `-q` flag to see if the load averages match
the CPU utilization:

```
# sar -q
```

Again, we can narrow events down even further:

01:42:01 AM	0	145	0.00	0.01	0.02	0
01:44:01 AM	0	145	0.00	0.01	0.02	0
01:46:01 AM	0	144	0.00	0.01	0.02	0
01:48:01 AM	14	164	4.43	1.12	0.39	0
01:50:05 AM	37	189	25.19	9.14	3.35	0
Average:	1	147	0.85	0.30	0.13	0

01:50:23 AM	LINUX RESTART

01:52:01 AM	runq-sz	plist-sz	ldavg-1	ldavg-5	ldavg-15	blocked
01:54:01 AM	0	143	0.01	0.04	0.02	0
01:56:01 AM	1	138	0.00	0.02	0.02	0
01:58:01 AM	0	138	0.00	0.01	0.02	0
02:00:01 AM	0	141	0.00	0.01	0.02	0

With the **load average** measurements, we can see that all was quiet at `01:46` even
though the CPU was high. However, in the next run at `01:48`, we could see the **run
queue** at 14 and the 1 minute load average at 4.

What are the run queue and load average?

Since we are looking at the run queue and load average, let's take a second to get an
understanding of what these values mean.

In a very basic concept, the run queue value shows the number of processes in an
active state waiting to be executed.

For more details, let's think about a CPU and how it works. A single CPU is able to perform only one task at a time. Most servers these days have multiple cores and sometimes multiple processors per server. On Linux, each core and thread (for hyper threaded CPUs) are seen as a single CPU.

Each one of these CPUs is able to execute one task at a time. If we had two CPU servers, our server could execute two tasks at a time.

Let's assume for a second that our 2 CPU system needs to execute four tasks at the same time. The system can execute two of those tasks but the other two tasks must wait until the first two are finished. When situations like this happen, the processes that are waiting are placed into a "run queue". When the system has processes in the run queue, they will be prioritized and executed once CPU's become available.

In our `sar` capture, we can see the run queue value was 14 at 01:48; this means that at that moment, there were 14 tasks waiting in the run queue for CPU.

Load average

The load average is a bit different from the run queue, but not very. The load average is the average run queue value over a given amount of time. In our preceding example, we can see `ldavg-1` (this column is the average run queue length for the last minute).

The run queue value and the 1-minute load average can be different because the run queue value, as reported by `sar` is at the time of execution where the 1-minute load average is the run queue averaged over 60 seconds.

```
01:46:01 AM        0      144      0.00      0.01      0.02       0
01:48:01 AM       14      164      4.43      1.12      0.39       0
01:50:05 AM       37      189     25.19      9.14      3.35       0
```

A single capture of a high run queue might not necessarily mean there is an issue, especially if the 1-minute load average is not high. However, in our example, we can see that at 01:48, our run queue had 14 tasks in queue, and at 01:50, our run queue had 37 tasks in queue.

On top of that, we can see that at 01:50, our 1-minute load average was 25.

Given the overlap with the CPU utilization, it seems that roughly around 01:46 - 01:48, something happened to cause a high CPU utilization. Along with this high utilization, there were also a lot of tasks that needed to be executed but could not be.

We should take a second and note down the times and values we saw in `sar`, as these will be necessary details for the root cause summary.

Investigating the filesystem being full

Earlier, we noticed that the filesystem was 100 percent full. Unfortunately, the version of `sysstat` we have installed doesn't capture disk space usage. A useful thing to identify is when the filesystem filled up as compared to when our run queue started to increase:

```
Jul  5 01:48:01 localhost auditd[560]: Audit daemon is low on disk space
for logging
Jul  5 01:48:01 localhost auditd[560]: Audit daemon is suspending logging
due to low disk space.
```

From the log messages we saw earlier, we could see the `auditd` process identified the low disk space at `01:48`. This is extremely close to the time our run queue spike was seen.

This is building towards a hypothesis that the problem's root cause was a filesystem filling up, which caused a process to either launch many CPU intensive tasks or block the CPU for other tasks.

While this is a sound theory, we have to prove it to be true. One way we can get closer to proving this is to identify what is utilizing the majority of disk space on this system:

```
# du -k / | sort -nk 1 | tail -25
64708   /var/cache/yum/x86_64/7/epel
67584   /var/cache/yum/x86_64/7/base
68668   /usr/lib/firmware
75888   /usr/lib/modules/3.10.0-123.el7.x86_64/kernel/drivers
80172   /boot
95384   /usr/share/locale
103548  /usr/lib/locale
105900  /usr/lib/modules/3.10.0-123.el7.x86_64/kernel
116080  /usr/lib/modules
116080  /usr/lib/modules/3.10.0-123.el7.x86_64
148276  /usr/bin
162980  /usr/lib64
```

```
183640    /var/cache/yum
183640    /var/cache/yum/x86_64
183640    /var/cache/yum/x86_64/7
184396    /var/cache
285240    /usr/share
317628    /var
328524    /usr/lib
1040924   /usr
2512948   /opt/myapp/logs
34218392  /opt/myapp/queue
36731428  /opt/myapp
36755164  /opt
38222996  /
```

The preceding one-liner is a very useful method for identifying which directories or files are using the most space.

The du command

The preceding one-liner uses the `sort` command, which you learned about in *Chapter 11, Recovering from Common Failures* to sort the output of du. The du command is a very useful command that can estimate the amount of space a given directory is using.

For example, if we wanted to know how much space the /var/tmp directory was using, we could easily identify that with the following du command:

```
# du -h /var/tmp
0    /var/tmp/systemd-private-Wu4ixe/tmp
0    /var/tmp/systemd-private-Wu4ixe
0    /var/tmp/systemd-private-pAN90Q/tmp
0    /var/tmp/systemd-private-pAN90Q
160K /var/tmp
```

A useful attribute of du is that, by default, it will not only list /var/tmp but also the directories within it. We can see that there are a few directories with nothing in them but the /var/tmp/ directory contains 160 kb of data.

```
# du -h /var/tmp/
0    /var/tmp/systemd-private-Wu4ixe/tmp
0    /var/tmp/systemd-private-Wu4ixe
```

```
0    /var/tmp/systemd-private-pAN90Q/tmp

0    /var/tmp/systemd-private-pAN90Q

4.0K    /var/tmp/somedir

164K    /var/tmp/
```

> It is important to know that the size of /var/tmp is the size of the contents within /var/tmp, which includes the other subdirectories.
>
> To illustrate the preceding point, I created a directory named "somedir" and put a 4 kb file within it. We can see from this subsequent du command that the /var/tmp directory is now showing 164 kb used.

The du command has quite a number of flags that allow us to change how it outputs disk usage. In the preceding examples, the values are being printed in a human-readable format, thanks to the -h flag. In the one liner, these values are being represented in kilobytes due to the -k flag:

```
2512948   /opt/myapp/logs

34218392  /opt/myapp/queue

36731428  /opt/myapp

36755164  /opt

38222996  /
```

If we go back to the one-liner, we can see from the output that from the 38 GB used in /, 34 GB is in the /opt/myapp/queue directory. This directory is pretty familiar to us, as we were troubleshooting issues with this directory in previous chapters.

From our previous experience, we know that this directory is used to queue messages received via a custom application.

Given the size of this directory, it's possible that before the reboot, the custom application was running on this server and filled up the filesystem.

We already know that this directory is consuming the majority of the space on this system. It would be useful to determine when the last file in this directory was created as this will give us a rough timeframe of when this application was running last:

```
# ls -l
total 368572
drwxrwxr-x. 2 vagrant vagrant        40 Jun 10 17:03 bin
drwxrwxr-x. 2 vagrant vagrant        23 Jun 10 16:55 conf
```

```
drwxrwxr-x. 2 vagrant vagrant          49 Jun 10 16:40 logs
drwxr-xr-x. 2 root    root    272932864 Jul  5 01:50 queue
-rwxr-xr-x. 1 vagrant vagrant         116 Jun 10 16:56 start.sh
```

We can actually do this by performing an `ls` in the `/opt/myapp` directory. We can see from the preceding output that the `queue/` directory was last modified on July 5th at 01:50. This correlates very nicely with our issues and at minimum, proves that the custom application was running prior to the reboot.

 The timestamp of when this directory was last updated and the fact that this application was running are both items we will notate in our summary.

Based on the preceding information we can, at this point, safely say that at the time of the incident, the custom application was running, and had created enough files to fill up the filesystem.

We can also say that around the time the filesystem reached 100 percent utilized, the load average of the server spiked suddenly.

From these facts, we can create a hypothesis; our current working theory is that once the application filled the filesystem, it was no longer able to create files. This might have caused the same application to block CPU time or spawn many CPU tasks, which caused a high load average.

Why wasn't the queue directory processed?

Since we know the custom application was the source of the filesystem issue, we also need to answer why.

In earlier chapters, you learned that this application's queue directory is processed by a `cronjob` that runs as the "vagrant" user. Let's take a look at when that cron job last ran by looking through the `/var/log/cron` log file:

```
Jun  6 15:28:01 localhost CROND[3115]: (vagrant) CMD (/opt/myapp/bin/
processor --debug --config /opt/myapp/conf/config.yml > /dev/null)
```

According to the `/var/log/cron` directory, the last time the job ran was `June 6th`. This timeline coincides roughly when this process was moved to another system, after this the server ran out of memory.

Could it be that the processor job was stopped but the application was not? Possibly, we know the application was running but let's check on the `processor` job.

We can check if the processor job has been removed with the `crontab` command:

```
# crontab -l -u vagrant
#*/4 * * * * /opt/myapp/bin/processor --debug --config /opt/myapp/conf/
config.yml > /dev/null
```

The `-l` (list) flag will cause the `crontab` command to print or list the cronjobs defined for the user executing it. When the `-u` (user) flag is added, it allows us to specify a user to list the cronjobs for, in this case, the `vagrant` user.

It appears from the list that the `processor` job hasn't been removed, but rather, it has been disabled. We can see that it has been disabled because the line starts with an `#`, which is used to specify comments in the `crontab` file.

This essentially turns the job into a comment, rather than a scheduled job. This means that the `crond` process will not execute this job.

A checkpoint on what you learned

At this point, let's do a checkpoint on what we were able to identify and gather.

After logging into the system, we were able to determine that the server had rebooted. We were able to see in `/var/log/messages` that the `watchdog` process was responsible for rebooting the server:

```
Jul  5 01:50:02 localhost watchdog[608]: loadavg 25 9 3 is higher than
the given threshold 24 18 12!
```

Based on the log messages in `/var/log/messages`, the watchdog process rebooted the server because of a high load. From `sar`, we could see that the load average went from 0 to 25 in a matter of a few minutes.

While performing our investigation, we were also able to identify that the server's / (root) filesystem is full. Not only is it full but also interestingly enough it was roughly 100 percent utilized just a few minutes before the system rebooted.

The reason the filesystem was in this condition was because the custom application in `/opt/myapp` was still running and creating files in `/opt/myapp/queue`. However, the job to clear this queue was not running as it has been commented out in the vagrant user's `crontab`.

Based on this, we can say that the root cause of our issue is most likely due to the filesystem filling up, which is due to the application running but not processing messages.

Sometimes you cannot prove everything

At this point, we have identified about everything we can as to what caused the high load average. Since we don't have a snapshot of what processes were running at the time of the incident, we cannot say for certain that it was the custom application. We also cannot say for certain based on the information we could gather that it was triggered because of the filesystem filling up.

We could test this theory by duplicating this scenario in another system, but that is not necessarily something to take on at 2:00 A.M. on a weekend. Duplicating an issue to that degree is usually something to perform as a follow up activity.

At this point given the data we could find, we can be reasonably certain as to the root cause. In many cases, this is as close as you will get as you might run out of time to gather or simply not have data to base your root cause on.

Preventing reoccurrence

Since we feel pretty confident about our hypothesis as to what happened, we now can move on to the final step of our root cause analysis; preventing the issue from reoccurring.

As we discussed in the beginning of our chapter, all useful root cause analysis reports include a plan of action. Sometimes, this plan of action is something to be performed immediately at the time of the issue. Sometimes, this plan is to be performed later as a long-term resolution.

For our issue, we are going to have both, immediate actions and long-term actions.

Immediate action

The first immediate action we need to take is to ensure that the systems primary function is healthy. In this case, the server's primary function is to serve the company's blog.

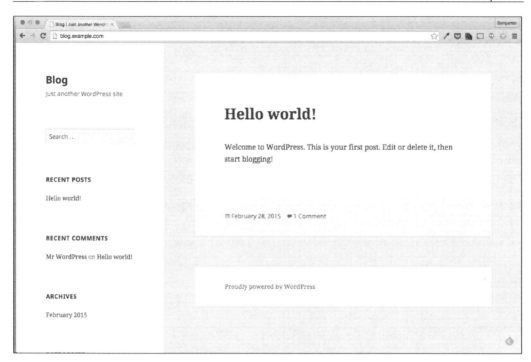

This is easy enough to check by going to the blog address in a browser. We can see from the preceding screenshot that the blog is working as expected. Just to be sure, we can validate that the Apache service is running as well:

```
# systemctl status httpd
httpd.service - The Apache HTTP Server
   Loaded: loaded (/usr/lib/systemd/system/httpd.service; enabled)
   Active: active (running) since Sun 2015-07-05 01:50:36 UTC; 3 days ago
 Main PID: 1015 (httpd)
   Status: "Total requests: 0; Current requests/sec: 0; Current traffic:
0 B/sec"
   CGroup: /system.slice/httpd.service
           ├─1015 /usr/sbin/httpd -DFOREGROUND
           ├─2315 /usr/sbin/httpd -DFOREGROUND
           ├─2316 /usr/sbin/httpd -DFOREGROUND
           ├─2318 /usr/sbin/httpd -DFOREGROUND
           ├─2319 /usr/sbin/httpd -DFOREGROUND
```

```
├─2321 /usr/sbin/httpd -DFOREGROUND
└─5687 /usr/sbin/httpd -DFOREGROUND
```

```
Jul 05 01:50:36 blog.example.com systemd[1]: Started The Apache HTTP
Server.
```

From this, it looks like our web server has been online since the reboot, this is good as it means the blog has been working since the reboot as well.

 Sometimes, depending on the criticality of the system, it might be important to first validate that the system is up and running before even investigating the issue. As with anything, this really depends on the environment as there are hard and fast rules about which comes first.

Now that we know the blog is working as expected, we need to resolve the disk being full.

```
# ls -la /opt/myapp/queue/ | wc -l
495151
```

As with earlier chapters, it seems the `queue` directory has quite a few messages waiting to be processed. In order to clear this properly, we will need to run the `processor` command manually, but there are a few extra steps we must take as well:

```
# sysctl -w fs.file-max=500000
fs.file-max = 500000
```

The first step we must take is to increase the number of files this system can have open at a time. We know this from past experience with the processor application and large amounts of messages.

```
# su - vagrant
$ ulimit -n 500000
$ ulimit -a
core file size          (blocks, -c) 0
data seg size           (kbytes, -d) unlimited
scheduling priority             (-e) 0
file size               (blocks, -f) unlimited
pending signals                 (-i) 7855
max locked memory       (kbytes, -l) 64
max memory size         (kbytes, -m) unlimited
open files                      (-n) 500000
pipe size            (512 bytes, -p) 8
```

```
POSIX message queues      (bytes, -q) 819200
real-time priority             (-r) 0
stack size              (kbytes, -s) 8192
cpu time               (seconds, -t) unlimited
max user processes             (-u) 4096
virtual memory          (kbytes, -v) unlimited
file locks                     (-x) unlimited
```

The second step is to increase the user limitations imposed on the vagrant user; specifically, the number of open files limitation. This step needs to be performed in the same shell session that we will execute the processor command in. Once the step is complete, we can manually execute the processor command to process the queued messages:

```
$ /opt/myapp/bin/processor --debug --config /opt/myapp/conf/config.yml
Initializing with configuration file /opt/myapp/conf/config.yml
- - - - - - - - - - - - - - - - - - - - - - - - - - - - - -
Starting message processing job
Added 495151 to queue
Processing 495151 messages
Processed 495151 messages
```

Now that the messages have been processed, we can recheck the filesystem utilization with the df command:

```
# df -h
Filesystem                Size  Used Avail Use% Mounted on
/dev/mapper/centos-root    39G  3.8G   35G  10% /
devtmpfs                  491M     0  491M   0% /dev
tmpfs                     498M     0  498M   0% /dev/shm
tmpfs                     498M   13M  485M   3% /run
tmpfs                     498M     0  498M   0% /sys/fs/cgroup
/dev/sda1                 497M  104M  394M  21% /boot
```

As we can see, the / filesystem is down to 10 percent utilization.

To ensure that we do not fill up this filesystem again, we validate that the custom application is currently stopped:

```
# ps -elf | grep myapp
0 R root      6535 2537  0  80   0 - 28160 -       15:09 pts/0
00:00:00 grep --color=auto myapp
```

Since we cannot see any processes running under the name application, we can be assured that the application is not running currently.

Long-term actions

This brings us to our **long-term actions**. The long-term actions are actions that we will recommend in our root cause summary, but aren't taken at this moment.

The first long-term action to recommend is that the custom application be permanently removed from this system. Since we know that the application has been migrated to another system, it should no longer be needed on this server. However, the removal of this application is not something we should take on at 2 A.M. or without validating that it is truly no longer required.

The second long-term action would be to investigate adding monitoring solutions, which can take periodic snapshots of running processes and the CPU/state of those processes. If we had that information available to us during this RCA investigation, we would be able to prove, without a doubt, which process was causing a high load. Since that information is not available, we are left to make an educated guess.

Again, this would not be a task that we would want to take on during a late night call but rather something for a standard work day.

A sample Root Cause Analysis

Now that we have all of the information we need, let's create a root cause analysis report. This report can be in any format, really, but I've found that something along the following lines works well.

Problem summary

At approximately 1:50 A.M. on July 5, 2015 the server `blog.example.com` unexpectedly rebooted. The `watchdog` process initiated the reboot process due to a high load average on the server.

After investigation, the high load average appears to be caused by a custom e-mail application, which was left in a running state even though it has been migrated to another server.

From the data available, it seems the application consumed 100 percent of the root filesystem.

While I was unable to obtain process states from before the reboot, it appears the high load average might have also been due to the same application being unable to write to the disk.

Problem details

The time at which the incident was reported—07/05/2015 at `01:52`

The timeline of the incident would be:

- An SMS alert came through at `01:52` stating `blog.example.com` was unreachable via the ICMP ping.
- The first troubleshooting step performed was a ping of the server:
    - The ping showed that the server was online
- Logged into the server at `01:59` and determined that the server had rebooted.
- Searched the `/var/log/messages` file and identified that the watchdog process had rebooted the server at `01:50:12`:
    - Watchdog started the reboot process due to the high load average at `01:50:02`
    - During investigation, we found that no users were logged in at the time of the incident
    - The server started the boot process at `01:50:32`
- During the investigation, it was identified that the server had run out of available disk space at `01:48:01`.
- The load average of this system started to increase at approximately the same time reaching 25 at `01:50:05`.
- We identified that the `/opt/myapp/queue` directory was last modified at `01:50` and contained roughly 34 GB of data creating 100 percent disk utilization:
    - This suggests that the custom e-mail application was running until the server rebooted
- We found that the `processor` job has not run since June 6th, which means that the messages were not processed.

Root cause

The filesystem reached 100 percent utilization due to the custom application running without the `processor` job being executed via cron. The data collected suggests this caused a high load average, which trigged the `watchdog` process to reboot the server.

Action plan

We should have the following steps in place:

- Validated that Apache is running and `Blog` is accessible
- Validated that the custom application is not running after system reboot
- Executed the processor job manually at 02:15 resolving disk space issues

Further actions to be taken

- Remove the custom application from the server to prevent the application from accidently starting
- Investigate the addition of process list monitoring to capture which processes are utilizing the CPU time during similar issues:
    - Will help in resolution of any similar situations should they occur

As you can see in the preceding report, we have a high-level timeline showing what we were able to identify, how we identified it, and the actions we took to resolve the issue. All key components of a good root cause analysis.

Summary

In this chapter, we covered how to respond to a very difficult issue: an unexpected reboot. We used the tools and methodologies we saw throughout this book to identify the root cause and create a root cause report.

We used log files heavily throughout this book; in this chapter, we were able to use these logs to identify the process that rebooted the server. We also identified the reason `watchdog` decided to reboot the server, which was due to a high load average.

We were able to use tools such as `sar`, `df`, `du`, and `ls` to determine the timing and cause of the high load average. All of these tools are commands you learned about throughout this book.

With this last chapter, we covered quite a few examples that were covered earlier in this book. You learned how to troubleshoot web applications, performance issues, custom applications, and hardware problems. We did all of these using real-world examples with real-world solutions.

While this book covers quite a few topics, the goal of this book was to show you the concepts of troubleshooting issues with Red Hat Enterprise Linux systems. The examples might be commonplace or somewhat rare but the commands used in these examples are commands that are used daily during troubleshooting. The topics covered all provide a core competency with Linux and will provide you with the knowledge necessary to troubleshoot issues not directly covered in this book.

Index

A

Adaptor troubleshooter 208
alert 396
Apache 61
Apache logs
  about 66
  location, finding of 66-68
  reviewing 69, 70
application
  about 334
  configuration file, using 316, 317
  running status, verifying 320, 321
  tracing, with strace 335
application programming
       interface (API) 324
application, starting issues
  about 310, 311
  application failing 314, 315
  exit code 311-313
  script failing 314, 315
arrays
  drives, re-adding to 302-305

B

bash one-liner
  about 377
  breaking down 377
basic troubleshooting
  about 209
  MariaDB service, validating 210-212
Bind 159
bound 278
buffers 108
bytes 227

C

caches 108, 109
captured data
  reading 173, 174
Character special file (CHR) 330
command flags 34, 35
command-line basics
  about 34
  command flags 34, 35
  command output, piping 35
common log files 26-28
configuration
  checking, of application 29, 30
configuration files
  about 31
  default system configuration directory 31
  finding 31
  finding, find command used 32
  finding, rpm command used 31, 32
conflict
  resolving 342-345
connectivity, testing
  about 150
  from db.example.com 182, 183
  telnet command, executing from
      blog.example.com 150, 151
  telnet command, executing from laptop 151
cores 101
cpuinfo file 101
CPU performance
  issues, identifying 105-107
CPU statistics
  viewing, with sar command 137-140

used, for identifying processes 132
used, for identifying processes
        utilizing I/O 126-129
using 102-104
Push (PSH) packets 175

Q

queue directory
reasons, for issues in processing 410

R

RAID 0 275
RAID 1 275
RAID 5 276
RAID 6 276
RAID 10 277
RAID recovery
working 278
read-only filesystems
about 236, 258, 259
disk issues, identifying 259-261
ro option 236
rw option 236
rebuild status
watching 306
Red Hat kernel docs 16
Red Hat package manager (RPM) 38
**Redundant Array of Independent Disks
        (RAID)**
about 274
troubleshooting 277, 278
reoccurrence, preventing
about 412
immediate action 412-416
long-term actions 416
reported issue 56, 347
reported issue, resolving
about 368
open files limitation 369
sysctl command, executing 369
reported problem
about 371
Apache, validating for down
        service 371, 372
reason, finding for down service
        of Apache 372-375

RESET packet 217
Resident Memory Size (SZ) 42
resources, troubleshooting process
about 10
books 10
Google 11
man pages 12, 13
people 16, 17
Red Hat kernel docs 16
Runbooks 10, 11
Team Wikis 10, 11
RHEL 7
reference link, for naming schema 45
root cause
establishing 21
Root Cause Analysis (RCA)
about 17, 18, 372, 395
actions, taken 19
anatomy 19
key data points, for validating 20
plan of action, for preventing incident 20
timeline, of events 19
root user 74
routing 191, 192
routing misconfigurations
looking for 196, 197
routing table
about 191
viewing 192-194
rpm command
about 38
files deployed by packages, listing 38
installed packages, listing 38
used, for finding configuration files 31, 32
rsyslog configuration files 28
Runbooks 10, 11
run queue 405, 406

S

sample Root Cause Analysis
about 416
action plan 418
problem details 417
problem summary 416
root cause 418

Thank you for buying
Red Hat Enterprise Linux Troubleshooting Guide

About Packt Publishing

Packt, pronounced 'packed', published its first book, *Mastering phpMyAdmin for Effective MySQL Management*, in April 2004, and subsequently continued to specialize in publishing highly focused books on specific technologies and solutions.

Our books and publications share the experiences of your fellow IT professionals in adapting and customizing today's systems, applications, and frameworks. Our solution-based books give you the knowledge and power to customize the software and technologies you're using to get the job done. Packt books are more specific and less general than the IT books you have seen in the past. Our unique business model allows us to bring you more focused information, giving you more of what you need to know, and less of what you don't.

Packt is a modern yet unique publishing company that focuses on producing quality, cutting-edge books for communities of developers, administrators, and newbies alike. For more information, please visit our website at www.packtpub.com.

About Packt Enterprise

In 2010, Packt launched two new brands, Packt Enterprise and Packt Open Source, in order to continue its focus on specialization. This book is part of the Packt Enterprise brand, home to books published on enterprise software – software created by major vendors, including (but not limited to) IBM, Microsoft, and Oracle, often for use in other corporations. Its titles will offer information relevant to a range of users of this software, including administrators, developers, architects, and end users.

Writing for Packt

We welcome all inquiries from people who are interested in authoring. Book proposals should be sent to author@packtpub.com. If your book idea is still at an early stage and you would like to discuss it first before writing a formal book proposal, then please contact us; one of our commissioning editors will get in touch with you.

We're not just looking for published authors; if you have strong technical skills but no writing experience, our experienced editors can help you develop a writing career, or simply get some additional reward for your expertise.

Learning RHEL Networking

Gain Linux administration skills by learning new networking concepts in Red Hat Enterprise Linux 7

Andrew Mallett

[PACKT] open source

Learning RHEL Networking

ISBN: 978-1-78528-783-1   Paperback: 216 pages

Gain Linux administration skills by learning new networking concepts in Red Hat Enterprise Linux 7

1. Discover how to deploy the networks services Chrony, Network Time Protocol (NTP), Domain Name System (DNS), and Dynamic Host Configuration Protocol (DHCP).

2. Deploy RHEL 7 into your Microsoft Active Directory Domain to utilize Single-Sign in Linux and Active Directory with a single account.

3. Master firewalling your network and server with Firewalld.

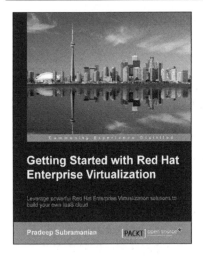

Getting Started with Red Hat Enterprise Virtualization

Leverage powerful Red Hat Enterprise Virtualization solutions to build your own IaaS cloud

Pradeep Subramanian

[PACKT] open source

Getting Started with Red Hat Enterprise Virtualization

ISBN: 978-1-78216-740-2   Paperback: 178 pages

Leverage powerful Red Hat Enterprise Virtualization solutions to build your own IaaS cloud

1. Build an agile, secure, and highly scalable virtualization foundation for your enterprise Linux and Windows workloads.

2. Explore how Red Hat Enterprise Virtualization positions itself as the strategic virtualization alternative to proprietary virtualization platforms.

3. Deep dive into its internal architecture and components and learn how to build and manage RHEV.

Please check **www.PacktPub.com** for information on our titles

Learning iOS Security

ISBN: 978-1-78355-174-3   Paperback: 142 pages

Enhance the security of your iOS platform and applications using iOS-centric security techniques

1. Familiarize yourself with fundamental methods to leverage the security of iOS platforms and apps.

2. Resolve common vulnerabilities and security-related shortcomings in iOS applications and operating systems.

3. A pragmatic and hands-on guide filled with clear and simple instructions to develop a secure mobile deployment.

Using Yocto Project with BeagleBone Black

ISBN: 978-1-78528-973-6   Paperback: 144 pages

Unleash the power of the BeagleBone Black embedded platform with Yocto Project

1. Build real world embedded system projects using the impressive combination of Yocto Project and Beaglebone Black.

2. Learn how to effectively add multimedia to your board and save time by exploiting layers from the existing ones.

3. A step-by-step, comprehensive guide for embedded system development with hands-on examples.

Please check **www.PacktPub.com** for information on our titles

50387010R00256

Made in the USA
San Bernardino, CA
21 June 2017